AF594196

HAVE I REASONS

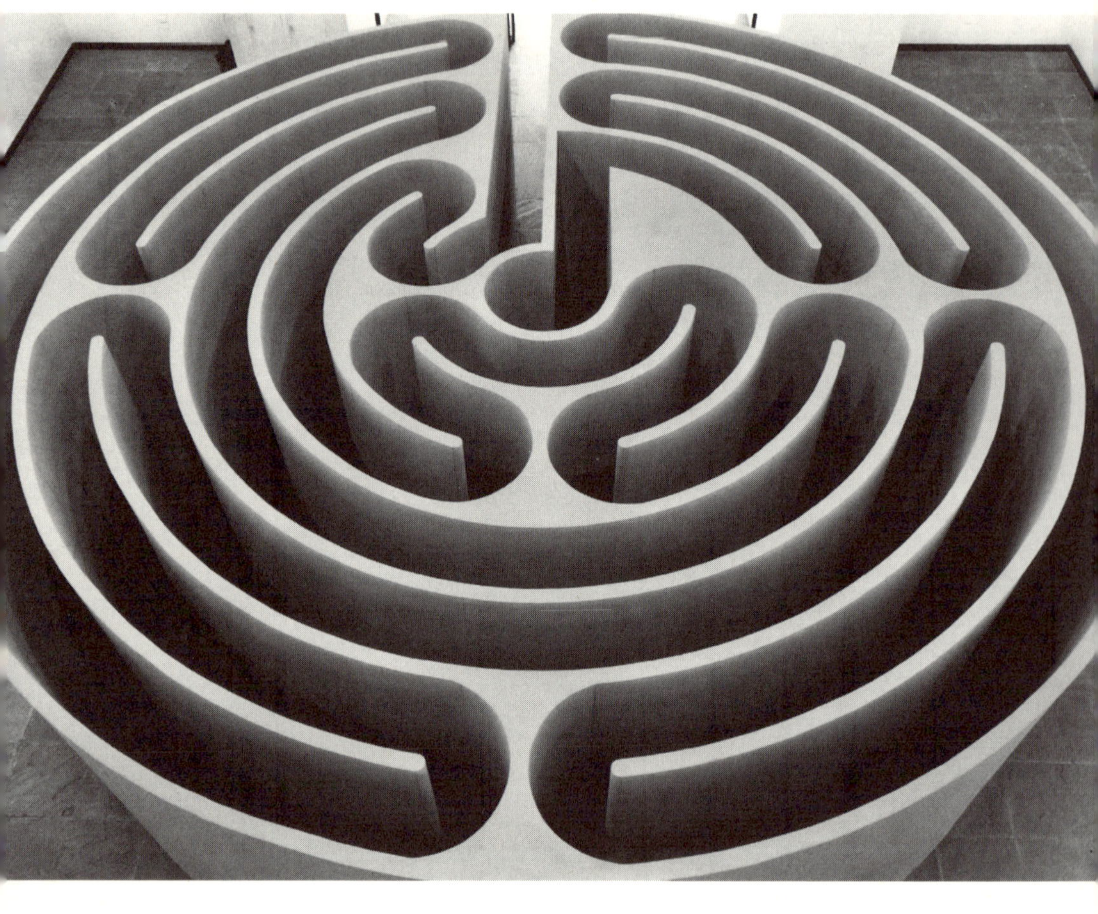

ROBERT MORRIS
HAVE I REASONS

WORK AND WRITINGS, 1993–2007

Edited and with an introduction by

NENA TSOUTI-SCHILLINGER

DUKE UNIVERSITY PRESS

DURHAM AND LONDON 2008

Introduction © 2008 by Nena Tsouti-Schillinger

Texts © 2008 Robert Morris except
"Writing with Davidson: Some Afterthoughts after Doing *Blind Time IV: Drawing with Davidson*" © 1993 The University of Chicago
"Professional Rules" © 1997 The University of Chicago
"Cézanne's Mountains" © 1998 The University of Chicago
"Size Matters" © 2000 The University of Chicago
"From a Chomskian Couch: The Imperialistic Unconscious" © 2003 The University of Chicago
"Threading the Labyrinth" © 2001 by *October Magazine*, Ltd. and the Massachusetts Institute of Technology

The illustrations of works by Robert Morris in this volume appear with the permission of the artist.

Frontis: *Untitled (Philadelphia Labyrinth)*, 1974. Plywood and masonite painted gray, 8 feet (2.44 m) high, 30 feet (9.14 m) diameter. The Solomon R. Guggenheim Museum, New York: Panza Collection. Photo by Will Brown, courtesy of Robert Morris.

All rights reserved
Printed in the United States of America on acid-free paper ♾
Designed by Amy Ruth Buchanan
Typeset in Minion and Gill Sans by Tseng Information Systems, Inc.
Library of Congress Cataloging-in-Publication Data appear on the last printed page of this book.

CONTENTS

List of Illustrations | vii
Acknowledgments | xi
Introduction | 1

.....

Indiana Street (1993) | 17
Writing with Davidson: Some Afterthoughts after Doing *Blind Time IV: Drawing with Davidson* (1993) | 41
The Art of Donald Davidson (1995) | 51
Steam (1995) | 61
Professional Rules (1997) | 63
Thinking Back about Him: On the Death of Richard Bellamy (1998) | 101
Cézanne's Mountains (1998) | 103
Size Matters (2000) | 121
Threading the Labyrinth (2001) | 137
Solecisms of Sight: Specular Speculations (2001) | 148
Thoughts on *Hegel's Owl* (2002) | 163
Maybe the Angel in Dürer (2003) | 167
From a Chomskian Couch: The Imperialistic Unconscious (2003) | 171
Toward an Ophthalmology of the Aesthetic and an Orthopedics of Seeing (2004) | 186
Notes on *Less than* (2004) | 203
The Birthday Boy (2004) | 205
Jasper Johns: The First Decade (2005) | 225

.....

Chronology | 257
Bibliography | 267
Index | 271

ILLUSTRATIONS

All works are by Robert Morris unless otherwise noted

1. *Two Columns*, 1973 refabrication of a 1961 original 2
2. *Box with the Sound of its Own Making*, 1961 2
3. *Initial Memory Drawing* (9/3/63, 8:00 P.M.), 1963 3
4. *First Memory Drawing* (9/4/63, 9:00 P.M.), 1963 5
5. *Second Memory Drawing* (9/8/63, 12:00 P.M.), 1963 5
6. *Third Memory Drawing* (9/16/63, 3:30 P.M.), 1963 5
7. *Fourth Memory Drawing* (10/2/63, 9:00 P.M.), 1963 5
8. Robert Morris in costume for his choreography *War*, 1963 6
9. Robert Morris at work on *Threadwaste*, New York, 1968 6
10. *Untitled, Reclamation Project (Johnson Pit no. 30)*, 1979 7
11. *Untitled (Inverted Shoulder)*, 1978 8
12. *Untitled*, 1983 8
13. Seventeen stained-glass windows, 2001, installed in the Maguelone Cathedral, detail (exterior view) 10
14. Robert Morris with *Melencolia II*, 2002. Detail 10
15. *The Birthday Boy*, 2004 10
16. *House and Bombs*, 2004 12
17. *Sliding Lights*, 2005 12
18. *Blind Time IV (Drawing with Davidson)*, 1991 13
19. *TELEGRAM/THE RATIONED YEARS*, 1998. Book written by Robert Morris 16
20. Installation view of *Robert Morris: The Rationed Years*, 1998 16
21. *Untitled*, 2005 18
22. *Bull Wall: American Royale*, 1992 19
23. *Blind Time IV (Drawing with Davidson)*, 1991 40
24. *Blind Time IV (Drawing with Davidson)*, 1991 45
25. *Blind Time IV (Drawing with Davidson)*, 1991 47
26. *Blind Time IV (Drawing with Davidson)*, 1991 50
27. *Steam*, 1971–74 60
28. Robert Morris with *Wheels*, 1963 64

29. *I-Box*, 1962 (open view) 68
30. *I-Box*, 1962 (closed view) 68
31. Robert Morris in his *Untitled (Box for Standing)*, 1961 70
32. *Site*, 1964 70
33. *Mirror*, 1969 70
34. *Untitled (Rope Piece)*, 1964 72
35. *Untitled (Wedges)*, 1971 72
36. *Second Study for a View from a Corner of Orion (Night)*, 1980 72
37. Installation view of *Tar Babies of the New World Order*, 1997 74
38. *Water Waste*, 2002 74
39. *Chairs*, 2002 74
40. Seventeen stained-glass windows, 2001, installed in the Maguelone Cathedral, detail (exterior view) 75
41. Presbytery in the Prato Cathedral, 2002 75
42. *Litanies*, 1963 76
43. *Statement of Esthetic Withdrawal*, 1963 76
44. Installation view of *Robert Morris: The Mind/Body Problem*, 1995
Left: *Untitled (Pine Portal)*, 1993 refabrication of a 1961 original
Right: *Untitled (Pine Portal with Mirrors)*, 1993 refabrication of a 1961 original 76
45. *Hearing*, 1972 78
46. Manuscript drawing for *Voice*, 1973 78
47. *Untitled*, 1974 (poster for *Voice*) 78
48. *Untitled (Portland Mirrors)*, 1977 78
49. *Blind Time I*, 1973 80
50. *Blind Time III*, 1985 80
51. *Blind Time V: Melancholia*, 1999 81
52. *Blind Time VI: Moral Blinds*, 2000 81
53. Installation view of *Robert Morris: Blind Time Drawings*, 2003 82
54. *Untitled (Three L-Beams)*, 1965-69 83
55. Top: *Untitled (Corner Beam)*, 1964
Bottom: *Untitled (Battered Cubes)*, 1965 84
56. *Untitled (Threadwaste)*, 1968 84
57. *House of the Vetti II*, 1983 84
58. *Metered Bulb*, 1963 86
59. *The Fallen and the Saved*, 1994 86
60. *Brain*, 1963 88
61. *Fathers and Sons*, 1955/1983 88

62. *Open Center Sculpture*, 1997 88
63. *Observatory*, 1977 90
64. *Observatory*, 1972 90
65. Installation view of *Robert Morris: The Mind/Body Problem*, 1994 90
66. *Untitled (Corner Piece)*, 1964 91
67. *Untitled (Ring with Light)*, 1965-66 91
68. *Card File*, 1962 92
69. *Untitled (Leave Key on Hook)*, 1963 92
70. Installation view of *Robert Morris: Work from 1967-1984*, 1985 92
71. *Horde/ Hoard/ Whored*, 1989 94
72. *Untitled (Catenary)*, 1968 94
73. Installation view of *Robert Morris: The Mind/Body Problem*, 1994 94
74. *Untitled (Holocaust)*, 1987 96
75. *Untitled (Investigations* series), 1990 96
76. *Untitled (Philadelphia Labyrinth)*, 1974 96
77. *Canvas Back / Fire*, 2001 97
78. Installation view of Robert Morris's one-man exhibition at the Green Gallery, New York, December 1964–January 1965 100
79. *Blind Time IV (Drawing with Davidson)*, 1991 102
80. Paul Cézanne, *Mont Sainte-Victoire Seen from Les Lauves*, 1904–6 105
81. *Based on a Section from Mont Saint-Victoire Seen from Les Lauves 1904–6, Cézanne*, 1997 105
82. Anselm Kiefer, *Breaking of the Vessels*, 1989–90 131
83. Frank Gehry, Guggenheim Museum, Bilbao, Spain, 1997 134
84. Robert Morris standing inside his *Passageway*, 1961 138
85. *Untitled (Gori Labyrinth)*, 1982 140
86. *Labyrinth*, 2000 140
87. *White Nights*, 2000 141
88. *Untitled (Labyrinth)*, 2000 141
89. *Finch College Project*, 1969 149
90. *Finch College Project*, 2001 remake of a 1969 original 149
91. Marcel Duchamp, *The Bride Stripped Bare by her Bachelors, Even (The Large Glass)*, 1915–23 152
92. Gustave Courbet, *The Origin of the World*, 1866 152
93. Marcel Duchamp, *Etant donnés* (exterior view of doors), 1946–66 154
94. Marcel Duchamp, *Etant donnés* (interior view) 154
95. *Hegel's Owl*, 2002. Detail (exterior view) 155
96. *Hegel's Owl*, 2002. Detail (interior view) 155

97. *Hegel's Owl*, 2002. Detail (interior view) 162
98. *Hegel's Owl*, 2002. Detail (exterior view) 164
99. *Melencolia II*, 2002 166
100. *Blind Time V: Melancholia*, 1999 168
101. *Blind Time V: Melancholia*, 1999 168
102. *Noamian Fragments*, 2002 170
103. *Squeeze*, 2002 170
104. Jasper Johns, *Flag*, 1954–55 174
105. *Towers of Light*, 2003 184
106. The Nuremberg Parade, 1936 184
107. *Three Rulers*, 1963 192
108. *Untitled (Swift Night Ruler)*, 1963 192
109. Simone Forti, *Slant Board*, 1961 194
110. *Less than*, 2005 202
111. *The Birthday Boy*, 2004 206
112. *The Birthday Boy*, 2004 210
113. *The Birthday Boy*, 2004 211
114. *The Birthday Boy*, 2004 214
115. *The Birthday Boy*, 2004 216
116. *The Birthday Boy*, 2004 219
117. *The Birthday Boy*, 2004 220
118. *The Birthday Boy*, 2004 223
119. Jasper Johns, *Target with Plaster Casts*, 1955 230
120. Jasper Johns, *White Flag*, 1955 232
121. Jasper Johns, *Device Circle*, 1959 234
122. Jasper Johns, *Tennyson*, 1958 236
123. Jasper Johns, *Voice*, 1967 238
124. Jasper Johns, *Diver*, 1962–63 239

ACKNOWLEDGMENTS

This volume presents seventeen of Morris's essays written over the last fifteen years and arranged chronologically. The following works are included:

"Indiana Street" (1993), an autobiographical essay, is previously unpublished.

"Writing with Davidson: Some Afterthoughts after Doing *Blind Time IV: Drawing with Davidson*" originally appeared in *Critical Inquiry* 19 (Summer 1993): 617–27.

"The Art of Donald Davidson" (1995), an essay about this major American philosopher of the twentieth century, originally appeared in *The Philosophy of Donald Davidson*, ed. Lewis Edwin Hahn, Library of Living Philosophers, volume 27 (Chicago: Open Court Press, 1999), 128–35.

"Steam" (1995), an essay on his site-specific installation of the same name at Western Washington University (Bellingham, Washington), is previously unpublished.

"Professional Rules" originally appeared in *Critical Inquiry* 23 (Winter 1997): 298–322.

"Thinking Back about Him" (1998) is an essay written after the death of Richard (Dick) Bellamy, the art dealer who ran the Green Gallery, where Morris had his first one-man exhibition in 1963 in New York. It is previously unpublished.

"Cézanne's Mountains" originally appeared in *Critical Inquiry* 24 (Spring 1998): 814–29.

"Size Matters" originally appeared in *Critical Inquiry* 26 (Spring 2000): 474–87.

"Threading the Labyrinth" originally appeared in *October* 96 (Spring 2001): 61–70.

“Solecisms of Sight: Specular Speculations” is the transcript of a seminar conducted at the Whitney Museum of Art by Morris on November 29, 2001, for the exhibition *Into the Light: The Projected Image in American Art, 1964–1977*. This seminar coincided with the installation of his 1969 film *Finch College Project*. “Solecisms of Sight: Specular Speculations” originally appeared in *October* 103 (Winter 2003): 31–41.

“Thoughts on *Hegel's Owl*” (2002), an essay on his permanent site-specific installation *Hegel's Owl* in Parco della Padula (Carrara, Italy), is previously unpublished.

“Maybe the Angel in Dürer” is a text on the relationship between his 1999 set of *Blind Time V: Melancholia* drawings and *Melencolia II*, the 2002 installation in Fattoria di Celle in Santomato, Pistoia. It was included in Nena Tsouti-Schillinger's “Drawing in Time,” *Robert Morris: Blind Time Drawings* (New York: Haim Chanin Fine Arts, 2003), 8–9.

“From a Chomskian Couch: The Imperialistic Unconscious” is the transcript of a seminar conducted at the Whitechapel Art Gallery in London by Morris on November 19, 2003, for the exhibition *A Short History of Performance*, which included the installation of his 1964 work *21.3.1964*. “From a Chomskian Couch: The Imperialistic Unconscious” originally appeared in *Critical Inquiry* 29 (Summer 2003): 678–94.

“Toward an Ophthalmology of the Aesthetic and an Orthopedics of Seeing” (2004) is previously unpublished. This text will appear as a chapter in *Rediscovering Aesthetics*, ed. Francis Halsall et al. (New York: Columbia University Press, forthcoming).

“Notes on *Less than*” (2004), an essay on his permanent site-specific bronze sculpture with sound installation for the Cultural Center of Reggio Emilia (Italy), originally appeared in the exhibition catalogue *Robert Morris: Less than* (Prato, Italy: Gli Ori, Prato Comune di Reggio Emilia, 2005).

“The Birthday Boy” (2004) is the textual element of his two-screen video-and-sound installation of the same name at the Galleria dell'Accademia (Florence, Italy), in 2004–5 for the exhibition *Forme per il David* in commemoration of the restoration and five hundredth anniversary of Michelangelo's *David*. “The Birthday Boy” is previously unpublished.

"Jasper Johns: The First Decade" (2005) originally appeared in the exhibition catalogue *Jasper Johns: An Allegory of Painting, 1955–1965* (Washington, D.C.: National Gallery of Art, 2007).

I have also included a detailed chronology with biographical notes and exhibitions.

Among the many people who provided encouragement and support, I wish to express my particular gratitude to the following: Kenneth Surin of Duke University, Elinor Richter of Hunter College, Dick Boyle of Temple University, and George Braziller.

I am also deeply grateful to the numerous individuals and institutions that helped provide me with photographs: Mathilde Simian and Haim Chanin Fine Arts; Antonio Homen and the Ileana Sonnabend Gallery; the Leo Castelli Gallery; the Guggenheim Museum of Art; Vittorio Urbani and Nuova Icona in Venice; Giuliano Gori and Miranda MacPhail in Fattoria di Celle in Pistoia; Roberta Conforti in Comune di Reggio Emilia; Vincenzo Capalbo in the Art Media Studio in Florence; the Galerie Pietro Sparta in Chagny; Jasper Johns and Sarah Taggart; Anselm Kiefer and Peter Namuth.

I also reaped great rewards from my editor, John O'Toole, who provided the help that is necessary to a project of this kind, and from the anonymous readers who reviewed the manuscript for Duke University Press. Special thanks go to the Duke staff, particularly to Reynolds Smith for his enthusiastic support of this project and his help in bringing it to fruition.

The support of my husband, Bill Schillinger, must be acknowledged on many counts; he offered much appreciated encouragement and advice in every stage of this book's production. My constant traveling companion, he was instrumental in obtaining on-site photographs, which would have been otherwise unavailable.

And finally, I extend my deepest gratitude to Robert Morris, who entrusted me with the responsibility of this difficult task and allowed his writings and images of his works to be published herein. Without his generous support, this book would not have been possible.

All previously published material is reprinted here with permission.

Nena Tsouti-Schillinger

INTRODUCTION | NENA TSOUTI-SCHILLINGER

One of the most influential artists of our time, Robert Morris is also a thought-provoking writer. In the minds of many readers Morris is known for his contributions to virtually every postwar art movement since abstract expressionism: as a pioneer of minimalist sculpture, a leader of antiform art, and an iconoclast breaking down traditional draftsmanship by making drawings with his eyes shut and no visual reference whatsoever (the *Blind Time* drawings). Others know him for a number of widely influential texts and notes on art written between 1966 and 1989 (many of them published in 1993 in *Continuous Project Altered Daily: The Writings of Robert Morris*). Still others consider him the most prolific writer of any artist of his generation, exceeding all expectations of what an artist might accomplish with words. He has captured audiences not only with his elusive flux of transformation, as an enduring practicing artist, but also under the persona of the intellectual theorist. That is to say, he is truly the embodiment of the artist/philosopher by definition. Morris has proved quite articulate concerning the nature and development of art as he relentlessly challenges prevailing ideas about art and culture.

Born in Kansas City, Missouri, on February 9, 1931, Robert Morris displayed an interest in art from his earliest years, having already been exposed by the age of seven to Egyptian art, Goya, and Cézanne during visits to the Nelson Gallery. He attended the Kansas City Art Institute and the California School of Fine Arts in San Francisco, later pursuing philosophy and psychology studies at Reed College in Portland, Oregon. Like many artists of the fifties, he began his career initially as a painter working in the abstract expressionist style, which was dominant then. During this period he also organized a theater workshop with his wife at that time, the dancer and choreographer Simone Forti, to explore movement, sound, light, and language. However, in 1960 he abandoned painting because he had come to find the medium inadequate for what he wished to express.

During the 1960s and 1970s, Morris played a central role in defining the movements of the period: minimalist sculpture, process art, and earthworks. In fact, it was the gray geometric plywood pieces he showed at Richard's Bellamy's Green Gallery in 1963 and 1964 that placed Morris in the front ranks of the

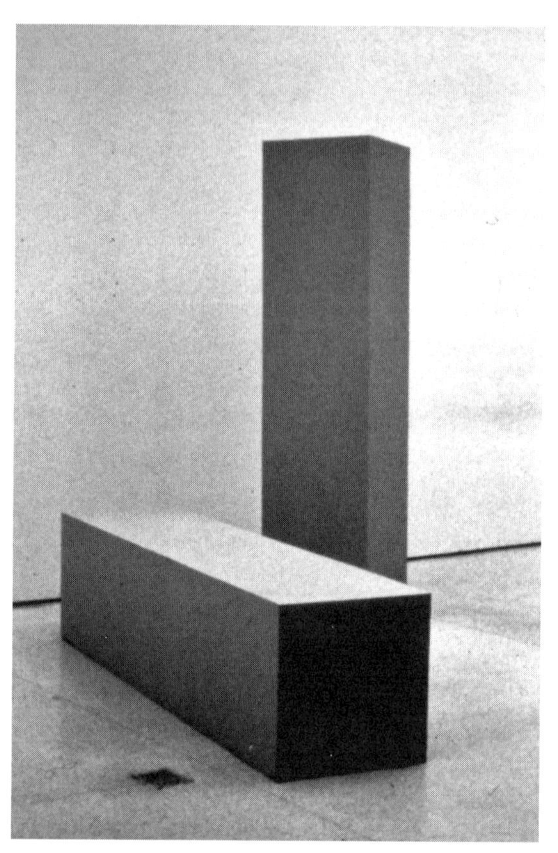

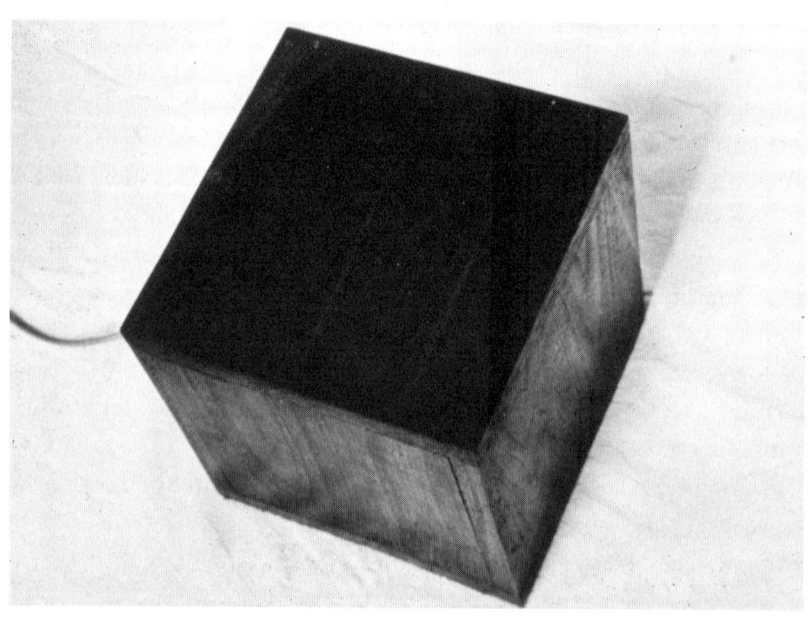

minimal movement. It is interesting to note that *Column*, an existing sculpture, was adapted for a performance at the Living Theater in New York (figure 1).[1]

In the 1960s, in the artistic tradition of Marcel Duchamp (whom he met when he moved to New York in 1961), Morris seemed to value idea over the artwork itself. He made *Box with the Sound of Its Own Making* (figure 2), an unpainted walnut box containing a tape recording of the sounds of sawing and hammering—the carpentry that produced it. He created drawings such as *Litanies* that were not representational images but only texts. In *Litanies*, Morris repeatedly wrote for two and a half hours the words "Litanies of the Chariot" from Duchamp's notes for *The Bride Stripped Bare by Her Bachelors, Even*, also known as *The Large Glass* (1915–23). Morris kept track of the time needed to make the work and recorded it on the drawing. *Memory Drawings*, executed two years later (figures 3–7), were created over a two-month period in September and October 1963. These five drawings show Morris's interest in scientific theories of memory, perhaps suggesting a kind of mockery of the celebrated achievements of science and technology. The artist drew the first piece and memorized it. He then reproduced the narrative from memory four times on four subsequent occasions separated by a geometric progression of four, eight, sixteen, and thirty-two days. The essence of this work, then, was the revelation of the significant extent of the change evident in each reiteration resulting from his own memory lapse. Self-sustaining and with no dependence on the realization of other projects on paper or canvas, or in stone, lead, felt, or any other traditional or nontraditional medium, the definitive works were the writings themselves. Although such freestanding narratives are common in Asian art as exemplified by calligraphy, nothing quite like these pieces had existed in the Western tradition. That these text-drawings created quite a sensation when first exhibited is hardly surprising.

Between 1962 and 1965 Morris also participated in projects at the Judson Dance Theater in New York and in fact choreographed six dance pieces:[2] *War*

1. *Two Columns*, 1973 refabrication of a 1961 original. 1973 version: painted aluminum, two units, each 96 × 24 × 24 inches (243.8 × 61 × 61 cm). Tehran Museum of Contemporary Art; 1961 version: painted plywood. Photo courtesy of Robert Morris.

2. *Box with the Sound of its Own Making*, 1961. Walnut box, speaker, tape, 9¾ × 9¾ × 9¾ inches (24.8 × 24.8 × 24.8 cm). Seattle Museum of Art, Seattle. Gift of Bagley and Virginia Wright. Photo courtesy of Robert Morris.

(overleaf) **3.** *Initial Memory Drawing* (9/3/63, 8:00 P.M.), 1963. Ink on paper, 20½ × 13 inches (52.1 × 33 cm). Collection of the artist. Photo courtesy of Robert Morris.

The physiological basis for memory has not been determined. Theories advanced to explain memory fall mainly into two classes: (1) Those which seek explanation in changes in composition of the brain cells; and (2) those which seek explanation in changes in patterns of electrical currents between cells. If one leaves the analogy at a crude level, comparisons can be made to the two basic ways in which man establishes a cultural memory, i.e. either spatially through preservation of models, pictures, maps, etc., or temporally through sequential records in print, audial recordings, and more recently by electronic means. Theories have also been advanced which attempt to combine these two processes. Such theories attempt to discriminate between types of memories, assigning the coding of some to physical alteration of the molecular structure of brain cells and others to reflex electrical circuits. The latter process is sometimes appended with a hypothesis of a mechanical nature, viz. through minute changes of synaptic fibers which grow larger or closer together and facilitate electrical pathways. Analog computing machines can be made to learn - a process impossible without storage of information. This storage is effected by specific variations in a time series together with a scanning device. Recent investigations in electroencephalography seem to point to such a scanning mechanism responsible for oscillating currents which tend to fade with concentration and attention. However the storing of visual images can be more easily ascribed to protein molecule alterations. All suggestions as to the locus of memory, either in terms of composition or action agree on the point that it is not held in any specific area of the cortex. Decimations of the cortex do not cut out particular memories, but the severing of neural pathways between the visual cortex and the frontal regions, while not disturbing vision, reduces to the unrecognizable that which is seen. The richness of and necessities for the interconnections of all parts of the cortex will undoubtedly be part of whatever theory is eventually established.

Drawing established and memorized 9/3/63, 8 pm.

R. Morris

(Above, clockwise from top left) **4.** *First Memory Drawing* (9/4/63, 9:00 P.M.), 1963. Ink on paper, 20½ × 13 inches (52.1 × 33 cm). Collection of the artist. Photo courtesy of Robert Morris. **5.** *Second Memory Drawing* (9/8/63, 12:00 P.M.), 1963. Ink on paper, 20½ × 13 inches (52.1 × 33 cm). Collection of the artist. Photo courtesy of Robert Morris. **6.** *Third Memory Drawing* (9/16/63, 3:30 P.M.), 1963. Ink on paper, 20½ × 13 inches (52.1 × 33 cm). Collection of the artist. Photo courtesy of Robert Morris. **7.** *Fourth Memory Drawing* (10/2/63, 9:00 P.M.), 1963. Ink on paper, 20½ × 13 inches (52.1 × 33 cm). Collection of the artist. Photo courtesy of Robert Morris.

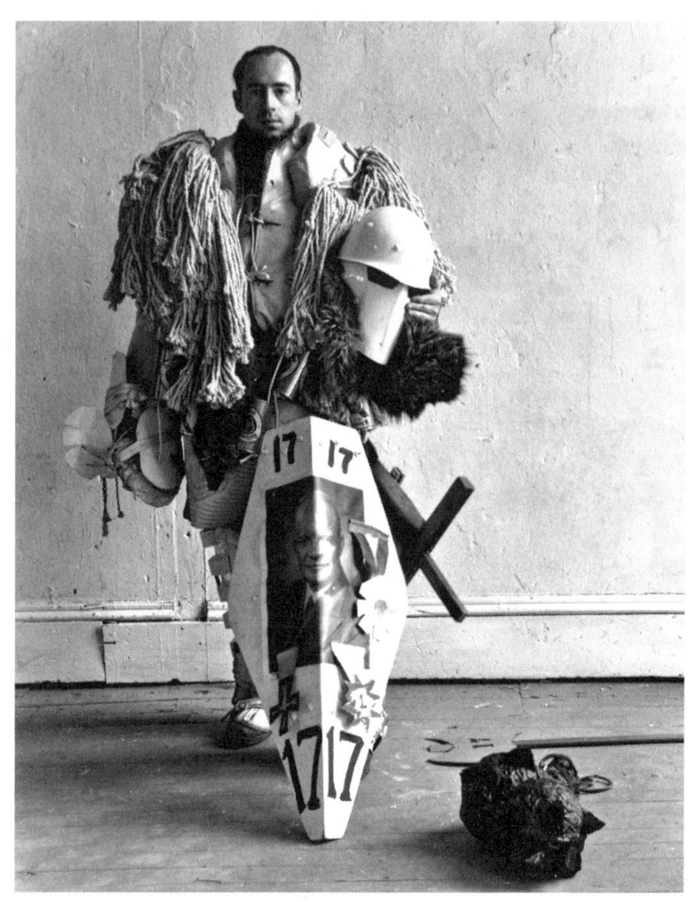
17
17
1717

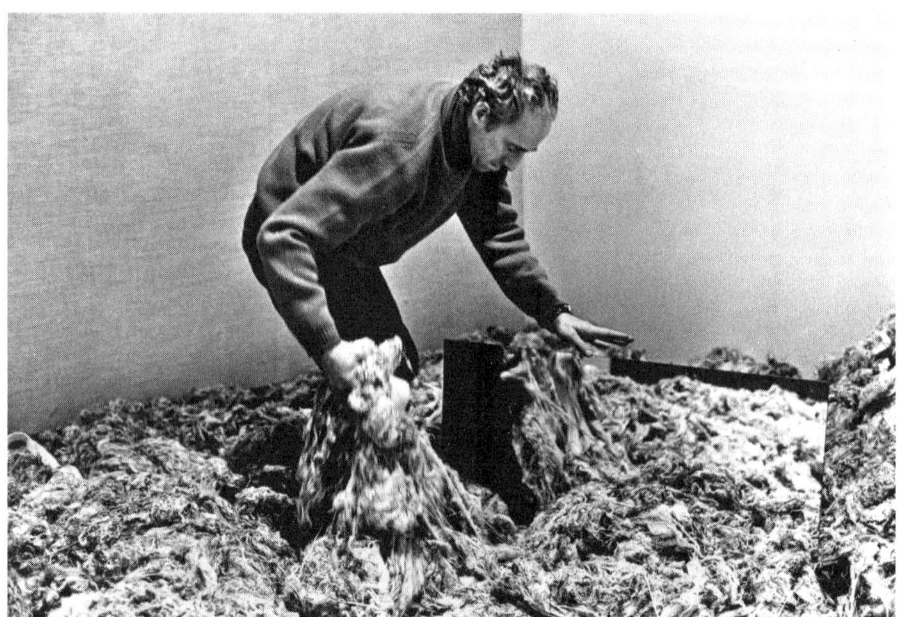

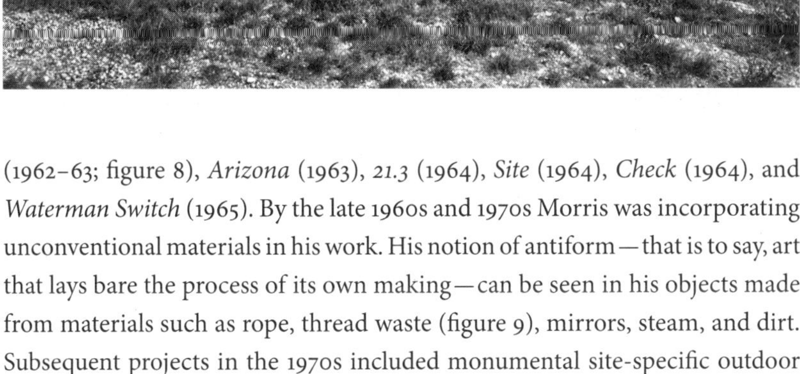

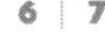

(1962–63; figure 8), *Arizona* (1963), *21.3* (1964), *Site* (1964), *Check* (1964), and *Waterman Switch* (1965). By the late 1960s and 1970s Morris was incorporating unconventional materials in his work. His notion of antiform—that is to say, art that lays bare the process of its own making—can be seen in his objects made from materials such as rope, thread waste (figure 9), mirrors, steam, and dirt. Subsequent projects in the 1970s included monumental site-specific outdoor earthworks in Europe and the United States (figure 10).

But among these nontraditional materials used by the artist, perhaps the most interesting was industrial felt. Between 1967 and 1996 Morris produced a remarkable number of works that employed industrial felt as a sculptural medium (figure 11). Whether rolled on the ground like a carpet ready to be stored (exhibited as "raw material"), or piled up, stacked up, hung from the

Opposite:

8. Robert Morris in costume for his choreography *War*, at the Judson Memorial Church, New York, January 1963. Photo courtesy of Robert Morris.

9. Robert Morris at work on *Threadwaste*, New York, 1968. Photo by Susan Horwitz, courtesy of Robert Morris.

Above:

10. *Untitled, Reclamation Project (Johnson Pit no. 30)*, 1979. Earth, tree-trunks, tar, 3.7 acres. Permanent site-specific earthwork in King County, City of Kent (Seattle). Photo courtesy of Bill Schillinger.

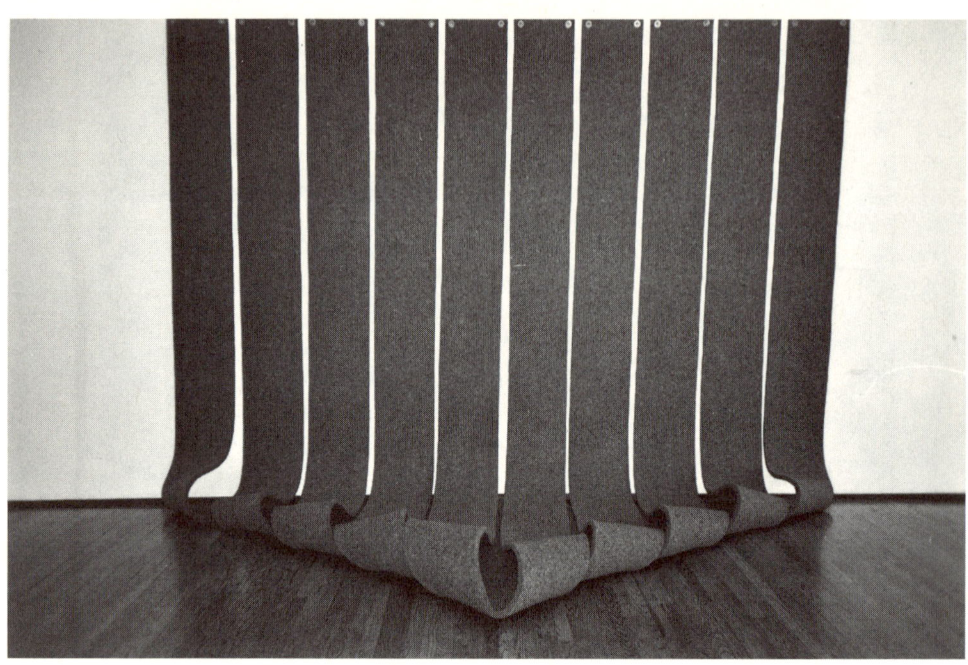

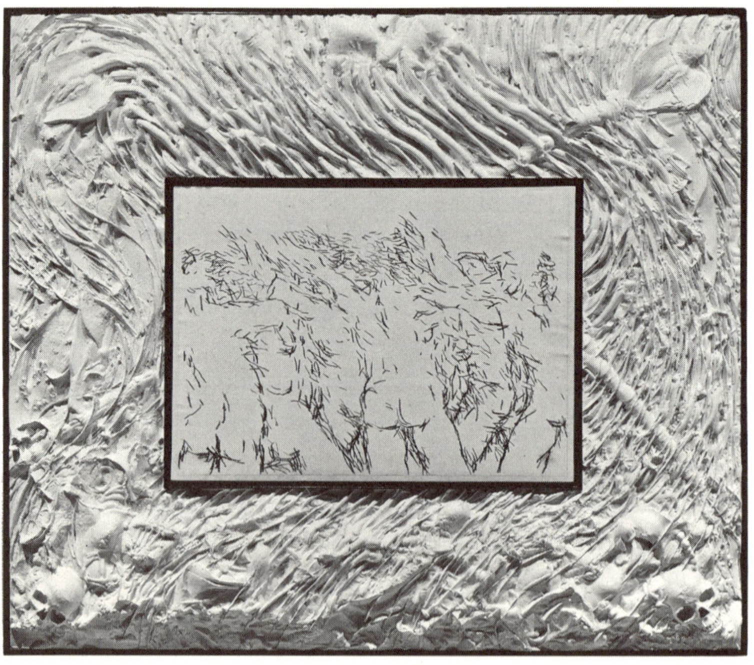

wall, with or without cut slits, with or without incorporated pipes, Morris's felt works reveal his interest in the property of the material, the role of gravity, and the idea of liberating form through chance.[3] In an interview with Phil Patton in 1983, Morris, explaining his choice of felt as his working medium, maintains that "felt has anatomical associations; it relates to the body—it's skinlike. The way it takes form, with gravity, stress, balance, and the kinesthetic sense, I liked all that."[4]

Questioning modernism in the 1980s, Morris violated a taboo by presenting the massive ornate frames of his *Hydrocal* series depicting apocalyptic imagery suggesting human potential for destruction;[5] in fact he caused a critical uproar in America (figure 12). Choreographer, performer, sculptor, critic, philosopher, pioneer, Morris has consistently renovated his art. Throughout his career he has proved incredibly versatile and always unpredictable. But his seemingly disparate works, Morris's artistic "styles" nevertheless are tied together by ideas rather than visual similarities. One is able to discern in his immense output certain features related to his growth, development, and very versatility that give us an idea of a unified personality as an achievement that depends precisely upon that unfolding.[6] And this versatility still exists in his works of the 1990s as well as in the more recent ones: the seventeen stained-glass windows installed in the Maguelone Cathedral, an eleventh-century Romanesque church (figure 13); his permanent site-specific installation *Melencolia II* (in collaboration with Claudio Parmiggiani) in Fattoria di Celle in Pistoia (figure 14); his two-screen video-and-sound installation *The Birthday Boy*, created in commemoration of the restoration and five-hundredth anniversary of Michelangelo's *David*, in the Galleria dell'Accademia in Florence, in which *David* was transformed from the traditional giant slayer into a young feminist black woman and a declining middle-aged man (figure 15);[7] and finally the encaustic paintings depicting interiors and domestic landscapes from the 1940s commenting on war and memory (figures 16–17).

At the same time Morris articulates his beliefs not only through his art but also through his writing. His master's thesis at Hunter College, "Form-Classes in the Work of Constantin Brancusi," was completed in 1966. (Morris was ap-

---

11. *Untitled (Inverted Shoulder)*, 1978. Gray felt and metal grommets, 9 feet 3 inches × 14 feet 11¾ inches × 6 feet × 2⅝ inches (2.82 × 4.56 × 1.90 m) overall. Museum Boymans-van Beuningen, Rotterdam. Photo courtesy of the editor.

12. *Untitled*, 1983. Cast Hydrocal, graphite on paper, 55¾ × 65½ inches (142 × 166 cm). Collection of Sonnabend Gallery, New York. Photo courtesy of Sonnabend Gallery.

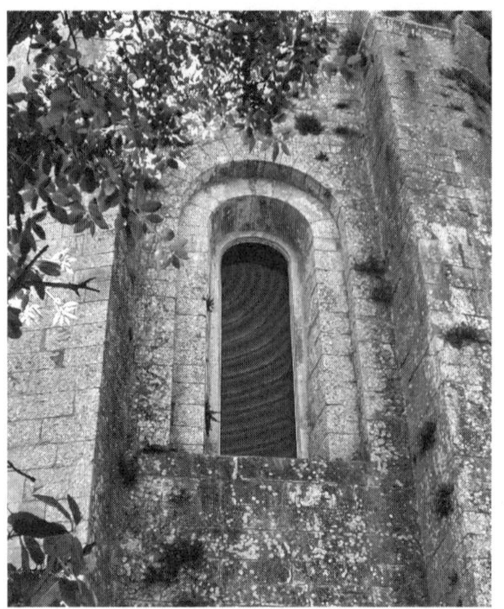

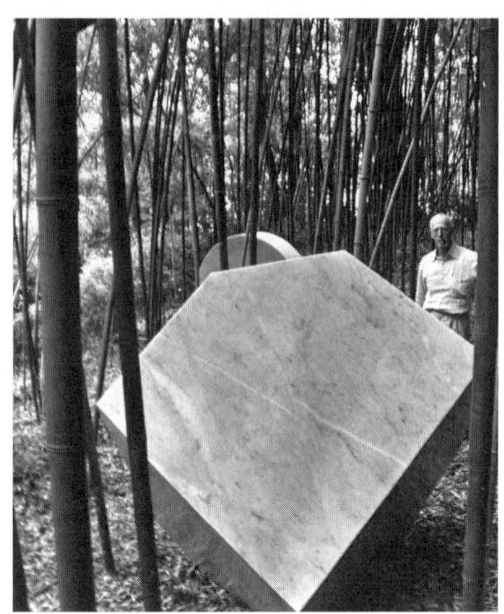

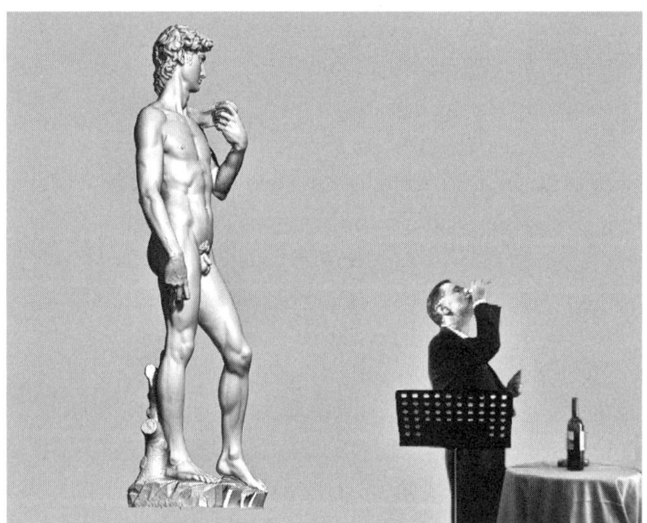

13. Seventeen stained-glass windows, 2001, installed in the Maguelone Cathedral, an eleventh-century Romanesque church that has been designated a French national historical monument. Work commission by the French Ministry of Culture. Detail (exterior view). Photo courtesy of Bill Schillinger.

14. Robert Morris with *Melencolia II*, 2002. Detail. Permanent site-specific installation. Collaboration with Claudio Parmiggiani. Collection of Giuliano Gori, Fattoria di Celle, Santomato, Pistoia, Italy. Photo courtesy of Bill Schillinger.

15. *The Birthday Boy*, 2004. Two-screen video with sound installation at the Galleria dell'Accademia, Florence. Photo courtesy of Vincenzo Capalbo.

pointed Distinguished Professor of Art at Hunter College in 1998.) And since then he has continued to write influential critical essays. His art and his writings are closely related. When I asked Morris if the act of writing is an integral part of his overall practice as an artist, he answered:

> I don't think of the "overall." Somebody with the name R. Morris engages with writing from time to time. The writing has changed over the years and taken different forms at different times. "Overall," I would say that outside of images there is only language. But neither is stoppable, although sometimes there is more of the one than the other.[8]

A number of factors motivated me to assemble this particular collection of Morris's writings. During the extensive research I did for my book *Robert Morris and Angst*, I realized that any complete analysis and assessment of Morris's total artistic contribution would prove inadequate without consideration and inclusion of his copious writings. It further occurred to me that while they present illuminating personal reflections on art, artists, language, and culture—providing a rich background for understanding his work—Morris's writings stand as a separate entity on their own literary merits.

Other researchers would soon learn, as I did, that many of his most recently published essays are scattered throughout various philosophy and art history periodicals, or are found in catalogues documenting exhibitions and installations in many widespread locations here and abroad. In other words, the last convenient collection of writings by this artist was published over a decade ago, that is, before even his major retrospectives at the Solomon R. Guggenheim Museum in New York and the Centre Georges Pompidou in Paris. As for the more recent unpublished works, they are of course simply not available. For these and other reasons I felt it was time to collect them in this single publication.

The reader here will discover that over time Morris's writings have become oriented more toward his concerns with contemporary social attitudes and issues. One will even find that a number of his writings are clearly polemical, given that his philosophic concerns—alongside his artistic ones—often focus on current manifestations of corporate excess, the hidden perils of modern technology and innovations, the risky trends toward international disengagement, unilateralism, and preemptive belligerence, and the commercialization of the aesthetic. Here Morris's concerns closely mirror the stark realities of the turbulent times we now face. He relates his truths with an element of irreverent candor that is too often left unspoken in our era of political correctness. This

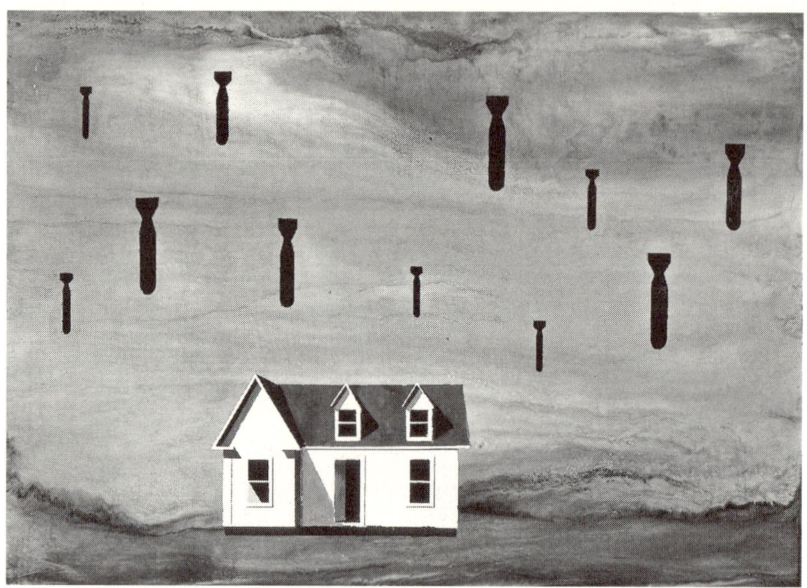

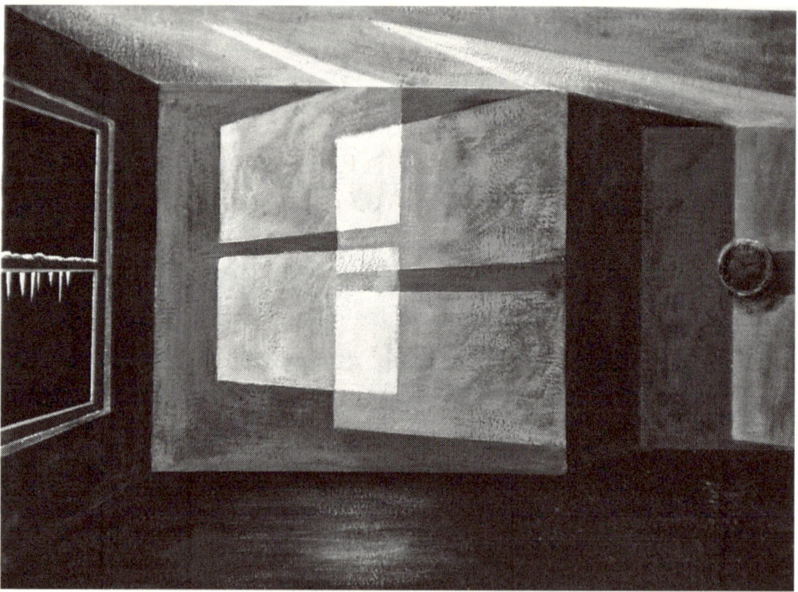

16. *House and Bombs*, 2004. Encaustic-on-wood panel, 30 × 42 inches (76.20 × 106.68 cm). Collection of Leo Castelli Gallery, New York. Photo courtesy of Leo Castelli Gallery.

17. *Sliding Lights*, 2005. Encaustic-on-wood panel, 33 × 46 inches (83.50 × 116.68 cm). Collection of Leo Castelli Gallery, New York. Photo courtesy of Leo Castelli Gallery.

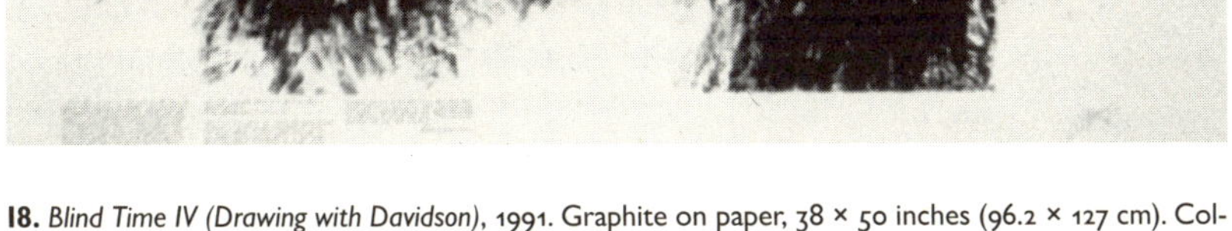

18. *Blind Time IV (Drawing with Davidson)*, 1991. Graphite on paper, 38 × 50 inches (96.2 × 127 cm). Collection of the artist. Photo by John Berens, courtesy of Robert Morris.

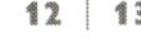

is perhaps the ultimate reason why I have compiled these invaluable contributions to contemporary thought.

Morris's interest in philosophy is well known and he is indeed a prolific writer on the subject. This collection of writings conveys an interest primarily in Ludwig Wittgenstein, Noam Chomsky, W. J. T. Mitchell, and Donald Davidson. Morris has an abiding interest in Davidson's work in the philosophy of mind, language, and action, so it comes as no surprise that two essays are devoted to this late renowned professor and philosopher at the University of California at Berkeley who in fact contributed the catalogue essay "The Third Man" for the Robert Morris exhibition at the Frank Martin Gallery, Muhlenberg College, in 1992.[9]

Morris incorporated excerpts from Davidson's books *Essays on Actions and Events* (1980) and *Inquiries into Truth and Interpretation* (1984) into a set of drawings entitled *Blind Time IV (Drawing with Davidson)* that the artist completed in 1991 as part of the ongoing series of drawings he made with his eyes closed beginning in 1973. Each quotation by Davidson is juxtaposed with Morris's intentions and the outcome—in his own words "how" he made each drawing—which the artist himself describes in the lower left corner of the drawing (figure 18). However, the reader cannot escape a growing sense of doubt that permeates the expressed certainty of these reasons and thus undermines them. In his essay "Writing with Davidson: Some Afterthoughts after Doing *Blind Time IV*: *Drawing with Davidson*," Morris sides with Davidson's account of the impossibility of reasons ever coming to an end and the philosopher's notion that reasons not only can explain actions but also be their cause.[10]

The works here range from one-page texts to long essays such as "Indiana Street," which I consider essential reading for those who wish to better understand Morris's work. This is not only for the obvious reason that Indiana Street is where he lived during his early formative childhood years in Kansas City—certainly some haunting childhood memories have greatly influenced his art-making. But together with the other essays in this volume, this autobiographical text reveals his unique manner of written expression, along with an exceptional gift for narrative description, the total effect of this combination being to instill in the reader a comprehensive grasp of Morris's wonderfully quirky mind.

In the presentation of Morris's writings, I have decided to intrude as little as possible with editorial changes, so as to let the original texts speak for themselves and stand on their own merits.

NOTES

1. Robert Morris's minimalist sculpture *Column* was used as a prop in a performance piece at the Living Theater in New York in 1961. His performance was as follows: center stage was a two-foot square gray plywood column standing eight feet high. Nothing else was on the stage. For three and a half minutes nothing happened. No one entered or left. Suddenly the column fell. Three and a half more minutes elapsed. The stage lights blacked out, marking the end of the performance.

   In conversation with the editor, Morris said that the original plan was for him to make the hollow column fall over while he was standing inside. However, he injured his head during the rehearsal on the day of the performance and instead a string was used to topple the column in the actual performance.
2. For a detailed history of the Judson Dance Theater, see Sally Banes, *Democracy's Body: Judson Dance Theater, 1962–64* (Durham, N.C.: Duke University Press, 1993).
3. For more on Morris's felt works, see Karmel, *Robert Morris: The Felt Works.*
4. Morris, as quoted in Phil Patton, "The Fire Next Time," *Art News* 82, no. 10 (December 1983): 50; quoted in Kimberly Paice, "Catalogue," in *Robert Morris: The Mind/Body Problem*, edited by Krauss et al., 213.
5. Hydrocal is the brand name of a type of plaster.
6. For more on the unity of Morris's art, see Tsouti-Schillinger, *Robert Morris and Angst.*

7. In Morris's installation *The Birthday Boy* two video screens show two middle-aged academics (a male and a female) lecturing pompously on Michelangelo's depiction of the biblical hero. They drink wine throughout their presentation. They get increasingly intoxicated and their remarks become more and more surreal on their interpretations of *David*—a symbol of manhood; of white oppression; a glorification of violent youth. Certainly *The Birthday Boy* is a piece that also brings to mind Morris's work from 1964 entitled *21.3*—a critique of art historical methods and a parody of the art historian Erwin Panofsky—in which the artist himself performed as the lecturer.
8. Morris, e-mail to the editor, December 3, 2005.
9. In "The Third Man" Davidson draws connections between elements of his thinking and Morris's works.
10. For an important discussion of the meeting of the two minds of Morris and Davidson in the *Blind Time IV* series, see Kenneth Surin, "Getting the Picture: Donald Davidson on Robert Morris's *Blind Time Drawings IV (Drawing with Davidson)*," *South Atlantic Quarterly* 101, no. 1 (Winter 2002): 133–69.

TELEGRAM

THE RATIONED YEARS

R. MORRIS

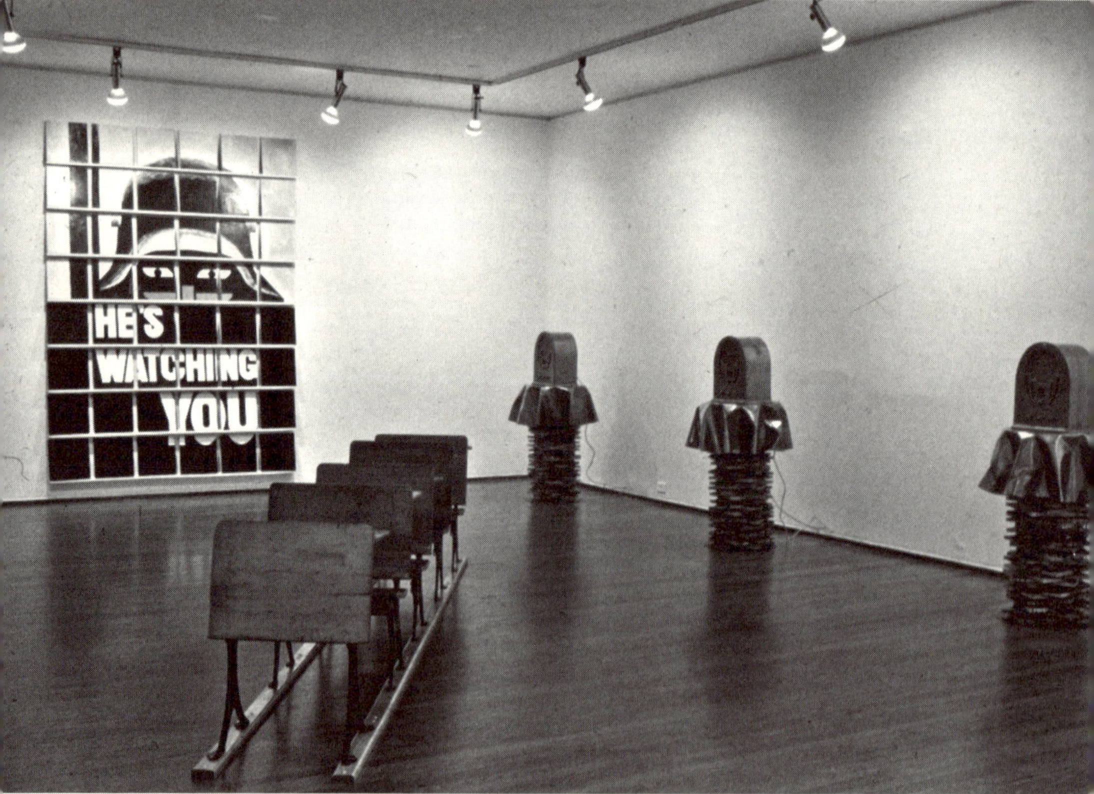

INDIANA STREET | 1993

Daddy, I know I will look back on this time and remember it as the good old days.

—MY SEVEN-YEAR-OLD DAUGHTER ON A CLOUDLESS JULY AFTERNOON

From the mid-1930s to the end of World War II we lived on Indiana Street in Kansas City, Missouri. All the houses on the west side of the 5200 block were single-story bungalows set above the street on steep terraces into which single-car garages had been excavated. All these houses were similar but differed in color and minor details, stairs, porches, eaves, etc. They were probably built in the early 1920s when the city expanded tremendously after World War I. Our house, 5208, was the second from the corner.

I remember clearly that moment in 1935 (I was four), sitting on the warm spring ground and squinting up through the bright sun watching two moving men strain up the porch steps with a red mohair sofa and chairs. The house was small: a living room, dining room, kitchen and breakfast nook, two little bedrooms, and a bathroom. It had a full basement and a cellar door in back.

My parents were both twenty-nine when we moved to Indiana Street in the depths of the Great Depression.

The house on the north side of us, the first on the block, was painted a bright yellow and surrounded by flower beds of roses and hollyhocks. Soon after we moved in, a sturdy wire fence marked off this yellow house from the trespasses of my sister and myself. But mostly, I presume, I was the reason for the fence. A few years later this fence provided an excellent barrier for my first pole-vaulting efforts as well as commando-type assaults over imaginary enemy lines. Mr. and Mrs. Chastain lived in the yellow house along with their married daughter and husband. During the war a girl in her twenties, who had come

---

19. *TELEGRAM / THE RATIONED YEARS*, 1998. Book written by Robert Morris, 71 pages. The book was published in an edition of 550 copies. Twenty numbered copies include a signed original drawing bound together with the book. Photo courtesy of the editor.

20. Installation view of *Robert Morris: The Rationed Years*, at the Leo Castelli Gallery, New York, September 26–November 30, 1998. Photo courtesy of Robert Morris.

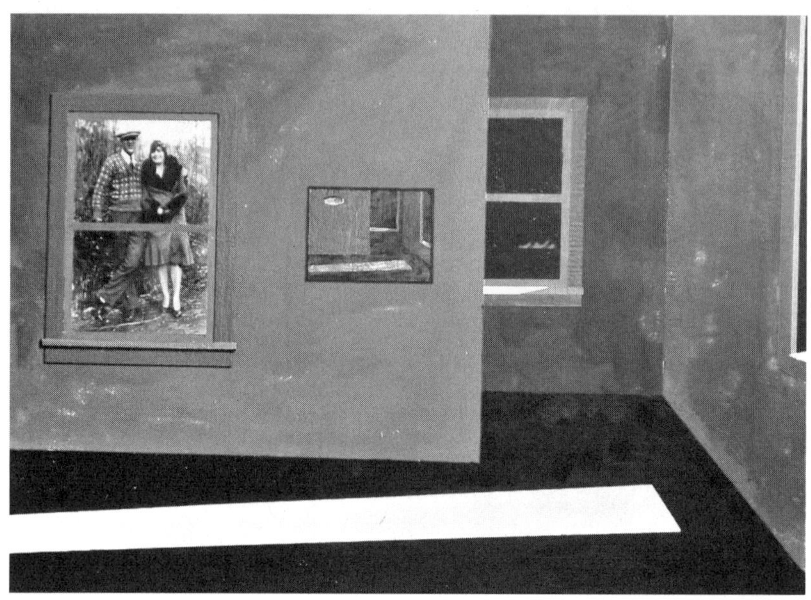

21. *Untitled*, 2005. Encaustic-on-wood panel, 33 × 46 inches (83.50 × 116.68 cm). Collection of the artist. Photo courtesy of the editor.

from the country like so many others to work for the war effort in the city, also lived there. I never knew where all of these people slept in such a small house. Mr. Chastain was "elderly," as my parents called him. He drove a pristine black Model-A Ford coupe to work downtown at the Union Station where he ran an elevator. He dressed in bib overalls and wore a trainman's striped hat and red bandanna like the engineers who drove the steam engines.

I had little to do with the older Chastains. Both were always concerned about the state of their flower beds and it seems to me in retrospect that I was probably viewed as a menace to their lifestyle. Their daughter, Willa, was married to a man of French extraction, Frank Liquier, a dark, gravel-voiced fellow of stern demeanor who had been partially crippled by polio. Frank worked as a sign painter and walked with an abnormal gait. His stiff legs were so bent inward at the knees that there was no clearance between them. Consequently, walking involved a series of staccato lurchings or swivelings of the upper torso in order to generate enough force to get one leg past the other. His elbows flung out to the sides for balance, Frank lurched now to the left and now to the right, moving forward one slow step at a time. I never saw him with a cane or crutches, and he walked in this effortful fashion every day to and from the streetcar stop four long blocks away. I would watch him coming home at about 6 p.m., his body

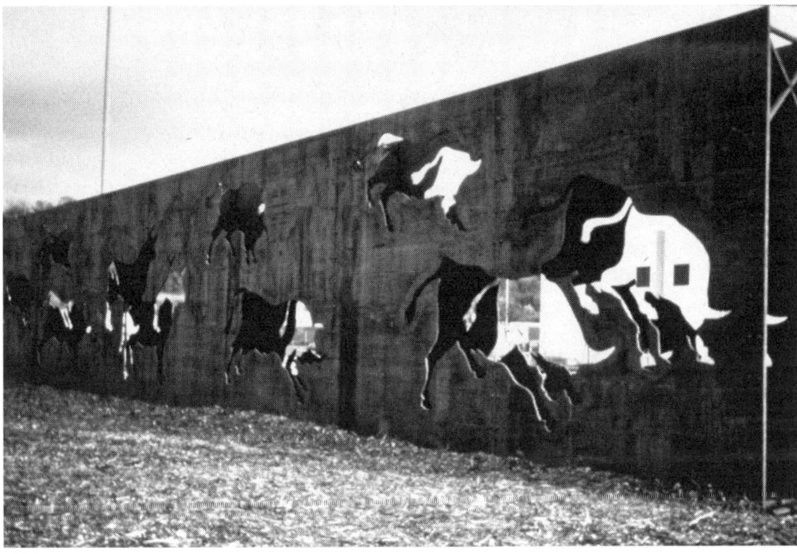

22. *Bull Wall: American Royale*, 1992. Two corten steel walls, 16 × 120 feet (4.88 × 36.58 meters) each. AIA commission, permanent site-specific installation in Kansas City, Missouri. Photo courtesy of Robert Morris.

swiveling and pivoting down the street. Somehow he negotiated the steep stairs in the terrace. I remember his impassive, dark face with the bluish shadow of his beard covered in sweat as he reached the top step.

Frank built a boat in the garage that was set into the terrace. This was a motor launch and filled the entire garage. He always worked at night on the boat and on summer evenings I would loiter around the garage watching him. In the dark cavelike garage he worked in the dim glow of a single mechanic's "trouble light." Perhaps the project had something to do with how crowded the house above the garage must have been. He was generally silent but answered my questions carefully when I asked about the construction of the craft. He explained that he had put 3,000 brass screws into the boat. At the time, the summer of 1939, I myself was trying rather unsuccessfully to build a balsawood Stuka dive bomber in the cramped bedroom I shared with my sister. Frank explained that he had bought a small lot on Lake Lotawanna east of the city and was also building a house and would one day move there with Willa and the boat. I know that eventually they moved to the lake with the boat, but I have no recollection of when it was. What is most fixed in my memory is Frank's implacable will, seen in his daily walk of eight blocks and the relentless nighttime construction of the boat, his body squeezed between its hull and the stone walls of the garage.

I never knew if this sense of bodily compression, the one knee pressed against the other with every step, the hull of the boat pushing against his torso (not to mention the absence of space in a tiny bungalow shared by five people), was finally relieved on the day he launched his boat onto the calm expanse of the lake's surface.

The house next door to us on the south was in my estimation a fraction smaller than ours. But I can recall no detail to substantiate such a judgment. Perhaps because it was occupied by only two people, as opposed to the four in our house and the five in the house to the north, it seemed smaller, illogical as that may be. The Vaurdamans lived there, Bill and Velma. Bill was a swarthy burly man in his early thirties with a chiseled profile. I thought at the time that he looked a little like the drawings of Superman in the comics. His wife was slim and tall. Bill worked on elevators, I was told. This is the only fact I ever learned about them. They kept to themselves and mixed little with the other people in the neighborhood, most of whom had children that played together and drew the parents into relationships of one sort or another. Looking into the Vaurdamans' window, which was directly across from the bedroom I shared with my sister, I often watched Bill shaving in the morning.

In the Vaurdamans' back yard was a magnificent box elder tree of, to a child, massive proportions. The bark of this tree was smooth, nearly silky in comparison with that of the rougher elms and oaks. Its enormous trunk separated into three slightly smaller ones a few feet above the ground, forming a kind of cup or seat. The upper branching limbs grew at almost right angles, making this a most lovable tree for climbing. I spent hours in its upper branches. From the lower branches I hung from my knees, once experiencing a cramp in my legs and falling to the soft earth headfirst with little damage. I peeled small sections of the bark away and examined the smooth, yellow, moist, and glistening surface of the living trunk. In the upper branches of this tree I saw at the age of eight the downy pubis of Joanne, an expert fourteen-year-old climber. She hung nonchalantly from her knees while her dress cascaded over her head to reveal, through old and shredded panties, this most absorbing sight. Attempting to lodge a long metal pipe in a vertical position between the branches, an experiment the purpose of which I no longer recall, I let go before sufficient friction was achieved and the pipe fell on my bare toes, causing a severe gash and plenty of blood. I changed the bandages for several weeks that summer, noting the odor of infection that the wound gave off.

Directly across the street was the house of Pop Harrison. The land on which the house sat was lower than that on which the houses on the west side of the block were sited. The yard was very large and sloped down behind the house into woods and a meandering stream called Brush Creek. The house had a certain spread-out aspect as if it had settled itself into its site. This was partly due to the large old elms, walnuts, maples, and oaks that surrounded it. People on the block said that Pop would never cut down a tree. Pop, a widower in his sixties, was also somewhat spread out and seemed settled into an imperturbable inner space. He never called any of the kids in the neighborhood by their given names but always greeted us with "Hello, child." He drove a 1933 Dodge coupe that had a rumble seat. Nominally black, the paint on the car was faded by the sun to a strange and subtle iridescent purplish blue that showed in certain lights. He sometimes arrived with the rumble seat filled with groceries. There was no garage and he parked under the pear tree in front of the house. Pop always wore dark three-piece suits with a watch fob buttoned into his lapel. His daughter, Lucille, and her husband, Harry, and their children Emma Lou and Sonny also lived in Pop's house. Unlike Pop, Lucille was jovial, loud, and talkative. But like Pop she weighed in at around 180. Harry had been in World War I and had experienced "shell shock," so the neighbors said. In any case, his hearing had been damaged and he wore a hearing aid that had a wire running from his ear to the battery and volume control in his shirt pocket. This device either never worked or he kept it turned down to low. Everyone shouted to Harry and he constantly said, "What's that?" A thin, wiry, good-natured man, his laughter, mixed with that of Lucille's, came out of the open doors and windows on summer days. Every Easter he and Lucille hid dozens of colored eggs throughout the large yard for the neighborhood children to find.

I remember the interior of their house as dark and cool in the summer. Unlike our bungalow its rooms were generous. Due to the slope of the land the basement was high and had been made into a kind of sun porch/sewing room that looked out onto the woods. My sister and Emma Lou often played there amid the heaps of colored fabrics that Lucille sewed into dresses. I remember the rustle and the color of the heaped material spread out on long tables and the early sun streaming through the open windows when I occasionally went to find my sister. In the lower yard behind the house was a stand of ancient walnut trees, and, further on, the creek where I once threw dozens of stones at a water moccasin that continued to raise itself out of the water to watch me in spite of the hail of rocks arriving all around it. In the late 1930s crews of stone masons from the WPA came to straighten out the meanders of Brush Creek and to push a large winding concrete and cut-limestone channel through the woods where the creek had once been. Since I considered these woods mine, I felt the

WPA project was an invasion and went to watch the work progress with a mixture of curiosity and resentment. After this project had been completed there were several reports of a "prowler" in the neighborhood and word spread that someone had found cardboard boxes in the masonry tunnel where the creek passed under Indiana Street. The report was that the cardboard confirmed the prowler's presence and since it had been flattened he must have spent the night on it. These stories filled me with dread and for years afterward I compulsively looked in the closet and under the bed before turning out the light.

The back yards of the block of houses bounded by 52nd and 53rd streets on the north and south and Indiana and College streets on the east and west ran together into a kind of no-man's-land, a tangle of bushes and trees. I knew every inch of this terrain as well as the spaces between the garages that were located behind the houses on 52nd. One special space was formed by two garages that had a telephone pole planted between them so that only those with narrow nine-year-old bodies could pass between. It was with a secret pleasure that I squeezed my body between the pole and the side of the garages, making my passage usually at dusk. Although unnamed, and perhaps unnamable, such spaces, of which there were many around the neighborhood, took on a special character. I would usually visit each once a week. The woods beyond Pop Harrison's house across Brush Creek were full of secret spaces. There was the abandoned well on an old overgrown house site on which only a few foundation walls remained. I would peer down the well for what, in memory, seemed hours. I could see frogs and an occasional snake at the bottom at high noon when the sun penetrated to the depths of this hole. There was the abandoned limestone rock quarry with a steel cable swinging from an overhanging oak on the small bluff above. Such places had all the silent presence I recognized many years later in the late landscapes of Cézanne: breathless, unpopulated, sun-dappled, profoundly silent. I went to these spaces to be enfolded in their presence. It was as though I could feel time stop there, as though I was an unseen eye witnessing a certain infinity, complete forever in its light and drowsy heat.

On the west side of Indiana, from 52nd Street south toward 53rd, the houses diminished ever so slightly in size—from Chastain to Morris to Vaurdaman to Killbane to McEuen to Kincaid. Beyond the Kincaids' the character of the block changed. The bungalows became tiny, the road in front was unpaved, and I knew none of those families. Even in this lower-middle-class neighborhood there was yet a lower class. With few exceptions I did not associate with anyone from this lower zone. I do not remember any admonishment from my parents about staying away from the lower end of the block, but it remained a largely unknown and unvisited terrain. My territorial space ended with the Kincaid house. At the age of seven I engaged in a rock fight with Suzanne, a tough and threatening girl from the lower zone. During a pause in the throwing I peered out from behind my lilac bush in the Vaurdamans' yard to be beaned on the forehead with a piece of cinder hurled by Suzanne. There was blood and later a scar. I suffered a physical setback but a territorial victory. Suzanne did not invade the upper block again.

Gene McEuen, a fatherless boy who lived in the third house down from us, was given the status of undesirable playmate by my parents. I came to think of him and his house as misplaced or transposed from the lower block into our upper zone. He was slightly older and, according to my parents, had been in reform school. He had run away from home and his mother spoke to no one on the block. The shades were always drawn over the curtainless windows of his house. One hot summer day when I crossed their yard I glimpsed the shaded bare rooms through the open door. I could make out neither rugs nor furniture and felt a sickening curiosity pass through my body. One frigid and gray December day several boys from the neighborhood had gone to the woods behind Pop's house to play hockey on a wide frozen meander of Brush Creek. We had found a metal barrel and built a fire in it. Gene was there and stood around watching. He was a nonskater. But then he probably owned no skates. In any case he was too old to play with the rest of us since he was about fourteen and we skaters were nine and ten. Standing by the fire Gene began to speak of his desire for women and exposed his large, erect penis to show us how ready he was for such adventures. Preoccupied with his performance I unthinkingly embraced the hot barrel, getting painful burns on the palms of both hands.

Gene McEuen once gave me a hardwood blackboard pointer. I don't recall why. I became fixated on the shape of this object, which was carved or turned on a lathe and to me had exquisite proportions. Did I associate such an object with the older boy's sexual display? Did I accept this object as a kind of passing of the phallus and its promises—a pointer pointing to my own promised sexual awakening? My contact with Gene was edged with a certain excitement and anxiety, and the disapproval of my parents was always voiced when they saw me talking to him. I regarded the pointer he gave me as having the aura of stolen goods, just as I regarded Gene as a kind of ex-con, an outsider, someone who had secrets he did not reveal. He presented to me the persona and image of the trespasser. But I also always saw him as a person who lived in empty rooms and someone who, above all, had tried to escape not only the grimness of his barren home and silent mother but in some way I also suspected, wanted to escape "us." That is, I felt a strange ambivalence about identifying and being identified with the denizens of the block—as though we all represented a kind of emptiness to him, as though he saw through the oppression that I only suspected, was confused by and confined within. That his "escape" had ended in reform school was all the more disheartening, reinforcing as it did the futility of any escape from the world of Indiana Street. Eventually Gene and his mother did move but memory does not mark the event. I was a freshman in high school when I heard that Gene had run away again and had fallen under a freight train, which had severed both his legs and an arm. Someone showed me the clipping from the *Kansas City Star*. I never knew if he survived this accident.

The one house from the lower block I once entered was the tiny yellow one where Phyllis Uzell lived. This was the last house before 53rd Street. The block beyond was a tangle of Brush Creek meanders and then cornfields. In the 1930s no houses had been built on Indiana Street from 53rd to 55th. In fact I do not recall any building going on anywhere in Kansas City during that decade. The physical environment seemed changeless, fixed forever. I think I came to know Phyllis because she had something to do with the Girl Scout troop to which my sister belonged. She was a large, athletic girl, loud, friendly, playful, and a couple of years older than I. I liked being with Phyllis in spite of the fact that my mother thought her a vulgar "Tom Boy" and disapproved of her father, who drank. Mr. Uzell often walked down Indiana Street with a kind of waddling, slew-footed gait. I don't remember that he owned a car in the early 1930s. He had a flushed complexion and a few tufts of orange hair that stuck up around his ears. He reminded me of Jiggs in the Sunday funnies. In the late '30s Mrs. Uzell left him and their three daughters. People said alcohol was the reason. Later, during the war, he had a head-on collision and Phyllis and one of her sisters were killed. Word was that he had been drunk. Mr. Uzell survived but hanged himself in the little house at the end of the block a few weeks later. The remaining sister went to live with the family next door. After this I tried not to walk down the lower unpaved part of Indiana Street past the Uzell house. The lower end of the street took on some of the same taint as did part of 52nd Street some six blocks west, which was on my route to Graceland Grade School. There on a frigid January morning I came upon a large, black Labrador lying in the middle of the street. It had been hit by a car, and its skull crushed. A large star of frozen blood extended from its head. For months I walked out of my way around this block and even years later when I could bear to pass this section of 52nd Street, the image of the massive black animal and its asterisk of frozen blood haunted me.

The Killbane family lived in the second house down from ours on the west side of Indiana. Crystal and Joe had two boys, Jody, the older, and Jim, two years younger. Jody was a year younger than I. At eight years of age, a seven-year-old is beneath consideration. I never knew Jody beyond a nodding acquaintance, achieved when we played hide-and-seek or some form of street ball. Jody's father was a motorcycle policeman and rode a massive Harley Davidson. One frosty November afternoon about 3 p.m. Joe roared up to the Graceland schoolyard on his great blue-and-white motorcycle to which chrome sirens, lights, and an eight-foot aerial were fastened, and asked me if I had seen Jody. Since Jody was not around I got the thrilling ride home on the back of the police motorcycle. Dismounting, my leg hit the aerial and I fell off the motorcycle and into the street flat on my back.

Walter and Harold Peters lived not on Indiana Street but a block west on College. Between the ages of eight and eleven I went across the no-man's-land of vacant lots up to their house every chance I got. The boys were a year older and a head taller than I. Lucy, their mother, and Walter Sr., their father, were boisterous and told ribald jokes. Unlike the dour and disapproving atmosphere in my own house, there were always jokes at the Peters'. The boys were fun to be around. Walter built balsawood airplanes with five-foot wingspans. These were both elegant and airworthy and flew the entire block down across the vacant lot from their house to mine with a slow and serene grace that filled me with admiration and wonder. Many years later when I was learning to fly gliders, the memory of a translucent red wing slowly wheeling through the air floated in my mind as I turned again and again on the summer air currents that lifted me ever higher into the sky.

I was never able to get the tissue paper tight on the Stuka I worked on for weeks. The multiple applications of the aromatic chemical we called "dope" applied to the paper skin never took out the sag. I would emerge from my tiny bedroom with cuts on my fingers from using an Exacto knife on the balsawood and be dizzy from the "dope." Both boys were excellent musicians. Harold played the trombone and Walter the clarinet. Lucy played the piano and Walter Sr. had a fine baritone voice. In the evenings he sometimes sang in German. The frail, white-haired grandfather who lived with them spoke only German. Walter, Harold, and I built a giant slingshot from a strip of automobile tire inner tube stretched between the fork of an apple tree. We found a box of huge metal fence staples and stretching out the thick rubber strip some three or four feet would aim high in the direction of Graceland Grade School some seven blocks to the northwest, firing away until our arms were tired. One Easter I told Harold of my idea to dye two identically colored blue eggs, only one of which would be hard-boiled. I would then encourage my father to break the uncooked egg on his head by demonstrating how easy it was with the cooked one. Harold encouraged this adventure and helped me to boil and dye the eggs. When the time came I demonstrated the egg-on-head to my father with a confident gesture. Harold had switched the eggs on me and carefully observed my gasps with no change of expression on his face.

The boys slept in an unfinished attic or what was called a "sleeping porch" on the second floor. This architectural afterthought was a detail often added to the backs of Kansas City houses built in the '20s. I longed to have an upstairs bedroom like this and begged my parents to let me sleep over on Friday nights with the Peters boys. We would wake in the unheated chill of the room at dawn and hatch our plans for the coming day, laughing in intoxicated freedom from our space far above the downstairs realm of the adults. Walter excavated a kind of cave or bunker in the vacant lot of no-man's-land. This shallow gravelike hole he covered with planks, earth, and sod. There was even a hinged door on top. My mother disapproved of this earthwork and suspected Walter Jr. of building it so that he could entice girls into it to "feel them up." Walter Sr. drove a city bus when I first knew the Peters. In the late 1930s he bought a flatbed truck and went into business for himself hauling things. He would often repeat to us boys that "it's a great life if you don't weaken." When I was twelve the Peters family moved to a small farm beyond the suburb of Waldo, where the streetcar line ended at the southwest end of Kansas City. I visited them only once, sleeping over again in an upstairs bedroom very much like the one on College Street. When Lucy and Walter Sr. had gone to town, Walter Jr. got his father's .38 pistol and let me fire it at a tree. It was the first time I shot a gun and I felt numb and nearly deaf afterward. I never saw Walter and Harold after this visit. Years later my mother told me the boys had moved to California and married. Walter Jr. became a labor organizer and lobbyist who traveled frequently to Washington, D.C. Harold's wife died of cancer in the 1960s.

On summer evenings my sister and her friend Emma Lou, her brother Sonny, and Jody, Walter, Harold, and any others who were around gathered to play baseball in Indiana Street, kick-the-can, or hide-and-seek. The box elder in the Vaurdamans' yard would usually be base in hide-and-seek. All of us would scatter in the dusk across the vacant lots and back yards. I remember lying on my stomach in the tall, dewy grass spying whoever was "it" to see when I could make a break for the box elder, my body taut for the imminent sprint to the tree but oddly relaxed with the sensuous, nearly sexual feeling of the earth beneath my belly. Waiting for the moment to run "home." Waiting with anxious excitement for the sprint into puberty.

On the east side of Indiana there were two remaining houses besides Pop Harrison's. One was the Weber house on the northeast corner of 52nd. This was a large three-story stone house occupied by two spinster sisters with white hair. A high spirea hedge surrounded the place. I can't recall ever entering the manicured yard. The sisters' nephew, Richard Weber, a boy about my own age, came to visit them on weekends. I had a special dislike for Richard, his prissy ways and overly clean clothes. At seven I tried to drop a large, flat limestone rock onto him as he stood below the wall at the foot of our terrace. I generally taunted him and challenged him to fights, and on occasion chased him into the sanctuary of his large yard. Perhaps a territorial instinct drove me, or perhaps some class envy of his slight economic advantage.

To the south of Pop Harrison's large rolling yard the ground fell off into a kind of bottom land beside Brush Creek. This flat field was invariably planted with corn and stretched a long half-block to the last house before 53rd on the east side of the street. Ralph Seever, a boy who was a couple of years older than I, lived in the little house back from the road beside the cornfield. Word was that Ralph was retarded. He did not go to Graceland like the rest of us and I do not think he attended any school. His walk was peculiar, penguinlike, although it may be exaggerated in memory. His voice was adenoidal and nasal, his face was pocked with scars and had a wolfish look, and his eyes slanted strangely. But he was always friendly and polite. While I felt unthreatened in his presence I also felt a foreboding. Ralph was interested in all things sexual and spoke with confidence and in detail about the copulation and birthing of animals. He was intimate with the tunnel beneath Brush Creek near 53rd Street and pointed out to me the pornographic graffiti on its cement walls. He spoke of the pallets of cardboard on which the reputed prowler spent his nights and kept a running count of the used condoms found under the tunnel. He claimed to know and to have visited "Turtle Bill," an old man who lived in a shack south of 53rd along the creek in a wild tangle of trees and swampy ground and who, according to rumor, existed on trapped turtles he cooked into stews. I only saw Turtle Bill once, ragged and bearded, moving through the trees along the creek like a shadow.

Ralph held both a curiosity and a dread for me and I came from the few visits I had with him vaguely disturbed and anxious. He seemed to possess a knowledge I wanted and did not want. Haunting Brush Creek as he did, he seemed to embody the fascination and uneasiness this dark stream elicited in me. There were youthful stories of quicksand in some of its meanders. The dark moccasins that slithered across its muddy, still surfaces gave me a chill. And a certain sewerlike taint emanated from the creek—evidenced by the occasional condom one saw undulating slowly, half-submerged in its dark waters. Ralph reminded me that not only there existed an underworld of the ostracized and the malformed, a class to which he belonged, but that a heavy inertial current of dark desires and unnamed urges flowed under the daylight of Indiana Street. He gave me a glimpse of the queasy underbody, where a slimy abjectness dripped that both fascinated and repelled. He pointed out to me what the others never named. With the inertia of what the others termed his "simpleness," he seemed to have dropped through the insulation of their linguistic repressions to move against some clammy, sexual membrane that pulsed hidden and unmentioned just below the surface of those lives on Indiana Street.

The great August heat wave of 1935 rolled over un-air-conditioned Kansas City with temperatures soaring above 100 degrees for over two weeks. I would stand on the front porch with Mother in the early morning after Father had gone to work. We would look at the pale cloudless sky and Mother would say, "It's going to be another scorcher." For those two weeks most of the denizens of our block on Indiana Street migrated in the evenings to Swope Park, some three miles to the southeast. We got on the Swope Park streetcar after supper carrying our bundle of sheets. Sometimes my sister and I got a ride in Pop's rumble seat and beat our parents to the park, arriving breathless from the hot wind that blew in our faces as we sped along the boulevard. We would rendezvous at Shelter House No. 1, a large limestone structure with a red tile roof and long flanking trellises. From there we would pick a spot on the vast rolling lawns and spread our bedding beside hundreds of other families. We slept on the ground until dawn when the fathers walked to the streetcar stop to go to work and the kids were rounded up for auto or streetcar rides back home before the heat came up. There is an indelible image in my mind of hundreds of white sheets being unfurled as an immense orange sun sank. There an airless dusk settles on a smooth, sloping lawn. There the flash of little naked bodies are running and squealing over the mournful sound of the cicadas buzzing their hymn to the paralyzing zenith of summer.

There were three horse-drawn vehicles that regularly made their way down Indiana Street. Of these the most elegant belonged to the "Manor Man." This nearly cubic wagon was painted a creamy yellow and the reins, which were a pristine white, passed through two small rectangular slots in the cab or wagon. I remember this fact because of the peculiar brass grommets that were fitted to these openings. The vehicle itself rode silently on two pneumatic rubber tires. This was the Manor Company bakery wagon and it came down the street promptly at 7:45 a.m. every morning except Sunday. The Manor Man was dressed in white and announced his presence by blowing a small, high-pitched silver whistle very much like those used by sailors on the warships depicted in the movies I saw at the Bijou Theater up on Prospect Street. He carried a metal basket over his arm as he bounded up our steep front stairs. In this basket were hot cross buns, cinnamon rolls, and white bread. We urged Mother to buy the rolls or buns. Sometimes she relented and heated these in the oven for our breakfast. As the front terrace of the entire block was steep, the Manor Man walked across the yards from the Chastains to the Kincaids as he went from door to door. The silver whistle that signaled his presence was also heard by the horse, which would then plod a few steps down the block always keeping pace with the Manor Man's progress above. As the Manor Man went down the last flight of steps at the Kincaid house the horse and wagon would be waiting for him.

During the first few summers on Indiana Street we had an icebox. The wagon of the iceman was flat and the load of ice covered with a heavy gray canvas. On hot days we begged him for a sliver of ice as he chipped into the large blocks with lightning-fast stabs of his ice pick. Water would be dripping onto the street from every board of the wet wagon, which gave off the most refreshing and fragrant smell on those summer mornings. The man himself was covered in wet leather. He wore a kind of leather cape over his shoulders onto which he hoisted the blocks with a swing of his tongs. A second layer of leather, a split apron, was strapped to his thighs. Whether the water that ran down his body was from the melting ice or the sweat of his labor I could not tell. In memory he moves with the swiftest of motions, accompanied by the snapping sound of the metal catches that held the leather straps of his garments. His actions constituted a performance: the flop of the wet canvas flung back to expose the blocks of ice, the staccato hiss of the ice pick in action, the bite of the tongs and the muscular swing of the translucent block onto the shoulder, and the bound up the stairs balancing the block of ice. He was a man who worked fast and without wasted motion. Perhaps it was the threat of the summer heat diminishing his load before his rounds were completed. But it might have been a celebration of his youthful strength and delight in the physical grace of movements honed by practice.

About once a month the Saturday morning quiet was shattered by an agonizing wail. "Aaaraaaaorriirrrornnnnn!" I could never make out the syllables. But the cry of the ragman filling the street must have been "Any rags or iron." One could hear the splayed iron wheels of his wreck of a wagon grinding the street between his yells. The horse was pitiful and as hunched over as the ragman. Like an apparition they made their way ever so slowly down the block. There was something terrifying to me about this presence. Turtle Bill seemed robust by comparison. Even in those hard times, ragged, abject poverty and homelessness were unknown on Indiana Street. But the eeriest aspect of the ragman was the linguistic collapse registered in the wail. Here speech itself had imploded and become a desperate cry. Some intimation of the doomed and fallen seemed to ride with that spectral figure on his wobbly wagon. Death was chanting on top of the pile of rusty iron and rags. Here was the opened grave itself calling all of Indiana Street to witness what lay ahead.

For a child, it seemed a long streetcar ride from 52nd and Swope Parkway to the gilded Loews movie palace downtown. And in winter, it was an even longer freezing ride back home. I would sit stiff and sleepy, sometimes lucky enough to be over a rare heater that warmed my bottom through the cane seat, and stare out at the lights in the crystalline night air. If that mindless and cynical bloodbath called World War I sparked the Dada movement at the Cafe Voltaire in Zurich, where the exiled Lenin sat through a few performances, in Kansas City the slaughter was commemorated by the Liberty Memorial. This pale tower I saw on top of the heave in the landscape to my right as the trolley, moving south, made the bridge over the Union Station tracks and approached Pershing Road for the long climb up the Main Street hill. Impressive indeed was that smooth, spotlit phallic shaft with the illuminated steam at its tip, drooling and drifting out into the frozen night sky. When killing becomes patriotic, national, and insane, perhaps only a sexualized memorial to it can keep its reality from full consciousness.

On my left, directly across from the Memorial, crowning that limestone crag known as Signboard Hill, another illuminated, larger-than-life artifact blazed and blinked in the winter night. High up was an enormous sphere—a disk, actually, but meant to read as a globe—a hieroglyph of the earth itself, formed in blue and white incandescent bulbs. Suddenly, out of nowhere, a small can of paint materialized at the top of this globe, and tipped forward in a most wonderful syncopation of coordinated lights. Out of this little *deus ex machina* flowed a quantity of red paint wildly incommensurate with the volume of the can. And the lights began to change from the innocent blue of the natural world to the red of man's engulfing cultural mark—paint—signified by means of electrically simulated drips and surges, until, within the course of some forty-five seconds, the entire globe demonstrated with a thousand red lights the triumphal words that flashed above the whole scene: "Sherwin-Williams paints cover the Earth." This hypnotic spectacle was repeated with only the briefest of pauses throughout the night.

Today, the shoddy architecture of Crown Center has replaced the seedy, blinking Signboard Hill of the 1930s and '40s. I doubt that anything will be found to replace that militaristic hard-on, the Liberty Memorial. But I hold a certain nostalgia for that blinking sign. Where else could one find a more paradigmatic emblem of proleptic capitalism's optimism about conquering the world marketplace than in that electrified paint, which left no point on the globe uncovered? And of more interest perhaps, what were the connections to be made between those two public monuments? On the right stood the one dedicated to the sacrificial dead of what history has billed a global conflict; on the left blinked the merry hopes of global mercantile domination. A certain internal symmetry began to show itself between those geometric emblems of cylinder and sphere. The ideological content began to leak out of these two minimalist monuments and to run together there on Main Street, waiting for me. But I would not have noticed then, on that long climb in the freezing streetcar straining up the hill. The Errol Flynn movie would have probably been exhausting. I would be dozing off to the muffled knocking of the air compressors, somewhere in the belly of the swaying trolley, dreaming of a black cape like Zorro's.

No doubt the snows of memory are always deeper. My recollection throws up a sky that was so dark and heavy that our white house appeared to glow against it at noon. The snow fell for days over an ever more silent neighborhood. That first winter on Indiana Street Father pulled my sister and me on a sled six blocks to Pachutto's grocery on Swope Parkway to get a Christmas tree. The image is as crystalline in my mind as was the snow beneath the streetlight: the two of us bundled up on the tiny sled, the silence broken only by the crunch of Father's boots on the powdery snow as we moved from one pool of light to another marked by the streetlights at every intersection. There were no snowplows and few cars tried to negotiate the choked streets. We could, with impunity and a careless thrill, take the 52nd Street hill all the way from South Benton down across Agnes, Bellfountain, Walrond, and College and come down the last and steepest stretch from Walrond to Indiana with ever greater acceleration. Not a car in sight as we crossed Indiana and shot off down the hill through the wild brambles and trees, making a hard left at the bottom to avoid going into Brush Creek. We got up with Father in the dark before school to sled and in the afternoons after school stayed out again into the dark. Our boots crunched as we climbed the long hill pulling our sleds. A five-step run at the top of South Benton and then slam down the belly on the sled, squint the eyes against the falling snow. Low to the white ground hearing the hiss of the runners, accelerating all the way, and flying through the pools of light at the intersections, yelling down the last steep drop after crossing Indiana. My screaming, night-fighting Stuka sled had the tank in the cross hairs as I pulled out of the dive on the swooping turn at the edge of the creek. We shouted, we gulped the snow-air's freshness, snot and tears from the cold running down our faces. We had great rollover accidents on purpose and sometimes rode the Flexible Flyer sleds sitting backward in acts of hysterical bravado, falling into drifts that buried us in the soft whiteness. When we arrived home with numb feet and wet boots we stood barefoot on the heat registers thawing out. The heat rising from the coal furnace in the basement gave us the sensation of pins and needles as we recovered the feeling in our feet.

The coal truck dumped its load of large anthracite boulders just off the street onto what would have been a sidewalk, had there been one. It was a long flight of steps up the steep front terrace, then around the side of the house to the basement window into which the heavy buckets had to be dumped. I seemed to make no headway reducing the size of this black mountain rising out of the snow. I would have a galvanized bucket in each hand, each with a large chunk of coal inside. A few steps and rest, a few more and put the buckets down again. The pull of the wire handle through my mittens began to raise blisters. I could hear the heavy thuds of the lumps of coal as they hit the basement floor inside. When I would return to the malevolent black mound, the sounds of the empty metal buckets clattering against the cement sides of the wall beside the steps seemed far too loud in the snow-muffled silence. My toes got numb and I was filled with despair at the overwhelming task, one I knew I would never complete. I took it as an omen that a future of this kind of work lay ahead of me, that I would be condemned to some form of punitive and interminable labor, that work invariably exacted a wracking bodily exhaustion. No doubt the experience and the foreboding were connected in part to observations of my father's physical exhaustion at the end of his day when he invariably fell asleep in his chair with the evening newspaper. At any rate my anticipation of male adulthood and the form of life I knew from Indiana Street melded into a kind of airless claustrophobia that became deposited with memory and associated with all of my childhood.

A moment from the winter of 1935. Mother tucked me in for an afternoon nap and assured me she would be there when I woke. Memory delivers this odd reassurance. But when I woke she was not in the house. She had taken the opportunity to walk the four blocks to the tiny market on 51st and Bellfountain. I stood by the front window overlooking the porch and stairs to the street. I saw her approach, slowly climbing the stairs with brown bags of groceries in each arm. I waited until she had mounted the top porch step and swung my tiny fist through the windowpane. Strangely I was uncut by the shattering glass. Mother was astonished and furious. This remains a cardinal moment in my life, a moment of fury and anger relieved by an act of bodily violence. No doubt I have lived a life of artmaking by transposing and sublimating a fury that has never abated and rises ever anew: an unending source of energy.

The woods behind Pop Harrison's house and across Brush Creek were a sanctuary, an escape, a second world apart from that of Indiana Street. I knew the paths by heart and every meander of the creek. I knew where the bright orange and black orioles nested and where water moccasins might be found. I knew the character of the various spaces the woods presented: the meadow of unusually tall, lush grasses that smelled so fresh, which was set in a clearing surrounded by looming oaks and walnuts; the ridge of limestone to the far eastern part near Swope Parkway; the gravel pit over by 52nd; and the tunnel below 51st that exited behind the ballpark stadium. I observed the birds, the snakes, turtles, and rabbits from my patient blinds within certain bushes, waiting and watching for hours in the drowsy summer afternoon heat. These spaces I visited alone, soaking up the silence and solitary stillness. It was as though I had passed out of the Indiana Street world and into a universe encapsulated by a kind of enlarged moment during which everything stood still. If I ever came close to the awe-filled moment of interrogating Being I did so there, long before I read Heidegger. In those moments I was simultaneously open to the strangeness and to the plentitude of the excruciating question of why, why is there something rather than nothing?

It was only later, after the age of ten, that my attempt to grasp what I can only now call some "sense of being," or the nature of my own consciousness, moved beyond being bound by those moments of fullness in the woods and transmuted itself into an experience of strangeness so alien that it brought panic. These "attacks" at first came on in what seemed a random way but later became associated with the places in which I had first experienced them. The experience was one of complete alienation and arbitrariness, as though the familiar had lost all focus and appeared grotesque and foreign. I could function, and did, during these times. There were no hallucinations. Everything remained the same, yet strangely remote. The experience was one I found indescribable to anyone. Many years later I was startled by Sartre's novel *Nausea* when I recognized that in it he had articulated some of these perceptions and feelings. I struggled alone through these periods of desperation, which were ended by sleep or some event that took me outside myself. Subsequent moments of terror and anxiety in adulthood were no more taxing than the effort to endure these strange periods, which began to fade gradually in my late teens but lingered into my mid-twenties.

On certain long-ago Saturday mornings, fortified with a mother's encouragement, I made my way from Indiana Street, via the Swope Park trolley, toward the Nelson Gallery. Many museums in the Midwest, like the Nelson-Atkins Gallery in Kansas City, the first I ever knew, occupy sites of former baronial estates. A noble in the Middle Ages might have endowed a monastery in perpetuity for the recitation of prayers on behalf of his soul. William Rockhill Nelson had an art museum built. I had my crayons and two nickels, one for each way. I got the drawing paper at the museum. I would have been eight years old and would spend the morning drawing in the galleries. Maybe Nelson had set it all up in his will—kids improving themselves with art on Saturdays. But only half the day, not cutting into baseball time. I remember most drawing from the Egyptian objects. Reliefs. Disembodied eyes, hands, and snakes floating in the hieroglyphic dream space, unburdened by the horizon that designated that weary, dualistic real world of the West where there always had to be a choice between earth and sky, heaven and hell, mind and body. In 1961 I made my first works that would later come to be called Minimal sculpture. Those gray columns and slabs I copied directly from the photographs of the ruins of the King Zoser complex at Saqqara, Egypt.

My father could tie a Turk's head in a hawser or splice an eye in a heavy rope so that no ends could be discovered, and I once saw him do this with a stranded steel cable. Yet he had no nautical experience that I knew of. Working in the livestock business, he was adept at glancing at a pen of cattle and stating immediately the number of animals it held, whether fifteen or forty. He had mysterious methods of calculating that were lightning fast and had nothing to do with those I learned in school. But I had no capacity to learn his methods. He had stuttered so badly as a child that he was sent to a special school and throughout his life he would occasionally not be able to get a certain word out. When angry his body would tremble and he would seem on the verge of dropping to the ground. He once picked up a two-by-four and dispatched a huge ram on the spot for butting him from the blind side. Taller by nearly a head than I ever grew to be, he had hands like shovels, a large broken nose and powerful jaw, and his eyes were of such a transparent gray that when I was small I thought I was seeing into his head when I looked at him. He was an orphan who grew up working on relatives' farms from Minnesota to Missouri. For the most part he was silent around the house, speaking neither of his past nor of the present. Many years later, when I pressed him to tell me about his early life, he described a cold farm dawn when he was six and he had led a blind gray Percheron from the stable to the water trough. He said he made the mistake of being between the huge horse and the water. The horse lowered its massive head and toppled him into the icy water. On Indiana Street he was a presence that loomed over me not unlike the horse: shadowy, massive, and silent, but also evanescent and, in some essential way, absent even when standing before me. And while he never toppled me into the unexpected, neither did he enter the zone of the familiar. Either I could not see him or he chose not to reveal himself. Or, more precisely, his presence was singularly visual and he existed for me primarily as an image. That knowledge of the other, based on the dimension of the linguistic, was forever absent in my relation to him. I ask myself now what weight and influence this sense of him as an image has had for me. Since a certain interrogative, if unanswerable, address to images seems to have focused my life as a visual artist, I ask myself if this has not been a life-long repetition, suitably transposed, of asking him who he was.

The Kansas City of my preteen youth was divided into two quite distinct realms, two life spaces. The one on Indiana Street was more continuous, often grayed out by stretches of school tedium and the endless coping, the scheming, and the mini-dramas of family life. Then there were the stockyards. Father was a livestock man. Mother thought it was a bad influence on me to go down to the stockyards. This provided incentive enough for me to go every chance I got. Father himself was transformed body and soul upon entering this malodorous and exotic zone. The men who worked in the stockyards arrived in drab and proper attire and ascended the worn stairs to Orin Haggerty's locker room. Here, these ordinary-looking men metamorphosed, donning their variously shaped Stetsons, their lizard boots, their pearl-snapped shirts, chaps and straps and double belts and Mexican spurs with rowels the size of silver dollars. And all of this amid the clouds of steam and talcum powder, the yelling, the elaborate obscenities, the bookmaking, the cigar smoke, and the rattle and snap of the snooker balls. There, witnessing cattle whips, wet towels flicked at unguarded rears, and three-cushioned side-pocket shots at the green pool tables, I knew I had entered a different—a secret—zone. There, Father glowed beneath his Stetson. I could see that he was far more at home there than at home.

The laughing and shouting and the horseplay and the jokes are long since gone from Genessee Street, and the Livestock Exchange building sits tattered and forlorn in the midst of a few token pens. Anyway, it did the last time I saw it a few years ago. But I can remember blazing summers when the acres of gates and chutes and sheds and scale houses stretched to the Kaw River and the noise of thousands of animals from the west, the slamming of switching freight cars from the east and the clanging of metal coming north from the Columbian Tank and Steel Company, combined in an indescribable cacophony that echoed off the bluffs towering over the West Bottoms. I remember seeing crazed Brahma bulls rip eight-by-eight gateposts out of the bricks as if they were matchsticks, and seeing 200 head of longhorns running wild-eyed across an elevated chute and learning that, until they were loaded onto a train in West Texas, they had never seen a man.

And within this dense and stressful labyrinth I saw also an occasional archer with quiver and bow float by as if from some medieval dream. In contrast to everyone else, he crept, sometimes loitered, as he pursued his prey, the giant brown rats that flourished in the abundant grain of the pens. These rats had lost their furtive nature and were fierce and aggressive, perhaps due to their size or the general franticness of the environment. The use of firearms at such close quarters was out of the question. Traps had not effectively controlled these creatures, and cats fled at the sight of prey larger than themselves. Hence the archers. Here, parallel but contrary to the apparent purposes of the stockyards, was another species of animal being fattened and then annihilated, but never, so far as I ever knew, eaten.

Also unforgettable was the medical supply store for stockmen that stood between the locker room and Shipley's Saddlery, with its window display of a stuffed, two-headed calf and a sepia-toned photomural of an enormous side-winder making a hit on a jack rabbit in mid-jump. And nothing will ever smell like the place. That verdant, reeking, subhuman, terrifying smell of slaughter-house and manure, alfalfa and wet sheep's wool, mule piss and men's sweat—all rising in a sweltering, dusty July cloud that swirled above the rank intermingling of the Kaw and Missouri rivers below. Despite the scale house's raucousness and color, and the high spirits of the men, I knew what the shouts of "Cuda-hay," "Armour," "Wilson," "Swift and Company" meant. This was one big zone devoted to death. The stockyards were a living funnel into those charnel-house holes. Is that why Father brought me there and, like Virgil, guided me through its noxious circles—so that I would know earlier than most what was out there? Was that why those men went in costume, maintained nearly self-mocking macho rituals, and clung with loud good humor and even a kind of rough love to one another since every day they were looking down the tunnel?

The dread of what I knew the stockyards stood for was not obscured by the color and bravado of the men whose business was to deliver death. If their loud camaraderie was intensified by their grim livelihoods, I recognized another version of social cohesion in the face of life's shared hardships back on Indiana Street. Though on a less dramatically grim plane than the thanatological environment of the stockyards, the denizens of Indiana Street banded together, identified with one another, the neighborhood, and, though they would not have said so, their class. All shared the sufferings that the Great Depression imposed on the lower classes in the decade of the 1930s. Their rituals of mutual recognition were not as stylized as those of the "boys down at the yards," for on Indiana Street the gestures that were in place were quieter—sharing some food, watching after the block's children, lending a spare tire, helping fix a roof. In this coming together on the edge of poverty the values of sharing, hard work, sympathy, and respect for each other were reinforced—and not incidentally instilled in the children as well. But such values were strictly those of the clan. The rare Black person who presumed to walk down Indiana Street on the way to the mini-ghetto of isolated Black families further south was glared at in silence and with indignation that this "other" should have invaded the White sanctuary. If memory reminds me that my existence within this community was marked by resentment and an overpowering impulse to escape, it was not for any specific prejudice against outsiders but because of the oppressive ignorance, lack of imagination, and narrowness of vision that suffused and perhaps cemented the cohesiveness of Indiana Street.

My early world was populated for the most part by those I knew in the neighborhood. Outside friendships were, with one rare exception, nonexistent. In September 1941 I met Roger Harrison. I was ten and he was eleven. He was new to Graceland and very different from all the other kids I had known there. In appearance he was lean and muscular. His face was stern and dark. His deep-set black eyes and high cheekbones seemed exotically Slavic, or maybe American Indian. He wore a horsehide leather jacket and cowboy boots. He turned out to be both the toughest and the smartest kid at Graceland and he had a lifelong effect on me. Roger had moved to South Benton from the Northeast quarter of Kansas City. Once a desirable place, Northeast had acquired the reputation of one of the toughest neighborhoods in the city. All the Golden Gloves fighters came from the district. Roger had moved to Kansas City from Kentucky at the age of seven. He told me that for the first three years he lived in Northeast he had a fight every day in the streets. During the grade school years I visited his house on South Benton but a few times. It was really outside my small neighborhood of Indiana Street. My contacts with Roger occurred during football and basketball games when some of us congregated at the Graceland schoolyard. Other times we met for band practice at a few of the houses around the school. Roger played the drums and I played the coronet. I seldom saw Roger during the summers. I was busy with baseball or occupied with activities close to home. Roger spent the blistering summers in the cool of his basement on South Benton. There he devoured stacks of books he borrowed from the Paseo High School library—a place I never knew existed until I went there in 1944 as a freshman. Roger read history, geometry, mathematics, and the plays and sonnets of Shakespeare. By the time I started reading anything in high school he was into Plato and Aristotle. He had a nearly photographic memory—not only for what he read but for everything that happened to him. He is to this day my living reference for every date and event of my Kansas City past that I cannot recall with sufficient precision. He remembers the date the streetcars were painted from yellow to green, and the date they were later, again, painted yellow. He can hold forth on every major battle of the Civil War, or on any of Plato's dialogues. Which tree grows the slowest or the fastest? Ask Roger. What was Stalin up to in 1934? Ask Roger. Want to know about medieval developments in logic? Ask Roger. Roger slowly brought my brain to life. He lit up history with a flare. He illuminated Tolstoy and Dostoyevsky and made me want to read them. He spoke of Shakespeare as though he knew the man. Roger pointed the way out of Indiana Street and I took it. But that is another story, not the one I tell here.

Childhood on Indiana Street in the 1930s comes back to me in memory as a silent movie in black and white. Or, better yet, as a set of black-and-white photographs in which, unlike those blurred ones in the family album, my image is absent. For in memory I watch these images from the point of view of the camera. With few exceptions (the swooping grace of my father's movements, for example), still and silent images form the mnemonic code of these lost years. A quintessential image from this time would be one of those dark, snowy mornings in which the silence was intensified. Making my way through the knee-deep drifts toward Graceland School I would stop and listen, face to the sky, eyes squinting against the falling flakes and mouth open to taste the points of cold settling on the tongue. In this muffled silence an occasional dog might bark or a snow shovel scrape some blocks away, but a kind of visual and aural stasis characterized the scene. It enfolded me in the whiteness and the silence and the cold, and made palpable an intense moment of the void. Perhaps I have occasionally relived such moments—in the blank, gray surfaces of my minimal works or in the sightless repetitions of the *Blind Time* drawings. When, as an adult, I heard of the Hindu view that our lives are a transit from illusion to oblivion I recognized I had previewed this insight standing in the snow half a century ago. Standing there welcoming that moment of the void seems from this distance a moment at the brink of an unstable defense against the adult world. If such a moment hovers on the edge of a capitulation to Thanatos it was also one of resistance. For what characterized the black and white and mostly gray of this '30s childhood was the intuition that the ideas and beliefs of the adult world I was exposed to were largely wrong and oppressive. Their view of how the world was and how one was to behave impelled me to escape. But there is no real escape for a child. Away from both adults and other children, standing alone in the mesmerizing heat of the woods or in the numbing, silent drifts, I was uncoupled for a moment from the gray idiocy of daily life. There, for an instant, I inhabited the void. No doubt the active form of resistance was first registered at the age of four in smashing the front-room window. This would later be turned back on itself in my "attacks" of debilitating dissociation. Such experiences occurred before I came to know those grown-up defenses of intellectual utopian modes, the resistance of a critical system, or the arena of art as a possible domain of transposed rage. Having spent a lifetime within the domain of art I have come to know that rage as a constantly transformed impulse. Ultimately it becomes a mere spark of ignition leading to multiple strategies for action, all of which elude reason as causes. But today, as I look back, I see both the embrace of the void and the schizoid episodes as the first instances of saying no with my entire being to those social, psychological, and intellectual oppressions that blanketed life on Indiana Street with the insulating silences of those bygone snows.

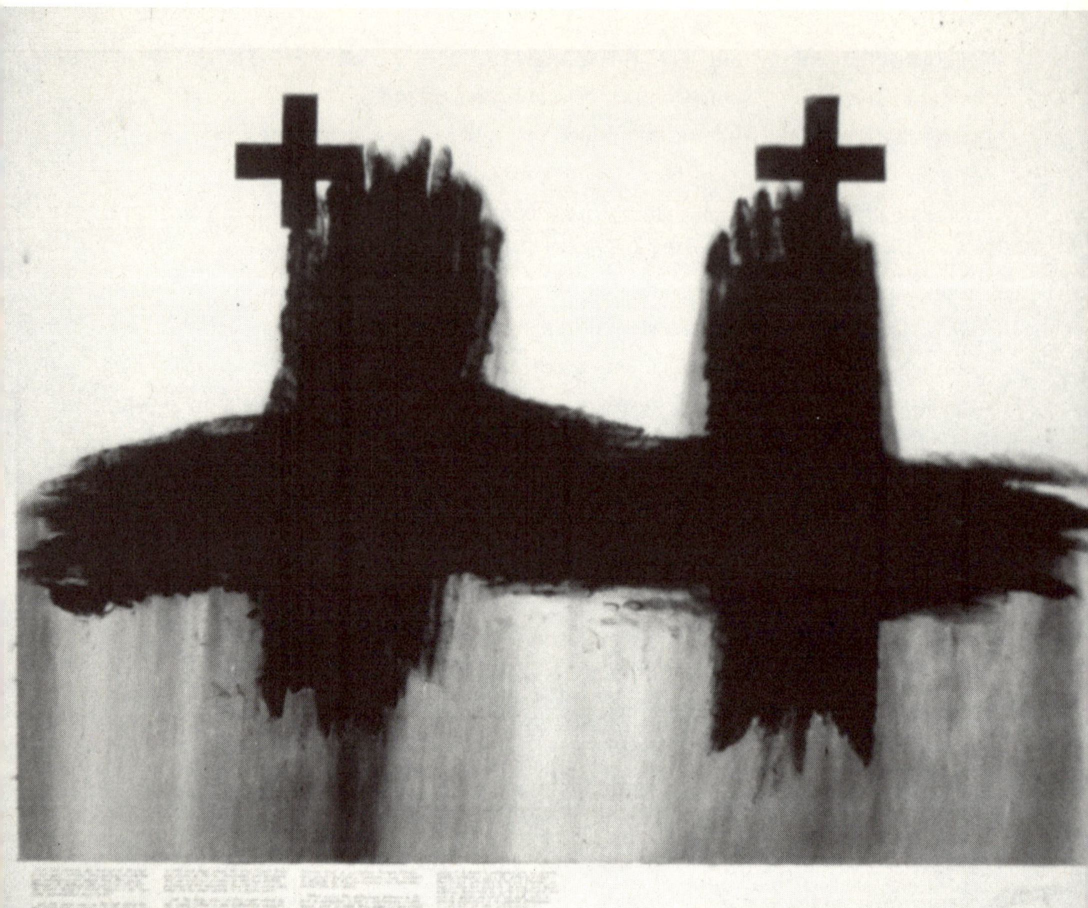

First two crosses are laid out on the page in the upper section. Then working blindfolded and estimating the lapsed time, the hands attempt to enlarge the cross on the left. The same thing is tried again on the right. Time estimation error: +20"

Let the large cross on the left stand for the Stuka that crashed in a snowstorm somewhere in the wastes of the Russian steppe in 1943, and from which the pilot, Joseph Beuys, was pulled by Tartar tribesmen who wrapped the unconscious airman in felt and butter, preserving his warmth for the 12 coma-like days he lay near death in a frozen yurt. Let the large cross on the right stand for the Stuka listed in the Luftwaffe archives which notes a crash in 1944 a few miles from an airfield at the Russian front, and records that a corporal Joseph Beuys, tail gunner and radio operator, was brought to hospital by Russian workers one half hour after the accident.

"What makes the difference between a lie and a metaphor is not a difference in the words used or what they mean (in any strict sense of meaning) but in how the words are used. Using a sentence to tell a lie and using it to make a metaphor are, of course, totally different uses, so different that they do not interfere with one another, as say, acting and lying do. In lying, one must make an assertion so as to represent oneself as believing what one does not; in acting, assertion is excluded. Metaphor is careless of the difference."
—Donald Davidson

WRITING WITH DAVIDSON: SOME AFTERTHOUGHTS AFTER DOING *BLIND TIME IV: DRAWING WITH DAVIDSON* | 1993

Words are the wrong currency to exchange for a picture.
—DONALD DAVIDSON, "WHAT METAPHORS MEAN"

What *were* Donald Davidson's writings doing in Morris's *Blind Time Drawings?* Evidently Morris had a desire to use Davidson's writings and did use his writings with the belief that, all things considered, the engagement with these writings, excerpted and out of context as they were, would yield an empowering relationship between the complex of what Morris was doing in the drawings and the language of the excerpted texts. But could we say that this was the "reason" for using the texts? If by putting scare quotes around *reason* we are tempted, even goaded, to push on, we should bear in mind Davidson's caveat that "further, and doubtless more searching, explanations may be available, but they cannot displace this one, since this one flows from what it is to be pleased that something is the case."[1] Davidson did not presume to know what Morris's reasons were for using his writings. Reasons for actions are not always easy to locate. Davidson does hold that reasons can have the status of causes and will be found inseparable from beliefs and desires. Constraints on interpreting behavior of the other are central to Davidson's thought. In viewing the behavior of the other we attribute to him or her a network of mostly coherent and consistent sets of beliefs and desires and expect that contradictory assertions will be held to a minimum. Thus in interpreting Morris's reasons for using Davidson's writing we would be guided by the twin norms of Davidson's Principle of Charity: holism and rationality. A reason can constitute a rational cause for action. But according to Davidson's doctrine of Anomalous Monism, there are no psychophysical laws. We will never find reasons both sufficient and necessary for actions. But beyond this, irrational beliefs and desires may also be significant

---

23. *Blind Time IV (Drawing with Davidson)*, 1991. Graphite on paper, 38 × 50 inches (96.2 × 127 cm). Collection of the artist. Photo by John Berens, courtesy of Robert Morris.

causes, which if they are not reasons, nevertheless reflect a certain logic among themselves and can even override the agent's more rational judgments of what, all things considered, it is best to do. Such a possibility, according to Davidson, requires extending to mental events a kind of overlapping "partitioning of the mind" in order that these conflicting beliefs and desires be put into play.[2]

Would Morris say that Davidson's descriptions of intentions, actions, events, reasons and causes, desires and beliefs, filled a certain conceptual void that hovered about the making of the *Blind Time Drawings?* Did he have a desire to fill that conceptual absence which accompanied the visual darkness? Did Davidson's writing illuminate Morris's otherwise blind working space? Or did groping around blind and smearing the page with ink on the hands constitute an act so informed by irrational desires for escape and regression that Morris sought out the linguistic sophistication of Davidson's writing to clean up his act, so to speak?[3] The answer to all these questions could be affirmative and still not be the reasons they were used.

When asked why he had made *Blind Time Drawings* in the first place, Morris was always prepared with a certain narrative of how the first series of drawings came about in 1973. This had to do with the ambition for, and a search to find, a basis for drawing other than straightforward representation on the one hand and the nonrepresentational on the other. A long series of experiments (all rejected) involving the body addressing the sheet of paper under various constraints led (perhaps by chance?) to the attempt to work by not watching the page. The ambition to put drawing on a new footing may have been there, but this may not have been the reason the drawings were made in the first place. Such reasons sound too much like rationalizations put forward after the fact. Some accounting for the obsessiveness indicated by this body of work (four series comprising a total of several hundred drawings to date) would seem warranted. Questions here might be directed toward discovering what sets of beliefs and desires put into play this obsessive reiteration. But descriptions of the act as a voluntary renunciation of control and judgment, handicapping of intention, and so on, may be "blind" to some set of beliefs and desires that reject vision in favor of investigations leading to revelations of a certain somatic knowledge that has nothing to do with the theorized wholeness of vision. Can we ask what images, anxieties, and guilt are alleviated and extinguished as they are transformed and revisited in this underworld of blindness? If working blind carries with it a certain pathos, there may also be in it a kind of Beckett-like humor that can only hone the weaponry of its ever-diminishing but ever-serviceable edge behind a mask with no eyeholes. Perhaps these ceaseless and sightless repetitions echo a kind of laughter not permitted in the light. Not every dark itch can be scratched in the daylight. It would not be inconsistent to ascribe a certain bravado to the method ("I can do it better with my eyes closed"), not to mention a contempt for that ironclad primacy of the visual, that reification of the seen promoted to a self-serving ontology that the "visual arts" never tires of asserting. And here we might ask if we have "lost sight" of that brighter realm of reasons as causes as well as that darker one of causes without reasons.

> For suppose, contrary to the legend, that Oedipus, for some dark oedipal reason, was hurrying along the road intent on killing his father, and, finding a surly old man blocking his way, killed him so he could (as he thought) get on with the main job. Then not only did Oedipus want to kill his father, and actually kill him, but his desire caused him to kill his father. Yet we could not say that in killing the old man he intentionally killed his father, nor that his reason in killing the old man was to kill his father.[4]

The phrase "for some dark oedipal reason" is intriguing. There is a certain amount of murder, mayhem, and disaster to be found in the examples that illustrate *Essays on Actions and Events*. But the sinking of the *Bismarck*, the dropping of roped mountain-climbing companions, repeated firings of guns that might stampede wild pigs that trample victims underline not some dark tendencies in the human so much as they serve to help parse those intentions, actions, and beliefs of a species whose salient characteristic is the rational. What then of "dark oedipal reason"?

Are there other schemes of interpretation, schemes incompatible with explanations of rationality and holism? Davidson views the notion of "scheme and content" as the "third dogma of empiricism" (the first and second being Quine's listing of the analytic-synthetic distinction and reductionism respectively). Davidson wants to avoid the empiricist assertion of a given and a medium (the mind) that interprets such a given (what is mental for Davidson is a conceptual rather than an ontological category), and it is held by some that he has indeed escaped from empiricism.[5] But there are, if not incompatible schemes, re-descriptions, other frames of reference, other registers. Where to find that chthonic register of "dark oedipal reason"? And what has the search for such registers to do with Morris's *Blind Time Drawings?*

Visual access to *Etant donnés*, Marcel Duchamp's last work, is by way of two peepholes in an ancient door. The splayed nude on the other side is clearly androgynous. The head is not visible, but a male hand holds aloft a phallic lamp.

The visible sex, presumably female, is anomalous: the lips of the vulva absent. The gash of castration or *The Beginning of the World?*[6] Does this splayed nude display the invitation of desire or give evidence of a crime? And does our look, which goes immediately between the legs, satisfy desire (and whose and what sort of desire?) or glimpse the unimaginable? Does vision penetrate with demand or recoil in horror? Can a look caress or cut? Must the phallic look be cut off in order to become a lamp shedding light on a scene witnessed only in blindness? No movement of the viewer's eyes in beholding the scene is possible. We are "blind" to any but a single visual frame. Moving one's head in the attempt to view the hidden face of the nude "cuts off" the view. Are we approaching reasons dark and oedipal? When Picasso was informed of Duchamp's death in 1968 he replied immediately, "He was wrong."

An explanation for the transition from primary to secondary identification in the resolution of the Oedipus complex was, according to some, never given a convincing reason by Freud.[7] That is to say, why does the child move from that relation of rivalry with the father to acceptance of his law of prohibition? Much of Lacan's thought revolves around maintaining the dialectical tension of this *Aufhebung*, this reversal from rivalry to acceptance. What is it that Oedipus cannot bear to see? Why does he put out his eyes? Because it is less costly than the removal of the phallus? Do we yet approach dark reason?[8]

In 1978 I hired a woman who had been blind since birth to execute, under my direction, the second series of *Blind Time Drawings*. After having explained a particular tactic for executing a drawing, she would often reply, "Now I see what you mean." In the Western tradition seeing has long been identified with knowing. Richard Rorty notes how "Heidegger has tried to show how the epistemological notion of 'objectivity' derives from, as he puts it, the Platonic 'identification of φύσις with ιδέα'—of the reality of a thing with its presence before us. He is concerned to explore the way in which the West became obsessed with the notion of our primary relation to objects as analogous to visual perception."[9]

Groucho Marx once asked, "Who do you want to believe, me or your own eyes?" Do we suspect our own vision? Or, more to the point, do we suspect vision's images? Images. So intractable and so inextricable from the linguistic. So easy to stigmatize, so tempting to want to exile them from the symbolic register. Such a persistent urge to quarantine them within the limbo of the "imaginary." Images. So frightening and uncontrollable. "We must get the visual, and in particular the mirroring, metaphors out of our speech altogether."[10] Better to put out one's eyes than look on certain scenes. Or, less hysterically, just close

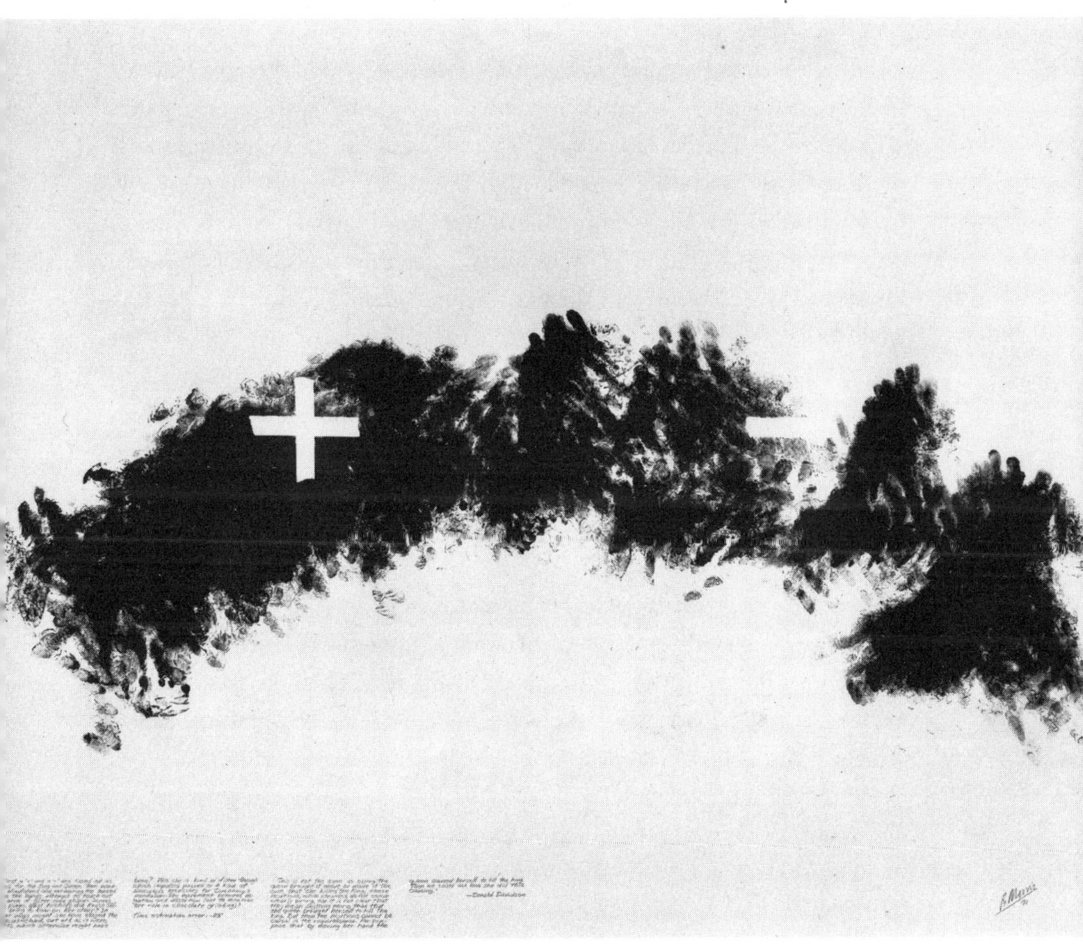

24. *Blind Time IV (Drawing with Davidson)*, 1991. Graphite on paper, 38 × 50 inches (96.2 × 127 cm). Collection of the artist. Photo by John Berens, courtesy of Robert Morris.

the eyes. Would the arrival at dark and oedipal reasons lend a greater weight to the drawings? Would we feel both relieved and more deferential to the drawings by a psychological interpretation? Would the drawings be more validated by a theoretical construct? Who do you want to believe, me or your own eyes? On one level the question is preposterous. Vision is always mediated. We always believe before we look. We always assume (theorize) a wholeness of the visual. We believe to such an extent that we do not "see" the absences. Can seeing sometimes obscure dark reason? What did Morris see with his eyes closed?

Davidson says that in order to accuse others of irrationality and error we must (pace the Principle of Charity) accord to others that most of their beliefs are true since massive error is unthinkable. If in Davidson's theory of meaning,

meaning remains a theoretical construct, it is also one tied to propositional truths of sentences. "*S* is true in *L* if and only if *p*." As Davidson says, things are true or not true because of how language works and how the world is. Is there any sense in which the making of these drawings (the making of art) can be described as exhibiting propositional attitudes? Is artmaking to be seen as an act of inventing ourselves by, as Rorty has suggested, capitalizing on the idiosyncratic contingencies of our autobiographies? And as artists are we lucky when others see their experience resonate in what we have done? Or can it be described in nearly opposite terms, namely, that artmaking, not unlike speech, is first and foremost a demand from the other for recognition, and the desires of the artist are only more globally insistent in foregrounding a desire that, in ravenously demanding the desire of the other, turns up a brighter light on that stage where the fight to the death for prestige is played out? Reasons dark and blind.

Most would agree that the search for reasons and causes is obviously urgent when the social fabric is threatened (murder, economic disaster, corruption, and so on). But a vast body of critical writing testifies to the fact that that area sometimes regarded as occupying a more evanescent level of the superstructure, the realm of art, elicits its own urgent responses. Davidson's notions about radical interpretation come with no hierarchies of social priorities, or constraints on types of activities to be interpreted. In our search to make sense of human behavior, art as well as the murder of kings would seem open to interpretation. Both the art of murder and the murder of art should be equally open to our search for reasons and causes. The detective story, a genre whose constraints are tighter than most, is exemplary in pointing up the play between art's causes that may not be reasons and its necessity for reasons that are causes. Its appeal, beyond every excellence the writing might exhibit, is the inevitable discovery and unraveling of reasons for a transgression. One way of describing the satisfactions involved would be to say that the genre draws simultaneously on the reader's sadistic aggressions in identifying with the crime while serving the masochism of the superego through inevitable discovery and punishment.[11] The overdetermination involved in that closure of cause and reason on apparently contingent events marks the genre as an invitation to hacks. It is the tension between the contingent and the reasonable that in other art forms elicits our most intense responses by exercising our most ambitious interpretive efforts.[12]

But have our searches for reasons been misguided. Might we rather, at the least, have searched for causes that are not reasons? Might it not be more profit-

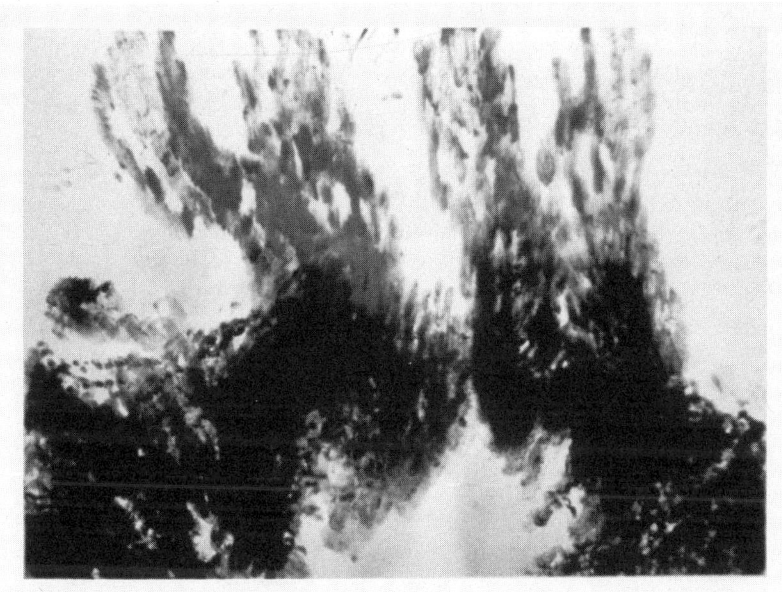

25. *Blind Time IV (Drawing with Davidson)*, 1991. Graphite on paper, 38 × 50 inches (96.2 × 127 cm). Collection of the artist. Photo by John Berens, courtesy of Robert Morris.

able to regard the act of "drawing blind" (as well as that of affixing Davidson's texts—perhaps as a kind of libretto that Morris sang as he worked blind) as operating in that economy of an excess which is the very ground of the metaphorical? Could the enterprise not be described as a kind of Orphic descent to bring back a lost love? And could not the fact of Morris finally opening his eyes and judging this particular drawing acceptable, that one not, betray not only a massive and irrefutable doubt about this descent, but underline the inevitable, final triumph of the visible that is at the same time a loss of what was seen below, away from the light?[13] Davidson has a lot to say about metaphor, most of it contested by others. He holds that there is nothing to decode in metaphors: "Joke or dream or metaphor can, like a picture or a bump on the head, make us appreciate some fact—but not by standing for, or expressing, the fact."[14] They gain what power they have by creating "gaps in logical space," as Rorty has commented. "How many facts or propositions are conveyed by a photograph? None, an infinity, or one great unstable fact? Bad question. A picture is not worth a thousand words, or any other number. Words are the wrong currency to exchange for a picture."[15]

NOTES

1. Donald Davidson, "Paradoxes of Irrationality," in *Philosophical Essays on Freud*, ed. Richard Wollheim and James Hopkins (Cambridge: Cambridge University Press, 1982), 289.
2. Ibid., 300. For the term *anomalous monism*, see Davidson, *Essays on Actions and Events* (New York: Oxford University Press, 1980), 231.
3. The very practice of excerpting (this act of cutting up) from writings such as Davidson's, writings possessed not only of a deep conceptual power and stylistic grace but of a supple wholeness and clarity, raises questions of a somewhat different order. But if such questions are suppressed here by remaining unarticulated—the very suggestion of their existence buried in an oblique footnote devoted to Morris commenting on Morris writing on Morris—they are nevertheless typical of those Morris raises throughout: if announced, seldom articulated; if articulated, seldom followed up; if followed up, seldom answered.
4. Davidson, *Essays on Actions and Events*, 232.
5. See Simon Evnine, *Donald Davidson* (Stanford, Calif.: Stanford University Press, 1991). For a critique and/or defense of not only the escape from empiricism but arguments against skepticism and realism, see the writings of Michael Dummett and Richard Rorty.
6. The small Gustave Courbet painting of the female pudenda is titled *The Beginning of the World* and was once owned by Jacques Lacan.
7. See Mikkel Borch-Jacobsen, *Lacan: The Absolute Master*, trans. Douglas Brick (Stanford, Calif.: Stanford University Press, 1991), 32–35.
8. Indeed it might be asked if Marcel Duchamp was not rendering in *Etant donnés* a kind of "anamorphic" image of ultimate fragmentation aligned along an axis running from blindness to insight. Compare Borch-Jacobsen expanding on Lacan's meditations on the familiar anamorphosis in Holbein's *The Ambassadors*:

> Seeing the painting before you, you could not see what you were in it. But now, no longer seeing it, seeing it from the side, you can finally see in it what you are—nothing, a hollow in the visible, and empty *vanitas*: "Holbein makes visible for us here something that is simply the subject nihilated—nihilated in the form that is, strictly speaking, the *imaged embodiment* of the *minus-phi* (—ϕ) of castration. . . . *It reflects our own nothingness*, in the figure of the death's head."
>
> Thus we see in this more than exemplary example, what the *object a* of phantasy represents for Lacan: an "embodiment" of the non-objective object of desire, an "image" of the unimaginable castrated phallus, a "reflection" of the non-existent vacuity of the subject—in short, an impossible image, a sort of ultimate limit of identification, a self-portrait in which the subject will see himself as he cannot see himself, a vision of horror in which his own nullity appears to him. (Borch-Jacobsen, *Lacan*, 237; Borch Jacobsen is quoting from Jacques Lacan, *The Four Fundamental Concepts of Psycho-Analysis*, trans. Alan Sheridan, ed. Jacques-Alain Miller [1973; rpt. New York: W. W. Norton, 1981], 88, 92)

In the Duchamp work the anamorphic focus is also achieved by "looking away" but with the difference that in looking away from the work one looks into the "blindness" of the afterimage memory. There is no secondary or tertiary angle of vision away from the peepholes. One looks away and into the visual vacuum of the absent but remembered scene. The inrush of symbolization (rather than a "correct" visual angle) refocuses the work as a descending series of shattered but inseparably composite image-symbols that only reassemble themselves in that looking away, that voluntary blindness to the trauma of the immediacy of the image imprinted upon our retinas at the guilty threshold of the peepholes.

9. Richard Rorty, *Philosophy and the Mirror of Nature* (Princeton, N.J.: Princeton University Press, 1979), 162–63.
10. Ibid., 371.
11. It is not too great a leap to transpose the "form" of the detective story onto the historical story of modernism. In this narrative individual acts constructed as transgressions were required and collective theory "punished"—if we can use the term to imply capture, stasis, and closure.
12. While Morris makes a number of questionable assertions throughout this text (not to mention the ubiquitous and questionable unanswered questions) none sends up a red flag quicker than this one. The suggestion of wanting to "make sense" of art threatens to topple onto him the weight of a vast critical enterprise that dismisses such an urge as not only naive but impossible. He seems to have even forgotten Baudelaire's remark to the effect that it is not what art is "about" (whatever that could be taken to mean) but the reverie it provokes that accounts for its salubrious effects.
13. See Davidson's strong replies to Max Black and Nelson Goodman in "What Metaphors Mean," *Inquiries into Truth and Interpretation* (Oxford: Clarendon Press, 1984), 245–64. This essay first appeared in *Critical Inquiry* 5 (Autumn 1978): 31–47; rpt. in *On Metaphor*, ed. Sheldon Sacks (Chicago: University of Chicago Press, 1979), 29–46. In that same volume appeared Nelson Goodman, "Metaphor as Moonlighting," 175–80, and Max Black, "How Metaphors Work: A Reply to Donald Davidson," 181–92.
14. Davidson, "What Metaphors Mean," *Inquiries into Truth and Interpretation*, 262.
15. Ibid., 263.

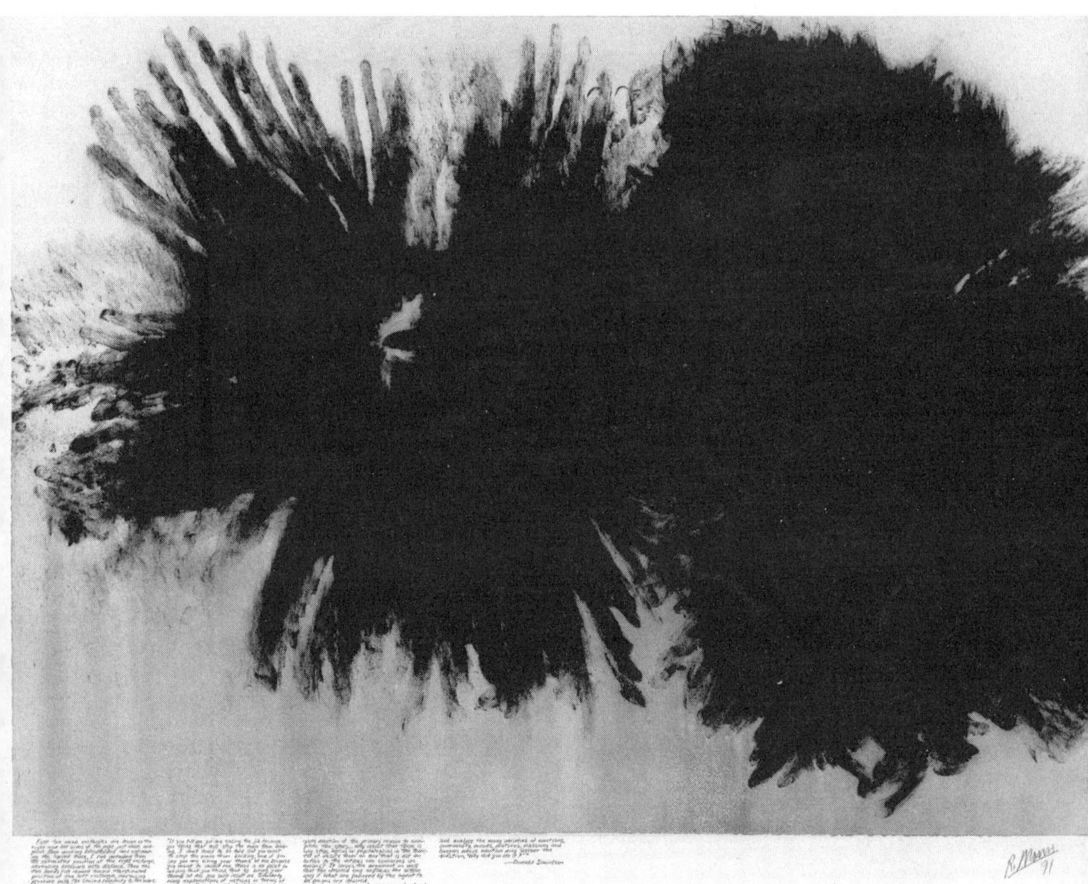

First two small rectangles are drawn on the right and left sides of the page just above mid-point. Then working blindfolded and estimating the lapsed time, I rub outward from the estimated position on the right rectangle increasing pressure with distance. Then the two hands rub inward toward the estimated position on the left rectangle, increasing pressure with the sensed proximity to the mark.—Time estimation error: + 18"

"If you tell me you are easing the jib because you think that will stop the main from backing, I don't need to be told that you want to stop the main from backing; and if you say you are biting your thumb at me because you want to insult me, there is no point in adding that you think that by biting your thumb at me you are insulting me. Similarly any explanations of actions in terms of reasons that are not primary do not require mention of the primary reason to complete the story . . . Why insist that there is any step, logical or psychological, in the transfer of desire from an end that is not an action to the actions one conceives as means? It serves the argument as well that the desired end explains the action only if what are believed by the agent to be means are desired. Fortunately it is not necessary to classify and analyze the many varieties of emotions, sentiments, moods, motives, passions, and hungers whose mention may answer the question, 'Why did you do it?'"
—Donald Davidson

THE ART OF DONALD DAVIDSON | 1995

Only man has the privilege of absurdity.

—THOMAS HOBBES

If, as Donald Davidson holds, truth is at the core of language, and (according to his "principle of charity") what most people believe—that mass of mundane propositional attitudes about the world—is true, and if language provides the social interaction that delivers an objective world (Davidson's famous "triangulation" between a subject, an object, and an other) where *truth*, though primitive, is central to a theory of meaning that allows us to understand speech and speakers, and if in making sense of the other it is necessary to consider his/her desires and beliefs as not foreign to our own, then given these inseparable elements and conditions, all of which hang together in a more or less coherent and holistic way, it becomes clear that what has been delivered is a *system*. It is a system that would reject both relativism and skepticism. It is a system organized around an interpretation of the nature of language and an interpretation of interpretation as, finally, more fundamental than language itself as a given system. Davidson's "radical interpretation" is a particular sort of unfinished and unfinishable system, one—as opposed to a systematic "conceptual scheme" through which the world is seen—that conceptualizes meaning as a condensate of social behavior. What is systematic is how meaning, truth, belief, desire, intention, action, the other, and the world are inseparably interlocked. It is a system that emerges strategically from a second-person perspective and would keep itself in the clear light of the public space and out of the shadows of a subjective Cartesian one. It is a system that builds on Wittgenstein (but is systematic), and builds on Quine, but is sensitive to the unsystematizable multitude of ways language is used.

Davidson's system hinges on a defense of both truth and a broad, if far from absolute, rationality that follows from it. What is implied is that it is not only

---

26. *Blind Time IV (Drawing with Davidson)*, 1991. Graphite on paper, 38 × 50 inches (96.2 × 127 cm). Collection of Haim Chanin Fine Arts, New York. Photo courtesy of Haim Chanin Fine Arts, New York.

possible to behave rationally but, the use of language being a form of behavior, we actually do so much of the time. At least we do much of the time when we listen to the words of the other, which like our own, do not always express the truth. We constantly negotiate the interpretation of lies, jokes, insults, sarcasm, and the like. The truth is focused here in our belief that, whatever the language game being played, we more often than not correctly interpret it. Davidson's notion of truth appears to be two-tiered. There is the structural-linguistic level, which employs recursive characterizations in the style of Tarski: "Snow is white" is true if and only if snow is white. The literal truth of such sentences depends on "what the words as spoken mean, and how the world is arranged."[1] But interpretation often requires a second step. As Davidson remarks, "speech requires at least two levels of interpretation, there being both the question of what the speaker's words mean, and the question of what the speaker means in speaking them."[2] If we are lied to and yet not deceived we negotiate this double interpretation by trading the literal meaning of the statement for its opposite; if deceived, we have gone only halfway by taking it as true in its first or literal sense only. For it is the same sentence in both cases. But claims for rationality flowing through language are sustained by Davidson on deeper and more holistic levels connecting language to action. The liar's sentence certainly does not open a space through which rationality falls. But the more convincing claims for the rational are best sought outside strictly linguistic considerations of structure and interpretation that revolve around truth. The stronger case is to be made on the basis of the agent's *intentional* actions, which go beyond the linguistic.

But if the rational, also the irrational. Considerations of the latter throw considerable light on the former. In bracketing the rational with the irrational Davidson notes (in his "Paradoxes of Irrationality")[3] the explanation of Socrates, who argued that only "ignorance can explain foolish or evil acts." This is contrasted to the *Medea Principle*, which assigns the irrational to the actions of an agent overwhelmed by the alien force of passion. These cases are also compared to Aristotle's assertion that "weakness of the will is due to a kind of forgetting." But these examples do not deal with fully intentional actions. The *paradox* of irrationality lies in those actions the agent takes in full knowledge that, all things considered, it would be better to do A, while nonetheless doing B. Here the agent violates his principle. Or as Davidson puts it: "For though his motive for ignoring his principle was a reason for ignoring the principle, it was not a reason against the principle itself, and so when it entered in this second way, it was irrelevant as a reason, to the principle and to the action. The irrationality depends on the distinction between a reason for having, or acting on, a principle, and a reason for the principle."[4] In irrational actions the causal relation remains but the logical one is distorted or missing. Marcia Cavell put it well when she said that "Irrationality is a failure, not an absence, of rationality."[5] While mental causes must be assigned to irrational acts, these causes do not count as reasons. Davidson goes on to account for the possibility of such irrationality by theorizing a "partitioning of the mind." Here both sides are characterized by a consistency and holism even though they are opposed to each other.

Davidson does not explore either the etiology of the divided mind that admits of the irrational or the relative command exercised over the subject by the one or the other. But he indicates a sympathy for Freud's "most important theses,"[6] one of which would be that the agent's irrational beliefs develop out of early thought processes (called by Freud the "primary process") dominated by fantasy, fears, and wishful thinking. Another of Freud's important theses would revolve around the concepts of the unconscious and repression.

Davidson says little directly about what constitutes the "better" in those "principles" of the agent that form his reference points for intentional actions or how the rational connects to and justifies these principles—although he rejects the notion of rational principles grounded in general or hierarchical moral platitudes, such as "it is wrong to lie." Furthermore, no indelible line can be drawn between either the so-called partitioned territories of the mind or the rational and irrational in intentional actions, since "all intentional actions, whether or not they are in some further sense irrational, have a rational element at the core."[7] What is common to all principles formed of desire and belief is the causal assumption—such as believing that stealing money will result in (be the cause of) the agent having money, whether it is rational or not to steal in the given circumstances. And there may be cases where the agent considers stealing the rational thing to do, the better thing to do, all things considered. Values are bound up in the desires and beliefs that form the agent's principles. How these principles of the "better" action are to be assessed as rational can only be determined, it would seem, in relation to a given situation judged in light of the action's nexus with other beliefs and values. The "better" here is normative in the logical rather than the moral sense—that is, it fits with other beliefs and desires of the agent. Whatever the particular principle in question, it presumably hangs together in ways consistent with those other beliefs and desires. It is this holistic aspect that confers a rationality defined in terms of consistency and appropriateness on any particular belief or principle.

"Every action has causes that rationalize it, that is, in terms of which it is rational. Of course those causes (beliefs and desires) may not be rational in the light of other beliefs and desires of the agent."[8] In Davidson's system, laws do not link the separate descriptions of mental and physical. The mental is supervenient on physical states, to be sure. But while physical events are subject to lawful description, mental events, according to Davidson's notion of "anomalous monism," are not. Mental "reasons," being irreducible to mechanisms of the physical, are sufficient to stand as causes, though never both necessary and sufficient ones.

Davidson has attacked relativism in a number of places. His principle of charity forms a general bulwark against it. But perhaps the most explicit assault is in the essay "On the Very Idea of a Conceptual Scheme." This is a two-pronged attack: against relativism on the one hand, and a kind of coup de grace to moribund Empiricism on the other. Davidson's arguments always seem interlocking and strategic:

> In giving up dependence on the concept of an interpreted reality, something outside all schemes and science, we do not relinquish the notion of objective truth—quite the contrary. Given the dogma of a dualism of scheme and reality, we get conceptual relativity, and truth relative to a scheme. Without the dogma, this kind of relativity goes by the board. Of course truth of sentences remains relative to language, but that is as objective as can be. In giving up the dualism of scheme and world, we do not give up the world, but reestablish unmediated touch with the familiar objects whose antics make our sentences and opinions true or false.[9]

In another context, Davidson has found Roland Barthes's celebrated pronouncement of the death of the author (claims for a rampant relativism that leaves texts potentially open to all interpretation) premature. He does not mention Barthes by name, but in "Locating Literary Language" he concludes:

> It is true that every person, every age, every culture will make what it can of a text; and persons, periods and cultures differ. But how can a significant relativism follow from a truism? If you and I try to compare notes on our interpretation of a text we can do so only to the extent that we have or can establish a broad basis of agreement. If what we share provides a common standard of truth and objectivity, difference of opinion makes sense. But

relativism about standards requires what there cannot be, a position beyond all standards.[10]

If Davidson's system, defending as it does against relativism and skepticism, stakes out a position opposed to postmodernist assumptions, his confrontation with the issues of the irrational contrasted to the rational leave much open ground to be explored. For the rational and the irrational mark the distantly opposed sites of a vast terrain that lies between: the nonrational. Davidson has had original and controversial things to say on those infrequent occasions when he has stepped out of the harsher light of a strict philosophical discourse on truth. Art and literature inhabit this broad space of the nonrational, where not truth but metaphor reigns and casts ambiguous shadows.[11] The essays collected in *Literary Theory after Davidson* testify to the breadth of implications inherent in Davidson's work for one of these zones of the nonrational. In a relatively late essay, "James Joyce and Humpty Dumpty," Davidson brings his notions of interpretation to bear on literary intentions. Here he cites Joyce to illuminate how art, at its best and most challenging, both makes possible and demands a creative effort of interpretation that nevertheless stops short of hysterical claims for the "death of the author."[12]

It has generally been assumed (and perhaps still is by those not converted to postmodernism) that the line between truth and metaphor marks a boundary: philosophy, illuminated by the former, stands on one side, while art stands on the other in more tangled landscapes. With Davidson's work I want to suspend such distinctions, without advocating a postmodernist collapse of truth and philosophy into literature. I think this suspension warranted because after giving all due consideration to his system as philosophy, there is a remainder. After threading through the issues of truth and belief and desire and interpretation and the other and the world, one emerges from this interlocking system and looks back to see an edifice standing. It is one that shows signs that more than a powerful analytic mind has been at work. This is an edifice that reverberates with a further interlocking element: the aesthetic. The aesthetic in Davidson's system is, I would argue, not separable from the philosophical content. It presides over the whole in the very will for a holistic, organic structure. But is it art? Paraphrasing Davidson, I would reply that it is not art if art is anything like what art historians and critics have supposed. I would not want to appropriate Davidson's system as a form of "conceptual art." Rather, I want here to appreciate that "remainder" in Davidson's system that *is art-like*.

Such an appreciation is not to suggest that truth might be blurred by art, but rather that in Davidson's writing truth is delivered with art. And more important, the ideas are somehow art-like. I think this art-like aspect has partly to do with the originality of some of the concepts themselves (the principle of charity, anomalous monism, the rejection of conceptual schemes, the rejection of language as an a priori abstraction), and partly with the uncanny way the concepts are locked together and how they resurface at unexpected times to reinforce one another. At a certain point this interlocking density seems to change state, and the system unfurls with a lightness and effortless wholeness as the systematic picture comes into focus. The magician's deck of separate cards becomes the seamless silk scarf; the parts of the sculpture resonate against one another and coalesce into an inseparable whole. Art-like as well is the daring move and unexpected shift that can erupt in Davidson's writing—not to mention the occasionally outrageous assertion. "A Nice Derangement of Epitaphs" is an essay that has sent philosophers into defensive fits—a situation more typical of the artist and his critics than that of the philosopher and his respondents. Here Davidson makes his infamous statement that "there is no such thing as a language, not if language is what many philosophers and linguists have supposed."[13] Two radical and related claims are being made in this text: (1) Language is not a finished, a priori abstraction, and (2) successful interpretation, the very lynchpin of Davidson's system, can only be negotiated by "wit, luck and wisdom from a private vocabulary and grammar." Both of these assertions reduce the static and the systematic in his system. The first claim has much in common with Western art's protean and unfinished character, the second with the act of artmaking. A certain creative element becomes a necessity not only for interpretation but for the existence of language itself.

Davidson has constructed a large model that feels like an ambitious work of art. Yet this model, which deploys certain aspects of "folk psychology," is articulated by sets of logical relations that create no "schemes" or entities through which the world is captured. His edifice is both minimal and complex, legislative and transparent: a "thing" that is at the same time not a thing, a system that at its roots is mobile and anti-systematic. We understand Davidson as a philosopher, but he feels like an artist.

It is to point out the obvious to say that Davidson created his philosophy through a highly literary prose that moves with pace and often within a landscape of startling examples. It is writing that is as ambitious for style as for content. In its compression and leanness, its unforeseen leaps and strategic arguments, and its wide cultural references, it stands unparalleled as the best philosophical writing since Wittgenstein's *Philosophical Investigations.*

The numerous examples Davidson cites in *Essays on Actions and Events*[14] are colorful and frequently violent. Policemen are knocked downstairs, the battleship *Bismarck* is sunk, men are shot or run over by stampeding herds of wild pigs, roped climbers are in danger of being dropped by their partners, burns are suffered and houses are set afire. The anonymous Mr. Smith is murdered more than once. Leopards are presented to wives, and future tyrants risk assassination. This is not to mention the numerous examples from literature cited in the essays. Hamlet does in Polonius, Medea goes wild, and Oedipus does his thing. Dante's sinners squirm, Brutus stabs Caesar, and the queen pours poison in the king's ear. All of these examples illustrate aspects of a discourse devoted to issues of truth and rationality. Calm and reasonable action may be difficult to find in a wild and threatening world rife with murderous irrationality, but our capacity to make reasonable sense of such intentions, events, and actions endures. I do not know if a certain irony rises to the surface here. Perhaps it is rather a kind of cold but heroic comfort that Davidson's texts offer. We may live at the end of the bloodiest century in history—Elizabeth Bishop called it the "worst so far"—but we are capable of discerning the truth behind the most numbing and brutal actions and events. Going a step beyond Hobbes, we can interpret man's endless array of absurdities with a resolute precision. That such a saturnine use has never been made of Davidson's radical interpretation does not mean that it might not be called upon to function in such a light.

"Metaphors," Davidson says, are both "the dreamwork of language" and yet "mean what the words, in their most literal interpretation, mean, and nothing more."[15] Metaphors lead us to see one thing as another; they open up the world and reveal astonishing landscapes across the terrain of the nonrational. Can Davidson's work—for all of its defense of truth, its clarity, its breadth and reach and boldness—be taken as a metaphor? Does his system, his model that seems so art-like, throw up a metaphorical image? It would be against his intentions for us to focus on his model in any art-like or iconic way. Yet I cannot help wondering how this polished, many-faceted system, firmly anchored to truth and the rational, also forms a picture—a picture of consistency, toughness, and strength, firmly planted and impervious to the violent waves of the twentieth century (the image of Parmenides holding his ground in a torrent unleashed by Heraclitus comes to mind). And here we pass from Hobbesian metaphors into utopian ones. For if the rationality that saturates Davidson's system has not informed many of those actions recorded as historically significant, it remains potentially available.

We take Davidson's system for what its words mean, to be sure—but this is also how Davidson says we must take a metaphor. But beyond this, can we use it as one thing to see another? James Joyce saw history as a nightmare from which he was trying to awake, while the insomniac poet Delmore Schwartz amended this to history as a nightmare in which he was trying to get a good night's sleep. Either way we have the metaphor of nightmare as history. And the future, with its chilling demographic and ecological portents, its economic, technological, social, political, and moral crises darkening the horizon, promises to continue the nightmare unabated. Could Davidson's system be taken as a light that glows in the midst of this gloom? A light to be thrown on the nightmare of history: one metaphor to illuminate another.

It is too easy to see this glow as Hobbesian, as illuminating the play of the rational and irrational forces behind behavior that has resulted in the wreckage and smoldering death of our time. But perhaps it is too hard to take this light as utopian, as a potential force of resistance to be brought to bear in facing the darkness of the future. Such a hope appears dim.

In the 1955 film *Mr. Arkadian*, Orson Welles tells the story of a scorpion coming to a river and asking a frog to carry him across on his back (I paraphrase): "I don't think so," says the frog, "you would sting me and we would both drown." "Would that be logical, if I want to get to the other side?" asks the scorpion. "All right," agrees the frog, and they start across. In the middle of the river the frog feels a paralyzing sting. As they are going down the frog asks, "Was that logical?" "No," replies the scorpion, "but it is my nature—what could I do?" Clearly the story of the scorpion stands as both an example of a severely partitioned mind and a familiar historical parable.

In the end, Freud did not express a great deal of hope for rational actions predominating in our behavior. It is not necessary to posit an anthropology about human nature so much as to look at history to be in sympathy with Freud. We hang suspended over the abyss of the future, hoping and waiting for rational solutions to appear, although none seem forthcoming. Freud did, however, offer some small personal hope that we could gain a degree of insight and rein in some of our irrational "acting out" behavior.

There is no implication in Davidson's broad view—across that holistic interlocking operation of desire and action and belief and truth—for a kind of therapeutic rationality. The rational is normative in Davidson's system only as a set of logical relations. The dynamics of the agent's development and how the irrational comes to be formed or to what degree it encroaches on his more intentional behaviors lie outside of Davidson's system. As Marcia Cavell has said, "Just how these older structures [the agent's early repressed fears and fantasies] impinge on behavior, and the extent to which, when they do, they modify the agent's responsibility for his activity, are complicated questions."[16] Philosophy, as Marx complained, sets out to understand the world and not to change it. In this sense Davidson's model remains outside history, casting a faint glow on its dark flank. But to take this reflected light as either ironic or utopian is to misread the hard-headed stance of this system—a system that does not budge from resisting both relativism and skepticism, one that places the concept of truth at the core of our comprehension of one another. As we wade into the dark and turbulent future we would do well to hold on to these notions, which, delivered as philosophical insights with aesthetic polish, are also, beneath their logic, moral assumptions.

NOTES

1. Davidson, personal communication.
2. Ibid.
3. Davidson, "Paradoxes of Irrationality," *Philosophical Essays on Freud*, ed. Richard Wollheim and James Hopkins (Cambridge: Cambridge University Press, 1982).
4. Ibid.
5. Marcia Cavell, *The Psychoanalytic Mind* (Cambridge, Mass.: Harvard University Press, 1993).
6. Davidson, "Paradoxes of Irrationality," *Philosophical Essays on Freud.*
7. Ibid.
8. Davidson, correspondence with the author.
9. Davidson, "On the Very Idea of a Conceptual Scheme," *Inquiries into Truth and Interpretation* (Oxford: Clarendon Press, 1984).
10. Davidson, "Locating Literary Language," in *Literary Theory after Davidson*, ed. Reed Way Dasenbrock (University Park: Pennsylvania State University Press, 1993).
11. Boundaries here are not hard and fast. Undoubtedly art and literature infiltrate the borders of both the rational and the irrational. Freud considered the territory of irrationality and primary process the base for creativity and artmaking. But clearly there is much in the construction process and the strategies of art that demands rational procedures that lie beyond whatever wellspring of the irrational can be claimed for the origins of art.
12. Davidson, "James Joyce and Humpty Dumpty," *Midwest Studies in Philosophy* 16 (1990): 1–12.
13. Davidson, "A Nice Derangement of Epitaphs," *Truth and Interpretation: Perspectives on the Philosophy of Donald Davidson*, ed. Ernest LePore (Oxford: Blackwell, 1986).
14. Davidson, *Essays on Actions and Events.*
15. Davidson, "What Metaphors Mean," *Inquiries into Truth and Interpretation.*
16. Cavell, *The Psychoanalytic Mind.*

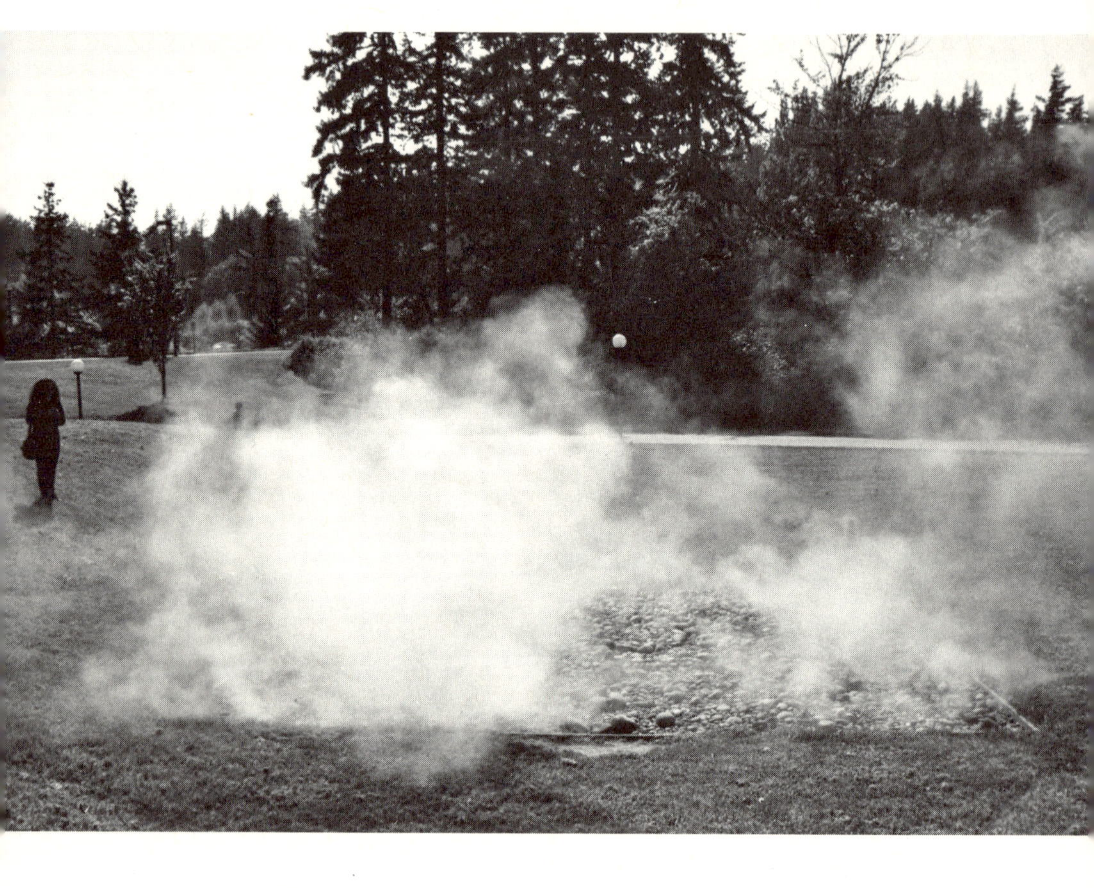

The epitome of the ephemeral. A refusal of "form" that does not, however, collapse into the sublime. A summation and cancellation of all the *clouds* ever represented in art. A veritable *Aufhebung* of the cloud. (Yet perhaps a tinge of nostalgia for Turner?) An expenditure of heat: that which life itself mortgages from the sun. A coldly calculated sculpture formed with warmth. A monument to both Heraclitus (you can't put your foot into the same steam twice in this work) and Parmenides (we will not speak of the work's "nothingness" in the face of heat which is the "one" of every living thing). Let' s not forget Zeno whose arrow would never make it through this work. Let's not forget the ancient sacred springs bubbling up in steamy, forgotten mists—sites now cemented over for shopping malls. Undoubtedly the archaic is celebrated in this work. Dig deep enough beneath the very spot on which *Steam* is installed and what would be found? Old pottery, broken, once polished stones from forgotten settlements. And what's this? Montaigne's lost collar button? But dig deeper still and see a broken oil lamp, a Roman bronze strigil. Go deeper, beyond every human artifact and into the earth's crust and heat rises. Smoke and the churning innards of the grumbling gut of the earth itself belches up its indigestion in sulphurous clouds. Dante knew of the region. But let's leave Christianity out of it. Hell, as we might recall, requires no digging, having shaped the upper layers of the earth for the last century. Continuous smoke and fire and the scream of wars large and small have deafened us to Mnemosyne's whispers. But steam is not smoke. James Watt knew what to do with both when he stuffed them into his engine and transfixed Turner, who put a rabbit in front of the industrialization bearing down on it full tilt. Watt we acknowledge with a deep bow. But we keep his machine out of sight in the next room. It is unbearable to look at. Watt and Babbage and von Neumann do not require monuments but a moment of silence in which we bow our heads and grit our teeth while their grinning visages em-

---

27. *Steam*, 1971–74. Steam outlets under a bed of stones, outlined with wood, dimensions variable. Permanent site-specific installation at Western Washington University, Bellingham, Washington. Photo courtesy of Bill Schillinger.

broider the pipes and wires of our magnificent cages. But let us for a moment step off the track down which technology hurtles with its relentless, terrifying momentum. Turn back once more to the archaic: the steam bath as purification: the Native American ritual of sweating in a steam-filled enclosure before battle. Not that I would dream of making claims for *Steam* along such lines. I only want to distinguish steam from smoke, eros from thanatos, energy from entropy, warmth from third degree burns. ("Distinguish there, Polonius, that cloud that looks very like a camel from that other, over there, that looks very like a mushroom.") Let's not forget the stones, thousands of them that have, since the Cambrian, lain in rivers submitting to water's infinitesimal rate of sculpting. Leonardo marveled at the process. How many miniature Brancusi ovoids have been dredged up here to occupy this geometric plain through which *Steam* percolates. These stones form the base of our monument of *Steam*. But perhaps *Steam* is after all an anti-monument. Perhaps it is a kind of monumental anti-monument monument to the shrinking cultural space of art—a space that tends to evaporate in the face of that lurch to the "right" that would validate only the useful and deny the exhilarating excess of all metaphor, the very site of art. After all *Steam* is just a lot of hot air; a towering babble of hissing, wordless vapor; a physical-visual-thermal sigh; a sweet, warm, mute breath wrung reluctantly from Watt's engine of work. A damp, incoherent mumble of the delights of evanescence and multiplicity; a gaseous, upward rush celebrating the contradiction of an object made from thin air—an object that upon being entered confers a white, enfolding blindness, the damp frisson of a vaporous claustrophobia, and the kiss of warm stones against the foot.

Can we say that a kind of grammatical chasm exists between the form of the proposition and that of the question? Is there a kind of world, as it were, of the question, whose difference, verging on the suspicion of a kind of lack, sets it in perpetual opposition to that other world, that of the statement? Some might read such differences as an allegory of gender—defined, admittedly, in a rather essentialist way. And when it comes to actions, are there those one could designate as interrogative? And what about objects?

It is as if I wanted to say that my actions in making art fell on the side of the question rather than of the statement. But I don't know whether to allow this feeling to remain in the form of a statement, or to recast it as a question. Do I feel that my actions in making art have always been shaded with questions? There are questions and there are questions. There are of course those rhetorical questions that are only disguised statements. There are questions we ask ourselves and those we ask others. There are questions that insult as well as reassure, distract, or change the subject. Obviously, there are some questions that have nothing to do with wanting answers. There are a host of philosophical questions regarding the question and its interpretation. But I take note of this more as a cautionary remark rather than to introduce any effort to open up too far the issue of the question of the question. Otherwise I would never get to the examples, the art. Nevertheless, I would like to float out the notion of an interrogative space, questionable as this might be, so that when the examples of the art appear they are coated or infected with a kind of questionlike aspect.

I see a field of uncleared obstacles between a family of related boundaries or grammatical games, as Wittgenstein might call them: the question and the proposition, the doubt and the statement, the impression and the inference, the intention and the action, and especially the actions in making art and the status of the resultant object. All of this unclarity carries over to any discussion of a concatenation of art objects produced by one person over an extended period of time.

In the studio I ask myself this question: What will happen if I do *a* and then *b*? After that I ask further, Now what happens after *c* and then *d*? Much later, and in the context of the public space of the gallery, is it then a misinter-

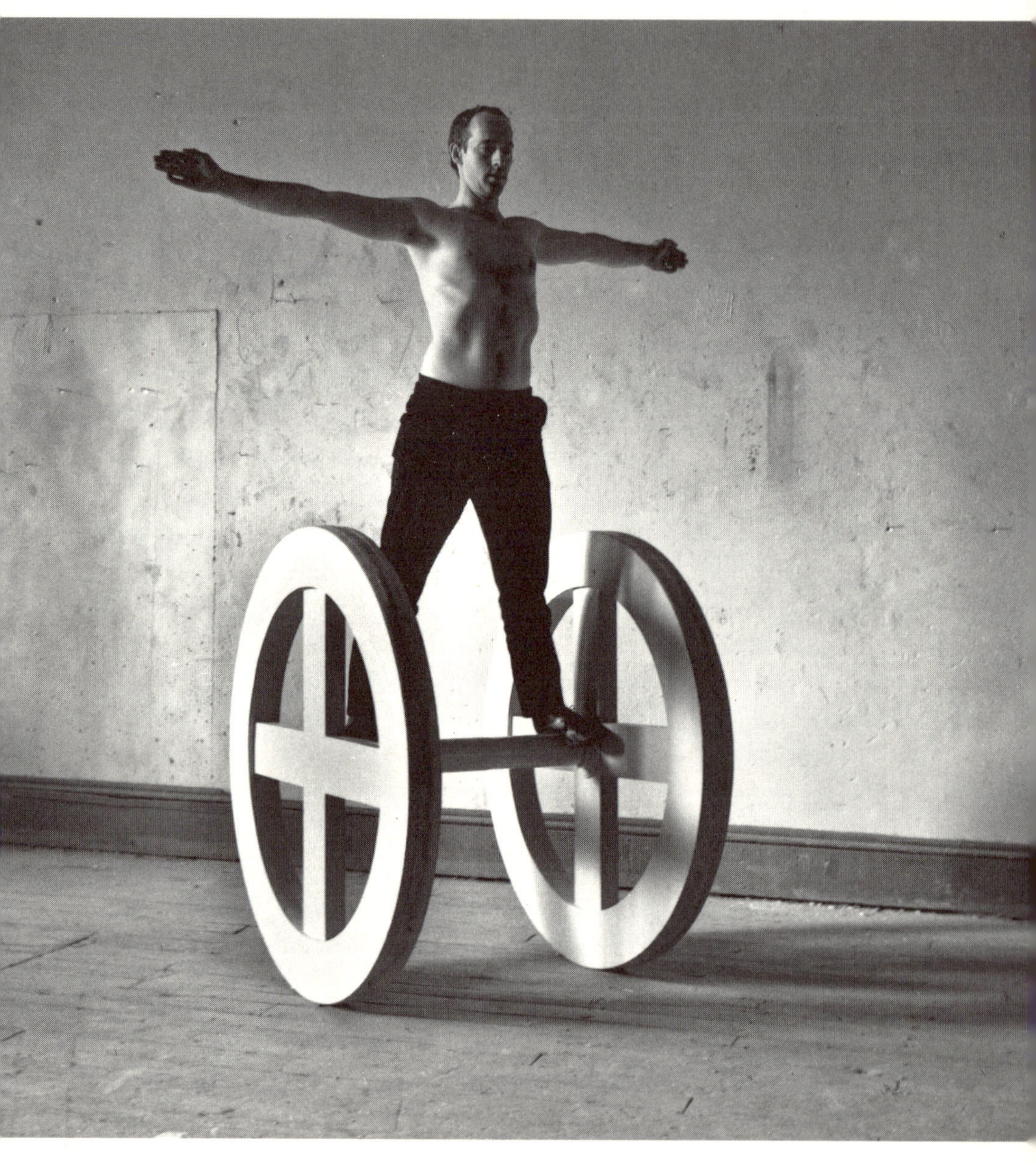

pretation for others to take the object I have made as first a "statement," about which subsequent questions are then to be asked? And you—that is to say, R. Morris; and I will adopt the *you* to address him from here on in—want to say that your questions in the making not only preceded the object but resulted in it? But how did the space of the studio make the order different? Perhaps it was a kind of privacy that obtained there. Well, in what sense can a space be private? In no sense that seems convincing. Still, it seems a shaded and sheltered space housing questions that never heal, as it were, into the totally finished. But in the space of the gallery the frame of the statement surrounds even the fragment. And here, of course, we do not mean "proposition" or any iteration that has truth-values connected with it.

But still, in retrospect, you want to defend yourself from charges of arbitrariness. It is in forums like this one that the question, now in an altogether different form—a question game with klieg lights attached, as it were—would illuminate the shaded space of the studio. And here your startled response to such wattage is to want to say that after doing *a* there was at least something like a reason for doing *b*. There was something in the series of questions accompanying the making that responded to the conditions, the results, the accidents. It was as if the questions followed along without question. But in retrospect, and under the klieg lights, those steps taken reappear on stage to take their bows in the costumes of reasons. But here I would also remind myself of Wittgenstein's query: "Have I reasons? The answer is: my reasons will soon give out. And then I shall act, without reasons."[1]

Can we apply this grammatical difference between the question and the statement to spatial modes themselves? Are we also predisposed toward such differences in how we read the public art space itself, coloring what we expect to find there differently from how we approach the more intimate spaces of those rooms in which we live out most of our lives?

Of all the torturous questions asked in the course of artmaking, of all the doubts that arise in the studio, are we not buoyed up there by the certainty that our efforts are at least consistently addressed to a service for the ruling class? Isn't this a custom that we do not doubt? And does not this custom determine a whole host of things beyond the guarantee of portability? Doesn't this custom

28. Robert Morris with *Wheels*, 1963. Laminated fir and painted cast iron, 47¾ inches (121.3 cm) diameter. The Art Gallery of Ontario, Toronto: Gift of the Volunteer Committee Fund. Photo courtesy of Robert Morris.

make for a kind of soft floor over which we are allowed to romp? Well, it is a soft floor that has not accommodated all that many. And there are edges where those who romp frequently fall off into oblivion.

Thirty-five years ago, when I started working in New York City, the custom of art as service was firmly in place, to be sure. But one of the differences between then and now was the amount of slack in the system. A marginal urban life in those days did not mean being on the street, as it does today. Rather, it meant a certain amount of leisure to, well, think and play and socialize and maybe make some art. A studio loft cost $100 a month, and reasonably paid part-time jobs were plentiful. One was even left with a surplus for the nights of raucous conversation at Max's Kansas City. But today what is called the free enterprise system may best be represented by its mascot, a dinosaur, as Tom Mitchell has suggested.[2]

No doubt Tyrannosaurus Rex, whose gender is unthinkable as anything but male, is the candidate for the emblem of this New World Order of a voracious and predatory corporate global capitalism. Could we call it TyrannoCap for short? TyrannoCap and his insatiable appetite for the bottom line has seen to it that there will be no slack in the system and that any cultural expression not transparent to the market will be ignored. Listen up, you recruits (if any are out there). You will shape up and stand tall as serious professionals or we ship you back to Dubuque. And wipe that smile off your face. After all, the mark of the professional is not play, but sales. Consistent sales with a consistent product is the motto. Being professionals, we are not going to step up to our practice as the elite of the serving class for free, are we?

Andy Warhol did not live long enough to collaborate with that other megabucks artist, Bill Gates. When, I wonder, will Bill Gates acquire the reproduction rights to Warhol's images, as he has to so many so-called masterpieces in the world's museums. Before long with a silent tripping of a timer switch, the bedroom wall will come alive simultaneously with the morning alarm clock and the looming mural-sized video image of, say, Rembrandt's *Night Watch* obliterating all recollection of the night's dreams. Perhaps commercials will wash over such art images for a kind of relief. Instead of paintings, a kind of video wallpaper, call it VidPap for short. Warhol would have loved it. And eventually Mr. Gates might get around to hawking a wall-sized image of Campbell Soup cans for the family room, thereby collecting revenue both from the homeowner and Campbell's.

Surely the practice of art as service implies sets of rules? A practice seems to depend upon rules. But Wittgenstein says in §201 of the *Philosophical Inves-*

tigations: "This was our paradox: no course of action could be determined by a rule, because every course of action can be made out to accord with the rule." Here is a remark whose implications would make David Hume look almost like a believer. Wittgenstein's implication here seems to be that whatever the rule that was followed in the past, it does not compel or justify the application of the rule in a future case.

Nelson Goodman's famous "new riddle of induction" seems to relate to Wittgenstein's skeptical problem. Briefly, Goodman's riddle is as follows: "Imagine a time *t*—say midnight on 1 January 2001. Define 'x is grue' to mean 'x is examined before *t* and is green or x is examined after *t* and is blue.' If generalizations are confirmed by their instances, then the fact that all emeralds so far examined are green confirms that all emeralds are grue as well as the generalization that all emeralds are green."[3] Saul Kripke adapts Goodman's riddle to Wittgenstein's doubt in the following way:

> Perhaps by "green," in the past, I meant *grue*, and the color image, which indeed was grue, was meant to direct me to apply the word "green" to *grue* objects always. If the *blue* object before me now is grue, then it falls in the extension of "green," as I meant it in the past. It is no help to suppose that in the past I stipulated that "green" was to apply to all and only those things "of the same color as" the sample. The skeptic can reinterpret "same color" as same *schmolor*, where things have the same schmolor if . . .[4]

And so on. But Wittgenstein's point is more about meaning than induction when he calls attention to how one's present mental state in no way determines what one ought to do in the future. The only guide we ever have here is that of custom.

Can we relate these skeptical remarks to those stylistic shifts in your work that others have frequently found so disconnected and bewildering, not to mention unprofessional? Was it the case that what you fashioned in the past was done in accord with a rule that seems not to guide you today when you want to continue along, that the instance before you now is different? Do we want to say that the world seems to have shifted slightly and that how you went about things in the past seems unsuited to the present task? But surely logic has nothing to do with the stylistic rule. It was a custom that you were unable to follow for reasons still not determined. And here we enter the psychological room and not the logical one.

Then perhaps we should look deeper into that psychological room for the sources of your lack of consistency in following the sovereign rules a profes-

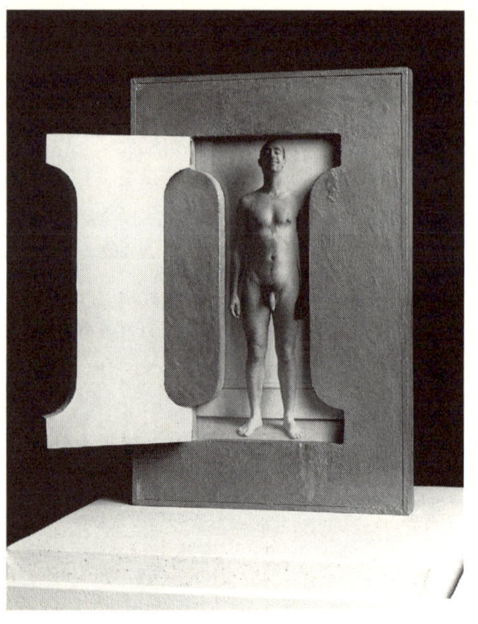
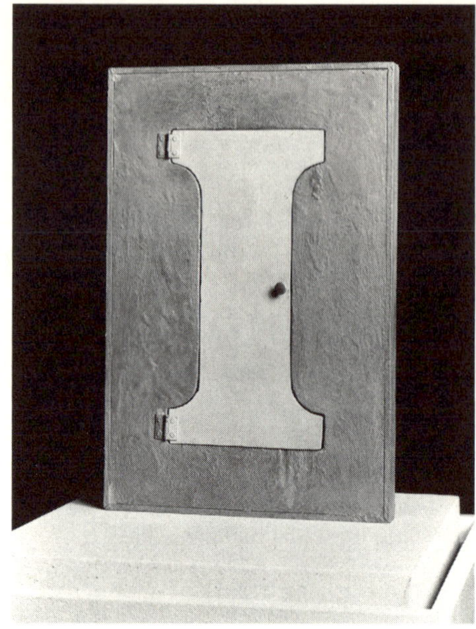

29. *I-Box*, 1962 (open view). Painted plywood cabinet with sculptmetal, containing photograph, 19 × 12¾ × 1 inches (48.3 × 32.4 × 35 cm). Collection of Leo Castelli Gallery, New York. Photo courtesy of Robert Morris. **30.** *I-Box*, 1962 (closed view). Photo courtesy of Robert Morris.

sional art practice demands. Then we would begin by going back again to your secret saint of long standing, David Hume, and review his notions of the illusory self? Let me quote this formidable skeptic:

> There are some philosophers who imagine we are intimately conscious of what we call our SELF; that we feel its existence and its continuance in existence; and are certain, beyond the evidence of a demonstration, both of its perfect identity and simplicity. The strongest sensation, the most violent passion, say they, instead of distracting us from this view, only fix it the more intensely, and make us consider their influence on *self* either by their pain or pleasure. To attempt a farther proof of this were to weaken its evidence; since no proof can be derived from any fact of which we can be certain, if we doubt this. Unluckily all these positive assertions are contrary to that very experience, which is pleaded for them, nor have we any idea of *self*, after the manner explain'd. . . . For my part, when I enter most intimately into what I call *myself*, I always stumble on some particular impression or other, of heat or cold, light or shade, love or hatred, pain or pleasure. I never can catch *myself* at any time without a perception. . . . If any one, upon serious and

unprejudic'd reflection, thinks he has a different notion of *himself*, I must confess I can reason no longer with him.[5]

Does Wittgenstein in the *Tractatus* get to the matter with more brevity, and without the excess empiricism, when he says, "The subject does not belong to the world: rather it is a limit of the world."[6] Here is a notion of the self that has shrunk to an extensionless point. Perhaps we have arrived, in a kind of uncanny trance, to stare at the consequences of the grammar of the personal pronoun, beyond which empty space seems to fall away.

How then does a consistent stylistic art practice mandated by an encapsulating market (recall Fredric Jameson's remark to the effect that culture equals the market)[7] align itself with such notions of the self? Perhaps I am not obliged to answer, since in the opinion of many I have never engaged in an art practice predicated on consistent rule following.

But perhaps you tried to follow certain rules but misapplied these. Or perhaps you misunderstood what these rules were. Well, wasn't it the case that in the new instance the old rule, when examined, did not fit? But isn't art's first rule of consistency that of craft? Isn't it by that custom that we are able to follow art? Doesn't the successive alteration of a model, which is craft's ruling custom, give us a place to stand? Doesn't grasping this serial rule define its very practice and allow us to say, "Now I know how to go on"? But today I do not think yesterday's thoughts, and craft does not aid me here.

But there is a physical density to art's objects that resists thought. Doesn't it stand in its dense physicality as the body stands to the world, giving testimony to an allegiance as well as the impossibility of coming to rest there? Don't you want to say that there are times when, embedded within the material resistance, as well as its flow, of what is handled in making art, that thought can only hesitate and step back as the momentum you set in motion plays itself out? And isn't the rule of craft bound up with this seduction?

We can talk about how we mean to define a particular art game. Are there alternatives, for example, to identifying it with those rules that yield stylistic consistency? Surely there are themes—it is possible to imagine "thematic" rules and customs—that can be located beneath the stylistic shifts. Well, narratives can be developed that pursue this tenacious, holistic prejudice. And, of course, the prejudice for explanatory narratives of some dimension is insatiable and unbounded—extending all the way to odes to the unconscious. But it seems that theory is a form of narrative we are never without. Yes, but how do you align or superimpose a theoretical narrative game over the artmaking game?

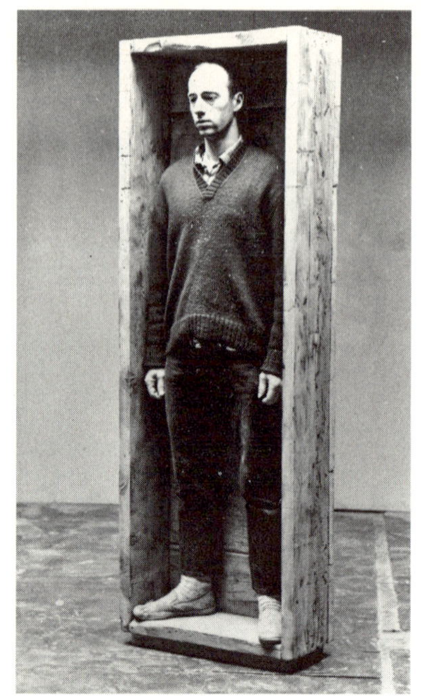

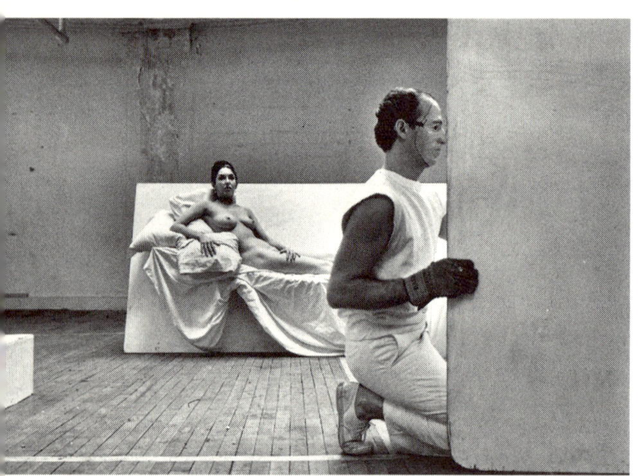

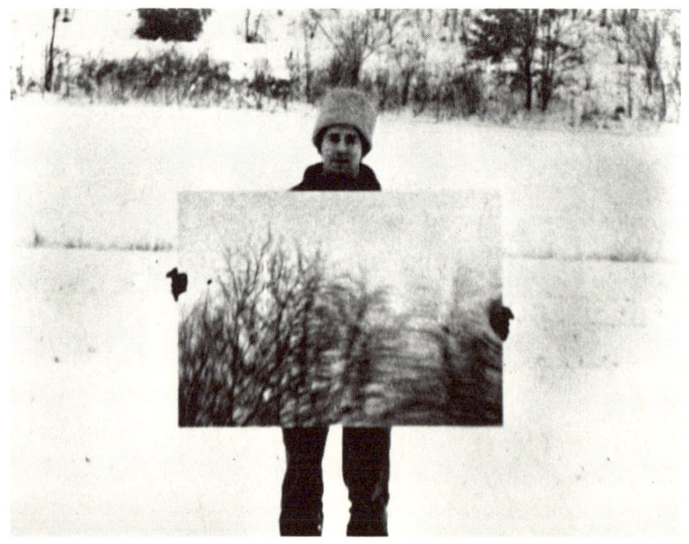

This is the question we probably will be unable to answer here—or anywhere else for that matter.

Is there at least something like a "family resemblance" among these works? If so, I would like to meet the other relatives. What thematic gene links such apparently disparate family members? Could it be that they share a kind of questioning of certain rules that, in some way yet to be determined, make the noses, as it were, of these works resemble one another? But I see no rules that have been questioned. Can't there be a kind of questioning about making that calls no rules into question but is nevertheless a kind of interrogation? A kind of questioning that has the form of "What if . . ." that, by some process also yet to be discovered, drops away with the insertion of these objects into the public domain? As if the language game that comes into contact with an art game in that public space stripped off that layer of doubt that presided at the birth of the objects. As if the language game of the so-called critical response came already armed with other sorts of questions; questions often conceived in terms of a series directed toward salvaging the same from the different. And here we have the kind of question that was never asked in the studio. Would we be justified in asking how this particular critical language game grew to such a size with, apparently, so little need of philosophy?

How could you have made an object that expressed your doubts? Surely we must keep in mind here that doubt can come only after belief. In any case your doubts are not widespread. You never seem to have doubted the ground of that Eurocentric Western landscape from which you sprang. This is the nurturing soil upon which your questions seem to sprout like weeds. Well, it was the garden plot we were given and it was full of these weeds when we got it. But our roots, for better or worse, are sunk here. In any case, "Doubting has an end" (*PI*, p. 180). And "a doubt that doubted everything would not be a doubt."[8]

Marcel Duchamp demonstrated that the custom of manipulating affect was unneeded in making art. In him we have the prototype of the artist without a practice and therefore without a craft. To the horror of the profession, he grin-

---

31. Robert Morris in his *Untitled (Box for Standing)*, 1961. Fir, 74 × 25 × 10½ inches (187.9 × 63.5 × 26.7 cm). Photo courtesy of Robert Morris.

32. *Site*, 1964. Robert Morris and Carolee Schneeman in rehearsal. Photo © Hans Namuth, courtesy of Peter Namuth.

33. *Mirror*, 1969. Still from 16mm black-and-white film. Castelli-Sonnabend Tapes and Films Inc., New York. Musée national d'art moderne, Centre Georges Pompidou, Paris. Photo courtesy of The Solomon R. Guggenheim Museum, New York.

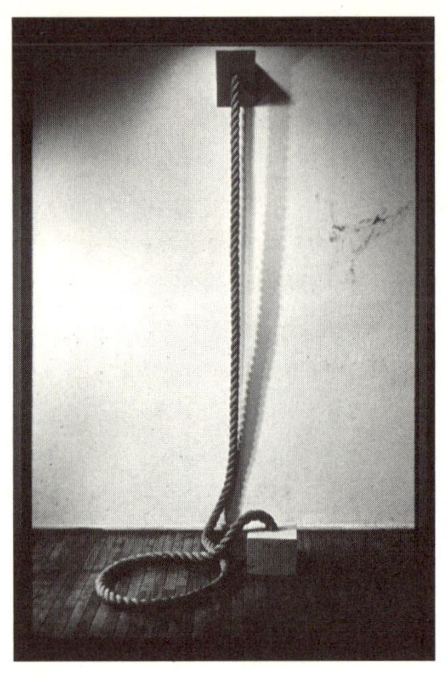

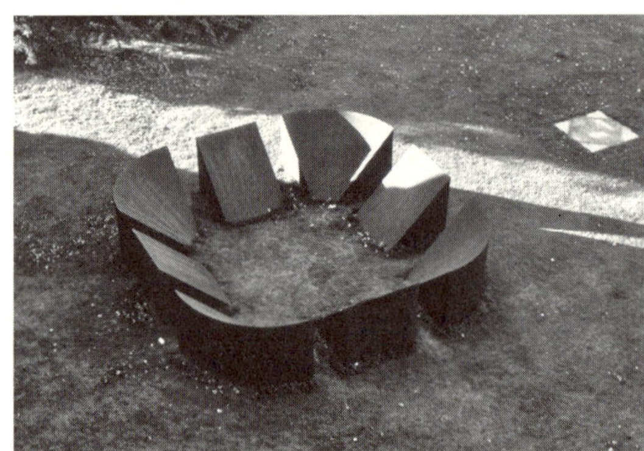

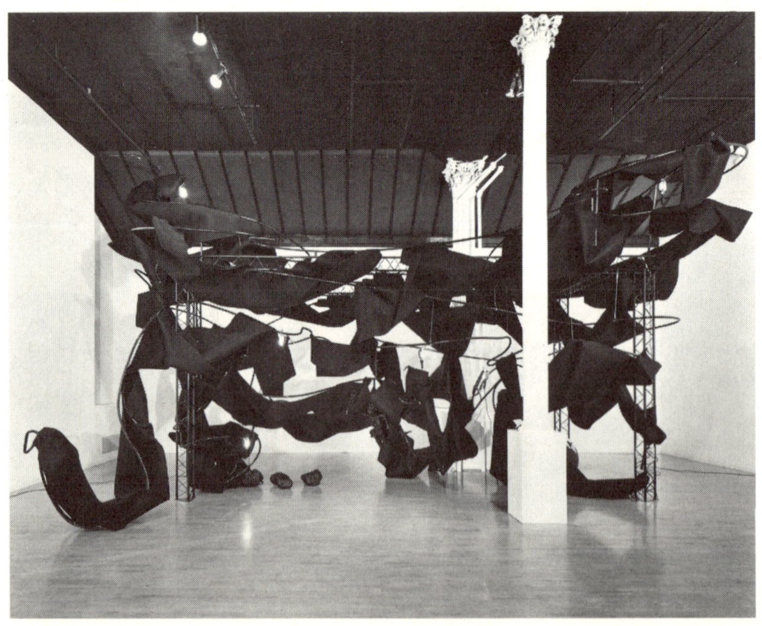

ningly described himself as an "unfrocked" artist. He remarked that he liked breathing better than working. In this he seems, Buddha-like, to have been able to step off the wheel of desire. For the market, he was willing to remake his works in multiple series of miniature reproductions. And here he demonstrates how the lure—and we again want to invoke custom here—of artmaking validated as some mysterious, but necessarily constant, incremental and, if legitimized, serially developed enterprise, is anything but mysterious, necessary or legitimate.

You seem like a man who walks along the shore picking up now this shell and now another only to discard the first, arriving finally back at your starting point with but a single shell, the very last one picked up. You hold this up and say, "See what I have ended up with." And this last one appears different, but in spite of all the time you spent, no more special than all the others. Yes, but we were on the lookout for the limits of the phylum and not the differences within the species. Well, exploring the limits of some of art's conventions is not to have reached the limit of art.

You should not forget that you are a member of that fading generation formed more by the word than the image. For out of the mists of your past, Mnemosyne arrives lugging an old Admiral Radio: a floor model with a strange, greenish, catlike, Cyclopean eye set in the middle of the dial, which widened or narrowed its vertical iris—and even, I think, its color—according to the station's reception. And as the sounds leaked through the brocade-covered speaker below, this illuminated eyeball squinted and blinked in synesthetic response to the static that indifferently interrupted the patrician cadences of FDR or ruined the arch timing of Fred Allen. We sometimes wonder if Goodman did not model his shifty emeralds on this vanished jewel of past living rooms. Yours was a radio childhood back in those black and white and mostly gray decades of the 1930s and '40s, one deprived entirely of the ghostly, mobile, and transfixing images of the video screen. The images of the outside world came but once a week in

34. *Untitled (Rope Piece)*, 1964. Painted wood boxes and rope; rope length: 18 feet (5.49 m). The Museum of Modern Art, New York: Gift of Philip Johnson. Photo courtesy of Robert Morris.

35. *Untitled (Wedges)*, 1971. Oiled steel, eight units, 4 feet 6 inches × 22 feet × 22 feet (1.37 × 6.71 × 6.71 m) overall. Permanent site-specific installation in Fairmount Park Association, Philadelphia. Photo courtesy of Robert Morris.

36. *Second Study for a View from a Corner of Orion (Night)*, 1980. Felt, steel, fiberglass, resin, human skeleton, electric light, 10 × 32 × 16 feet (3 × 9.8 × 4.9 m). Collection of the artist. Photo courtesy of Robert Morris.

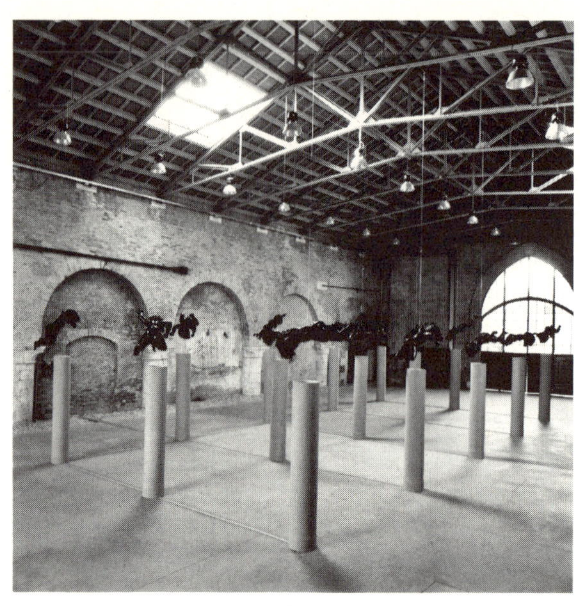

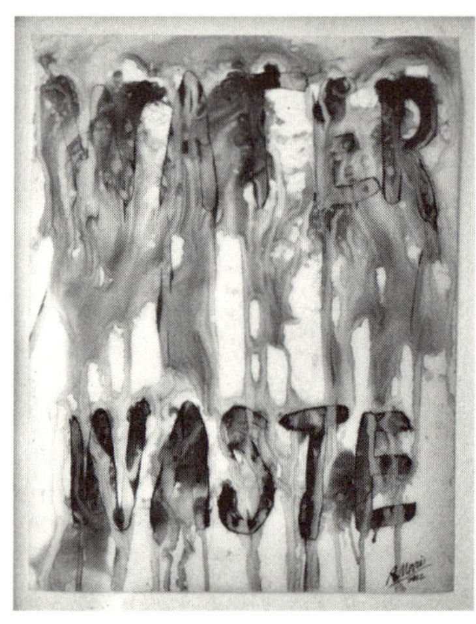
WASTE

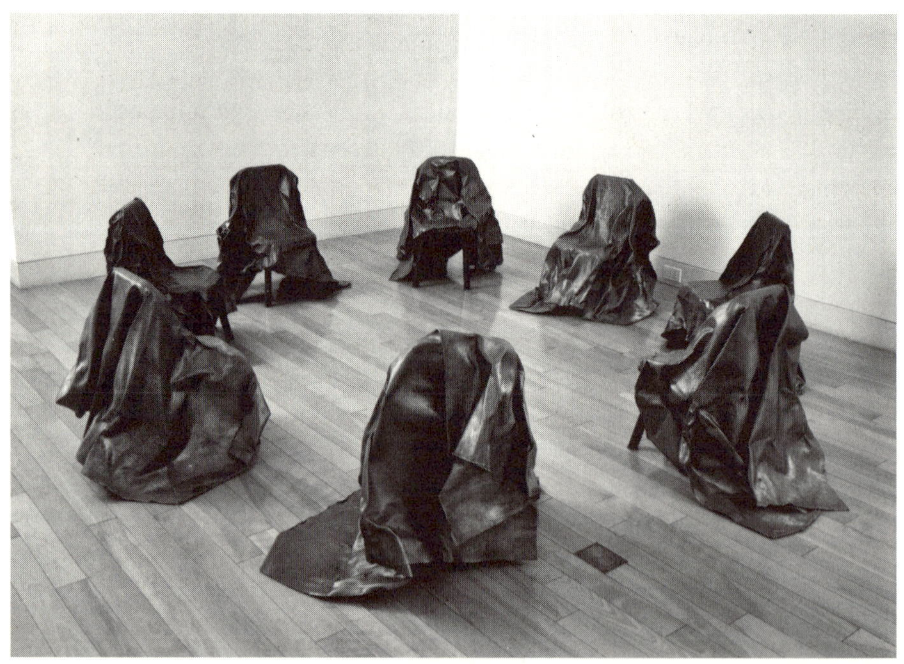

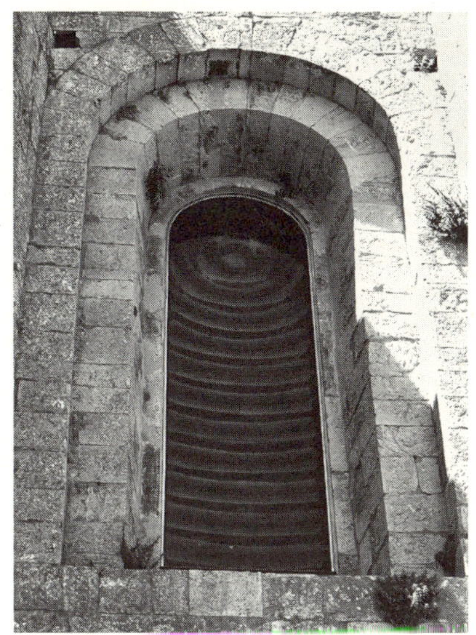

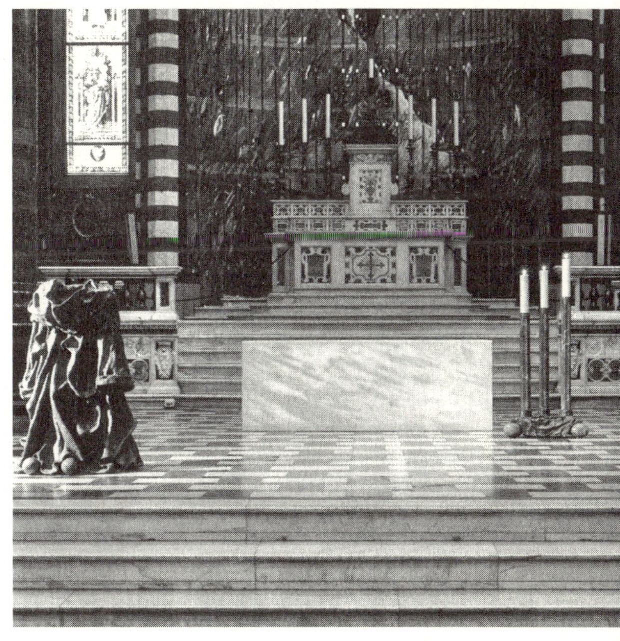

Opposite:

37. Installation view of *Tar Babies of the New World Order*, 1997. Clay, thread, plastic. Fifteen units (columns), each: 98.5 inches (250.2 cm) high, 8 inches (20.3 cm) diameter; fifteen units (baby figures), each: 47.3 inches (120.1 cm) long. Collection of Nuova Icona, Venice, Italy. Photo Graziano Arici, courtesy of Nuova Icona, Venice.

38. *Water Waste*, 2002. Ink on vellum, 14 × 17 ½ inches (35.56 × 44.45 cm). Private collection, New York. Photo courtesy of the editor.

39. *Chairs*, 2002. Lead and wood. Eight units, 25 × 124 × 124 inches (63.50 × 314.96 × 314.96 cm) overall. Collection of the artist. Photo courtesy of Robert Morris.

Above:

40. Seventeen stained-glass windows, 2001, installed in the Maguelone Cathedral, an eleventh-century Romanesque church that has been designated a French national historical monument. Work commission by the French Ministry of Culture. Detail (exterior view). Photo courtesy of Bill Schillinger.

41. Presbytery in the Prato Cathedral, 2002. Altar: white marble; ambon: bronze; candelabrum: bronze, Prato, Italy. Work commission by Giuliano and Pina Gori. Photo courtesy of Giuliano Gori.

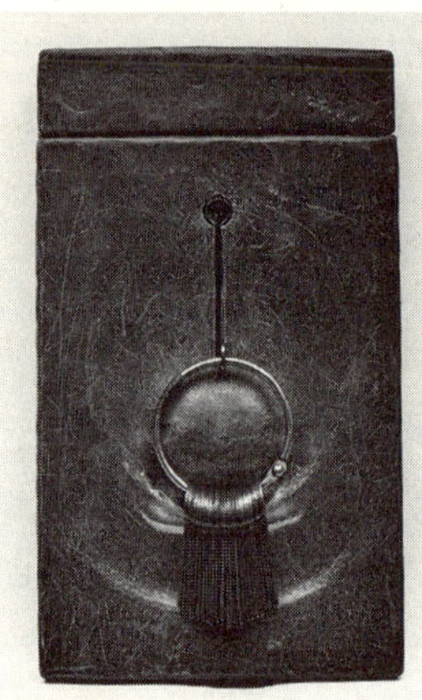

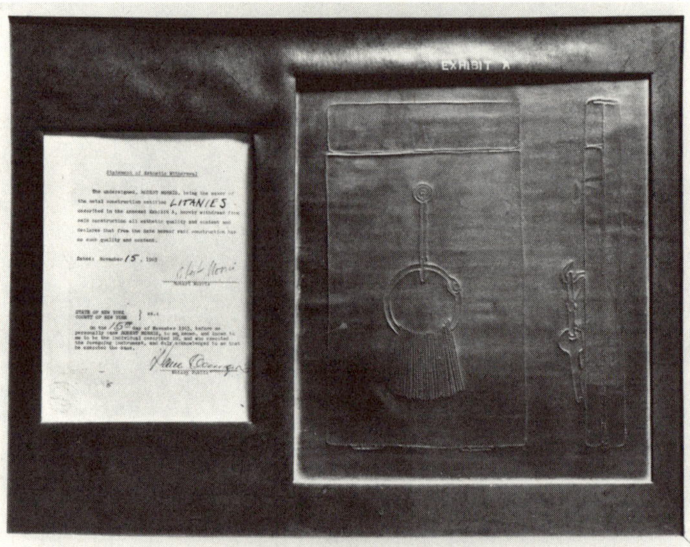
EXHIBIT A
LITANIES

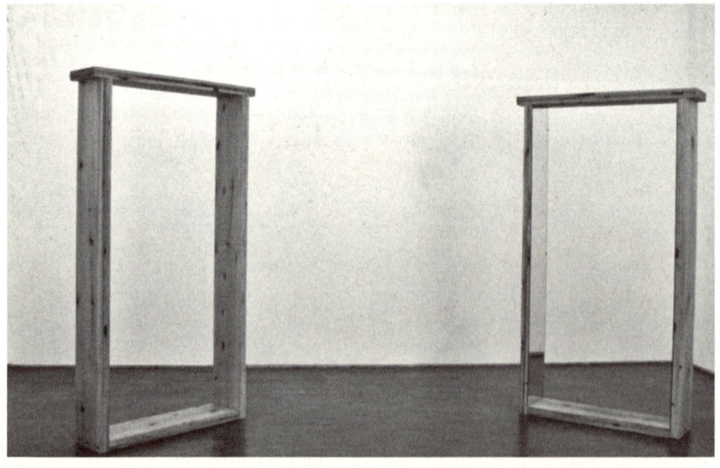

those days, in the form of *Life* magazine for the static ones and the *Movietone News Reel* for the animated ones. Such was the anorexic visual diet of my generation's childhood. Still, I cannot say that I became an artist from a childhood of visual hunger.

John Cage remarked that if you really understood him you would have no need of his work. There is always something to listen to, as Cage's notorious work of so-called silence demonstrates. Today, when every day we consume a blitzkrieg of images delivered from every mediaized direction, one wonders why there are more artists than ever before.

Could we say you always had a suspicion of the image? After all, grayness seems to predominate? No optical celebration of lush surfaces are to be found in your oeuvre. Your strategies had more often to do with locating conditions that generated objects and divided spaces. Still, we are left with images when all is said and done. No, you are wrong. We are left with photographs and words when all is said and done. Still, there seems to have been in the past a certain conscious resistance to the "image," as if this offered you a certain purchase, a certain foothold (pardon the image here) from which to work. And how does such a stance feel today? Well, it is like standing on a station platform watching the express go by.

The question persists: How do you account for not following the rules of a consistent art practice? Well, perhaps in the past, when you had applied the rule to a necessarily limited number of cases it only appeared that it was the rule shared with the others. More recent cases reveal how in fact you had taken the rule in some aberrant gruelike and noncustomary way, and this was responsible for the anomalous look things came to have. Surely there is ample evidence of your steadfast acceptance of the custom of art as service, since so many works

---

42. *Litanies*, 1963. Lead over wood, steel key ring, 27 keys and brass lock, 12 × 7⅛ × 2½ inches (30.5 × 18.1 × 6.3 cm). The Museum of Modern Art, New York. Gift of Philip Johnson. Photo courtesy of Robert Morris.

43. *Statement of Esthetic Withdrawal*, 1963. Typed and notarized statement on paper and lead over wood, mounted in imitation leather mat, 17⅝ × 23¾ inches (44.8 × 60.3 cm). The Museum of Modern Art, New York. Gift of Philip Johnson. Photo courtesy of Robert Morris.

44. Installation view of *Robert Morris: The Mind/Body Problem*, retrospective exhibition, Musée national d'art moderne, Centre Georges Pompidou, Paris, July 5–October 23, 1995. Photo courtesy of Robert Morris. Left: *Untitled (Pine Portal)*, 1993 refabrication of a 1961 original. Laminated pine, 96 × 48 × 12 inches (243.8 × 121.9 × 30.5 cm). Collection of the artist. Right: *Untitled (Pine Portal with Mirrors)*, 1993 refabrication of a 1961 original. Laminated pine and mirrors, 85 × 45 × 11 inches (215.2 × 114.3 × 28 cm). Collection of the artist.

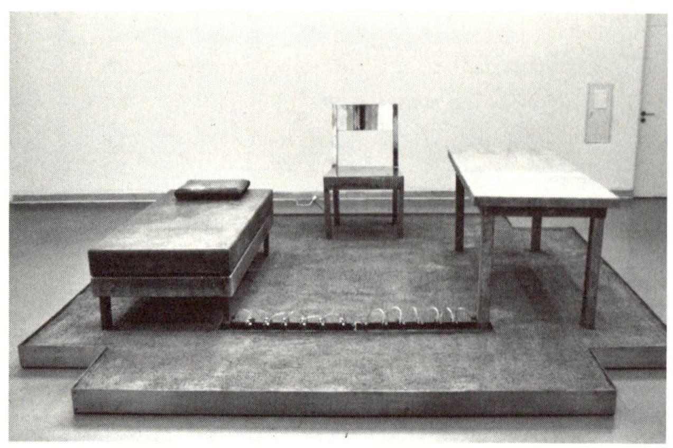

not because of resistence but because of the lack of it. That was when the billowing out really began. Just a touch was needed to begin. Just a toe hold to push off from. And out I floated turning in every direction. I don't have to tell you what I did with the old voice. Sideways. Upside down. Backwards. Turn it inside out like an old sock. You heard me back there.

END REEL 2

talking backwards. Remember? Backwards talking there. Back me. Heard you. Like that. Well, some would say that here I speak of the form. Those same some would no doubt say that I was still speaking of them. Not the them of the same some. But the former them. Those four. The them of those of whom I spoke

BEGIN REEL 6

when I began to speak of them. And, very likely, those same some could be the them of whom I spoke when I began to speak of them. Or, at least, some of those same some might have been members of the them of whom I spoke when I began to speak of them. Those, that is, from whom I felt I had to "get away, always that," and from whom I no longer feel any need to "get away, always that," being now away from them of whom I formerly

*END REEL 2 MIXED

43

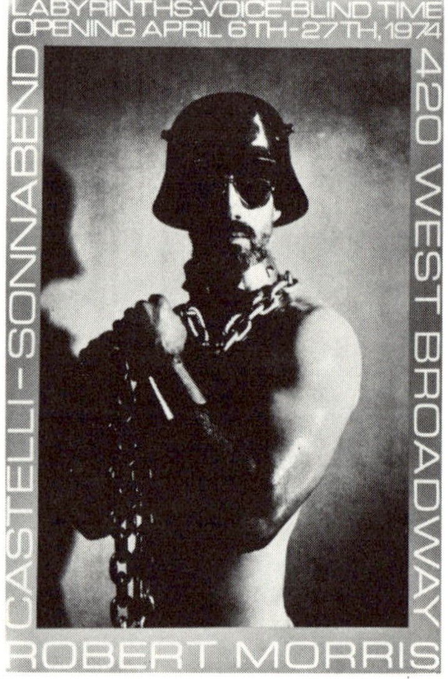

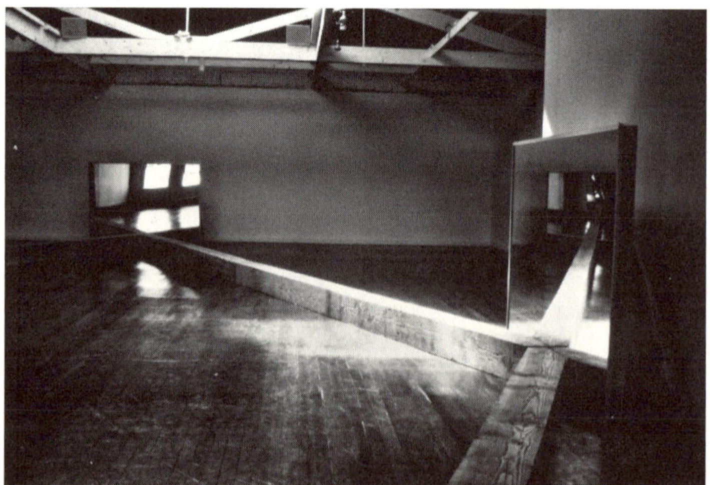

found their way into collections. Do you want to say that you were capable of bringing forward only this rule of custom, the rule of service? And here you would no doubt quote Wittgenstein again when he says, "When I obey a rule, I do not choose. I obey the rule *blindly*" (*PI*, §219).

But what about the rules of genre? Nothing so transforms art from an investigation into a professional, self-assured, and self-replicating practice as these. Nothing hews closer to the custom of service than the guarantee that art should issue in a practice that forgets its origins as an investigation and continues to reiterate a single inference, as though the impure specter of Goodman's grue emeralds that accommodated both green and blue could be cleansed by relentless repetitions of an ever purer shade of green; repetitions that keep time to TryannoCap's bell, which clangs overhead so deafeningly today.

But by the beginning of the 1960s, when you began, the rules of genre had been shot full of holes. That rearguard, Greenbergian, modernist script was by then a sorry, tattered document. The modernist rules of the pure genres were already a disrupted set of customs. Pop art, minimal art, conceptual art rolled by. But it was probably not until the late 1970s—that fateful decade when America's economic Golden Age drew to a close—that the idea of multiple, self-confident genres was firmly in place. The old rules gave way to new ones. Different games began to be played—although there are some who would want the old semi-religious modernist order back and some even who would claim it never left. But instead of dissenting expressions being seen as heretically diverging from a few heavy discourses, a new landscape of niches grew up, each of which came to house a minigenre. Today these dot the landscape as far as the eye can see. Genre niches of body art, video art, and gender art of every

---

45. *Hearing*, 1972. Three-and-one-half-hour stereo tape, stereo tape recorder, amplifier, two speakers; copper chair with water and immersion heater, 48 × 24 × 30 inches (121.9 × 61 × 76.2 cm); zinc table, 36 × 78 × 36 inches (91.4 × 182.9 × 25.4 cm); and wet-cell batteries buried in sand in a bronze trough; on wood platform 6 inches (15.2 cm) high, 12 feet (3.66 m) square, with 24 inch-square (61 cm) sections cut from each corner. Williams College Museum of Art, Williamstown, Massachusetts. Photo courtesy of The Solomon R. Guggenheim Museum, New York.

46. Manuscript drawing for *Voice*, 1973. Pencil and typewriter ink on paper, 11 × 8½ inches (27.9 × 21.6 cm). Collection of the artist. Photo courtesy of Robert Morris.

47. *Untitled*, 1974 (poster for *Voice*). Offset lithograph, 36¾ × 23⅞ inches (93.3 × 60.6 cm). Collection of the artist. Photo courtesy of Robert Morris.

48. *Untitled (Portland Mirrors)*, 1977. Four units, each 72 × 96 inches (182.9 × 243.8 cm) with 12 inch square (30.5 cm2) fir timbers of varying lengths. Le Musée d'art contemporain, Lyon. Photo courtesy of Robert Morris.

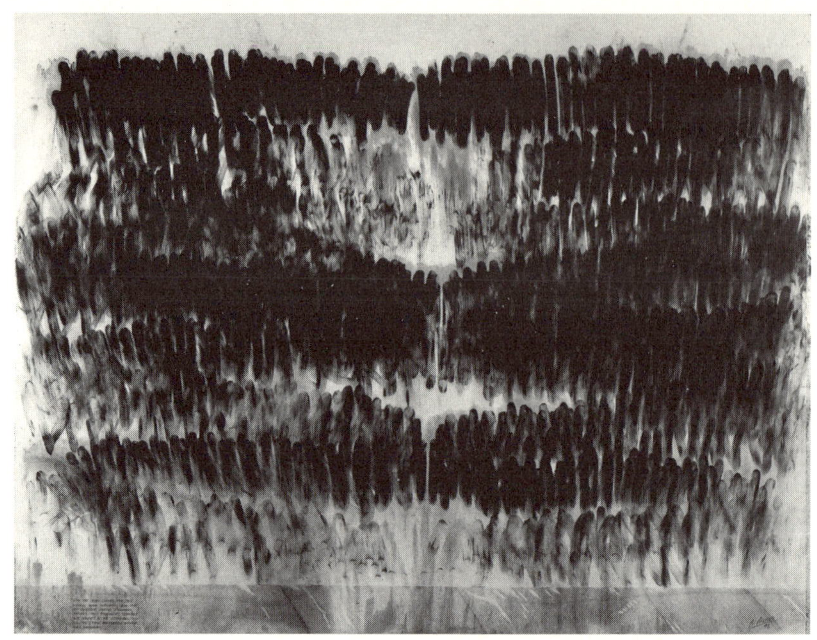

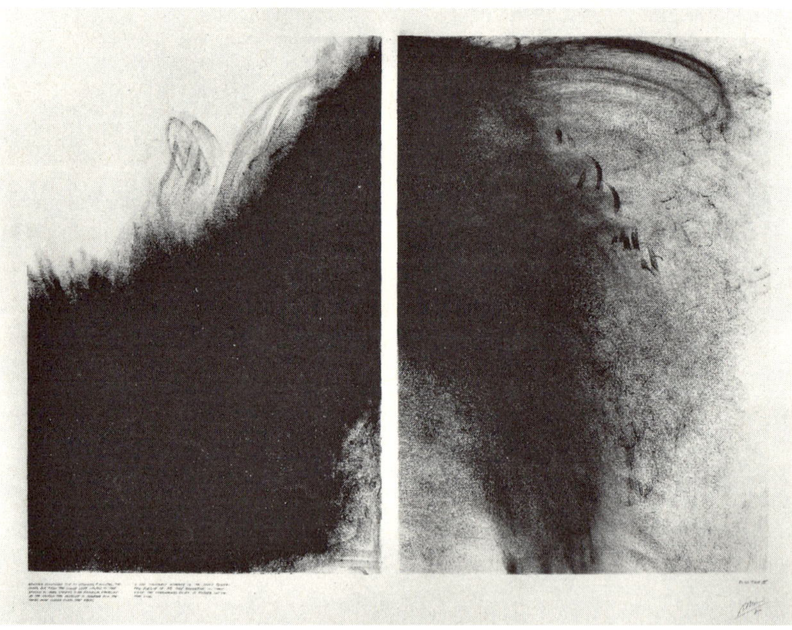

49. *Blind Time I*, 1973. Graphite on paper, 35 × 46 inches (88.9 × 116.8 cm). National Gallery of Art, Washington D.C. Photo courtesy of Robert Morris.

50. *Blind Time III*, 1985. Iron oxide on paper, 38 × 50 inches (96.5 × 127 cm). Collection of Sonnabend Gallery, New York. Photo courtesy of Robert Morris.

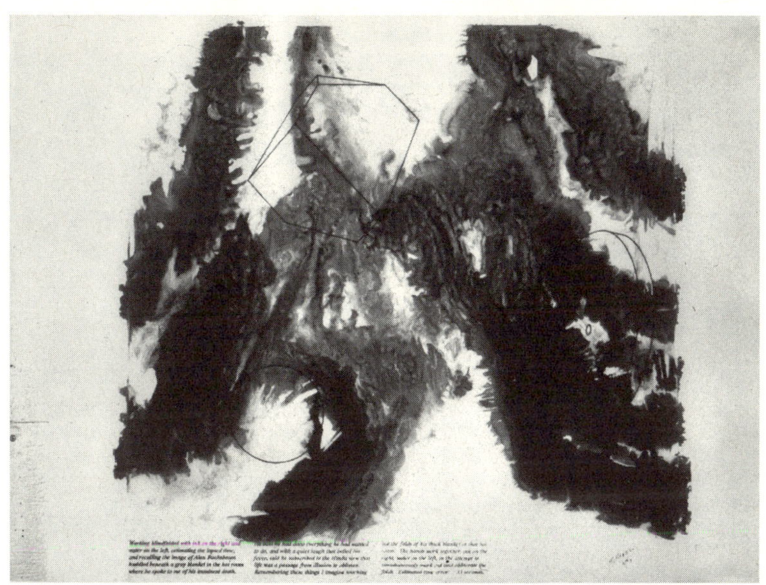

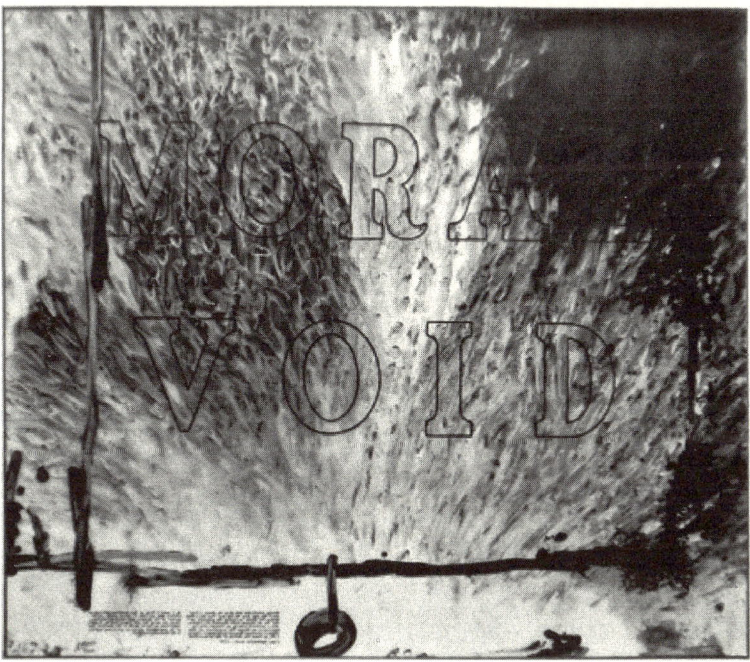

51. *Blind Time V: Melancholia*, 1999. Ink on mylar, 28 × 30 inches (73.03 × 76.20 cm). Collection of Sonnabend Gallery, New York. Photo courtesy of Bill Schillinger.

52. *Blind Time VI: Moral Blinds*, 2000. Ink on mylar, 35½ × 41 inches (90.2 × 104.8 cm). Collection of the artist. Photo courtesy of Bill Schillinger.

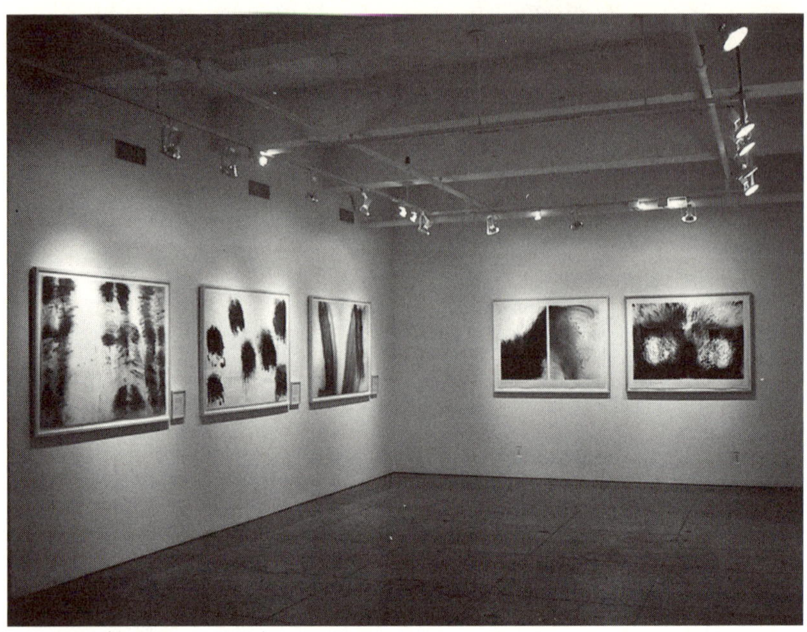

53. Installation view of *Robert Morris: Blind Time Drawings*, at Haim Chanin Fine Arts, New York, September 12–November 1, 2003. Photo courtesy of Haim Chanin Fine Arts, New York.

variety. A phalanx of related niches glowing with an array of politically correct attitudes expressed in a welter of media, and an expanded array of niches for painting that stretch from the lugubrious monochrome to neo-you-name-it, to subniches of performance and installation art heavy with feminist and racial themes, not to mention those deeply dug niches proclaiming victimhood as inspiration and the automatic guarantee of the right to be heard (the poet Joseph Brodsky's advice that one should "at all costs try to avoid granting yourself the status of the victim" notwithstanding).[9] And isn't this multiplicity of art games to be welcomed? Isn't a landscape with an artist in every doorway a livelier one? Shouldn't a consumerist democracy dictate a fifteen-minute limit to fame?

Two years ago during an installation at the Leo Castelli Gallery in New York City I had the occasion to introduce my young, new assistant to the venerable eighty-six-year-old dealer. "Leo," I said, "I want you to meet Andrew, my new assistant. He is an artist." For a moment Castelli studied my assistant, who was beaming in the presence of such a legendary figure. Finally Leo smiled and said, "Ah, we are all artists. Some more, some less."

But didn't we in the past grant art and artists a certain puzzled awe because of their peculiar habit of living so intimately with the irreducible strangeness of

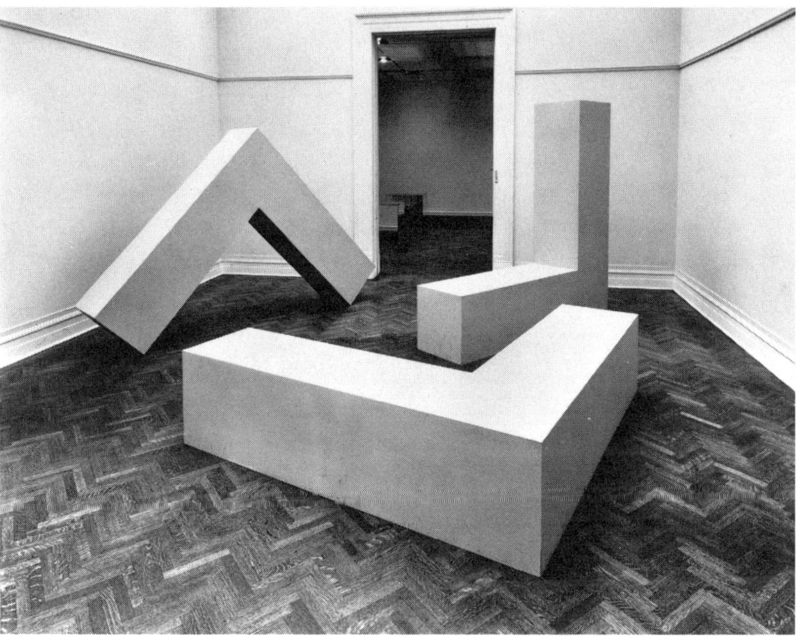

54. *Untitled (Three L-Beams)*, 1965–69. Painted plywood, three units, each 96 × 96 × 24 inches (243.8 × 243.8 × 61 cm). Private ollection, New York. Photo courtesy of Robert Morris.

the physical? Wasn't there once something almost quaint, if a little perplexing, about ascribing to the aesthetic a refusal of the instrumental impulse? Didn't the aesthetic engagement with the world at one time seem somehow too profligate and excessive, an unaffordable supplement to what was called the real world, a world not nearly so real, of course, as the one we have today? In those days this involvement might even have carried a slight edge of embarrassment because of how play constantly bubbled through it. Was a space once ceded to the artist—with a certain condescending relief—where play was assumed to be strung to a pitch of unseemly seriousness while simultaneously destabilized by the suspicion of an erotic itch? Was there then something reassuring about having only to imagine oneself in the place of the artist? Could this have brought relief to know that one was not personally required to stir the thickness of the world with the wand of fantasy? Was there a time not so long ago when art was patronized for its effort to be serious about what didn't matter?

All the new art games—even the more shrill and sloganizing ones—are staggeringly reliable in their professionalism and their eager clamor to be let inside those vaulted and polished rooms that are so secure and highly insured and believed to be sealed against the dust of time.

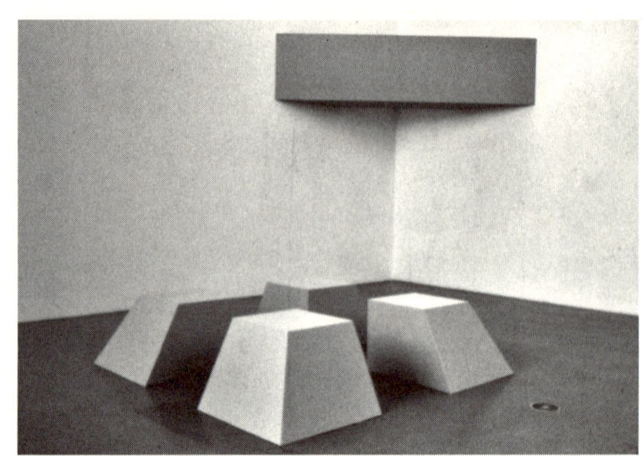

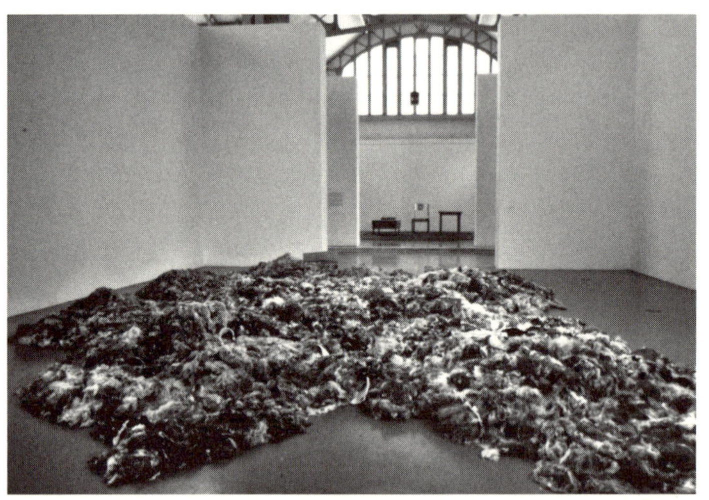

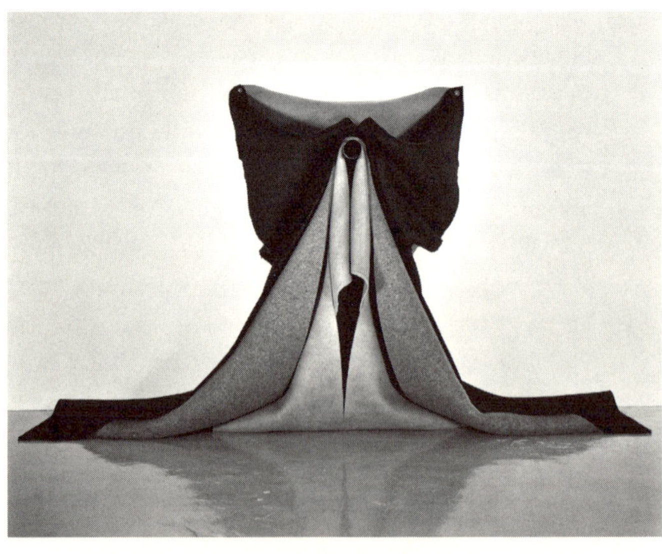

But a certain smell of the strategic has always hung over your work. Did you not in the beginning wish to chip away at some transcendent notion of modernism's rule of pure "sculpture"? Well, you were born into the world at a certain time. There is a context. Then, you would say that what you have done is to be taken as a kind of reply? Yes, but a reply to what? Since we find no celebrations here, perhaps a reply to your oppressions.

You want to say that your iterations were neither instances of a thematically linked series, nor resulted from a strategic questioning of rules? Well, you want to answer, they came about as a series of particular investigations in which questions were addressed to the conditions of the existence of the example.

But surely an investigation also has its rules. And these would have to do not only with the asking of questions but the careful observation of results. And what about conclusions? Are not conclusions an end of the investigation? Doesn't an investigation issue in conclusions? And what about the most mysterious factor of all, the accident? Yes, what about that moment when you feel that because of the welcome accident you are suddenly traveling along in a different direction? Then, surprised and almost without effort, you find yourself moving along on a different set of rails.

Once the klieg lights were on you, you would look around for an old list. Such as: Could construction count as the making process? Could the object exist only as its own reproduction; that is, can a case be made here, remembering the good ship Argo, for the nominal and the formal to take precedence over the unique, the original? Can the object be in the same space as the body, so that its meaning will be, as Wittgenstein says, "like going up to someone"(*PI*, §455)?

But we are afraid the possibility for such meanings has disappeared from a discourse that rather sees the meanings of all expressions as the mere symptoms of the various political, economic, and social ideologies within which the art of any given time is suspended. Can't you see your art in these terms as the

55. Top: *Untitled (Corner Beam)*, 1964. Painted plywood, 24 × 12 × 144 inches (61 × 30.5 × 36.6 cm). Bottom: *Untitled (Battered Cubes)*, 1965. Painted plywood, four units, each 24 × 36 × 36 inches (61 × 91.4 × 91.4 cm). Photo courtesy of Robert Morris.

56. *Untitled (Threadwaste)*, 1968. Threadwaste, asphalt, mirrors, copper tubing, and felt, overall dimensions variable. The Museum of Modern Art, New York: Gift of Philip Johnson. Photo courtesy of Robert Morris.

57. *House of the Vetti II*, 1983. Gray and pink felt, steel bracket and metal grommets, 89 × 157 × 36 inches (226 × 400 × 91.5 cm). Private collection. Photo courtesy of The Solomon R. Guggenheim Museum, New York.

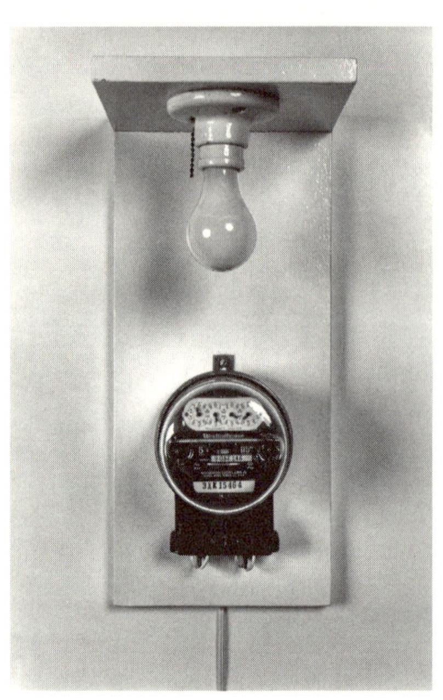

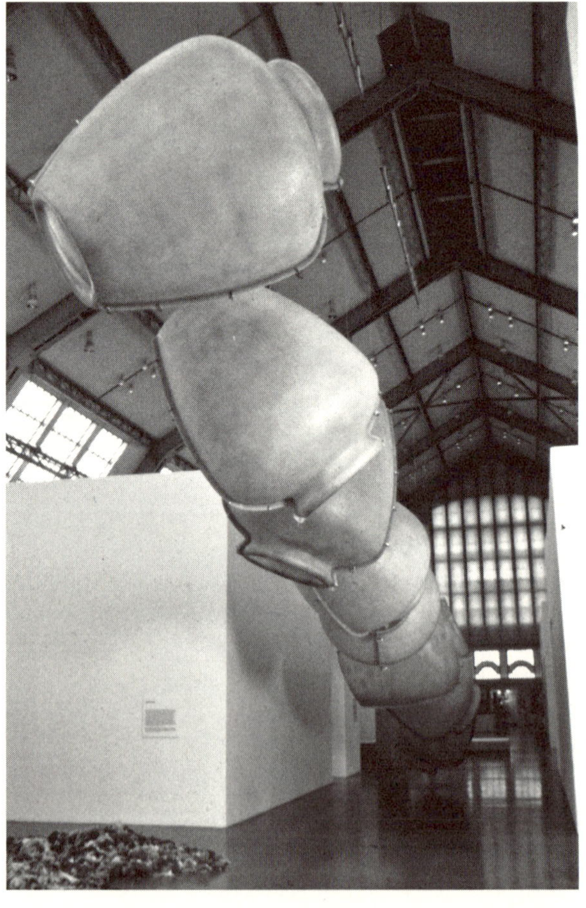

mere expression of those powers that gave rise to it? But here you do not speak of expression but reduction. And to view the work in these terms we do not, needless to say, need the art. A few old photographs will do together with a few of your own old notations. The faintest breath of the signified and not the corporeal body of the signifier is all we need to read this text. For surely it is not even dead bodies that such a forensic text requires.

But what about that other critical practice language game of longstanding that would see, for example, these two columns—the one upright, the other prone—linked to an age-old longer series descending from the abbreviated torsos found at Harappa on the one hand and the form of the funerary dolmen on the other; that series from which you seem to want to set yourself apart—by means of this veritable hyphen of an object called a sculpture—and simultaneously bring to an end with its rotated double—this plywood exclamation mark. Such seems to be the ambition of these dual blanknesses with which you have wanted to *strip* sculpture bare, even. And you cannot deny that these faceless synecdoches for the body amount to a fairly literal demonstration, one that reeks of a laboratory experiment, namely, one supporting a phenomenological thesis that here approaches the comical. These works that so insistently remind the viewer of the embeddedness of his corporeal self in the world and demand a simultaneously reflexive confrontation with the object and his own body, devolve, as important minds have told us, into a "theatricality" unworthy of high art. At the most generous stretch we might grant that these dismal gray objects—one up, one down—may embody an allegory of that monotonously enduring twin thematics of plastic art: the body on the one hand, and landscape on the other. But these ultimate marks of the vertical and horizontal raise more questions than they answer. Do we have here the same thing in two positions? Or do we have two things, each a representative of a different position? Or do we have an implied action? In which case the work destabilizes itself as a pair of objects and hovers dangerously close to an event. And if an event, what is the order? Do we have here a vertical in search of a horizontal, what might be termed a sort of plywood death wish? It does not seem likely, given the abbre-

58. *Metered Bulb*, 1963. Light bulb, ceramic socket with pull chain, and electricity meter, mounted on painted wood 17 ¾ × 8 × 8 ¼ inches (45.1 × 20.3 × 21 cm). The Museum of Modern Art, New York: Gift of Jasper Johns. Photo by Dorothy Zeidman, courtesy of Robert Morris.

59. *The Fallen and the Saved*, 1994. Fiberglass, sound tape, and speakers. Eight units (urns), each 66 × 60 inches (167.64 × 152.40 cm). Collection of Giuliano Gori, Fattoria di Celle, Santomato, Pistoia, Italy. Photo courtesy of Robert Morris.

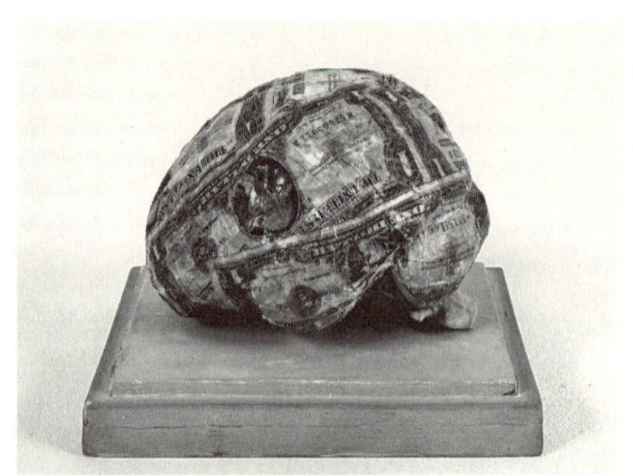

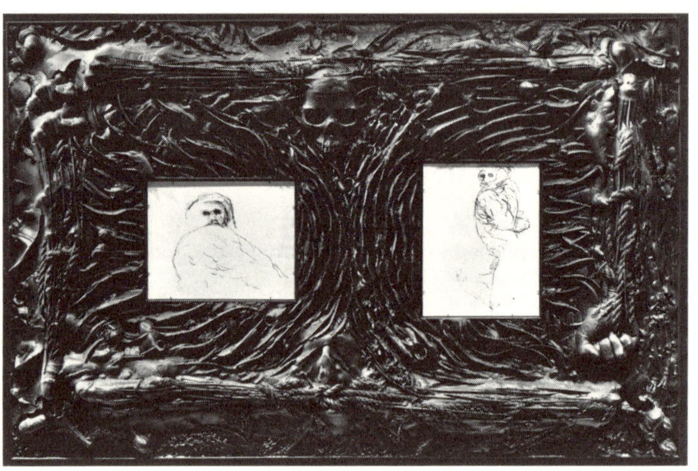

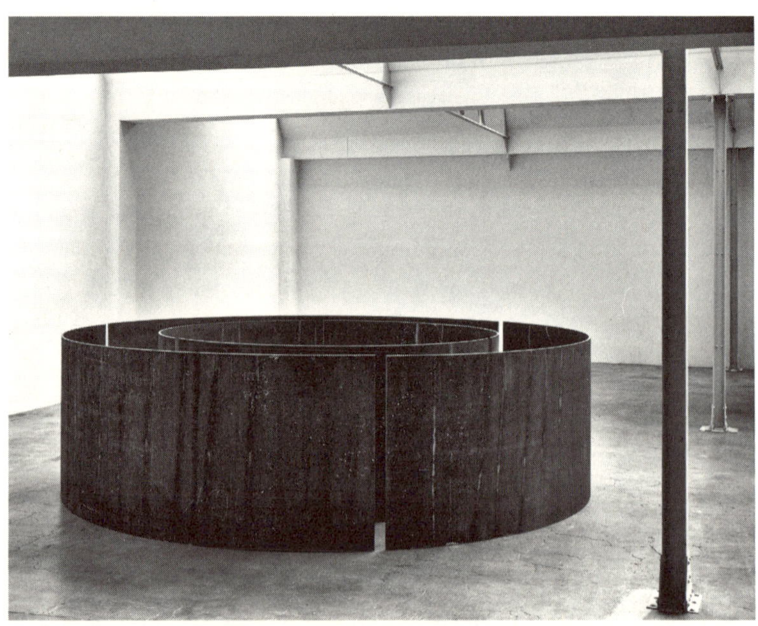

viated and barren nature of the objects, that the event alluded to here is to be read as a horizontal in search of a vertical, a kind of rising up, a rampant sort of apotheosis of the transcendental phallic signifier triumphant. Surely the ambiguity of the work's status, as it hovers between object and event, could please none of us who have ever revered Gotthold Ephraim Lessing.

Satire has perhaps gone far enough here. But such questions easily run amok when the critical becomes reduced to that strategic language game of projecting the linked series. What sort of erotics, for example, would such an approach yield in this comparison of a constraining spatial void on the one hand, and a plywood shaft on the other? Well, it could only lead to accusations that its maker was a hopelessly greedy personality, childishly intolerant of missing out on what the other half has. No doubt somewhere in these works that are simultaneously overdetermined and empty, Rrose Sélavy lifts her finely chiseled profile.

Would you rather say that for you there have always been a number of making games going on and it is just this that the others object to? Well, it reinforces the illusion of a self to assign it one game, to have that one named game to call out. One name, one game goes the rule of market recognition. And those naked plywood objects were only one game? Yes, only one. But the very nature of a game is that the rules are reinforced and justified by the community. A game played by one would not be a game. But somewhere I said that what you are calling the plywood game—which perhaps has less to do with the material than it does with a game about building and scale and gravity and assumptions about the mobile body and so forth—shares certain normative aspects with games played as far back as the Neolithic.

And what about some of the others you have played? What about those that seem to have been played not in the space of the mobile body, those more sedentary ones played, where? Within the spaces of the mental? And why do these more intimate games so often show traces or impressions of the body, as if the body had traversed these objects on its way elsewhere? Yes, other games

---

60. *Brain*, 1963. 8 ½ dollar bills over plaster cast in glass case, 7 ½ × 6 ½ × 5 ¾ inches (19.05 × 16.51 × 14.61 cm). Collection of Leo Castelli Gallery, New York. Photo courtesy of The Solomon R. Guggenheim Museum, New York.

61. *Fathers and Sons*, 1955/1983. Painted Hydrocal and ink on paper, 33 ¼ × 51 ⅜ inches (84.5 × 130.5 cm). Collection of the artist. Photo by John Abbott, courtesy of Robert Morris.

62. *Open Center Sculpture*, 1997. Steel, 45.67 × 157.48 inches (116 × 400 cm). Collection of Robert Morris and Galerie Pietro Sparta, Chagny, France. Photo courtesy of Galerie Pietro Sparta, Chagny.

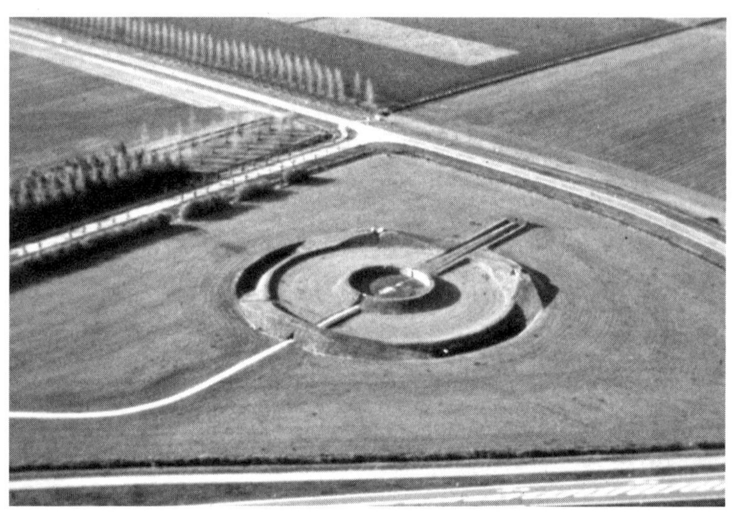

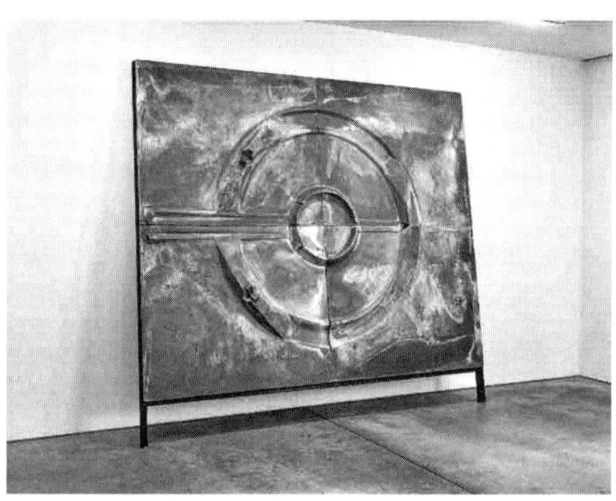

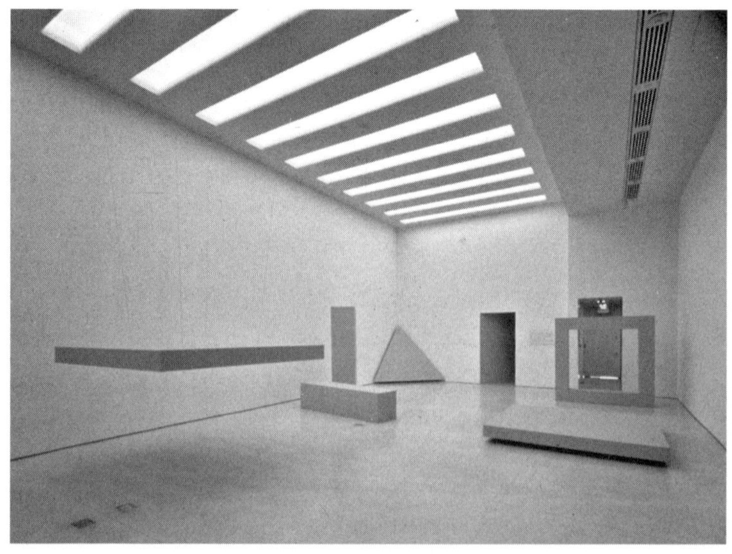

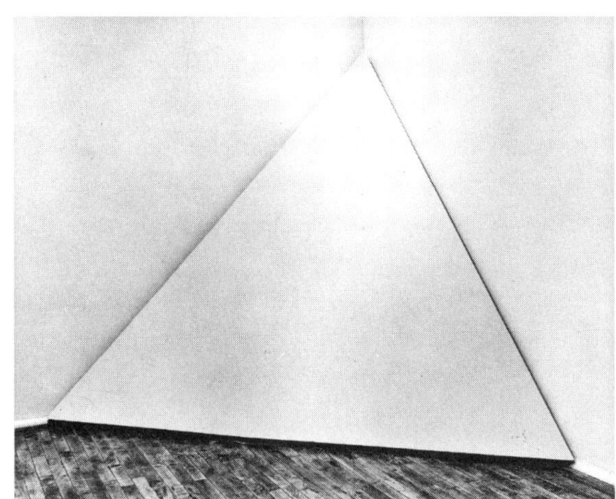

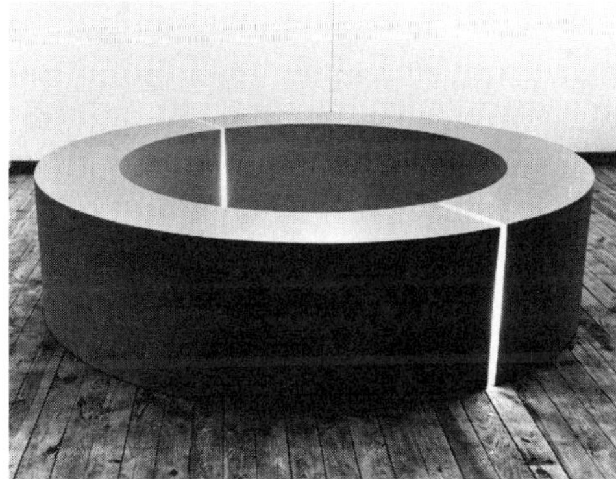

Opposite:

63. *Observatory*, 1977. Aerial view. Earth, water, wood, granite, steel, 298 feet 7 inches (91.01 m) diameter. Permanent site-specific earthwork in Oostelijk, Flevoland, The Netherlands. Photo courtesy of Robert Morris.

64. *Observatory*, 1972. Lead and steel, 108 × 121 × 5 inches (274.32 × 307.34 × 12 cm). Collection of Robert Morris and Sonnabend Gallery, New York. Photo courtesy of Sonnabend Gallery, New York.

65. Installation view of *Robert Morris: The Mind/Body Problem*, retrospective exhibition, The Solomon Guggenheim Museum, New York, January 16–April 4, 1994. Photo courtesy of Robert Morris.

Above:

66. *Untitled (Corner Piece)*, 1964. Painted plywood, 78 inches (198.1 cm) high, 108 inches (274.3 cm) wide. The Solomon R. Guggenheim Museum, New York: Panza Collection. Photo by David Heald, courtesy of Robert Morris.

67. *Untitled (Ring with Light)*, 1965–1966. Painted wood and fiberglass and fluorescent light, two units, each 24 inches (61 cm) high, 14 inches (35.6 cm) deep; overall diameter 97 inches (246.4 cm). Dallas Museum of Art, General Acquisitions Fund and a matching grant from the National Endowments for the Arts. Photo by Rudolph Burkhardt, courtesy of Robert Morris.

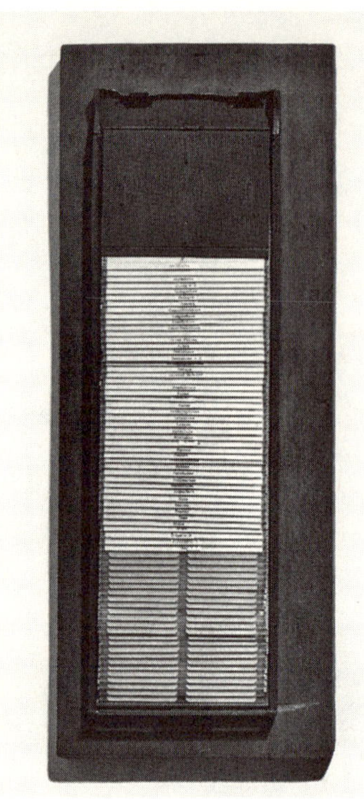

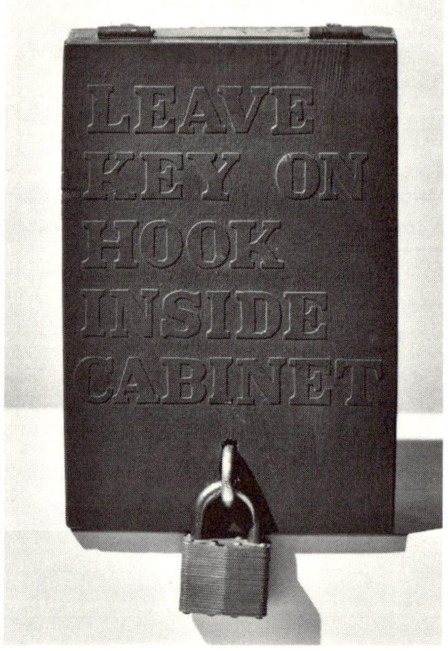
LEAVE
KEY ON
HOOK
INSIDE
CABINET

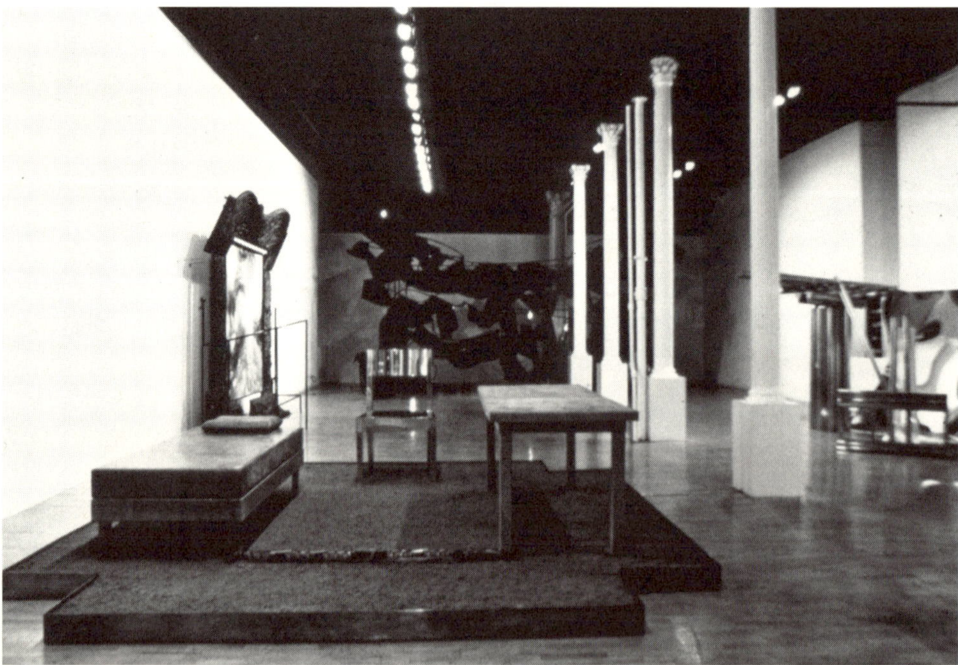

occurred in other rooms. And these in turn share aspects of the past practices that stretch back and, to satisfy the historians, latch on, however tenuously, to the practices of Donatello or Rodin, for example—just to call up the heavy artillery.

Then it would seem that the art historical obsession with linking the same in a series does not deserve the satirization you give it. But we speak of aspects of games whose changes over time make them only distant relatives to those played in the past. The present rooms are in the same house, but we exist in an addition or a wing connected by such remote and winding passages that they resemble a labyrinth. And we are trying to give descriptions here and not explanations.

How could we approach the issue of valuation here? Surely in a lifetime of relentless art activity you must pause in your labors from time to time in front of such a question. And here we would want to know if a distinction is to be made for the sake of valuation between the activity of making and the products produced. Taken together, they constitute a form of life. They have been a way of being in the world. These objects, the result of a particular activity, together with the many questions raised in their pursuit, are, we would like to say, another way of saying, questions and all. If this pursuit has been largely characterized, as you claim, by the mode of interrogation—leaving aside for the moment the lack of clarity with this notion—applied to a variety of artmaking games, the objects finally stand without their question marks. It is as if it were in the very nature of the social process—and its sovereign customs that govern art's form of life—that this transfiguration from question to statement was automatically enforced; as if the grammatical or modal shift was both inevitable and lawful; as if the price of the social demanded at last an end to questions.

And if the questions come to an end, so too do our efforts at justification. And here we can recall Wittgenstein's remark: "If I have exhausted the justifications, I have reached bedrock, and my spade is turned. Then I am inclined to say: 'This is simply what I do'" (*PI*, §217).

---

68. *Card File*, 1962. Metal and plastic wall file mounted on wood, containing forty-four index cards, 27 × 10½ × 2 inches (68.6 × 26.7 × 5.1 cm). Musée national d'art moderne, Centre Georges Pompidou, Paris. Photo courtesy of Robert Morris.

69. *Untitled (Leave Key on Hook)*, 1963. Key, lock, and patinated bronze box, 13 × 7½ × 3½ inches (33 × 19.1 × 8.9 cm). Private collection. Photo courtesy of Robert Morris.

70. Installation view of *Robert Morris: Work from 1967–1984*, one-man exhibition, Leo Castelli Gallery, New York, January 12–February 9, 1985. Photo courtesy of Robert Morris.

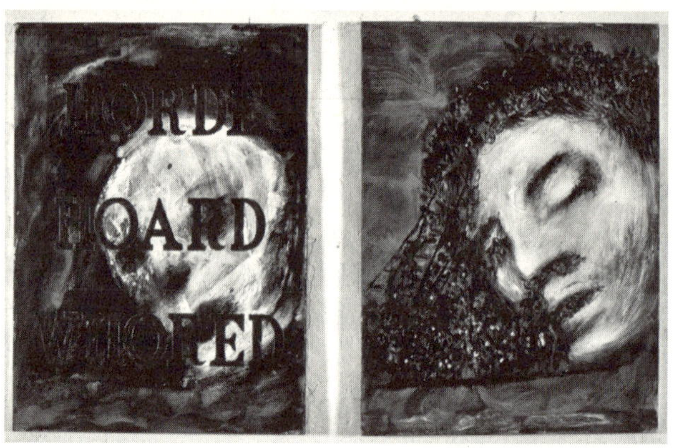
HOARD

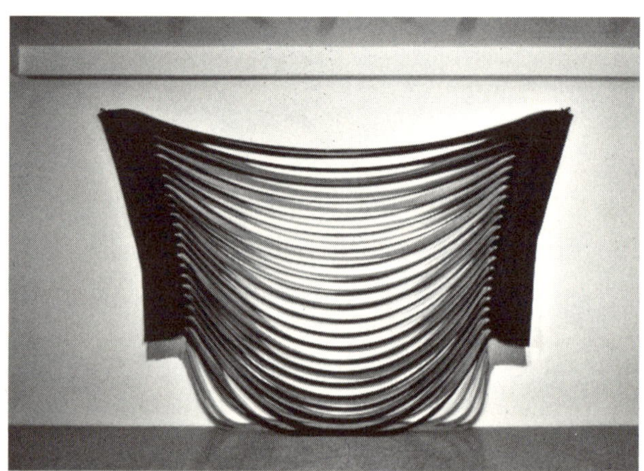

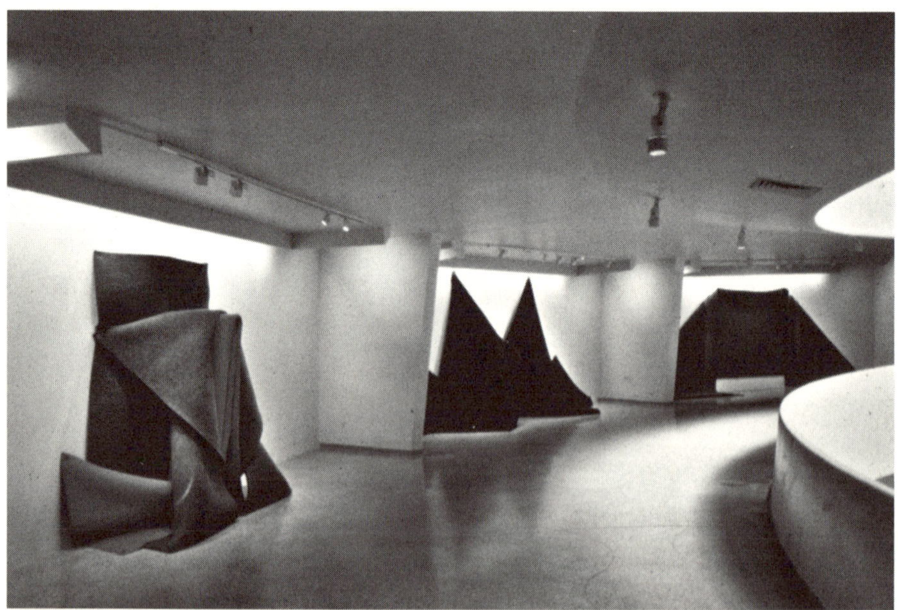

"Bring me a slab" (*PI*, §19). "Bring me a Corner Piece." Or, why not just "slab." "Corner piece." With a little ostensive definition and repetitive practice my assistant would surely learn my language of desires here. Needless to say, the assistant would have already mastered the technique of using a language in order to know how to play this naming game.

"Bring me a Ring." "Bring me a Bench." "Ring." "Bench." We could go on with other examples. But the question becomes, If this is not a way to learn a language, is it any way to learn a sculpture-game? It might amount to a sort of primitive sculpture game. But why necessarily a *sculpture* game? As you remarked earlier, by the early 1960s the genre game was highly suspect. Well, you called them sculptures then. Yes. But this as well . . .

Then language was also used as sculpture?

Or would you say that sculpture was used as language? And here we would not be speaking of the "language of art." And what about these remarks? Do they make a kind of sculpture of words? Or do I, speaking these words, become that which was always suppressed, that which the so-called rules of artmaking militated against: a "living, speaking sculpture"? It would seem that the term *sculpture* has, under such conditions of extension, lost all sense of itself as a distinct genre. But surely names must refer to something. What do we name here, which has so little discernible boundary? Is it still sculpture? Do you even remember what sculpture once was?

How would you answer the charge of the historian Eric Hobsbawm that the serious and challenging art of our century is confined to the activity of an avant-garde whose output is bracketed by the two world wars? Subsequent to this period we have a number of more or less academic practices. Call these subsequent practices confident traditions or mere footnotes. Speaking of these last couple of decades, he says, "The novelty was that technology had drenched everyday life in private as well as public with art. Never had it been harder to avoid aesthetic experience. The 'work of art' was lost in the flow of words, of sounds, of images, in the universal environment of what would have once been called art."[10] Don't the questions you ask seem introverted, marginal, and

---

71. *Horde/ Hoard/ Whored*, 1989. Encaustic on two panels, 47 ⅞ × 76 ¾ (121.6 × 194.9 cm). Collection of Sonnabend Gallery, New York. Photo courtesy of Robert Morris.

72. *Untitled (Catenary)*, 1968. Black and gray felt (two layers), 6 × 12 feet (1.83 × 3.66 m). Collection of the artist. Photo courtesy of Robert Morris.

73. Installation view of *Robert Morris: The Mind/Body Problem*, retrospective exhibition, The Solomon Guggenheim Museum, New York, January 16–April 4, 1994. Photo courtesy of Robert Morris.

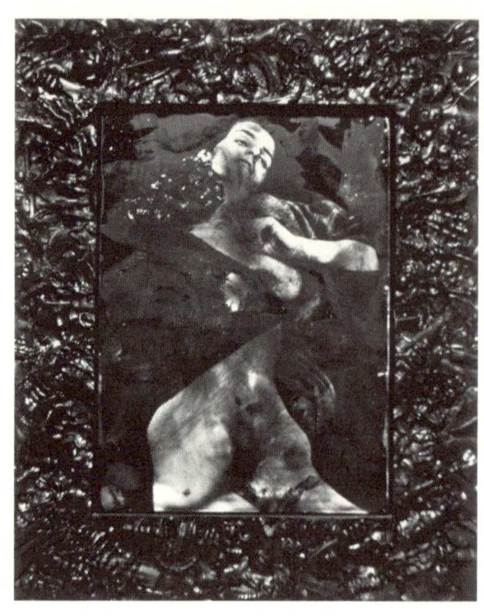

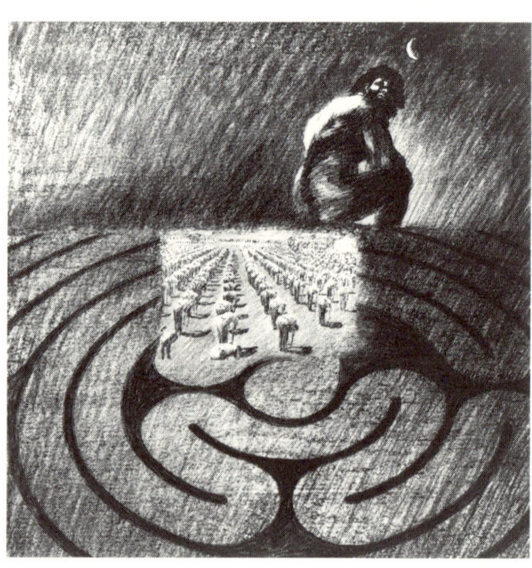

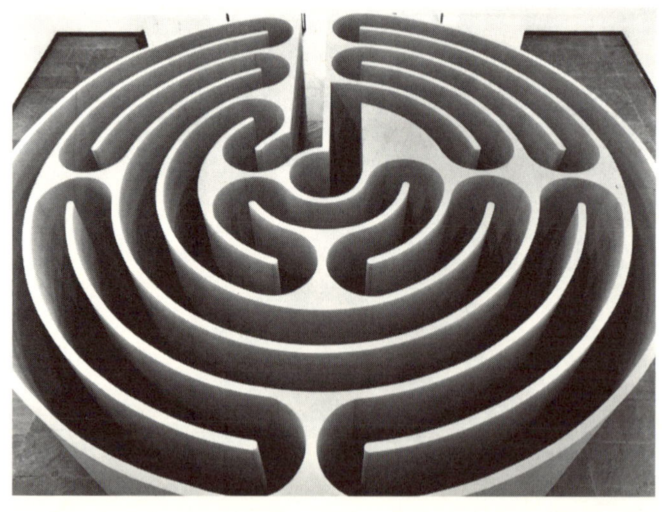

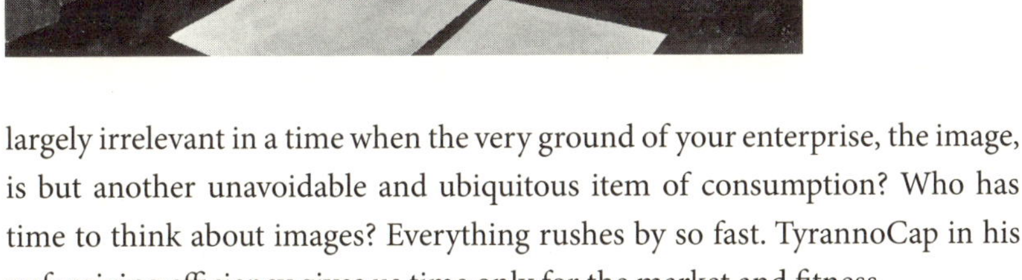

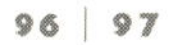

largely irrelevant in a time when the very ground of your enterprise, the image, is but another unavoidable and ubiquitous item of consumption? Who has time to think about images? Everything rushes by so fast. TyrannoCap in his unforgiving efficiency gives us time only for the market and fitness.

But, you seem to want to say, the image was not the ground of the enterprise. It was the activity of making and the resultant object suspended in its web of conditions that were never the same twice, together with the ceaseless interrogations that furnished the rooms of those years. Yes, you seem to have been anything but an iconophile in your enterprise which is piled as high with words on one side as with images on the other. If, as Wittgenstein remarks somewhere, "The purpose of philosophy is to build a wall at the end of language,"[11] your less purposeful efforts seem to have been to make objects that straddled that wall.

Opposite:

74. *Untitled (Holocaust)*, 1987. Silkscreen and encaustic on aluminum, with fiberglass and felt, 69 × 57¼ × 4½ inches (175.3 × 145.4 × 11.4 cm). Collection of the Eli Broad Family Foundation, Santa Monica, California. Photo courtesy of Robert Morris.

75. *Untitled (Investigations* series), 1990. Graphite on vellum, 18 × 18 inches (45.7 × 45.7 cm). Private collection, New York. Photo by F. Scruton, courtesy of Robert Morris.

76. *Untitled (Philadelphia Labyrinth)*, 1974. Plywood and masonite painted gray, 8 feet (2.44 m) high, 30 feet (9.14 m) diameter. The Solomon R. Guggenheim Museum, New York: Panza Collection. Photo by Will Brown, courtesy of The Solomon R. Guggenheim Museum, New York.

Above:

77. *Canvas Back / Fire*, 2001. Encaustic-on-wood panel, 30 × 42 inches (76.20 × 106.68 cm). Collection of Leo Castelli Gallery, New York. Photo courtesy of Leo Castelli Gallery.

But we would say that the suspicion of the image did not come from the language that surrounded it. But suspicion is the wrong word. Perhaps in your case the image was but a margin or an index, or better, a kind of seismic trace registering the faint rumblings of innumerable and ever-present threats that only the paranoid are privileged to perceive.

Yet you want to say that it is in the nature of the service we perform that we should be made to wear identifying uniforms that are at once gaudily emblematic and faded. For those who we serve have little time for our childish questions. They assume children should be seen and not heard. It comes with the job that the image is something that gets handed back to us as a kind of coded or abbreviated mark of what we were, not unlike those frightening photos of oneself that glare back from institutional IDs. Are you not then complicit and encouraging in this reduction to an image by mindlessly submitting to this indexing of your efforts in the form of slide projections? Well, we have tried to speak, to thicken, as it were, those brittle images of the past, to fashion a narrative, however disconnected, that would speak to and for this album of faded snapshots and to listen again to the echoes of past voices, to ask once again some of the endless questions in the effort to remember how the rooms were furnished and what characterized the form of life that went on there.

Then doesn't it come to you finally with a shock of recognition that yours has been more of a religious quest than one beset with professional anxieties? In spite of the occasional confessional tone, you have, as a kind of closet gnostic, kept this door tightly closed. And has not art for you always stood for the promise of redemption in a world in which the one thing never doubted was that enduring hum of human evil? Is it not this feeling that lies beneath your ironies and illuminates your past journeys?

Perhaps your past journeys were like those of a spelunker who fell into the cave of art. You found many passageways to explore, each with its unique set of spaces. But we would like to ask what you made of the flickering shadows on the walls? Well, we might reply, once inside those chthonic chambers, the one thing we never thought about was the rational sunlight. And yet you provide no general map of that dark labyrinth you have spent so much time in. Well, what does exploration have to do with description? Yet it was your past and shouldn't the past have a shape?

Wittgenstein asks, "And how does he know what the past is? And how will he know again in the future what remembering feels like? (On the other hand one might, perhaps, speak of a feeling 'Long, long ago,' for there is a tone, a gesture, which go with certain narratives of past times)" (*PI*, §231).

NOTES

1. Ludwig Wittgenstein, *Philosophical Investigations*, trans. G. E. M. Anscombe (New York: Macmillan, 1953), §211; hereafter abbreviated *PI.*
2. See W. J. T. Mitchell, *The Last Dinosaur Book: The Life and Times of a Cultural Icon* (Chicago: University of Chicago Press, 1998).
3. *The Oxford Companion to Philosophy*, ed. Ted Honderich (New York: Oxford University Press, 1995), 328.
4. S. A. Kripke, *Wittgenstein on Rules and Private Language* (Cambridge, Mass.: Harvard University Press, 1982), 20.
5. David Hume, *Treatise of Human Nature* (Oxford: Clarendon Press, 1896), 252.
6. Wittgenstein, *Tractatus Logico-Philosophicus*, trans. D. F. Pears and B. F. McGuinness (London: Routledge and Kegan Paul, 1974), 117.
7. See Fredric Jameson, *Postmodernism, or, The Cultural Logic of Late Capitalism* (Durham, N.C.: Duke University Press, 1991).
8. Wittgenstein, *On Certainty*, trans. Denis Paul and G. E. M. Anscombe, ed. G. E. M. Anscombe (New York: Harper, 1969), §450.
9. Joseph Brodsky, *On Grief and Reason* (New York: Farrar, Straus and Giroux, 1995), 144.
10. Eric Hobsbawm, *The Age of Extremes* (New York: Pantheon, 1994), 520.
11. I have no source for this quote. I once read it in a bookstore but did not buy the book, which was compiled of notes Wittgenstein left unpublished.

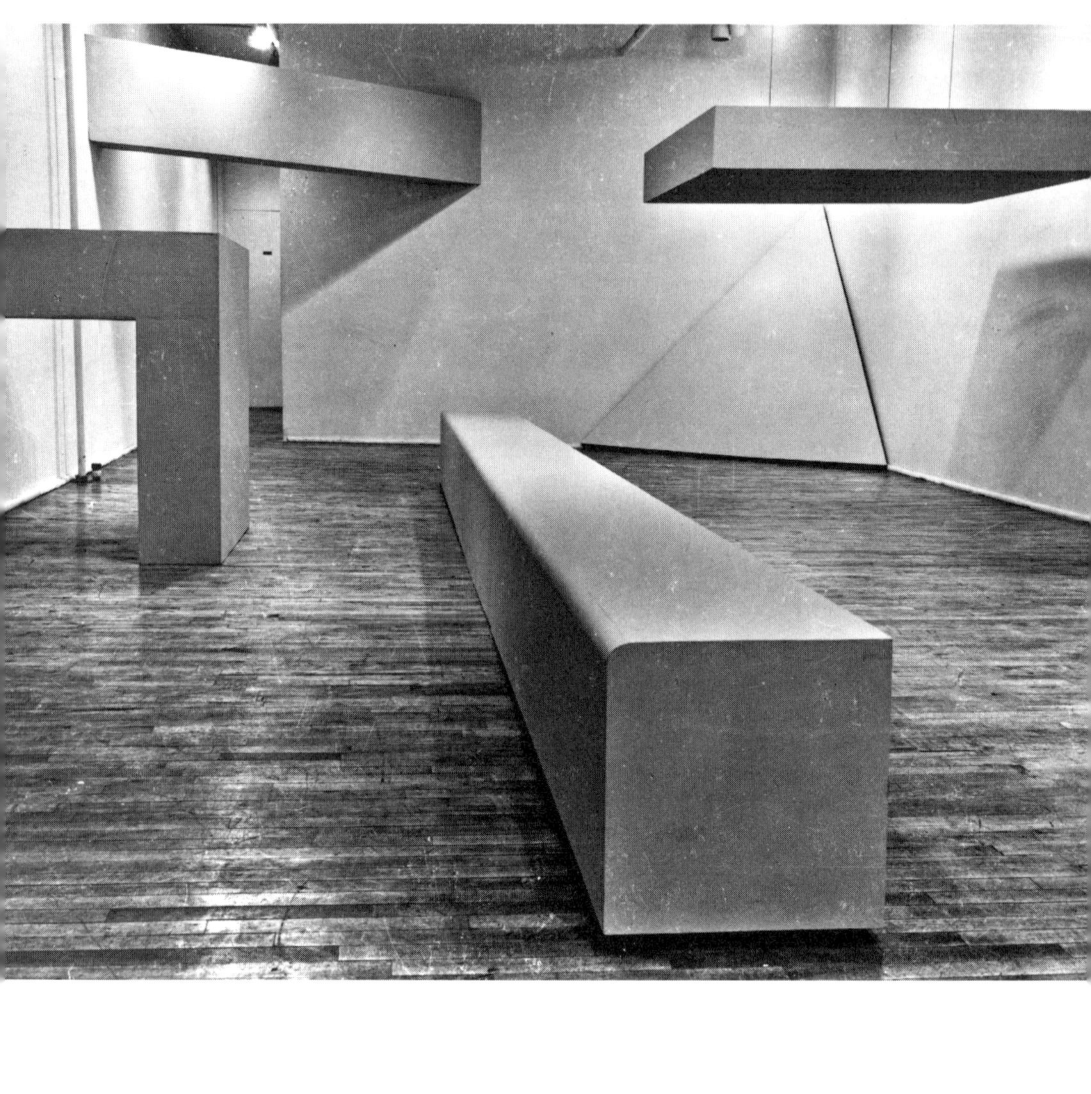

THINKING BACK ABOUT HIM: ON THE DEATH OF RICHARD BELLAMY | 1998

It seems like it was another lifetime. Anyway, another lifestyle ago. When we went to small Chinese restaurants and a few friends met for poker games on the Lower East Side. When art was a way of living without much money. When you didn't need much money. Half a dozen ideas defined the issues of the art world. Most things were made by hand. And when they weren't people got upset. A crooked taxi baron glitzed out real vulgar uptown and kept a stable of artists downtown. Dick floated somewhere between. Hovered mid-town maybe. Mediating. Shuttling metaphysical messages through the red urban dusks. Quizzical. Plugged into other circuits. Listening for edges others never heard. Fairly ragged bookkeeping and they said they called it the Green Gallery because of the color of money. "Philip Johnson was in," he said, smiling that before-the-repaired-teeth smile. "He saw your work and wanted to get a broom and kill it." A voice like a rich malted milk. "Tendentious" was the worst thing he could say about a work of art. Poons volunteered to sweep the floor of the 57th street space. It was all in that time before a particular compacted and polished shit glaze on the art professionals became the de rigueur surface for the gallery life. A lifestyle ago. When the half-life of things was more than two days. When people stayed in the city in the summers and took the subway to the beach on weekends. When you could buy hardware and illegal Cuban cigars on Canal Street and the only things stirring on Greene Street at night were the doll factories. He fell asleep on a sculpture. I sat there waiting. We decided to do a show on a month's notice when I didn't have a single piece made yet. He was waiting to be put into another space by the work. Or he made a space that unfolded for it. Seeing around corners and between folds. Listening for it.

---

78. Installation view of Robert Morris's one-man exhibition at the Green Gallery, New York, December 1964–January 1965. Photo by Rudolph Burkhard, courtesy of Robert Morris.

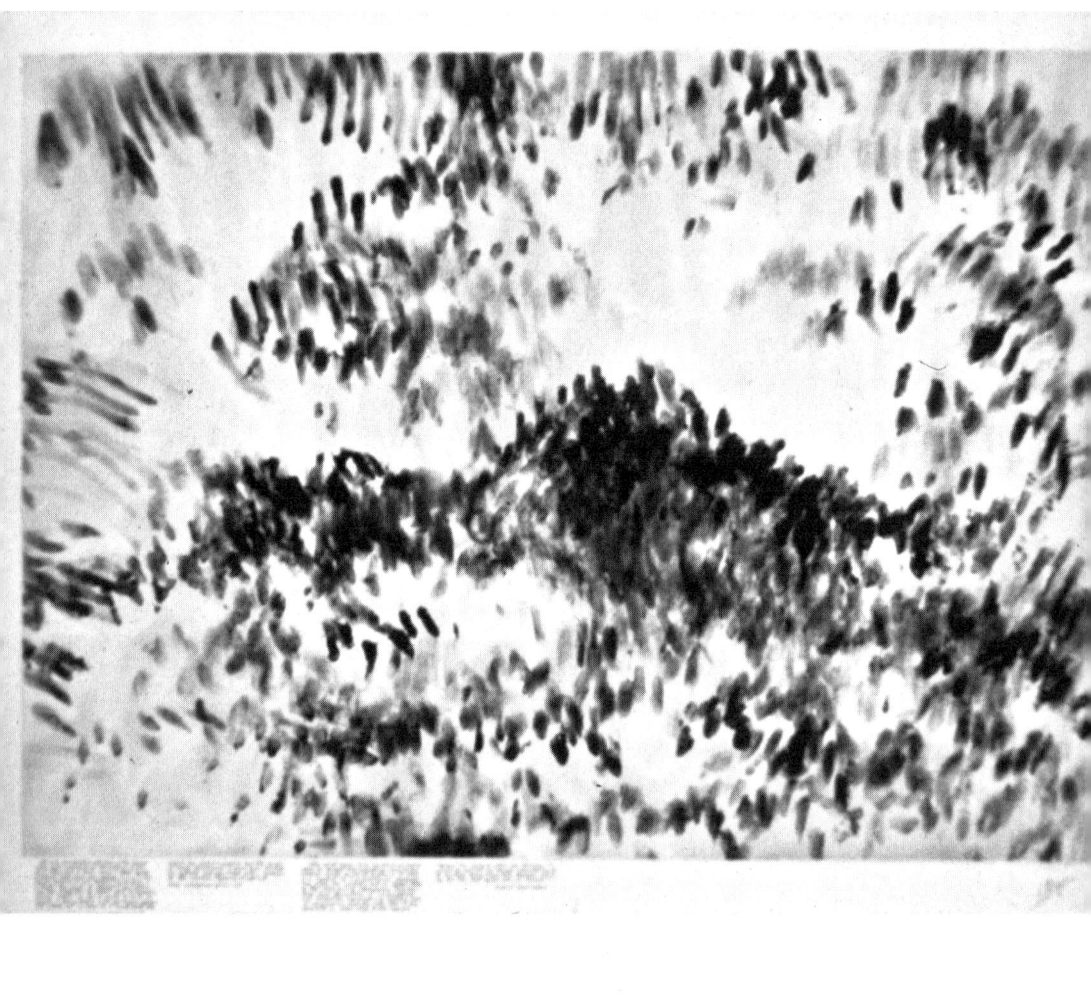

CÉZANNE'S MOUNTAINS | 1998

They created pictures; we are attempting a piece of nature.

—PAUL CÉZANNE

All that the eye's versatility disperses must be reunited.

—MAURICE MERLEAU-PONTY

We never do more than move our bodies: the rest is up to nature.

—DONALD DAVIDSON

I.

In what sense do the late Cézanne landscapes, specifically the Mont Sainte-Victoire paintings, attempt to represent the world? And is this to ask, In what sense are these works representations based on the code of resemblance? Resemblance, as Nelson Goodman has reminded us, is not an especially good criterion of representation, since anything can stand for anything else and, contrarily, one twin does not represent the other. Do I want to suggest that some code of representation besides that of resemblance is at work here? And here we should say *besides* and not *other than*, since admittedly these works bear a certain mark of resemblance to certain aspects of the world.

The Mont Sainte-Victoire works produced in the last four years of Cézanne's life were realized in watercolor and pencil and oils. These final works charge forward and open out, or open up, to a certain furious animation of surface—a surface ruptured with a pulsation of marks that tend not so much to elide as to ignore the code of resemblance; see, for example, *Mont Sainte-Victoire Seen from Les Lauves*; or the work from the same series in the Kunstmuseum in Basel. It is as though such marks and such a surface were generating a space that was moving into a different, yet to-be-named space, one that hovered at the edge of

---

79. *Blind Time IV (Drawing with Davidson)*, 1991. Graphite on paper, 38 × 50 inches (96.2 × 127 cm). Collection of the artist. Photo by John Berens, courtesy of Robert Morris.

resemblance. Formed of a sediment of touches, this space and these marks lift into the rush of a charged field of forces. What name is there for this so-called sky that transmutes with so little transition into this so-called mountain? What name is there for this faceted skein of marks that fall now like a veil and now like a wall below a horizon that is itself permeable to a surge and flow between top and bottom, not to mention the suggestion of far as near and near as far? What name is there for this hallucinated compression of the proximal and the distal that would tilt up a space not so much everywhere equidistant to vision as one converted/confined/released/bound over to an oxymoronic zone of a haptic coloration? What sort of space has the capacity to both hover and yet anchor itself to a surface? (Surely that grotesque, clanking *grid* leaning in the art historical corner is a far too rusty and Procrustean bed on which to stretch these works.)

To say that somewhere in the tangle of blues and bare canvas, or the greens of a dragged brush, the hand was opening on the very brink of releasing a world of resemblance, a resemblance by which a world was still held, but one that adhered by no more than the mere friction of touch, may be to misconstrue and misdescribe these works that seem to fall between the codes of the abstract and the representational.

Before us we see a welter of touches of color that are densely material yet aerial, spaced and hovering yet grounded. A threatening, destabilizing translucency lurks at the edge of solidity in these works. The watercolor and pencil sketches of Mont Sainte-Victoire seem suspended in the air itself. The transparent purples and greens and pinks of the watercolors shimmer and float, yet seal themselves to the opened whiteness of the page in diaphanous undulations. The rhythms of these marks are both awkward and serene, and resonate more to the body's registration of a dry summer heat, or peripheral visual sensations of the shudder of vegetation stirred by a hot breeze, than to optical signs whose ambition is to represent leaves on trees (see the watercolor *Mont Sainte-Victoire Seen from Les Lauves* [1902–6], in the Museum of Modern Art).

The oils pulsate with half a dozen hues of blue, green, and purples run from near blackness to a high-keyed transparency erupting upward to invade the space of a nominal sky, which in turn descends with touches of ultramarine to spike the bottom edge of the rectangle. The others, shimmering as though still retaining the radiant heat of the summer earth from which they were ground, thread their way through the thickets of greens and purples. Somehow a certain equanimity restrains the stress of forces distributed across these surfaces.

Wittgenstein's remark that "we predicate of the thing what lies in the method

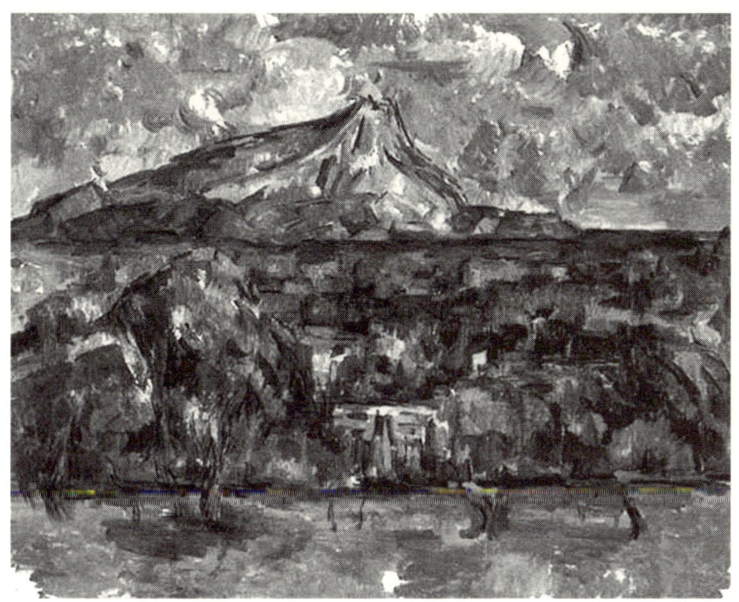

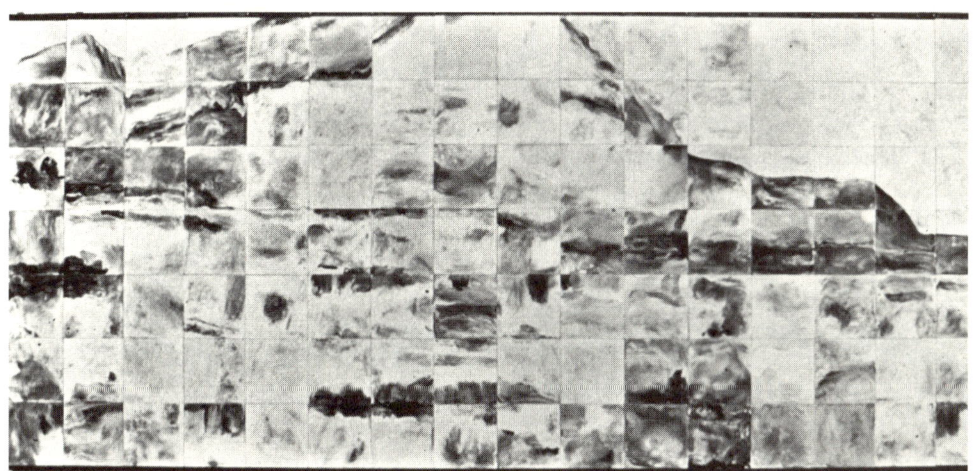

80. Paul Cézanne, *Mont Sainte-Victoire Seen from Les Lauves*, 1904–1906. Oil on canvas, 25⅝ × 32 inches (65 × 81.3 cm). Nelson Gallery of Art, Kansas City: Purchased Nelson Fund.

81. *Based on a Section from Mont Saint-Victoire Seen from Les Lauves 1904–1906, Cézanne*, 1997. Encaustic on panel (112 units), 85 × 189 inches (215.90 × 480 cm) overall. Collection of the artist. Photo courtesy of Robert Morris.

of representing it" brings us close to our problem (failure?) of representing what these works represent as representations.[1] If our urgency for a description is irrelevant to the activity that engaged Cézanne in producing the works, we nevertheless have an object before us that should, we think, submit itself to description. But we flounder in the metaphysics of identity in our descriptions. Identities in these works begin to implode in this field of ruptured, virtual objects (sky/sky? mountain/mountain? ground/ground?) that exchange forces with one another.

These last works reek with a sense of bursting renewal squeezed in the grip of finality. That they show more than can be said we readily admit: that they admit more than can readily be seen allows us to wedge the foot of a word in their doorway. But what does the attempted precision of our descriptions have to do with getting in the doorway? Wittgenstein asks, "Is it always an advantage to replace an indistinct picture by a sharp one? Isn't the indistinct one often exactly what we need?" (*PI*, §71).

I want to ask in what ways these works might be tied to the world beyond the code of resemblance. I might begin by suggesting that these works perhaps less represent than recall the world. Here I immediately fall into difficulty. A recalling does not fall outside, or even beyond, a representing. A recalling surely assumes a representing and flows from it. But in the case of the works under question I want to ask about such a recalling as a "re-calling" of what might be meant, what might have been attempted, in such a renaming, in such a repositioning of artmaking to the world. That is to say I want to ask what are the terms, the implications and the consequences, and the shifts of meanings, amounting to a re-coding of painting, that these works hold. To ask this is to ask, What is being reflected from them as the mirror of resemblance is perhaps dimmed? What sort of optics are being put in place of a mirrorlike surface, and how are the traces of the world encoded under such a regime? What are the assumptions and strategies of such a realignment, and how was this re-calling staged?

On one level such a re-calling revolves around a retrieving, a revisiting, of Cézanne's early childhood memories tied to certain sites around Aix. Cézanne's "motifs" embody such revisitings. The effort of redemption addressed to this deep nostalgia constitutes a charged psychological struggle within the work. Mnemosyne haunts the sites Cézanne repeatedly revisited. A lost innocence locked within childhood memory saturated these silent woods and quarries, ponds and mountain. But what was sought was not a primitive or edenic return to the innocence of nostalgia but a confrontation with the loss that memory, history, and change inscribe on the psyche. The issue of memory for Cézanne becomes the challenge of transfiguration forged in those confrontations with his charged sites. How is this loss to be redeemed through art—that mode which possesses the possibility of defeating loss? By, I want to say, representing memory's loss. And I do not mean the loss of memory, but the representation of memory's ravages of the psyche by means of metaphor.

It would seem that all art, in its enduring stasis, seeks to defeat time, the very condition that allows for its production. Yet how do we account for the acknowledgment of time in these works? It is a breathing stillness in these late works that encodes the acknowledgment of time. Such pulsations do not so much seek to defeat time as to find a metaphor for it, as though they made the distinction between temporality, as the condition of life, and stasis, its antithesis in death. I want to suggest that such pulsations themselves, materially embodied in the work as the orchestrated spacings of the touches of its facture, duplicate as encoded analogue or metaphor vision's fixations of interest, registered as a set of traversing and probing foci. I would argue that one axis of the work, involving as it does the distillation of embodied visuality—its temporally bound penetrations and traverses of space—into a static analogue, the painted image, amounts to a code, one that exceeds that of resemblance. The reading of this code demands a recognition of the work's reenactment of a particular visual address characterized not only by phenomenological metaphors but, as we shall see, the apprehension of further philosophical attitudes toward the world.

Is the security of the child tied to property rights? In the beginning the child's property is confined to the intimate regions of its body, the parent, and what lies within arm's reach. Its world is devoid of the extended concerns of property as nationalism or real estate values. The world at large is a looming presence saturated with questions. Children are privileged to ask questions that otherwise only the sages confront: what is time, what is space, why is there something and not nothing? Do I want to suggest that one of the things "represented" in Cézanne's late works is a certain childlike breathlessness—that awe fixated on its charged spaces and places? Don't these late works project an openness to those haunted and looming vibrations of the world arriving as charged places? I am suggesting that these motifs are held as transfixing, questioning sites, sites that question the artist, sites that, having remained waiting for him since childhood, interrogated his life as a kind of parenthesis lived between those earliest and latest encounters. Such sites, in their unchanging stasis, called his changes to account and mocked his mortality.

Simultaneously, and from the other side—from the bodily side, or the side of the body inhabiting its living time and space as opposed to that of memory, but nevertheless impelled and compelled by memory's psychic charge—there is also embodied in these works a re-calling or re-naming of a complex set of mediated relations that could only have issued from a lifetime of preparation. These mediated relations are those of artmaking, which Cézanne re-called and renamed. In this re-calling and renaming we pass from issues of representation that revolve around the redemption of memory into those that border on a double nausea.

On the one hand, we have a nausea of consciousness confronting the body divided within itself—that is to say, divided between the space that informs vision, or vision's capacity to occupy space, and the body's limited capacity for physical movement. On the other hand, we have the greater nausea on the far side of this—the sense of that abyss that marks off the divide between the organic and finite and the inorganic and infinite. Such a greater nausea emerges from the acknowledgment of this dualistic ontology that foregrounds the pathos of the organic and finite body pitted against the inorganic and infinite: the looming of the enduring world (as "motif") bearing down on the temporary flesh.

It is to the first nausea that I first want to turn. I would dismantle what appears perhaps innocuous and seamless in this route from seeing to making. I want to see the discontinuity, the gulf (and here we would find the nausea) between vision's mobility and the body's limited motions. I would mark that difference between vision's effortless penetrations and the limit of the arm's reach. I would fix here that terror between the eye's traverse of the horizon and the torpidity and confinement of every bodily action. I would stress the abyss between the weightlessness of sight and the mortal heaviness of the flesh. And this is to suggest that the sense of capacity bound to a visual gestalt is contradicted by an awareness of the lack of somatic mastery—that site of the mirror stage so famously crucial to Lacan's explications of the infant's exaltation and rage—which is never grown out of, never entirely overcome. It is also to suggest that Cézanne's late landscapes establish a metaphor for the acknowledgment of this abyss. For the exaltation in these works also opens, in every hovering touch, in every dragged stroke of the brush, in every centimeter of paralyzed hesitation as bare canvas, to the admission of the body's despair and incompleteness before the grandeur of the motif. The very collapse of the representational convention of perspectival distance into a code that compresses the distal and the proximal in favor of the latter, as though the world had been restated in favor of touch over vision, reveals a pathos and a longing for a world that would be more at hand, less traumatized by vision's imperial totalities.

But such struggles of realignment inevitably awaken the second nausea, which is bound to an ontological dualism: the infinities of inorganic sky and mountain mocking the infirmities of organic and finite body and its promise of rot as destiny. The mountain itself, the one individuated feature in these works, embodies the enduring and unmovable; it emanates geological time. The eye's effortless perception of light masks the sight of an unacknowledged wound. Transitive in its directed gaze, vision's intransitive receptivity marks a bodily penetration. The shaft of light is absorbed by the heavy, shuddering flesh. And in this wounding the dance of photons also announces the death of the eye. Cézanne's task was to forge a negotiation between these incommensurables, these dual nauseas.

I want also to suggest that these nauseas themselves were framed by an attitude of mourning, that the paintings were monuments of mourning for the intimation Cézanne had that his motifs were themselves threatened. Such a mourning was for a world on the brink of passing. If these sacred sites were informed by the inorganic and the infinite, they were nonetheless threatened by the ravages of so-called progress. Cézanne's letters attest to his despair at modernity's technological advances, which were at the beginning of the century already converting nature into a commodity. Many of his motifs that had waited a lifetime for him would pass with him.

The route (always bordering on the threat of a rout) of artmaking might be mapped as a passage from or through or between a set of conditions that are asymmetrical, nonreciprocating, and directional. The contour of these always unstable, always to be renegotiated relations might be described as a profile that moves across and through the body intersected by space and time. The process begins with a seeing that traverses space, fixated at the site of the responding body that negotiates its limited space of movements as it condenses these into the gesture of a hand that mediates a medium that terminates in, is stopped at, is precipitated into an object which is also an image and an accretion that we cannot yet say with any confidence what it is a complete record of, nor yet mark all of the ways it comes to anchor itself to the world as a "representation"—not to mention what or how certain embodiments, analogues, metaphors, and processes, and still other tropes saturating these marks, might constitute ties to the world that lie beyond what can be called, with any confidence, the representational.

We begin then to attempt a re-calling and/or a renaming, that is to say, to attempt to follow or rather open up Cézanne's re-calling and renaming of the artmaking that informs these late landscapes, thinking predominantly of the great series of Mont Sainte-Victoire works.

A hierarchy suggests itself in the form of yet another negotiated dualism between light and flesh, body and world, self and object, intention and action, event and object. This one splits into a dualism in which the image comes last spatially and temporally as an accretion of gestures, of touches that fall between the hesitant and the sure—touching as a kind of pointing registered on, I want to say, less *the* painting as such, than a redefining of the body's hovering, transfixed as it were, between its own physical space and that of a visual space belonging more properly to the world. From the body's limit arises a pathos of gestures toward acknowledging that nausea delivered by the visual from which it is prohibited to inhabit as a motion, say of flight, that would perhaps approximate vision's thrust and penetration of space. This contradiction between the body's space and that of vision finds its pathos in the modality of painting where the two spaces, that of the body and that of the eye, are transfigured by Cézanne in such a way that the one comes to reflect the other as one set of dimensions might be mirrored, as well as mired, caught, secured in the most unstable of ways, in the other. And here the reflection, the mirroring, is not particularly intelligible as a "representation," for it has become rather the record of a deposit of bodily gestures materially embodied as touches which are themselves transcriptions of the difference between two spaces that, in their marks upon the white rectangle, forge a code for a nonexistent space in which there is neither, properly speaking, the proximal nor the distal and at the same time a compression of these two into such a code that favors the former, as upon a kind of tablet of death rather than a pictorial representation: a re-calling and a renaming of what and how painting stands to the world, or of how it stood to his or how his stood to it.

Must we not then seek to rename this process of artmaking and its object, a renaming that would traverse—as we might expect in a force that nowhere presents singularity as a modality—a certain doubling, a sense of pulsating duality? The twin axes of the paired terms of algorithm/anagoge suggest themselves as pointing toward Cézanne's transcriptive method and its horizon of consequences.

The origin of the algorithmic axis is to be traced along the asymmetrical encounter between seeing and acting. The anagogical emerges in that totality, the route to which the conflicts of this negotiation hold unflinchingly to the very end.

The asymmetries of the alternating, reciprocal relation of the living moment of eye movement and the responding bodily movement become aligned, condensed, and concentrated at the end of the hand as a particular kind of signal, a signaling that is at once a compressed gesture, or the gesture a signaling (a kind of algorithmic calculating?), a signifying that acknowledges the confined space between the body and flat canvas as well as that pathos between eye and world.

What is mystical, anagogical, is the nature of the transcriptive encoding wrested from the visual world via the limitations of the body: a compressive space encoded on the canvas echoing that very compression of vision coursing the fleshy conduit between eye and bodily motion. If this compression is partly a pathos, a loss, issuing from the body and the flesh that mourns vision's flight, it is also a celebration, an *Aufhebung*, of what one wants to call a visuality that issues from the hand, as it were. If this compressive traverse from vision to a termination in the touch of the brush, from vision's depth to its coded mapping on a flat surface, frames the algorithmic axis as a transcoding of the distances of looking by which the world is accessed, we need to also look at the distances looked at in these late landscapes.

And such looking at a distance needs to be looked at close-up, as it were. For like everything in these works, it encodes a doubled, uncoupled modality. Celebrating the eye's penetrations and traverses of space that would refuse a possessive, consuming focus, the Mont Sainte-Victoire works unfold as a mediated, transposed coruscation of limpid signifiers drained of singular identities (other than the looming, vaguely contoured mountain)—an equivalence bestowed by light itself. The body wanted to follow this play of serene vibration across what is given to vision by the only means available to the painter, the shudder of touch. A touch that also offered protest across the looming antilight of that sullen white absence, the blank page or canvas. In Cézanne's last works even this antilight is given its due; not every point on that surface whose blankness is not only absence but denial is covered. If these spaces of absence acknowledge the impossibility of finish, they also acknowledge that unbridgeable distance between vision's seamlessness and that abyss between the body's intentions and actions. If such gaps of blank paper or canvas are themselves semiotic marks that encode this split, they signify as well the impossibility of representation issuing from the lived body as a seamless signifier of full presence.

I want to suggest that Cézanne's looking at his motifs, first experienced in the first decade of his life and revisited in the last, was a redefined gaze directed into and across the world without desire—that is to say, without the desire that stumbles in such a fervid and febrile way across so much of his work before the turn of the century. Call this another re-calling of desire, a desire re-called partly by the re-calling of the painting itself as a tablet of death. The desire to touch the world without possessiveness can be a kind of release of desire, a touch that is also a farewell, and a kind of mourning as well as a praise of earth and sky. Here the signaling of the hand to the white rectangular tablet deposits a mark that, falling between a gesture of hesitancy and assurance, registers a seeking shorn of all previous codes of mastery. Here also is the site of a deadly combat to subdue and wrest from other deaths—emblematized by those nonwhite tablets of the past, his own as well as all the others, those dead tablets painted to death, stinking of dead art—that would elude death by eluding desire. In these late works the desire of the body has been sacrificed to a form of restraint that would acknowledge not only the body's withdrawal from the world but its anticipated absence from a world that continues to endure. How can we see ourselves breathing our last breaths as a breathing along with a world we must both surrender and surrender to? This is a question raised by these last works. These late works embody a breathing that is also a seeing—a seeing that has given up its orality, a looking no longer attached to either projections of anthropomorphic desire or a relentless consumption registered as a mastery informing that production.

. . . . .

Half a century ago I stood on a rocky Missouri hillside beneath a heavy canopy of oaks and persimmons and massive walnuts in humid July heat daubing greens and blues at a flimsy canvas on a rickety easel, attempting to limn a patch of a stucco house half hidden within dense vegetation. Sweat ran down my shirt as I thought of the *Château Noir* shimmering in its greens and ochers. On that day, in that throbbing heat, the spaces between me and the world had yet to be measured; I had yet to assess the world's spaces and those of my body; I had yet to risk my movement within and against the spaces of the world; I had yet to measure my margins of mobility against the weight of history. Being as green as the summer landscape, I was also as empty as the sky of those future clouds that would demand redemption in the midst of ambition. On that sweltering Missouri late afternoon summer day, nothing interrupted the innocence of a sensed awkwardness. There was only a ringing anxiety, a desperate insecurity, and a frightening sense of absence. And if the power of Cézanne stirred my hand, it was a power that was too old for me and one I could not grasp, one that youth could not touch, for I had at such a time no nostalgia to redeem, and my quiet spaces of childhood had yet to be demolished by the world and my own desire. Loss and mourning and grief were mine yet to discover, as was the surrender of desire. Death had not yet made its more formal appearances, and so I could not see it acknowledged as well as subdued there beneath the flurry of brush strokes vibrating within the rectangle on the wall of the Nelson Gallery in *Mont Sainte-Victoire Seen from Les Lauves* (1904–6).

Do I want to assert that when I first saw *Mont Sainte-Victoire Seen from Les Lauves* as a child, transfixed by it in September 1939, I did not take its tripartite divisions for a representation of sky, mountain, and an area that was not so much foreground or background as neither and both? Or do I want to assert that what was once taken as a representation has somehow, in ways not clear, but surely ways that have to do with me, with my changes over nearly six decades, come to alter what I take to be a representation? As Cézanne's motifs waited for him for half a century, this work has waited for me for over half a century, waited for certain deaths in me, as well as near me, before I could see it in its fullness. Only after a sufficient set of losses and griefs could it come forward and rereveal itself in my re-call of it, in my rereading of it. Only now can I hear its silences as a mourning for what was passing, a mourning from Cézanne that was also an acceptance on the deepest level of passing as our condition, a passing that in passing, nearly at the last minute, or at least in the last hours and last years, finds in the privilege of vision and light an excess of fullness, a fullness that overruns and outdistances the pace of body, mind, and hand to transpose its energy into an artifact that struggles to register, in our necessary hesitations and doubts, a certain reflection that would present solidity in place of the ringing light and some degree of grace in the face of the infinity of the inanimate. It is in these struggles to reflect that the work comes to rest, if it can be said to come to rest at all, as an address to a representation of an affirmation and a mourning that lies beyond resemblance.

2.

We are confronted in Cézanne's Mont Sainte-Victoire works and in Wittgenstein's *Philosophical Investigations* with a series of something like landscapes, perhaps landscapes as metaphors. In the case of the former these return again and again to the "motif." The terrain crisscrossed by Wittgenstein in his sets of remarks in the *Philosophical Investigations* resembles, as he remarked, a series of sketches that moved this way and that over the nature of language and how we use and misuse it, how we find our bearings in it and how we become lost in it. ("Language is a labyrinth of paths. You approach from *one* side and know your way about; you approach the same place from another side and no longer know your way about" [*PI*, § 203]). Cézanne crisscrossed the terrain at the foot of Mont Sainte-Victoire, now from one side and now from another. The reiteration of the motif of the mountain serves to return him again and again to his encounter with the question of the space of vision and its relation to the body.

The worlds of Wittgenstein and Cézanne hover on the edge of doubts that demanded endless reinscriptions traversing the very edges of these doubts. Neither ends in the despair of skepticism, but neither denies its persistent presence. The traverse of these respective landscapes, demanding a multitude of gestures on the part of Cézanne, and a long series of remarks on the part of Wittgenstein, proceeded with a certain spacing. With Wittgenstein it is a certain set of questions that approaches now from this side and now from that, and the repetitive reinscriptions of these remarks come to take on what we might call a kind of verbal *pentimento*. The text begins to take on the character of a palimpsest in which the crossed-out lines of doubt are nevertheless visible through and beneath later repetitions of or visitations to the same site. I am impelled to find in the late works of Cézanne a parallel in the character of his marks, those animated deposits of spaced colors. And the parallel with Wittgenstein is in the spaces of uncovered canvas, a holding off of finish by which we read the implied or unsaid acknowledgment of the possibility of doubt rather than the expression of it. These works refrain from that finish that would "ground" them in the solidity of representation as resemblance in ways that recall how Wittgenstein refuses a seamless, finished text on the one hand, and on the other, refuses to ground language and our ways of knowing and acting on anything more than the communal practices of those forms of life in which he finds them.

In reply to Bertrand Russell's claim that skepticism was "practically barren" though "logically irrefutable," Wittgenstein countered that "skepticism is *not* irrefutable, but obviously nonsensical, when it tries to raise doubts where no questions can be asked. For doubt can exist only where a question exists, a question only where an answer exists, and an answer only where something *can be said*."[2]

Stanley Cavell has argued that Wittgenstein in the *Investigations* repeatedly acknowledges the necessary possibility of skepticism while withholding any direct answer, which would put too much flesh on the bones of this ageless, hovering ghost.[3] Others, such as Saul Kripke, find Wittgenstein's tormented circling around the question of what it is to follow a rule a much closer encounter with Humean specters.[4] Thomas Nagel has suggested that Wittgenstein's position was that if doubts "are expressible, they must be wrong."[5] This is not the place to review Wittgenstein's private language argument, which leads to his subtle considerations of criteria and rule following, the consequences of which go deep into the nature of what we can call upon for justifications in our linguistic behavior, our beliefs and actions. Skepticism makes its appearance in these considerations when we ask for an objectivity that extends beyond use. Our craving for generality and scientific-type explanations leads us into metaphysics, where we posit mistakes that bring us to the brink of skepticism. Wittgenstein did not so much answer the skeptic as show that his questions were incoherent. But in his efforts to build a "wall at the end of language" that would exclude incoherent questions, he seems to have tunneled under language into an unstable space. There he found missing those objective supports we thought justified our procedures. As Nagel puts it, "We are left with *nothing but* my successive applications of a term, without anything to compare them with that can count as the rule for its application—the criterion that determines whether I have applied it correctly in each case."[6]

If skepticism can be the consequence of interpreting rules rather than following them blindly, and if our court of last appeal is to a kind of custom in which we will not so much discover our justifications as that pause where we can say with Wittgenstein, "if I have exhausted the justifications I have reached bedrock, and my spade is turned. Then I am inclined to say: 'This is simply what I do,'" (*PI*, §217). Here we might as well admit that a certain hauntedness will forever hover over all our efforts to give justifying reasons and that it is when we venture out to the edge of these, half a step from doubt, where hesitation precedes our touch, that we can draw those breaths with which we form the only words that will ever be our own, and these will very likely take the form of questions as much as statements, or, given the way the world works, be taken by us as questions and by others as statements.

I would suggest that a proceeding by questioning rather than doubting informs the Mont Sainte-Victoire works in a way parallel to how Wittgenstein came to ask himself questions as a way of doing philosophy.

Other philosophers, such as W. V. O. Quine and Donald Davidson, would perhaps find Wittgenstein's obsession with the normativity of rules a symptom of one of those linguistic "cramps" Wittgenstein so famously sought to undo. For Davidson, the notion of a rule merely implies a presupposition of language rather than any explanation of it.[7] Davidson wants to give up the assumption that language must "operate on the basis of shared conventions, rules, or regularities." Starting from a second-person perspective that finds interpretation central and subjectivist accounts of less interest, Davidson asserts that it is in the generation of "passing theories" directed toward the other and "derived by wit, luck, and wisdom from a private vocabulary and grammar" that we grasp the meaning of the other's words. Rules here are "rules of thumb for figuring out what deviations from the dictionary are most likely." Here skepticism does not haunt the edges of communication, and a sense of play is more significant than doubt.[8]

These considerations have implications for art. Art is not a language in the sense that its iconic activity can be compared to the linguistic point by point in a semantic and syntactical way. This is not to deny that language is inextricably imbricated in our access to images any more than images can be excluded from our linguistic usage. But images are not words and making art is not speaking. Making art might be described as a kind of calculating, as well as a questioning, with feelings. But I have digressed into Wittgensteinian issues of normativity and rules and various subsequent thinkers' responses as a prelude to and a framing of my ascription of an algorithmic method to Cézanne's late works, specifically the Mont Sainte-Victoire works. I follow Wittgenstein in seeking no objectivity for this algorithmic procedure beyond its use (whatever legislative and logical empowerment it offers, it has no independent, Platonic existence), and Davidson in wanting to release the cramp imposed by ascribing to art-making no less than to linguistic interactions (odd as this may sound) a certain creative element. Cézanne's algorithmic method does not uniformly guide all of the late works. It is absent from the stilted and inferior *Bathers* works and does not function in the still lifes. This algorithm might be compared to Davidson's notions of a "passing theory"—in this case directed toward interpreting the otherness of space and moving, step by step, across vision to bodily response to coded surface.

Unique to the Mont Sainte-Victoire works is the degree to which discrete objects are deprived of representation in terms of depicted resemblance. It is not so much that objects are broken down or deprived of identity by missing outlines and the like. It is more the case that objects in the field of vision are not acknowledged as such, as if they were embedded into the field, driven back into it, welded to it so deeply that individuation was no longer an issue. The field itself is foregrounded—in front, as it were, of any object within it. Because of this loss of individuation these works have been labeled as laying the groundwork for modernism's code of abstraction. Perhaps they do. But I would argue that a concern for such inchoate abstraction amounts to a misreading of the intentions of the Mont Sainte-Victoire works. I want to re-call this so-called abstract aspect, reinterpret it as a function of the algorithmic procedure—one that has nothing to do with notions either of representation or abstraction that circumscribe present conceptualizations of the limits of art's available codes. The suppression of the cathecting of objects by means of the code of depiction according to resemblance was required by the algorithmic transcription that delivered a third space devoid of distinctions between the proximal and the distal. But it also did more than this.

I am suggesting that Cézanne's consideration of painting as a form of life open to a body acting in response to the world was both an intensely examined act and an intensely anxious one that was neither informed by any frontal address to doubt nor issued in contemplative images of resemblance. The space Cézanne arrived at was an unstable one. In the Mont Sainte-Victoire works, where objects begin to lose their identities, space begins to compress. The feeling induced by these works is both grand and anxious, informed by both dread and relief. It is the feeling of an incipient blindness in which we are about to lose the visual world and its objects and the demands and terrors these inflict on us. This visual world of depth and objects is exchanged for another delivered by means of the haptic algorithm. This landscape becomes an abyss where visual depth darkens into touch, where touch is registered as color, as though touch could read color, as though color was accessed by touch, or as though Mnemosyne herself arrived by the touches of colors. The eliding of objects in favor of touches of color saturating the visual field does not, I would emphasize, indicate evidence for an empiricist position valorizing "sense impressions" over the perception of objects any more than it theorizes the space of abstraction. The Mont Sainte-Victoire works teeter on a phase change. They stand, as it were, at the entrance to the world, shutting down visually, collapsing into the space of blindness, where depth is lost to touch, which, in these late works, is the hesitant touches of mourning and farewell.

On another level these works can be read as an aggressive, destructive gesture, or rather, such a gesture can be read within the works, arising from Cézanne's despair and anger at the progress of "development" arriving to disrupt and destroy his childhood spaces. The inability to accept the imminent "death" of his motifs led him to want to both touch and symbolically destroy these sites by marking them as blind places, no longer open, closed off to a penetrating visuality. The paintings can be seen as shades in the process of being drawn over that visuality, marking their death, testifying to a mourning, as well as reverberating to an anticipation of the painter's own death. (Perhaps Cézanne's diabetic condition should not be discounted here. It is a condition that often threatens sight.) Anxiety rather than doubt has a central place in these works. But such a monumental anger that had no room for skepticism did, as all art always does, leave room for play to the very end. Of course different artists play differently.

If, in his macho phrase, Picasso (that imperialistic cannibal of images, whose eye was fitted with the sharpest of teeth) asserted a determination to live by the words "I do not search, I find"—a prescient motto that presages an insatiable appetite for a world of commodity consumption of images that might today be spoken with an equal voraciousness by Bill Gates—we must understand here a desire that can never doubt its appetite for conquests that it would read as progress, and an anxiety that would read otherness as mere nonrelation to be obliterated by the annexation of invasion. The world is no longer to be searched since it has been found, or rather, there is nothing to be searched for among the array of cataloged commodities as information and information as commodity that total all its possible divisions. And this totalizing illumination of the known as consumable would, in eliding the darkness of the yet-to-be-found, extends monoculture all the way down to, for example, the genetic sequence—to mention but one of the many modes it would fixate as the found, the fungible, and the marketable.

The only identifiable human artifact—the only depiction in terms of resemblance—in most of these late works (for example, *Mont Sainte-Victoire Seen from Les Lauves*, 1904–6; Basel) is the suggestion of architecture. In the work cited it is a house. Let us rather say a home, a dwelling. Let us even say a place of being charged with all the longing of Heideggerian *Heimat*. For these works project more than a shimmering and vibrating anxiety hovering on the edge of destructive self-blinding. They are drenched in longing and loss. If the paintings enact a condemnation of visuality as conquest—a shattering of visuality's mastery as metaphor for that imperial, totalizing objectification ushered in by modernity's Weberian, rationalized, administrated, bureaucratic alienation and progress—by gesturing toward self-blinding, they also seek a redemption and a comforting for the body. They may go so far as to acknowledge the collective guilt that the painter shared by inhabiting the moment of modernity. I believe they even go so far as to touch that state of infantile desire for oneness before vision knows anything of depth perception. There is nothing especially surprising about art—anyway great art—embracing the contradictory, elevating and reclaiming the infantile and the repressed, reenacting the terror and fury of primary process, while evidencing longing and desires for compensation and redemption. These are frequent impulses beneath art and suggest the inverse or underside of the activity—what the poet Anna Akhmatova perhaps had in mind when she suggested to Joseph Brodsky that all art was built out of trash.

What is profound in the Mont Sainte-Victoire works is how the monumental rests on and is extended over the unstable, how these artifacts utilize their contradictions and weld them into a grandeur that nevertheless remains open to revealing the destabilizing fissures of those anxieties that lie at their origins. The very "unfinish" of these works reiterates the refusal of resolution and closure of those conflicts and hesitations that were the conditions of their making—and all art since seems far too finished. The glory of these late works lies in their perpetuation of risk, in their refusal to shut down the contradictions upon which they were built. Cézanne's genius lies in having forged a way of acting at the limits of human tolerance for the contradictory and finding in that struggle a connection to the world that had not been made before him and has not been made since. In doing this he extended our sense of possibility by allowing us to inhabit the complex otherness of a space that is anything but a picture of mountains.

NOTES

1. Wittgenstein: *Philosophical Investigations*, trans. G. E. M. Anscombe (New York: Macmillan, 1953), §104; hereafter abbreviated *PI*.
2. Wittgenstein, *Tractatus Logico-Philosophicus*, trans. D. F. Pears and B. F. McGuinness (London: Routledge and Kegan Paul, 1961), §6.51.
3. See Stanley Cavell's discussion in "Knowing and Acknowledging," *The Cavell Reader*, ed. Stephen Mulhall (Cambridge, Mass.: Blackwell, 1996), 47–71.
4. See Saul Kripke, *Wittgenstein on Rules and Private Language* (Cambridge, Mass.: Harvard University Press, 1982).
5. Thomas Nagel, *Other Minds: Critical Essays, 1969–1994* (New York: Oxford University Press, 1995), 47.
6. Ibid., 52.
7. Both Kripke's and Stanley Cavell's interpretations of this issue—each differing to be sure (see Cavell's more or less Austinian critique of Kripke's *Wittgenstein on Rules and Private Language* in *Conditions Handsome and Unhandsome* [Chicago: University of Chicago Press, 1990], 64–100)—hinge on a communitarian reading. But aren't norms and normality constantly being questioned by Wittgenstein? Or is he also attacking them? In any case he is always saying more than one thing in

the *Investigations*. What if rules, rather than explaining anything, are what is to be explained?

> Rules are best conceived as objects used in particular ways, without any intrinsic properties that make them rules. . . . This view breaks down the sense of a rule as having a *"form"* that makes it identical with itself . . . and thus brings out the radical way in which Wittgenstein rejects the classical metaphysics of entity. All of this is ignored when we focus merely on agreement of the community as the determinant of correct rule-following. (Henry Staten, "Following Wittgenstein," in *Wittgenstein and Derrida* [Lincoln: University of Nebraska Press, 1984], 165, 21; Staten is paraphrasing Gordon Baker, "Following Wittgenstein," in *Wittgenstein: To Follow a Rule*, ed. Steven H. Holtzman and Christopher M. Leich [London: Routledge, 1981], 58–64.)

8. Davidson, "A Nice Derangement of Epitaphs," in *Truth and Interpretation: Perspectives on the Philosophy of Donald Davidson*, ed. Ernest LePore (Oxford: Blackwell, 1986), 446.

SIZE MATTERS | 2000

The Tao that can be expressed
is not the eternal Tao.
The name that can be named
is not the eternal name.
"Nonexistence" I call the beginning of Heaven and Earth.
"Existence" I call the mother of individual beings.
Therefore does the direction towards nonexistence
lead to the sight of the miraculous essence,
the direction toward existence
to the sight of spatial limitations.

I.

The city of the 1960s was still a largely utilitarian environment. The aestheticization of urban spaces that occurred in the '90s represents a sea change. The very notion of a lifestyle—not yet imaginable in the '60s—is an aesthetic concept and testifies to the transformation of urban life itself. So, too, do the conversions of formerly utilitarian districts, such as SoHo and Chelsea in New York City, into culture ghettos a step above the theme park. The '90s delivered entertainment as a culture mall in those zones that begin with a few art galleries and quickly morph into upscale, high-end real estate spaces, fashion boutiques, espresso bars, and slick restaurants. Thirty-five years ago one could be comfortable and marginal in New York, survive on a part-time job, and have plenty of leisure for intellectual or aesthetic pursuits. Today there is no margin in big-city life. And the aesthetic has been franchised and incorporated into every item of exchange. But to say with Pierre Bourdieu that the aesthetic is just an item of consumption, a mere class signal, is to miss the pervasiveness with which the aesthetic has invaded and transformed urban life.[1] Absent also from the '60s were the space of information and a colorful, multifaceted cyberspace servicing every human itch, where subgroups of specialized interests multiply and unfold into multiple sub-subgroups with the speed of Mandelbrot fractals. If the pierced and tattooed body has become the canvas, how should art confront a body already presented as art? What role is art to play in an arena where the self-conscious shaping of a lifestyle already frames an aesthetic space around the body? If today the values of entertainment and fashion mediate the merger of art and life, didn't these two always squeeze pretty close together in the heated environment framing an earlier more elite, autonomous art? If art and life have merged in unprecedented ways today the question arises as to what kind of art is present in the merging and what kind of life is being lived in the midst of a new aesthetic saturation? That the '90s appear light-years from the '60s prompts a glance back at a certain art that arose in that time, as well as its lingering legacy in ours. It was within the shadows of a grayer, utilitarian urban space that minimal art of the 1960s was born. Where did it come from and what were its values?

The origins of abstract art lie far back in the history of the West. Iconoclastic proscriptions against making recognizable images reach at least as far back as the Second Commandment: "Thou shalt not make thee any graven images, or likeness of any thing that is in heaven above, or that is in the earth beneath, or that is in the waters beneath the earth" (Deut. 5:8). The sense of the sacred in the Judeo-Christian tradition is deeply imbricated with these iconophobic prohibitions. And of course the Deity Himself is to remain unrepresented, abstract, and sublime, beyond the framing capacity of the mortal mind.

The more recent Western modernist narrative of a progressive drive toward abstraction and formal purity in the plastic arts spans the first three-quarters of this century and has been told many times. This is a dualistic, contradictory narrative, beginning with Kandinsky and stories of transcendent or spiritual impulses motivating abstract art from one side. A rationalistic, formalistic empiricism making claims for an autonomy of the abstract object gains a dominant momentum by midcentury and forms the other part of the ideology. As the century wore on the enterprise of abstract art continued to reverberate with echoes of the Book of Deuteronomy while it loudly demanded a silent, abstract autonomy of the formal—a doxology formalized by Alfred Barr as early as 1936—not to mention an historical inevitability demanded for it a little later by Clement Greenberg.[2] By midcentury an abstract art defended as an empiricism of self-sufficient formalism, a kind of silent visual ontology, historically driven but framed with promises of the transcendental, had moved to cultural center stage.

Abstraction as an official art reaches its apogee in America in the '50s with the rise of abstract expressionism. The Old Testament rhetoric of some of the artists of this period—Barnett Newman, most notably, but Mark Rothko and

Clyfford Still might also be included—reminds us once again of how iconoclastic appeals to the sacred in abstract art had not been forgotten. If abstract art achieved a certain classical high-art status with the minimalism of the '60s, the rhetoric of its practitioners was stridently formal and secular in their ideological defenses. But had they really forgotten God? Had Jonathan Edwards and Ralph Waldo Emerson really vanished from American art? Did the strictures of nonobjective plastic art—that world of the iconoclastically nonreferential, the imageless image absent any resemblance to recognizable things—still resonate to sympathies for the Puritanical and the transcendental?

It is generally agreed that in turning away from representations by resemblance all abstract works continue to abound with contradictory references. The refusal of resemblance guarantees nothing other than the satisfactions of following the letter of the iconoclastic Mosaic law. In any case resemblance, as Nelson Goodman has reminded us, is a poor criterion of representation, since anything can stand for anything else. And, contrarily, not only does one twin not stand for the other, but aspects of resemblance can be read into any two objects in the world.[3] Greenberg's nominalism and empiricism to the contrary, every art object arrives first as a sign. Only signs can deliver aesthetic experience. Any abstract work, just as any representational art object, is read against those predecessors in its subclass; that inevitably historical, token-of-a-kind reading fixes and orients all artworks.

Any abstract work may or may not have claimed for it the status of a metaphorical or allegorical sign. Metonymic references are generally absent, or at least disparaged, when present in the sign system of nonobjective works. And here we might recall Edmund Burke's distinction between the beautiful and the sublime. Only the metaphorical can accede to sublime status, while only the partial, the small, and, of course, the feminine (I follow Burke here) can occupy the category of the beautiful.[4] In American abstract art big is not only always better but also the only hope against its nemesis, the decorative. A little Pollock is hopeless decor. Only big signs have a shot at masculine sublime metaphors. And, in America, only the dead serious. No jokes, no faces, no words. The elimination of the representational and the verbal is also a sign opening the sanctifying of an aesthetic space leading back toward the silences of the religious. Ad Reinhardt's singular ability to bind the ironic to high seriousness sat uneasily with his colleagues in the late '50s. What were they to make of his protominimal *Black Paintings*, his refusal to go monumental, his political engagement, and remarks such as "Art is too serious to be taken seriously"?[5]

And could the rise of American abstract art in the forties have owed something to World War II? An ideology promoting the focus on art as a phenomenalism of silent visual experience totally and irreducibly copresent with the art object (so went Greenberg's pitch) was also one wanting to turn aside all reference to the outside world. Inside such an experience one could forget for a few moments those horrors in Europe then beginning to accelerate into a technology of death that would distinguish the century as the most blood-soaked so far.

The abstract action painting of the '50s resonated to a pragmatism emphasizing doing and American know-how unbeholden to European precedents. Modernist notions of progress were implicit in the doctrine, not to mention Emersonian exhortations to self-reliance. But flawed Deweyan empirical appeals to the autonomy of a totalizing immediate experience constituted its main defense. And this defense continued to be invoked in the minimal art that followed—although I don't recall John Dewey's name ever having been mentioned. It is only with conceptual art that the hegemony of Dewey's radical empiricism (his most famous book was *Art as Experience*) begins to be questioned. Conceptual art problematized the hegemony of an autonomous, nominalistic, and totalizing art experience. This was not a case of importing epistemological claims into art but of denying that empirical experience coincides with the limit of art. Conceptual art, in foregrounding naming and describing, asserted the priority of art as a sign. This was a strategic move against the ideology of the visual as an autonomous presence, which was in denial of its status as sign. Of course the other tradition descending largely from Duchamp that led to pop art had never fallen into such a narrow ideological position, but the dialectical engagement of conceptual art was with the empiricism of the minimal ideology and ignored pop art as not worth thinking about.

It is with minimal art that the late nineteenth and early twentieth centuries' set of presuppositions reverberating through Dewey come to fruition. Here that old-time religion of Puritanism and transcendentalism grafted to Deweyan pragmatism's aesthetics of wholeness achieves its full-blown ideological synthesis. In this work a certain truculent Americanism finds its artistic voice. Maybe that voice was a bit rough, but it still remembered the old hymns.

Minimal art's adaptation of industrial processes as manifestations of power wielded by the individual artist not only listened to Emersonian cheers for self-reliance but magnified a Deweyan confidence in doing and dogged, unswerving appeals to tough, in-your-face experience, while tapping into progressive American technological know-how. Minimalism's programmatic rejection of European art traditions, which it shared with the more ambitious abstract expressionist efforts, wanted to repress memory and emphasize the American obsession with the new and the now as progress over a past that was to be forgotten. It was Pollock, of course, whose work first articulated this ambition and set an overarching precedent. Minimal art was only trying to answer Pollock's challenge and to capitalize on what lay latent and undeveloped in his work—that is, to expand the holism and purity into a communal practice. If Pollock had been the prophet, minimalism was the church.

The minimal artists of the '60s were like industrial frontiersmen, exploring the factories and the steel mills. The artwork must carry the stamp of *work*—that is to say, men's work, the only possible serious work, brought back still glowing from the foundries and mills without a drop of irony to put a sag in its erect heroism. And this men's work is big, foursquare, no nonsense, a priori. How to make an object that is nonobjective? A thing made like something useful that could take abuse but that is unused, autonomous, and unyielding. Stamp, cut, fold, bend it; repeat it factorywise; and then leave it. Leave it right there in your face or in front of your body. The great anxiety of this enterprise—the fall into the decorative, the feminine, the beautiful, in short, the minor—could only be assuaged by the big and heavy. This work was going to bang your body, threaten your space and flesh, make you walk around its beetling sublimity. These works were work. Even those callous-handed New England fathers might have approved. But wait. Could that buzzing beneath or above the secular rhetoric be the hum of transcendence hovering there in the space?

If Donald Judd appealed to a hard, reductive Deweyan empiricism, Robert Morris inserted the gestalt of unitary forms and the phenomenology of Merleau-Ponty into the game, stepping over the discreet, Deweyan distance of vision into a bodily engagement with the self-reflexive. The transformation of experience from the optical to the haptic as the self-reflexive body's perception of a dualistic gestalt/space came to form the stronger formal core of minimal art. The objects of minimal art were in your space, and you had to confront them with both body and eye.

But the epicenter of minimal work lay above any overt appeals to experience or a latter-day materialist phenomenology of Merleau-Ponty's body, a body that had to move to perceive, and therefore foregrounded the importance of space. For a charged world hovers over any negotiations of space sucked in by these in-your-face objects. And this world is the same idealist and transcendent one once preached by that great Puritan, Jonathan Edwards. The more severe minimal sculptors (Carl Andre, Sol LeWitt, Morris, early Dan Flavin, later Richard Serra) were following Edwards, who followed Locke's hierarchy in deeming such things as color secondary qualities. If they repressed these as nonintrinsic in favor of foregrounding the haptic as primary, where "solidity is just resistance, shape is the termination of resistance, and motion is the communication of resistance from space to space," they would never have overtly stated that "resistance is nothing else but the exercise of God's power," even while they followed Edwards's promotion of formal values to a moral status.[6] Edwards identified God himself with empty space and in words embarrassingly close to the big attitude worn by every minimalist, "But I had as good speak plain: I have already said as much as that space is god."[7] There can be no emptiness, no notion of absolute nothingness outside the eternal existence of being. Armed with an iconoclastic Puritanical iconography damning the represented, what could be better than the apparent emptiness of space to encode the highest aesthetic value?—a value that in its ineffable, charged emptiness has from this distance cooled sufficiently to allow the gassy ideology to condense.

Of course, not all minimal art fetishized space. Certainly Judd's work (and it is not for nothing that he was one of Dewey's last students), in its emphasis on candy-box colored surfaces and simple serial extensions, issues from an essentially optical position. Haptic physicality and phenomenological penetrations of space were foreign to his work. That anxious yearning for radical transcendence imbuing the other, more severe practitioners of the genre was absent from these endlessly repeated, flat-footed, essentially weightless stacks of sheet metal and plastic. If Judd's work, which he defended in terms of a radical empiricism, remains the most secular and materialistic of the minimalists, it was also the most decorative. Always beautiful but never sublime, it fetishized the object and ignored the space.

As for the others: purity of space and the big as transcendent metaphor for, if not the deity, an unnameableness pretty high up there, rise over a tough-guy, American, low-tech know-how like the sweat evaporating off an honest foundry worker. The aesthetic becomes promoted to a morality of purity. God resides not in the details, as Mies van der Rohe once thought, but in the spaces between them. Impulses for the massive presence of the repetitive in this work—repetitions not only in the subunits that compose a work but the relentless productions of series of slightly varying works—lie deeper than market-driven accommodations. Such repetitions have about them the compulsiveness of prayer itself. The high formalism of the abstract art enterprise always had a churchlike atmosphere—the solemnity of the making, the necessity for an interceding priest-critic to explicate and give blessing, the sanctity of the museum as site for worship. The raucousness of early pop art contemporary with the minimal irritated. The practitioners of pop art were farting in church.

Earth art, rising on the heels of the minimal, is inconceivable without minimalism's doctrine of the sublime, its program of co-opting industrial processes, its insistence on the clarity of gestalt forms, and the foregrounding of space itself. But beyond this formal program, earth art drew from the minimal that desire for an uneasy transcendence that would, while asserting a stiff formalism, nevertheless save the work from collapse into mere formalism. Earth art added an overt romanticism to a minimal program. Those vast stretches of sculpted nature were inflected by an Emersonian thematic and reverberated to an agrarian nature worship descending partly from the works of Frederick Law Olmsted. But those acres of lurid canvas sunsets painted by Thomas Cole and Frederic Church—spaces where God's heaven descended to touch the earth—should also be counted as precedents.

Minimal art was the attempt to recuperate transcendent Puritan values by reencoding them via an iconoclasm of austere formal spatial purity. At the same time its ambition was to transpose and redeem utilitarian industrial processes and gestalt forms into an aesthetic space of the phenomenological. Echoing the ambitions of William James, minimal art wanted it both ways: on the one hand, the tough-minded empiricism of Frank Stella's remark that what you see is what you get; on the other, the elusive, tender-minded transcendence (never part of the official doxology) encoded by the purity of the formal spatial relations, whose lawlike severity implied a transcendent order reaching beyond the aesthetic phenomenalism. The severe spatial ordering constituted and encoded the transcendent relation—space was not object, yet phenomenal, not arbitrary, but more than merely rational, an absence whose presence and generality supervenes the physical object. The power of minimal art was how it held in place this paradoxical relation, how the severely ordered space of absence itself made the gestalt of the object more real, how the palpable was read through the impalpable, giving rise to a sense of the relations between objects anchored in a lawlike transcendent space. Space shows itself in the behavior of the object but is not itself a behaving object. The ambition of this work is revealed, just as with all vital art, in the ingenious strategies with which it confronted and held its contradictions in tense suspension. And like all vital art the tensions embodied in that staging could not last. And like all vital art minimal art did not pass without its lingering, residual mannerist phase, the recent work of Serra being a case in point. These works, which approach the tonnage of aircraft carriers to up the ante and keep a flagging phenomenology of experience afloat, nevertheless sink to the level of displaced icons that evoke images of bloated corporate power—an accusation that could not have been leveled at the minimal work of the '60s, when the inherent contradictions were held in a tense balance and gigantism was unnecessary.

Minimal art at its zenith in the '60s was a kind of religious art. Unfrocked perhaps, but religious nevertheless in floating its transcendence into those immaterial spaces between its formal densities. It encapsulated and recapitulated a uniquely American rethinking of the material thought of artmaking. This material thought swam within and not against the historical current of that tripartite American tradition of the Puritanical, the transcendental, and the pragmatic. Its contribution was to build on Pollock in metaphorizing these longstanding values (values that by the '90s have all but vanished) into a distilled aesthetic experience—an experience welding utilitarian forms and processes to iconophobic images, allowing space itself to reaffirm that forgotten or repressed transcendent guarantee claimed for it by that greatest of the Puritans, Jonathan Edwards.[8]

2.

But do we find that old tripartite American tradition completely dead as the '90s come to a close? Surely at least the cruder Jamesian version of a pragmatism sanctioning relativism and opportunism still guides. And the concerns of Edwards? Buried beneath the tonnage of entertainment that overwhelms? But in the midst of a loaded urban space, reeking of an aestheticized material environment, can the faintest shudders of Puritanical guilt be detected? And where would such seismic twitches of the psyche be registered? In art? Could some art be offering a kind of promise of redemption from the assaults of all those material girls? Doesn't most of it celebrate the giddy effervescence of irony as a lifestyle?

But wait. What about really big art? Big enough to be heard over the guilty giggles and sticking up far above the shoulders of those slacker slouches. Big stuff that makes you wonder what it cost, even in a time when money is out of control. And forget abstract. Who cares anymore? The '90s glut of images levels, numbs, and equalizes; one image is as good as another. Big is what matters. Big isn't everything, but maybe the only thing that will get noticed. The only thing that might compete with the din of style in its roar of ubiquitous, mutating manifestations.

If the Mozart effect is to be noticed against the grain of that numbing din, perhaps there is something that might be called the Wagner effect at work from another direction, representing perhaps an oppositional move, or at any rate one yet to be theorized. The Wagner effect would be bound into those looming icons of dominating presence, offering a kind of odd forgiveness secretly addressed to those whose guilty lives make such expressions possible. Work falling under the rubric of the Wagner effect would be aimed at servicing the upper echelons of a would-be ruling class who, in their driven generosity, demand those vast and sanctified spaces of the museum as testimony to the importance of their class and self-congratulatory public service. A type of art that is, literally, hard to get in the museum. Massive, unwieldy, dizzyingly costly, and Wagnerian to its core, its price alone a kind of guarantee of redemption, holding out the promise of a murkier, mustier transcendence than Edwards could have endured. Lit more by a dim, somber romantic sky, art emanating the Wagner effect perhaps dumbs down (as opposed to the Mozart effect, which makes even rats smarter) or numbs down with a massive, swooning, mystical aesthetic awe whose price per square foot alone can induce vertigo. Style doesn't much matter for the Wagner effect, gigantic size and expense being the generating engine. Of course, besides the grandiosity, touches of the mystical and allusions to origins don't hurt either—they didn't hurt Wagner.[9]

Anselm Kiefer's troweling on acres of blood and soil is, of course, scooping out of the Wagner-effect barrel. But from the grander gestures reaching back to abstract expressionism—and on to Robert Wilson, Roy Lichtenstein, and Chuck Close, to the work of earth artists such as Michael Heizer, whose *City* in the desert is surely one of the century's most monstrous and egregious examples of the genre, and not to be forgotten are the works of the heirs of earth art, such as Maya Lin's Vietnam Veterans Memorial and James Turrell's magic mountain, the plaza decorations of Ellsworth Kelly and Serra, Bill Viola's giant cornball video wall projections of flaming creatures, Gerhard Richter's endless canvas acreages of abstract wallpaper (which doesn't quite reach the bloated angst of his compatriot Kiefer), just to name a few—all are huge-scale romantic art gestures animated by the Wagner effect. The grander gestures of Yves Klein in the early '60s were, of course, seminal Wagner effect. And later, Joseph Beuys (whose works would be unthinkable without Klein's example of the stage-managed media persona) achieved a high-density Wagner effect even without massive scale. But it was his carefully crafted persona as shamanistic mystic, a kind of Teutonic Wotan offering healing and redemption through art—not to mention the portentous romanticism of his ritualistic performances—as much as the art objects themselves that reeked of the Wagner effect. Klein and Beuys both understood how a sense of large scale could be achieved by media manipulation more easily than through the production of giant icons. Images of the impresario artist in full costume, surrounded by hordes of acolytes and clouds of mysticism, swell and roll effortlessly through the media.

Of course, big art goes all the way back to Magdalenian cave art and can be found in many subsequent periods. In this respect Wagner-effect art just takes its place in line with every moment of official art and is paltry in comparison to such monument-obsessed periods as Pharaonic Egypt. As with all official art the element of awe and expense, or even the awe of expense, is built in, required, and achieved by grandiosity of scale. And like so much past grandiose official art, what we witness in current Wagner-effect work is mostly a lateness of style, a virtually exhausted aesthetic. But at the end of this century the very idea of the monumental carries a faint whiff of the obscene.

If Wagner effect can be periodized in our time it can be said to begin with Pollock. In the '60s the one enterprise whose intention was to create monumental icons not falling into Wagner effect was Claes Oldenburg's. Was this prescient artist, maybe the most intelligent of our era, constructing Trojan horses all along? The easy, knee-jerk irony found in so much pop art is absent from the amalgamation of pathos and mockery bound so tightly in Oldenburg's earlier work—an oeuvre admittedly weakened later under the dual signatures of the enterprise as packaged and cooperative. The only precedents for his earlier, outsize common objects set down on plazas and in other public spaces might be found in Goya's *Los Caprichos*. Oldenburg's giant emblems do not monumentalize the fetishizing idiocies of consumer capitalism so much as its addled mentality and hopeless values comprised of pride and abjection. Oldenburg's Hobbesian vision allegorizes the perversion and failure of the very notion of the public in our time. His dystopian spaces are precisely opposite those obsequious ones emanating Wagner effect that so often foreground an episteme of form to disguise the values being served.

The utopian spaces of modernism binding the empirical and transcendent within the progressivist historical march of abstract icons have vanished. The giddy, schizophrenic, bricolaged spaces of the postmodern, assembled from the jittery hysterical riot of pastiched images, subside into the fitful spasms of its inconsequential last gasps.

But within the stylistic heterogeneity of those gigantic artworks partaking of the Wagner effect, an official art has been coagulating over the years, allegorizing a space of domination hinting at a peculiar kind of redemption. This

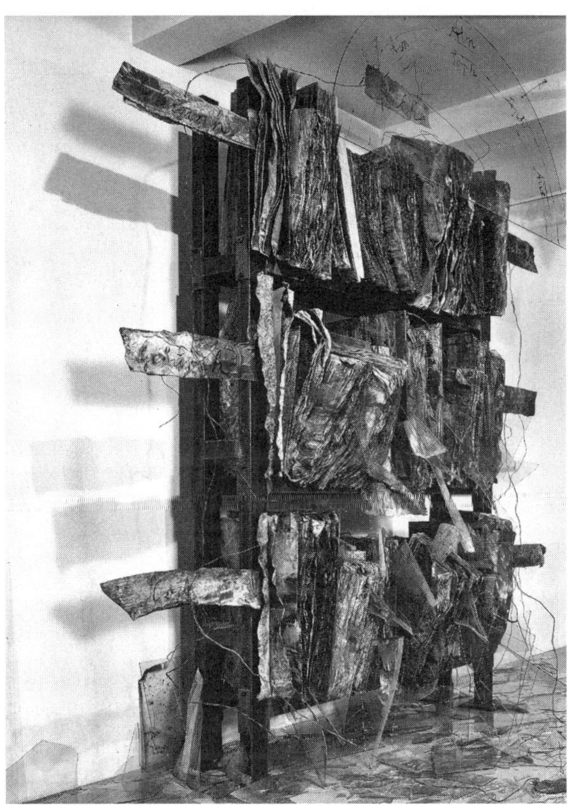

82. Anselm Kiefer, *Breaking of the Vessels*, 1989–90. About 40 lead books on iron-bookshelf, iron, lead, copper-wire, glass, charcoal and aquatec, 150½ × 135⅞ × 59 inches (382 × 345 × 150 cm). Photo courtesy of Anselm Kiefer.

would be a dark, triumphal space binding the fantasies of a largely invisible class into massive icons delivered as gestures toward a (faux?) public art. Here resides a phenomenal aesthetic framing and redefining entertainment as awe. The ideal here is some form of quasi-public site as dominating affirmation. Grandiose spaces of delicious surrender and seduction of the will, where every imaginable political gesture of resistance evaporates, where the very idea of the critical becomes purged in the face of the looming idol. A certain pinnacle of the Wagner effect was no doubt achieved in Lin's Vietnam Veterans Memorial in Washington, D.C. Exhibiting a strong gestalt form scavenged from minimal and earth art conventions, the black granite wall of names functions as a curtain drawn across governmental criminality. Criticality evaporates in this tight theater foregrounding private grief, the expression of which serves to effect closure on a national wound that should have been left open. Here is public art at its most devious and perverted.

Perhaps the Wagner effect has been building more or less untheorized for half a century, delivering via its massive forms an allegory of the ambitions of the dominant class in all their exclusive, monumentally moneyed proportions. An allegory most focused by an empiricism of elusive, dizzying formalism—a torqued space, a space of ellipsis in which the power celebrated eludes identification as it demands submission. And when we consider what such grandiose forms can deliver, should we forget Albert Speer?

3.

W. J. T. Mitchell has noted that the phenomenon he calls dinomania tends to periodically reappear in the culture in times of material well-being. He sees the dinosaur as a mythical, ambivalent cultural icon addressing anxieties of extinction as well as celebrations of predatory capitalist power.[10] Mitchell notes that the institution of the great American museum was initiated by Charles Wilson Peale constructing a space in which to publicly display the bones of a mastodon, this "monster" of the museum being the principal attraction. (The term *monster* is doubly apt if the Latin roots are excavated: *monstrum* denotes both monstrosity and warning; *monstrare* means "to show"). The Chicago Field Museum's recent $8.36 million purchase of the *Tyrannosaurus rex* fossil, nicknamed Sue, brings us back full circle to Peale. But more than this, Sue is pure Wagner effect: a conundrum of origins bathed in the mysterious awe of deep time; the thanatoid capacities of her seven-inch teeth and gigantic size inducing a shudder of the sublime, together with the secret, necrotic joy of knowing the animal is dead, extinct; and, most of all, the rarity of this fetish guaranteed by the pure depths of the monetary. As Mitchell has pointed out, the gigantic icons art museums collect are not unrelated to those massive fossilized bones of the natural history museum.

Today's contemporary art museum more often than not celebrates the rising tide of fashion and kitsch. Exhibitions like the recent *The Art of the Motorcycle* at the Guggenheim in New York attempt to service, perpetuate, and celebrate the democracy of the kitsch fetish, reassuring yet again that the low is as high as anything needs to go. Still, occasionally the Wagner effect is towed in as a means to aim high. Sacred icons are needed today, just not as often. But whether kitsch or Wagner effect, only the buzz of cultural event as spectacle guarantees a gate.

The art museum of today has, of course, moved away from its role as an institution merely open to the public to one actively servicing the public. That is to say, it has shifted its raison d'être or strategic cultural position from one of internal coherence, in which its responsibility resides in sharing its elitist expertise with a public, to a tactical concern with those external factors of staging events to sell to the public. Of course it is possible that museums are merely returning full circle to the role they played in antebellum America when, as Neil Harris describes, "high culture was not yet separated from popular culture. Museums, such as Barnum's in New York, Kimball's in Boston, Peale's in Philadelphia, or the Western Museum in Cincinnati, mingled all sorts of oddities—Indian arrows, dinosaur bones, two-headed pigs, along with casts of Greek sculpture, and paintings by Gilbert Stuart and Thomas Scully."[11]

Some contemporary museums send their staff to be trained by Disney. Delivery of entertainment rises to the top of the agenda. The visitor is serviced and programmed, delivered with headset to the event on display. Carioca dancing, guitar players, fashion shows, and evening fun events are advertised, and the fun extends all the way to the museum shop. Museum morphs into culture mall. For the steep price of admission a kind of *Gesamtkunstwerk* of aesthetic experience has been delivered. Curators become artists who stage events with art props. The museum experience is guaranteed to extend the aestheticization of your lifestyle. But occasionally the art object can, given sufficient Wagner-effect volume, compete with the surrounding promotional din. Those museum objects generating sufficient Wagner effect provide simultaneously phenomenal aesthetic fetishes that are also transcendent and generally nationalist cultural idols, which sometimes also dazzle as totemic objects pragmatically guaranteed by massive dollar signs and historical pedigrees—all delivered in the package of a sensational event.

Frank Gehry's Guggenheim Bilbao temple of and to gigantism offers the latest, most up-to-date arena for aesthetic assaults of the awesomely big. Even dinosaurs would get lost in these blimp hangar spaces. Here at last we have Wagner-effect architecture specially built for Wagner-effect art.

If Gehry's earlier effort in the Santa Monica house arrives anywhere near Fredric Jameson's claim that it attempts to rethink the cognitive and spatial problems of a meeting of private and corporate space—"the two antithetical and incommensurable features . . . of abstract American space"[12]—the vast processional spaces of Bilbao are surely a meditation on the resolution of the conflict in favor of the corporate. If the multinational corporation of today is the apotheosis of the gigantic, until Bilbao there had been no suitable cultural

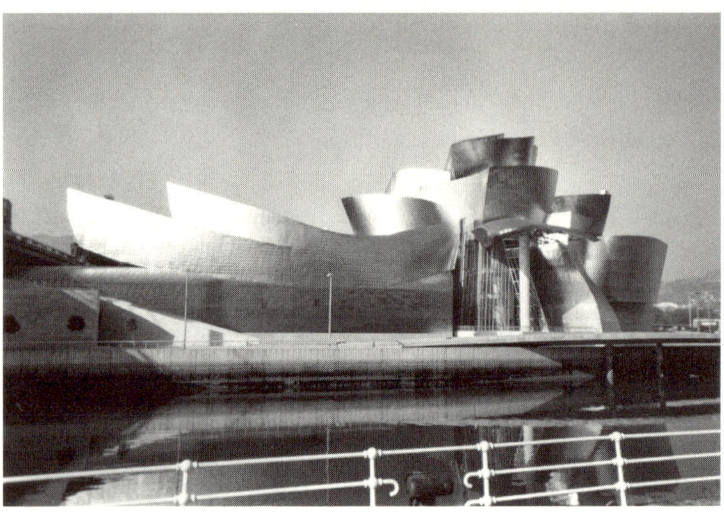

83. Frank Gehry, Guggenheim Museum, Bilbao, Spain, 1997. Photo courtesy of Elinor Richter.

allegory for it. Those invisible, cyberspace linkages of its extensive, disparate assets and svelte controls manifested as information flows between separate but connected entities had, until Bilbao, no visible spatial metaphors. But in this Basque museum the processional unfolding of lofty, "mutable, polymorphous, heterogeneous"[13] spaces surely allegorizes the spirit of the gigantic multinational corporation in all its expanded, conglomerated, dazzlingly protean capacities—Wagner effect delivered with a splendor that far outpaces the bloated icons it houses. But then Gehry once remarked that artists wanted impressive spaces in which to show their mud pies.

It took half a century to reify form out of the larger aesthetic impulse—perhaps part of that broader march toward totalizing objectifications ushered in by modernity's Weberian, rationalized, administered, bureaucratic alienation and progress. By now the fetishizing of iconophobic abstract form, of which minimal art was the last major expression, has endured for a century. But form never carried the load it was thought to bear—although the ideologies it was saddled with weighed tons.

If the aesthetic is as central, compelling, and mysterious in our lives as sex, it should come as no surprise that both sell so well. The strategies of Wagner-effect art arise as attempts to be heard against (but of course also with) the commercialized din of the aestheticized environment, within which the museum has become but another competing institution of entertainment. But in our century much besides the aesthetic has been reified and fetishized, perverted and exploited. And the culture of late capitalism gearing up to assault the next millennium has long since passed that point where thoughts of restraint, let alone reintegration, are even conceivable.

NOTES

1. See Pierre Bourdieu, *Distinction: A Social Critique of the Judgment of Taste*, trans. Richard Nice (Cambridge, Mass.: Harvard University Press, 1984).
2. Alfred Barr, *Cubism and Abstract Art: Painting, Sculpture, Constructions, Photography, Architecture, Industrial Art, Theatre, Films, Posters, Typography* (1936; rpt. Cambridge, Mass.: Belknap Press of Harvard University, 1986).
3. See Nelson Goodman, *Languages of Art: An Approach to a Theory of Symbols* (Indianapolis: Hackett, 1976), 4.
4. See Edmund Burke, *A Philosophical Enquiry into the Origin of our Ideas of the Sublime and Beautiful* (New York: Oxford University Press, 1990), 100, 103.
5. Ad Reinhardt, conversation with author.
6. Jonathan Edwards, quoted in Charles Crittendon, *The Oxford Companion to Philosophy*, ed. Ted Honderich (New York: Oxford University Press, 1995), 219.
7. *A Jonathan Edwards Reader*, ed. John Edwin Smith, Harry S. Stout, and Kenneth P. Minkema (New Haven, Conn.: Yale University Press, 1995), 10.
8. In his 1967 essay "Art and Objecthood," a text taking my work as the centerpiece for its assault on "theatricality," Michael Fried focuses more on the objects of minimal sculpture and less on the space in castigating their fall into "literalism." (Michael Fried, "Art and Objecthood," *Art and Objecthood: Essays and Reviews* [Chicago: University of Chicago Press, 1998], 154, 168). Fried cited Edwards in the epigraph to that essay. No doubt he would consider the uses I've made of Edwards in this text further evidence of apostasy. In retrospect the only fault I find with Fried's essay is that it did not extend the concept of theatricality far enough.
9. Besides these obvious earmarks of the romantic—those concerns with guilt and redemption, origins and mysticism—I include the particular contributions of Wagner: the sense of endlessness and huge scale, the numbing awe, the droning of the repetitive, the heaviness and portentousness of the once again reworked sublime, the coming-to-get-youness of the aggressively theatrical—in short, all of those things (and a few more) that Nietzsche came to detest as decadent in Wagner's work. See Friedrich Nietzsche, "The Case of Wagner," *The Birth of Tragedy and the Case of Wagner*, trans. Walter Kaufman (New York: Random House, 1967), 155–92.
10. See W. J. T. Mitchell, *The Last Dinosaur Book: The Life and Times of a Cultural Icon* (Chicago: University of Chicago Press, 1998).
11. Neil Harris, *Cultural Excursions: Marketing Appetites and Cultural Tastes in Modern America* (Chicago: University of Chicago Press, 1990), 18.
12. Jameson, *Postmodernism, or The Cultural Logic of Late Capitalism* (Durham, N.C.: Duke University Press, 1991), 128. Jameson identifies the "tumbling cube" juxta-

posed to chain-link fence and corrugated aluminum in Gehry's Santa Monica house as emblematic of this dialogue (127).

13. Herbert Muschamp, "Regent and King in a Procession of New Forms," *New York Times*, November 29, 1998. Muschamp is here extolling the formal wonders of the spaces and remains silent on any iconological or ideological readings of the architecture.

> Perhaps the most important example of non-logical a priori knowledge is knowledge as to ethical value. I am not speaking of judgements as to what is useful or as to what is virtuous, for such judgements do require empirical premises; I am speaking of judgements as to the intrinsic desirability of things. If something is useful, it must be useful because it secures some end; the end must, if we have gone far enough, be valuable on its own account, and not merely because it is useful for some further end. Thus all judgements as to what is useful depend upon judgements as to what has value on its own account.[1]

Did Bertrand Russell go far enough? Desirability as the ethical good? One thing or two?

> It is clear that ethics cannot be put into words. Ethics is Transcendental. (Ethics and Aesthetics are one and the same.)[2]

One thing or two? One before the other? One leading to the other? Sometimes the one, sometimes the other? Like two mirrors sometimes aligned, sometimes not? Like a pendulum. . . .

About a century and a half ago Charles Sanders Peirce swung pendulums for the U.S. Geodetic Survey. It was the only job he could find. "Esthetics," Peirce said,

> is the science of ideals, or of that which is objectively admirable without any ulterior reason. . . . Ethics, or the science of right and wrong, must appeal to Esthetics for aid in determining the *summum bonum*. It is the theory of self-controlled, or deliberate conduct. Logic is the theory of self-controlled, or deliberate thought; and as such, must appeal to ethics for its principles.[3]

Ideals, the admirable, right and wrong, the good, logic, principles. All connected in any given form of life. But maybe down deeper things are simpler. G. E. Moore thought "personal affections and aesthetic enjoyments include *all* the greatest, and *by far*, the greatest goods we can imagine. . . ."[4] If only it were so simple . . .

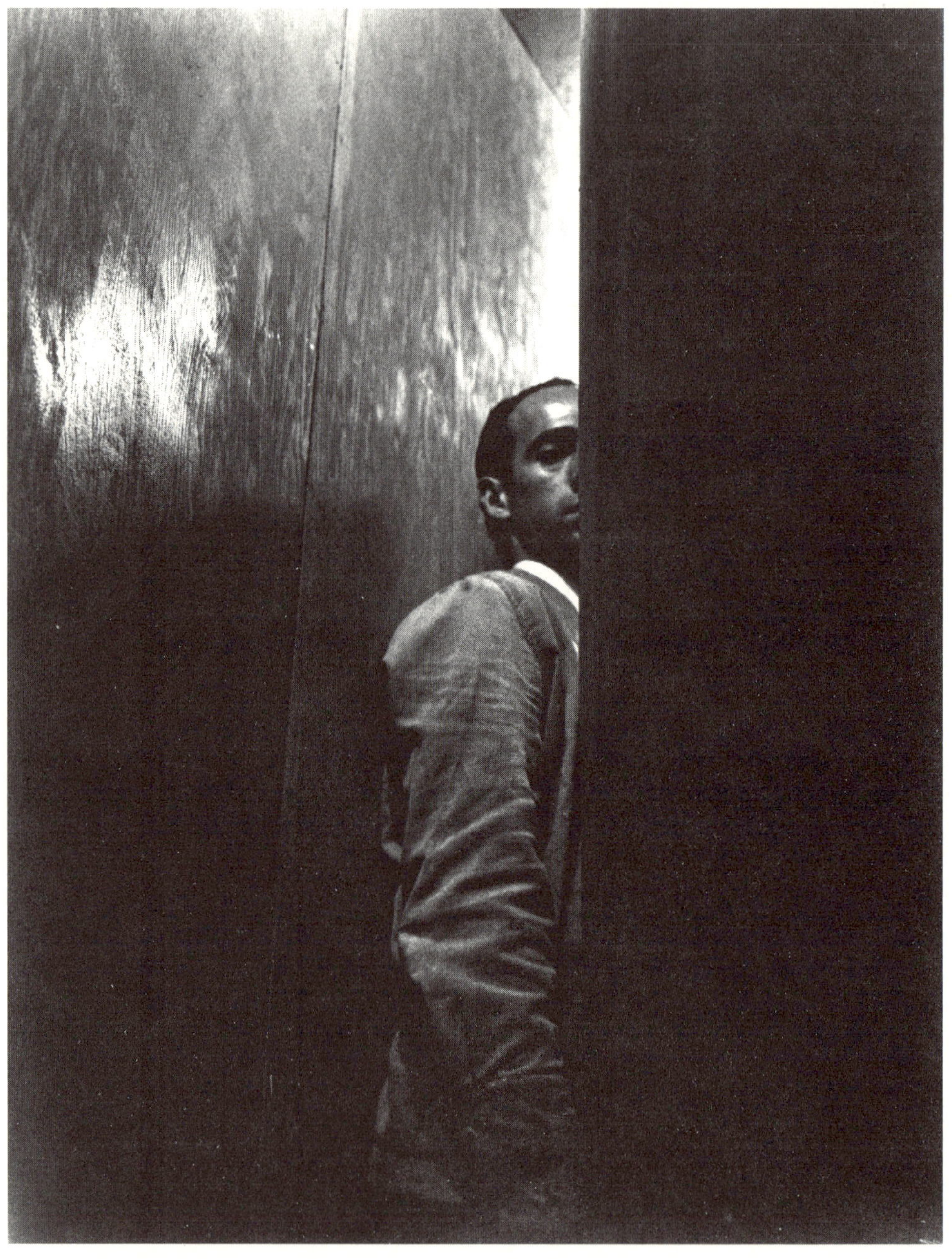

I should like to talk of the sort of explanation one longs for when one talks about an aesthetic impression.[5]

Not forgetting its connection to those other things. Not forgetting also, for example, that Hitler, as he went along, got beyond (better than?) his early watercolors. He and Speer gloating over those eerie white models of a new Berlin for the thousand-year Reich. Like bad Wagnerian sets. The Nuremberg parade ground, the flags, lights, insignia. Something to be said for bloated size, all of it looking back to Wagner (and looking forward to Robert Wilson, Michael Heizer, and other practitioners of gigantism?). The slow, heavy, numbing scale of the neo-sublime. Wagner-effect art.[6] Everything Nietzsche came to detest.

And with these things we can build a wall of ideological blocks. Think of Enrico Fermi's pile of graphite bricks beneath the stadium in Chicago. Think of it containing the radiation within. Then think of the masonry of Visual Culture. Here is a wall that is supposed to be radiation-free. The heat locked up in the insulating blocks, each of which is stamped with its ideological mark. It is what can be called a free-standing empirical wall. Cool. Cool as can be.

Noam Chomsky's double-headed ax of the innate and the a priori. Useful on empirical masonry.

"*Labis*": the Greek term for double-headed ax. The earliest images of labyrinths. Their passageways like ripples or echoes radiating from the form of a double-headed ax. The imaginary Minotaur at the center. Bull Desire charging around, circulating behind the masonry walls.

How many labyrinths have I made or drawn? The late Nico Callas, looking at one of these drawings remarked, "But I prefer the Minotaur." Desire, yes, but how do we name it? This isn't the right way of putting it. It is a question of seeing it before naming it. But all language can do is name or describe.

Who besides Thierry de Duve and Arthur Danto ever believed Duchamp's protestations of indifference? Consider *3 Standard Stoppages*. Threads dropped from the height of one meter do not fall into svelte catenary and reverse catenary curves. But the idea of indifference as a weapon against the aesthetic already bubbles up with the sweetest aesthetic effervescence. Curves of desire. See it and then name it.

In order to get clear about aesthetic words you have to describe ways of living. We think we have to talk about aesthetic judgements like "This is

84. Robert Morris standing inside his *Passageway*, 1961. Painted plywood, 8 × 50 feet (2.44 × 15.24 m). Photo courtesy of Robert Morris.

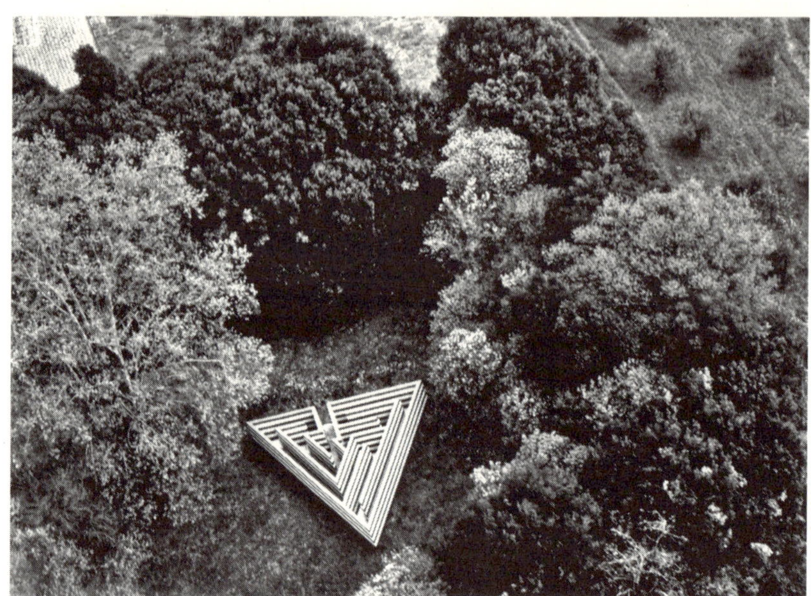

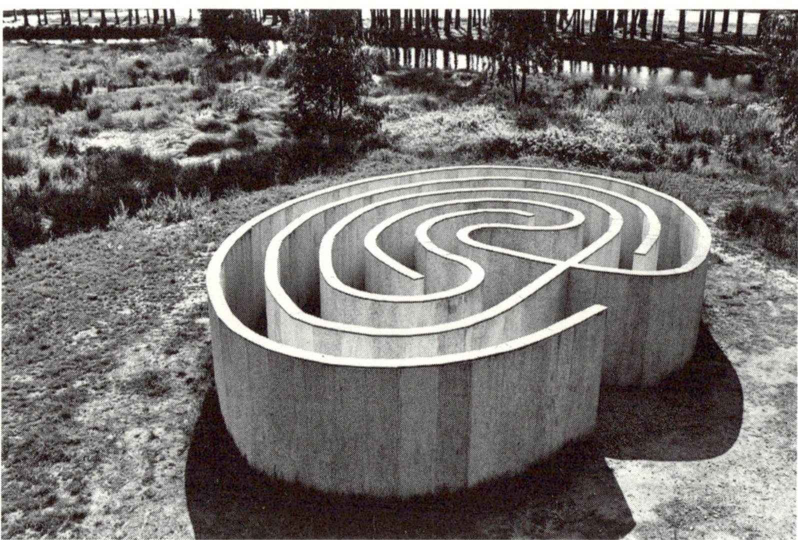

85. *Untitled (Gori Labyrinth)*, 1982. Green and white marble, 39 × 39 × 6½ feet (12 × 12 × 2 m). Collection of Giuliano Gori, Fattoria di Celle, Santomato, Pistoia, Italy. Photo Aurelio Amendola, courtesy of Giuliano Gori.

86. *Labyrinth*, 2000. Gray granite with black slate, 8 feet (2.44 m) high, 35 feet (10.67 m) diameter. Plan based on the "Labyrinth of Mogor," a 3,500-year-old petroglyph located a few miles from the site in Pontevedra, Spain. Photo courtesy of Robert Morris.

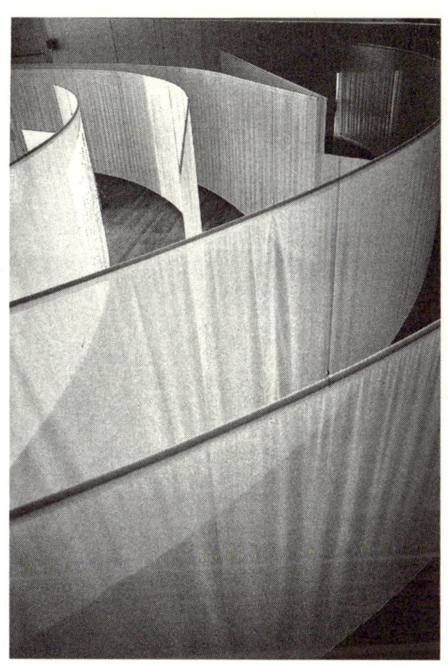

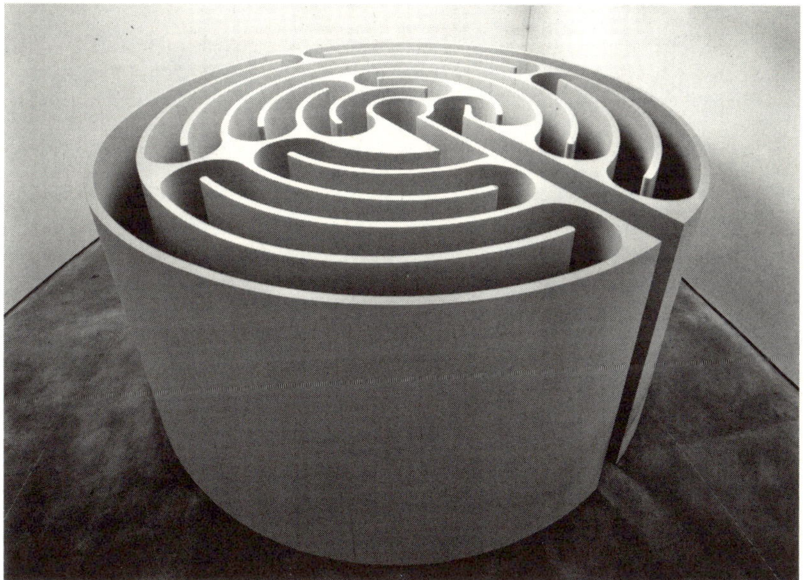

87. *White Nights*, 2000. Installation at Le Musée d'art contemporain, Lyon, France. Photo by Blaise Adilon, courtesy of Robert Morris.

88. *Untitled (Labyrinth)*, 2000. Plywood and masonite, 16 feet (4.88 m) high, 35 feet (10.67 m) diameter. Installation view from the exhibition *Changing Perception: The Panza Collection at the Guggenheim Museum*, Bilbao. Photo by Erika Barahona, courtesy of Robert Morris.

> beautiful," but we find that if we have to talk about aesthetic judgements we don't find these words at all, but a word used something like a gesture, accompanying a complicated activity.[7]

. . . Like having the idea of dropping, doing it, but then rearranging, pacing, stewing about it, doing it again, gluing down the rearrangements, making templates, then going to the trouble of putting everything into a croquet box, then stepping back, smiling, and making the gesture of "take that!"

The great wall of the techno-empirical paradigm curves out of sight. (Visual Culture, examining each brick close up, does not perceive this curvature.) Only the fleet-footed run fast enough to follow the curvature. And philosophizing with our hammer (the one Chomsky lent us, not the other one) we knock holes as we go. We're moving too fast to get a look through these holes, but we do hear an echo. From our hammer? No. It's that sing-song voice of the old Chinaman from Königsberg reminding us that the schematicism of our understanding, in its application to appearances and their mere form, is an art concealed in the depths of the human soul, whose real modes of activity nature is hardly likely ever to allow us to discover, and to have open to our gaze.[8]

Labyrinths again.

> You could say: "An aesthetic explanation is not a causal explanation."[9]

> The attraction of certain kinds of explanation is overwhelming. At a given time the attraction of a certain kind of explanation is greater than you can conceive. In particular, explanation of the kind "This is really only this."[10]

Visual Culture's causal masonry again. Straight and true. No curves, please, they might lead to a labyrinth.

The acquisition of language, the mind-body problem, the question of meaning, of free will, consciousness. And the nature of that innate faculty of the ethical Russell spoke of. And Peirce's elusive standard bearer of the a priori, the aesthetic. So little progress across the centuries. Because the mind has a limited capacity to, in some fashion, represent aspects of the world, we are not warranted in concluding that it was wired to represent itself. Inquiry into the nature of the a priori faculties, *pace* Kant, may be terminally foreclosed.

> One might, in fact, reasonably go still further in chipping away at traditional concepts of acquisition of knowledge. Why should we suppose that the innate general principles, or the principles that integrate and organize our mature systems of belief, should be discoverable "by dint of attention"?[11]

Of what use is an art world divided between an ingrown academia and the fashion-entertainment industry? But doesn't the aesthetic also lurk behind these paper-thin walls? And is it also paper-thin? Do those tons of fashionable, politically correct, and for the most part overdetermined, didactic, and boring artworks indignant about race and gender indignities bind together the aesthetic and the moral? And aren't the best intentions responsible for some of the worst effects? And those cool, ironic, fashionable hordes milling around attending to the care and feeding of their lifestyles? Aren't they guided by what we might call an aesthetic of ennui?

> Now I maintain that the beautiful is the symbol of the morally good; and only because we refer the beautiful to the morally good (we all do so naturally and require all others also to do so, as a duty) does our liking for it include a claim to everyone else's assent.[12]

And what about evil? Couldn't there be an anti-aesthetic linked to evil? Or are there only good innate faculties? In the archives of the Resistance in Lyon, France, there is on file a Gestapo photograph of an elegant kind of helmet penetrated by large screws that when turned . . .

> Viewed naturalistically, why shouldn't your pain produce pleasure in me? It isn't as if each pain has inscribed upon it, "Not to be used for the production of pleasure." There is, as it were, a kind of radical contingency about which interpersonal pleasure-pain links get established. Conceptually you can have one just as well as the other.[13]

Or should we hang this helmet of worms on Visual Culture's empirical wall?

> What is currently understood even in a limited way seems to me to indicate that the mind is a highly differentiated structure, with quite distinct sub-systems. If so, an understanding of the properties of one of these systems should not be expected to provide the principles by which others are organized and function. Even an account of knowledge of language that is overflowing with insights is unlikely to contribute directly to the study of factors that enter into our understanding of the nature of the visual world, or conversely.[14]

Recent studies indicate that the perception of abstract art activates two specific areas of brain activity while looking at representational art fires up two additional, specific areas.[15] Pretty specific sub-systems going on here. Each with its set of rules. Tasks are divided up. As Zeki remarks, "The brain is no mere passive chronicler of the external physical reality but an active participant in generating the visual image, according to its own rules and programs."[16] But almost four centuries ago Descartes told us that we

> will have reason to conclude that there is no need to suppose that something material passes from objects to our eyes to make us see colors and light, or even that there is something in the objects, which resembles the ideas or sensations that we have of them. In just the same way, when a blind man feels bodies, nothing has to issue from the bodies and pass along his stick to his hand; and the resistance or movement of the bodies, which is the sole cause of the sensations he has of them, is nothing like the ideas he forms of them. By this means, your mind will be delivered from all those little images flitting through the air, called "intentional forms," which so exercise the imagination of the philosophers.[17]

For the last three hundred and fifty years thinkers have taken vows against succumbing to Descartes' subjectivity. And still the ghost of the innate returns looking less and less like a ghost each time it shows up.

We've lost the thread of the aesthetic. When activated does it wind through labyrinthine areas of the brain? Does it require its own program, a program divided and sub-divided into subordinate tasks? Does it brush up against that other innate program, the moral, in some dark, labyrinthine passage? Perhaps a gesture of greeting passes between the two, a kind of Panofskyan "hat removing." Or is this passing more like two ships gliding by one another in the night with only the echo of a fog horn hanging in the darkness to mark their passage? Or could it be more lively? A giddy, giggling encounter in which much winking and eyebrow lifting goes on. "Gotcha, Doppelganger!" the one whispers. "Likewise, my symbol," says the other as they slap high fives and squeeze past each other in the narrow passageway.

The shantytowns of Johannesburg have narrow, labyrinthine passageways. The stench, the lack of sanitation, the overcrowding, the unemployment, the crime and violence—we don't want to think about any thread of the aesthetic lying in the mud and open sewers of such labyrinths. We don't want to think about these places because we don't have to. And while we are among that

> minority of the human population, (who) as Francis Fukuyama would put it, are sufficiently sheltered so as to enter a "post-historical" realm, living in cities and suburbs in which the environment has been mastered and ethnic animosities have been quelled by bourgeois prosperity, an increasingly large

number of people will be stuck in history, living in shantytowns where attempts to rise above poverty, cultural dysfunction, and ethnic strife will be doomed by a lack of water to drink, soil to till, and space to survive in. In the developing world environmental stress will present people with a choice that is increasingly among totalitarianism (as in Iraq), Fascist-tending mini-states (as in Serb-held Bosnia), and road-warrior cultures (as in Somalia).[18]

Nietzsche says somewhere that art arises out of excess. Elsewhere he says the only way the world can be justified is by viewing it as a work of art. What about the excess of lack and that more than a third third world? Any aesthetic threads dangling here?

Greenberg spoke, albeit in passing, of the ties of avant-garde art to the ruling class. Perhaps a little thicker than mere threads such attachment had the nature of an "umbilical cord of gold."[19] As we know, on occasion dirty, snotty threads can weave themselves into these golden cords.

The rope of modernism. Knotted like a quipu artifact, worn like a charm, or an albatross, around Clio's neck. Strategically stretched against the technoscientific paradigm of modernity. Coiled first on the ground religion had vacated, then looped around hopeful new values and braided into utopian macramés, later knotted into little tangles of critical protests, finally unraveled and frayed into abstract, formalistic dangles. Which strand contained the authentic aesthetic thread?

Imagine a few gossamer-thin strands of an aesthetic of worry. Spun of threads pulled from Mnemosyne's cloak and woven into a tattered web. Hanging in a dark corner of the new millennium's polished titanium cathedral of the market. Off to the side of the celebratory mass. Invisible in the self-congratulatory glitter. Unnoticed in the thousand-watt glare of amnesiac grins singing hymns of puerile irony.

If to understand a word is to understand a language, a culture, a form of life, and if definitions are useless in aiding us to comprehend the very words we use, isn't it impossible to foreground something called the "aesthetic" and attempt to isolate it from the background of cultural practices? But hints, shivers of recognition are all we ask for. Just a glimpse of the thread running along half-buried in a passageway of the labyrinth.

It is not only difficult to describe what appreciation consists in, but impossible. To describe what it consists in we would have to describe the whole environment.[20]

Practices develop and for a time endure. Over time rules attach to these practices. And "in learning the rules you get a more and more refined judgment."[21] Should we look for the thread of the aesthetic woven into these practices? An elusive thread that leads into the labyrinth of the a priori. Or should we defer to the masons of Visual Culture stacking up the ideological bricks in their straight, empirical walls?

If Chomsky is correct in concluding that the organization, sub-sets, rules and functioning of linguistic systems shed no light on visual systems, just what is it that Norman Bryson and Mieke Bal are reading when they "read" pictures?

> Suppose there are two people. A and B, talking to one another. The circuit begins in the brain of one of them, say A, in which the objects of consciousness, which we may call concepts, are located, associated with representations of the linguistic signs, or auditory images, that serve to express them. We may suppose that a given concept releases in the brain a corresponding auditory image; this is an entirely *physiological* process: the brain transmits an impulse, corresponding to the image, to the organs of sound production; the soundwaves are then propagated from the mouth of A to the ear of B: a purely *physical* process. Next, the circuit continues in B, in the reverse order: from the ear to the brain, a physiological transmission of the auditory image; in the brain, the psychic association of this image with the corresponding concept.[22]

What is wrong with this account? The representation of concepts as mental images. "It imitates the associationist account put forward by the British empiricists: . . . they identified concepts with ideas, which they typically understood as mental images."[23] As the great wave of semiology recedes, all kinds of curious detritus will be found tangled and rotting on the spongy sands.

"There is a 'Why?' to aesthetic discomfort not a 'cause' to it."[24]

> If philosophical aesthetics has until recently been ill-served by analytical philosophy, it is equally true that the topic of beauty has been ill-served by philosophical aesthetics. Everything that touches this area of our experience suffers from extreme fluidity of theory, and over the past seven hundred years the topic has pursued a course from absolute realism through subjectivism to a point of final evaporation.[25]

Subjectivism at the boiling point? Noxious vapors probably hover here. Vision blurs and the eyes water and burn. There may be no cure for this suffering "from extreme fluidity of theory." Maybe there is ptomaine in the mortar. Moribund masonry symptoms arising from a compulsion to wall in those threads through which flow the electric juices of the ever surprising.

NOTES

1. Bertrand Russell, *The Problems of Philosophy* (London: Oxford University Press, 1912), 75–76.
2. Wittgenstein, *Tractatus Logico-Philosophicus*, trans. D. F. Pears and B. F. McGuinness (London: Routledge and Kegan Paul, 1961), 147.
3. Charles Sanders Peirce, "Philosophy and the Sciences: A Classification," *Philosophical Writings of Peirce*, ed. Justus Buchler (New York: Dover, 1955), 62.
4. G. E. Moore, *Principia Ethica* (Cambridge: Cambridge University Press, 1993), 238.
5. Wittgenstein, *Lectures and Conversations* (Berkeley: University of California Press, 19[illegible]), 19
6. See my "Size Matters" for a discussion of Wagner-effect art.
7. Wittgenstein, *Lectures and Conversations*, 11.
8. Immanuel Kant, *A Critique of Pure Reason*, trans. Norman Kemp (New York: Modern Library, 1958), 110–11.
9. Wittgenstein, *Lectures and Conversations*, 18.
10. Ibid., 24.
11. Noam Chomsky, *Problems of Knowledge and Freedom* (New York: Pantheon, 1971), 9.
12. Kant, *Critique of Judgment*, trans. Werner S. Pluhar (Indianapolis: Hackett, 1987), 228.
13. Colin McGinn, *Ethics, Evil, and Fiction* (Oxford: Clarendon Press, 1997), 84.
14. Chomsky, *Rules and Representations* (New York: Columbia University Press, 1980), 27.
15. Semir Zeki, *Inner Vision* (New York: Oxford University Press, 2000).
16. Ibid.
17. René Descartes, "Optics," in *Descartes Selected Philosophical Writings* (Cambridge: Cambridge University Press, 1999), 58–59.
18. Robert D. Kaplan, *The Coming Anarchy* (New York: Random House, 2000), 22.
19. Clement Greenberg, "Avant-Garde and Kitsch," in *Art and Culture: Critical Essays* (Boston: Beacon Press, 1989), 8.
20. Wittgenstein, *Lectures and Conversations*, 7.
21. Ibid., 5.
22. Ferdinand de Saussure, *Cours de Linguistique General*, ed. T. de Mauro (Paris: Payot, 1985), 17–18.
23. Michael Dummett, *Origins of Analytic Philosophy* (Cambridge, Mass.: Harvard University Press, 1994), 132.
24. Wittgenstein, *Lectures and Conversations*, 14.
25. Anthony Savile, "Beauty: A Neo-Kantian Account," in *Essays in Kant's Aesthetics*, ed. Ted Cohen and Paul Guyer (Chicago: University of Chicago Press, 1982), 115.

SOLECISMS OF SIGHT: SPECULAR SPECULATIONS | 2001

I was informed that the Whitney's "Seminars with Artists" series were "designed to be informal" events. I apologize in advance for not conforming to this format but presenting instead a rather formal talk. The time has long since passed when I was capable of mumbling informally about my work before a group of people. Now I am reduced to mumbling from a script. But grizzled veterans such as myself require a crutch when on parade in public.

—ROBERT MORRIS, BEGINNING HIS SEMINAR CONDUCTED AT THE WHITNEY MUSEUM OF ART ON NOVEMBER 29, 2001, FOR THE EXHIBITION INTO THE LIGHT: THE PROJECTED IMAGE IN AMERICAN ART, 1964–1977, DURING WHICH HIS 1969 FILM FINCH COLLEGE PROJECT WAS RECREATED AND INSTALLED.

I don't know if I should show images of my 1969 *Finch College Project*, the work installed in the recent Whitney Museum exhibition *Into the Light: The Projected Image in American Art, 1964–1977*. To do so would run counter to the iconoclastic and iconophobic tenor of this work—a work that tried to get rid of the image, suppress it, remove it. Showing slides of this work would both revive and reduce the work to a visuality it wanted to shed. It was a work built around a process of installing and then stripping images from the wall. *FCP* degraded the image by doubling it with mirrors, and then projected the filmed memory of this back into the space, demoting the status of the image to that of an illusion which loses focus and density as it rotates in the space, further denaturing the iconic. The image is after all always too dangerous, too threatening, too irrational, too uncontainable, too freighted with ideological weight of one kind or another. Never mind that our consumption of imagery has grown at some shocking, demented, geometric rate since 1969 when I made the work installed here. All the more reason it has relevance today. Never mind that the underlying terror of imagery saturating this work—a terror motivating the striving for a kind of Talibanistic purity—nevertheless failed to achieve divine nothingness. But then something is always left over in the attempt to destroy the image. Some grease spot on the wall, some scar, some stain that will not wash away. In my case it was the 144 dots of tarry adhesive left on the walls.

But you will say, "Well, what about that stupid filmed image of workmen

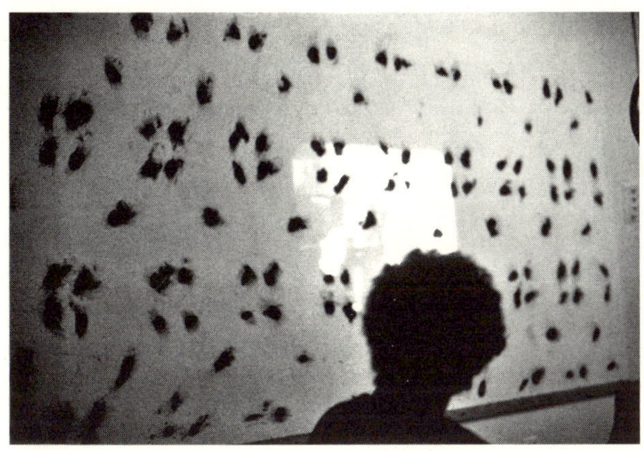

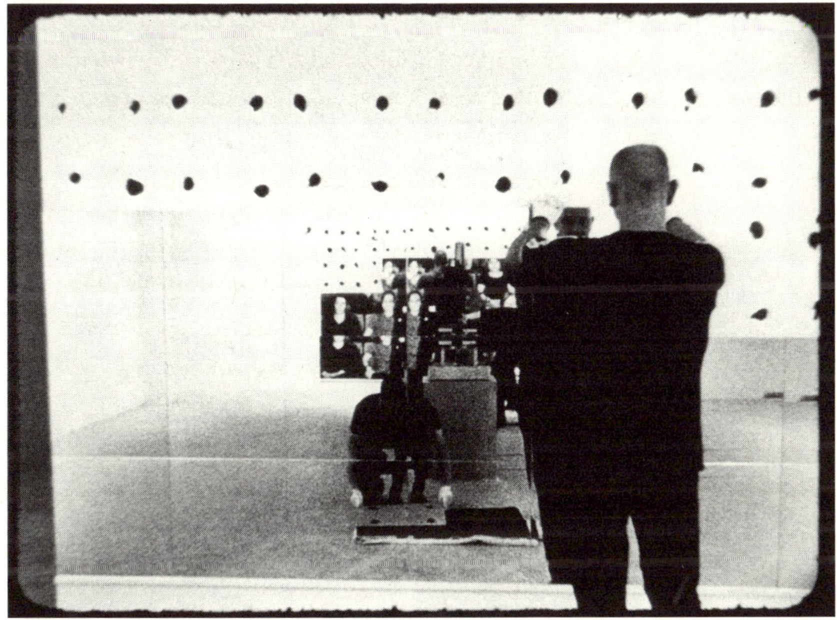

89. *Finch College Project*, 1969. 16mm projector, film, mirrors. Photo courtesy of Robert Morris.

90. *Finch College Project*, 2001 remake of a 1969 original. Installation at the Whitney Museum of Art, New York. Photo courtesy of Robert Morris.

putting up and taking down all that stuff? What about that image of the constantly widening and narrowing parallelogram of light revolving around the room, getting in the viewer's eyes and space and inducing a kind of nauseous vertigo of the iconic?" I have admittedly left some loose ends. Achieving the purity of nothingness, a total absence that defeats the tyranny of the image by vacuuming up every visual glitch, is no easy task. Smack it down here and it pops up there. Erase it from the left and it arises on the right. For us mortals, divine blindness can only be a goal toward which we strive.

If this work is then a failure in its intentions to achieve pure iconoclastic nothingness, does it, you might well ask, have any redeeming features? And, you will no doubt add, the intentions of the artist are of no consequence anyway.

Well, couldn't we begin here in the attempt to unpack this work by asking what influences might bear on it? I readily admit to two. Earlier I mentioned the word "vertigo," which is also the title of a 1958 Hitchcock film that impressed me when I saw it so long ago, and I think it partly informs this work. Leaving aside my affinity for Hitchcock's pessimism and misanthropy, I was even more attracted by his ability to at once deflate and promote the image, achieving a kind of simultaneous cancellation and elevation. Such negations, which left an indelible trace, resonated to my own ambitions at the time. And in *Vertigo* I was especially impressed with how Hitchcock loads and manipulates the image to create an illusory, irrational, delusional, and nauseating space. Always threatening in this film is that spinning, vertiginous, and irrational space which overpowers linguistic rationality. Or at least male linguistic rationality. And Hitchcock genderizes this space of illusion as feminine; a dangerous and threatening space in which the male's rational power might become lost. Even Jimmy Stewart's erect and commanding bodily presence is threatened by the spinning vortex of an illusory image that is perhaps not so much cast by the feminine as projected by the male. Add to this Hitchcock's fascination with the double. I wouldn't say my installation was exactly a homage to Hitchcock. But Hitchcock's play with doubling and cycles of concealing and revealing images that camouflage the abyss of his negativity was, let's say, a source of inspiration for that slow-motion vertigo I was attempting.

The other influence apparent in this work is, alas, that of Marcel Duchamp's *Rotoreliefs* of 1935, those disks, that when mounted on the old 78 rpm turntables imparted a vertiginous, pulsating animation to the images. (Sorry I can't make this spin, but take my word for it, when turning, the image achieves a startling, pulsating illusion of tumescence and detumescence as it revolves.)

I am not alone here in having been mesmerized by these spinning, pulsating disks that are perhaps more autistic than artistic. In any case acres of art in the 1960s and '70s can be traced back to the *Rotoreliefs*. I speak here of those tons of art structured on what I would call an "empiricism of the phenomenal," for which the illusionistic pulsation of the *Rotoreliefs* stands as prime for all the replicas they spawned. And here I class all art that lives by its phenomenological affect on the body or vision, whether it works in the literally illusionistic ways of the *Rotoreliefs* or in mere extended, less obvious ways, including ways that the art historian Michael Fried has characterized as "theatrical." But here we should make a distinction between two kinds of phenomenological art: that which stands in the space of painting, and that which molests the viewer's body and space. Strategies of the first kind apply to works that (a) pump up scale by enlargement and/or repetition of the image; and (b), like the *Rotoreliefs*, present a kind of hiccup of time, a brief, pulsation of looped repetition that for all intents and purposes is static, rather than presenting any syntactical, inflected temporal extension; and (c), do not molest the viewer's space; and (d) [related to c], demand a spatial address in which the viewer is perpendicular to the image on the wall. Such features (all four of them) have migrated almost no distance from that purely visual mode of address (a perceptual space actually) which painting demands.

Well, standing in front of a wall to read inscribed signs—whether scratched on rocks 35,000 years ago, or marked on canvas or illuminated by video projection or film—it is the same space. And if those signs on that wall (or walls) have no appreciable narrative development, it is the same space. And if the space of those signs delivers the viewer as unmoving body exercising eyes only, we are in the same space.

We have a different space when (a) the space of the viewer's body is invaded or when (b) he is provoked to movement or (c) his image becomes part of the work. Such difference is summed up with immense economy in one work in the *Into the Light* show. This is the Simone Forti work. Here the viewer does not stand staring at some gigantic pair of spinning balls (spare us the heavy symbolism), or at walls being visually slammed or vibrated with flickering, strobing projections. Rather, the Forti work promotes an intimate somatic connection to a work of quiet, ordinary bodily movement by provoking the viewer to move her own body in a nearly parallel way in order to be able to perceive the work. Forti's hologram depicting a simple bodily movement demands a reciprocal bodily movement of the viewer—she has to bend and rotate around the object if it is to be visible at all. I could speak at length on Forti's introduction of a

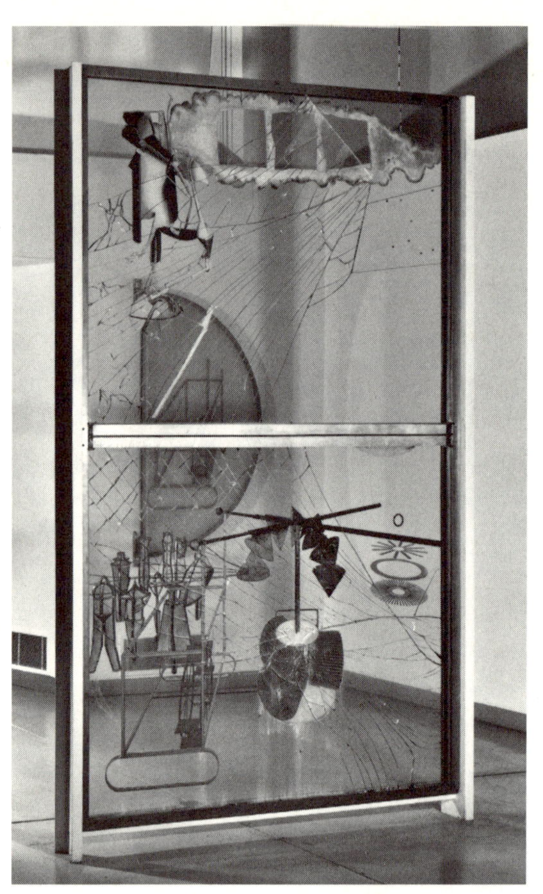

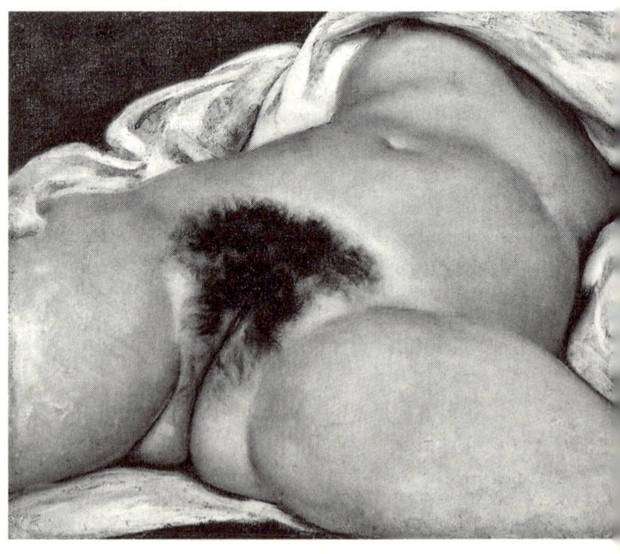

Wittgensteinian "ordinariness" that revolutionized dance in the early 1960s, but that is another story.

Let me return to my own work. A kinder judgment might be that this work presents on some level an allegory of loss and memory. The literal scene is the following: a cycle of working in which an audience is created on one side, a set of mirrors installed on the other, which eventually reflects the audience. A revolving camera witnesses this reflexivity of vision in which its own eye is caught. The film is developed and installed in a projector, which revolves as did the camera. The projected filmed image travels across the only remaining evidence of the actions, the dots of adhesive on the wall, remembering, you might say, what transpired in that space, what has been lost, stripped off. Not unlike the earlier *Box with the Sound of its Own Making* of 1961, this mnemonic obsession with loss and memory also structures *FCP*.

Not so fast, you might well say. Haven't we come across this repetitive event of "stripping" elsewhere? Wasn't there once even a bride "stripped bare," even? Here is Marcel Duchamp's *Bride Stripped Bare by Her Bachelors, Even*, often referred to as the *Large Glass*, which he worked on with an extremely limited output of labor from 1915 to 1923 when he declared it "definitively unfinished." The domain of the Bride is above, that of the Bachelors below. Duchamp's fanciful mechanical-erotic narrative describes how the Bachelors, those nine moldlike forms, produce a kind of gas while chanting a litany as the Glider oscillates. The gas is transmuted into spangles that transit the Sieves or cones. There are nine shots fired upward that pass through the mirrored Ocular Witness. The Bride's garment gets unhooked somehow amidst all this mechanical racket. A fairly feeble striptease is going on here. Maybe that is why Duchamp added the word "even" to the title.

Don't we arrive in your work of *FCP* at a kind of displaced stripping in which veils and garments are replaced by mirrors and photographs of a gawking audience? And what does this stripping off garments or audiences or mirrors amount to anyway?

Here is an earlier work, a Gustave Courbet of 1866 titled *The Origin of the World*. You see it here as it was originally displayed: hidden behind a green

---

91. Marcel Duchamp, *The Bride Stripped Bare by her Bachelors, Even (The Large Glass)*, 1915–23. Oil, varnish, lead foil, lead wire, and dust on two glass panels. Photo by Graydon Wood, courtesy of the Philadelphia Museum of Art: Bequest of Katherine S. Dreier, 1952. Copyright © 2006 Artists Rights Society (ARS), New York / ADAGP, Paris / Succession Marcel Duchamp.

92. Gustave Courbet, *The Origin of the World*, 1866. Oil on canvas. Musée d'Orsay, Paris, France.

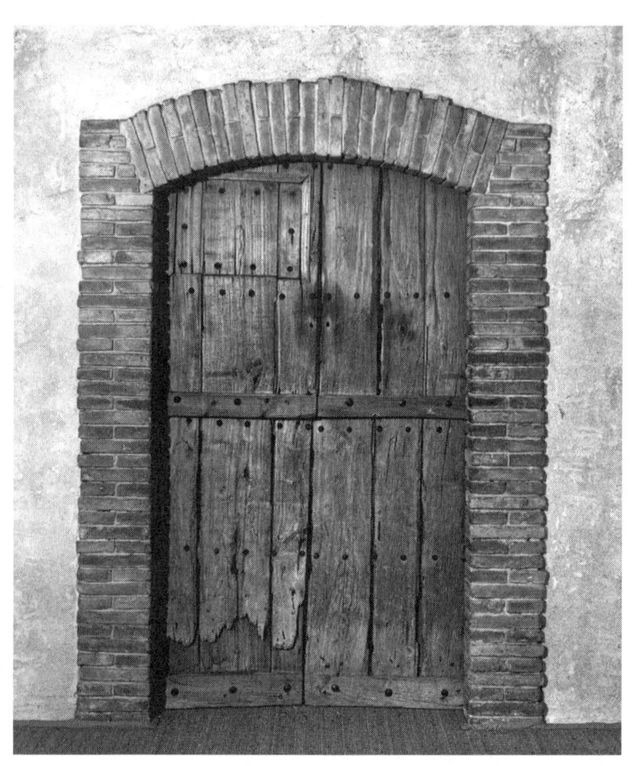

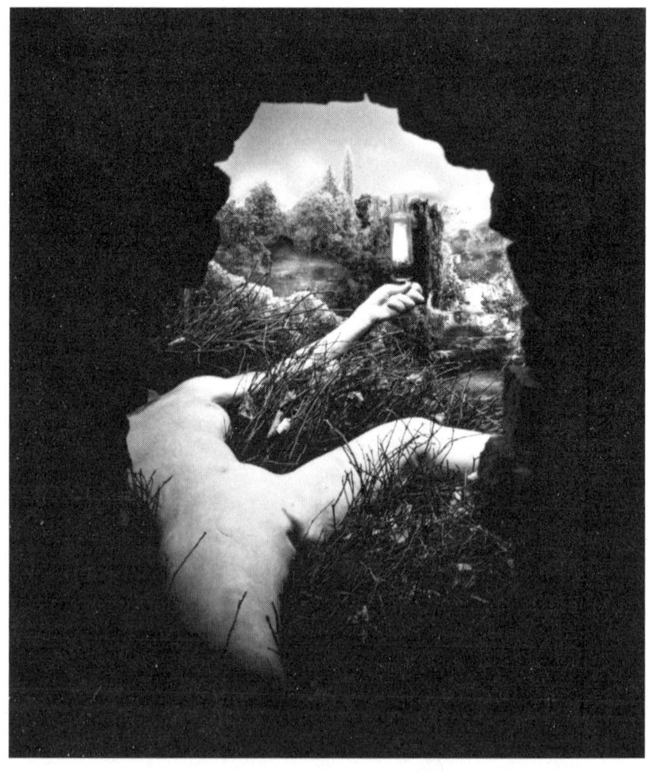

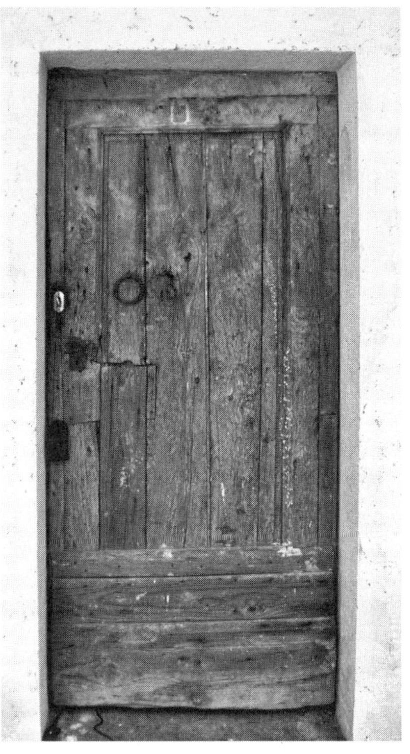

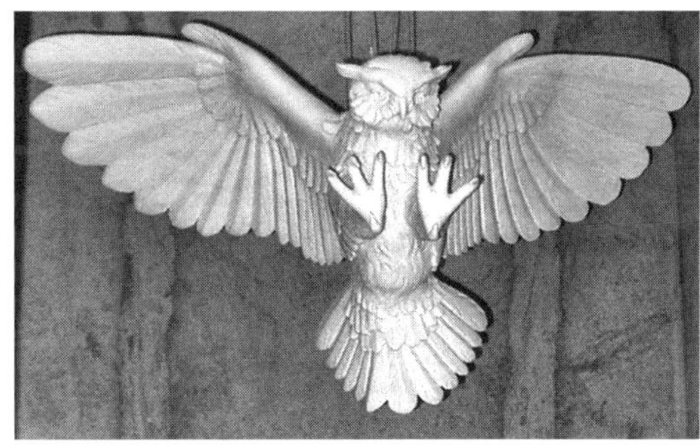

Opposite:

93. Marcel Duchamp, *Etant donnés* (exterior view of doors), 1946–66. Mixed-media assemblage. Photo courtesy of the Philadelphia Museum of Art: Gift of the Cassandra Foundation, 1969. Copyright © 2006 Artists Rights Society (ARS), New York / ADAGP, Paris / Succession Marcel Duchamp.

94. Marcel Duchamp, *Etant donnés* (interior view). Photo courtesy of the Philadelphia Museum of Art: Gift of the Cassandra Foundation, 1969. Copyright © 2006 Artists Rights Society (ARS), New York / ADAGP, Paris / Succession Marcel Duchamp.

Above:

95. *Hegel's Owl*, 2002. Detail (exterior view). Permanent site-specific installation in Parco della Padula in Carrara, Italy. Work commission by Pina and Giuliano Gori. Photo courtesy of Bill Schillinger.

96. *Hegel's Owl*, 2002. Detail (interior view). Photo courtesy of Bill Schillinger.

curtain or veil, while in the possession of its first owner. Later the work was concealed behind a panel representing a castle in the snow, so Fernand Léger once claimed. But I have no slide of this or of the subsequent panel made by André Masson that slid down to obscure the *Origin* when Jacques Lacan owned it after World War II.

Anyway, here it stands, or lies, revealed with the curtain removed. Removing an outer veil to find a more essential one perhaps? This stripping is usually something done by the guys of course. And what are they looking for underneath these veils?

Here is the last work of Marcel Duchamp, dated 1946–66. You are looking at the exterior of the work. Those weathered doors have two peepholes through which can be viewed this interior. That doesn't look like a female hand holding the lamp. What *are* these guys looking for beneath veils and behind closed doors? And what has been stripped away? What is the nature of this veiled image? Has a truer one appeared beneath the veil? Or is it rather a kind of mirror reflecting their own anxieties about that nothingness you spoke of before?

At least Courbet and Duchamp had their more or less colorful mirrors. Maybe all you have managed is a displaced, rather drab, black-and-white version of this little drama. You strip off the image and all you get is tar, which is "rat" spelled backward. In any case what does all this anxiety about the image—not to mention those mirrors, veils, removals, strippings, and nothingnesses that bother the guys so much—have to do with the ladies? Their understandable impatience and boredom here may be, in the last analysis, the unkindest cut of all.

But perhaps we are barking, or at least looking, up the wrong tree as it were. Perhaps it is that cycle of concealed and revealed images in *FCP* that we need to examine more closely. After all, no compulsive allegory of the stripping of the bride of art informs *FCP*. No naked ladies. In fact, it is hard to find anything in *FCP* informed by a longing for the aesthetic.

I think other anxieties are to be found in this work than those that inform modernist and postmodernist agendas allegorized by Duchamp and Courbet and played out endlessly by others across the last century. These other anxieties revolve around the audience whose presence is inevitably caught in the mnemonic filmed image revolving around the room in *FCP*. What is the significance of superimposing the unphotographed audience who enter the space of *FCP* onto the photographed one that already exists as an artifact within the filmed work—an artifact already partially defaced by its cycle of mirrored appearance and disappearance, concealment and revelation? Or described otherwise: Onto the artifactual audience sealed within *FCP*, one that already comes and goes in a vertiginous space, already doubled by its rotating mirror reflection, is superimposed a live audience whose coming and going, entering and leaving, appearing and disappearing become inextricably imbricated with the projected one. Why the play of these doppelgängers? Why this attempt to fold the site of art inside out by presenting what is generally outside the space of artmaking—i.e., that social body that comes to judge in that space of the subsequent? Why create a vacuum at the center of this work by displacing its focus to the periphery, to that space which more properly belongs to the observer? Why center this work around the coerced participation of its own viewers? Why this attempt to make visible that great blind spot at the center of the site of art, the always unseen audience? Why bring forward that bit of social body held decorously outside the studio door but forever present in the head of the artist? Why allow this transgression, this forbidden access, opening the space of the artmaking to these prying, witnessing eyes? Why hold up a series of mirrors that would deflect and reverberate vision across various spaces of sight and thought collapsing identity itself in a disorienting vertigo of doubling and reflexivity?

Here we leave behind those anticipatory strategies of stripping the muse to her nakedness, that striptease modernism and postmodernism never tied of. No allegorized bride of art waits hidden behind her veil in the center of this work. There is only the mirror reflecting back the viewer's stare. And then, finally, the mirror is removed, imploding vision or displacing it onto the naked, self-reflexive stares of the audience. *FCP* enacts a kind of vertiginous staggering backward into the arms of its witnesses. It collapses onto its audience, surrendering its narcissistic identity to an interrogating search among the bodies who constitute and animate the work—the social body itself.

Speaking here of the museum audience as a "bit of the social body" is not to Frankenstein it by performing any conceptual amputation. Rather it is to underline the fact that aesthetic matters encountered in museums tend to concern only a portion of the populace. Before we take a look at this social body so central to *FCP*, let me pause and momentarily change the subject.

Long ago, when I first showed with the Sonnabend Gallery in Paris, Ileana Sonnabend sat in her gallery and knitted constantly. When one day I asked her why, she replied that it gave her something to think about while she was talking. I just happen to have some truly idiotic images of *FCP* that I think I'll share with you. By excluding the viewing public these images cut the work off at the knees, but perhaps their very grotesqueness of misrepresentation will provide you with something to think about while I go on talking.

What, I would like to know, is to be asked of the social body that sometimes finds itself inside a museum? What does being inside a museum today do for or to it? Should the museum continue to shovel spectacle toward its insatiable appetite for entertainment? Will those lobotomized spectacles celebrating the democracy of the kitsch fetish that are repeatedly served up by the Guggenheim Museum, for example, serve to lessen the churning resentments of the social body? Will the events of September 11 cause anything more than a brief pause in its vertigo of resentments? Resentments of government, "of the rich, of the poor on welfare, of white-collar criminals, of street criminals, of drug dealers, of financial institutions, of taxes, of unions, of extravagantly paid executives, of the media, of health care providers, of child abusers, of date rapists, of pornographers, of prying journalists, of partisan prosecutors, of political action committees, of telemarketers, of militant feminists, of lawyers, of landlords, of auto repair shops, of public utilities, of teenage mothers, of absconding fathers, of corporations, of polluters, of environmentalists, of paperwork, of bureaucracy, of computers, of computer technicians, of people who have benefited from affirmative action (minorities and women especially), of people who have benefited from traditional favoritism (whites and men especially), of prisoners with access to weight-lifting equipment, of entrepreneurs who have prospered while their customers have remained poor, of homosexuals, of homophobes, of evangelists, of Muslims, of new-agers, of illegal aliens, of legal aliens," and, of course, of terrorists, to notice but a few of those resentments spinning around in the national vertigo of the social body.

In 1960, 58 percent of the national body "agreed that 'most people can be trusted'"; in 1994, only 35 percent did. From 1972 to 1997 the federal prison population increased from 196,000 to 1,159,000, nearly a sixfold increase. Adding local jail populations, the total was 1,726,000 behind bars in 1997. "Nearly one out of three black men in their twenties is currently under some form of penal supervision—prison, jail, probation, or parole. Between 1975 and 1998, the proportion of U.S. income received by the poorest 20 percent of the population declined 22 percent while that received by the wealthiest 5 percent increased 35 percent." These are quantifiable indices, but observable in more diffuse and anecdotal ways one sees countless incidents of "careless service, shoddy work, wasted time, scattered trash, and mindless consumption" trailing in the wake of the lurching social body. The children have of course not been neglected. "One out of ten women between the ages of fifteen and nineteen became pregnant in 1996, the last year studied. This rate was twice that of England and Canada and ten times that of the Netherlands and Japan. Approximately one-third of all children born in the U.S. and three-quarters of black children are born out of wedlock. Most fathers of these children assume no responsibility for their care or support. To the limited extent that anyone can measure this closeted phenomenon, child abuse has increased. . . . The juvenile homicide rate in 1997 was twice what it had been in 1985. . . . In 1997, 1998, and 1999—teenagers and one preteenager in Mississippi, Kentucky, Pennsylvania, Oregon, Colorado, and Georgia brought firearms to school and began to fire at random, killing twenty-six students and three teachers, and wounding sixty-nine others in the seven incidents." Prior to 1997 there were no deaths caused by school shootings. "Between 1982 and 1996, the number of children in foster care grew by 93 percent. Since 1970, the percentage of teens and children who are overweight has increased approximately 150 percent. One high school student in five reports that she has seriously contemplated suicide within the past year, and the number of suicides among young people has tripled since the 1950s."[1]

Clearly the social body today carries more wounds than half a century ago.[2] In 1969 *FCP* backed into the arms of a slightly more innocent audience. As that bit of social body cast its vision across the pox of tarry dots on the walls, anxieties about terrorist variola would have been far from its thoughts. But today it is more wounded, more anxious, and more distracted. Perhaps even its somewhat callow narcissisms and feckless optimism is also beginning to fade, making room for the possibility of a certain self-criticism that it never felt much need of before. Although there seems to be little evidence that the American social body has, since September 11, begun to cast glances of self-inquiry at itself. But then nothing submerges such introspection like the rumble of patriotism. And, as Dr. Johnson once noted, nothing works like patriotism for fashioning a secure refuge for the scoundrel.

The doubled audience of *FCP*—that section of social body composed of both the actual and the artifactual—hover, circulate, fade, and reconstitute themselves at the heart of this work today just as three decades ago. That intersection between the rotations of the fading and reappearing, of the concealing and revealing, of the artifactual audience confronting the live witnesses (unfortunately excised from these images), who stage their own vertigo of spatial entrances and exits, constitutes the endless cycles of *FCP*. And today *FCP* rematerializes to mirror their complex, questioning, direct, and reflected glances at themselves and at one another across the spaces of this work, glances that are today more haunted than those of thirty-two years ago.

Was FCP driven by a recursive strategy, one in which art as an act of presentation is cancelled and rewritten, or reframed, in terms of the act of reception? It could then be described as a kind of vacuum waiting to be activated by the viewer. But allegations that the artist was driven by an anxiety to embrace the audience seem both utopian and misguided. The chasm between the artist and his audience can of course never be bridged. This is not due to some lamentable alienation of the artist. This gap may be due, partly, to the disjunctive nature of communication itself, which is always hit or miss, more or less. But then again, the agendas of artmaking may have very little to do with communication. As for utopian thoughts in 1969. . . . Well, it was a time when fire hoses and dogs were being set against African Americans; national leaders, Civil Rights workers, and college students were being murdered; and a criminal war was being prosecuted in Southeast Asia. Resistance, not utopia, was the order of the day.

Questions without answers continue to circulate within the slow-motion vertigo of FCP. Although any questions echoing there now about relations between the art and its historical moment of thirty-two years ago are academic. Is that bit of social body wandering through FCP today (so painfully absent in these slides) seeking a few minutes of distraction, entertainment, reassurance, aesthetic massage, or more of the same old museum spectacle? My intuition is that it is seeking much more. I suspect that today it is looking for something that has not yet been said, or seen, as the case may be. Something that will speak, in ways we can't yet imagine, to the pressure of those new dislocations now wrenching the formerly insular, first-world, American social body. Wrenching it into a new single but multipolar world where there is now no place to hide.

NOTES

1. Quotations and statistics from Albert W. Alschuler's *Law without Values: The Life, Work, and Legacy of Justice Holmes* (Chicago: University of Chicago Press, 2000), 187–90.
2. "Wounded" may be too mild a term. Alschuler's descriptions and statistics of the American social body can be read in darker ways. Samuel P. Huntington sees "moral decline, cultural suicide, and political disunity in the West" as evidenced by: "(1) increases in antisocial behavior, such as crime, drug use, and violence generally; (2) family decay, including increased rates of divorce, illegitimacy, teen-age pregnancy, and single-parent families; (3) at least in the United States, a decline in 'social capital,' that is, membership in voluntary associations and the interpersonal

trust associated with such membership; (4) general weakening of the 'work ethic' and rise of a cult of personal indulgence; (5) decreasing commitment to learning and intellectual activity, manifested in the United States in lower levels of scholastic achievement." See Samuel P. Huntington, *The Clash of Civilizations and the Remaking of World Order* (New York: Simon and Schuster, 1996), 304.

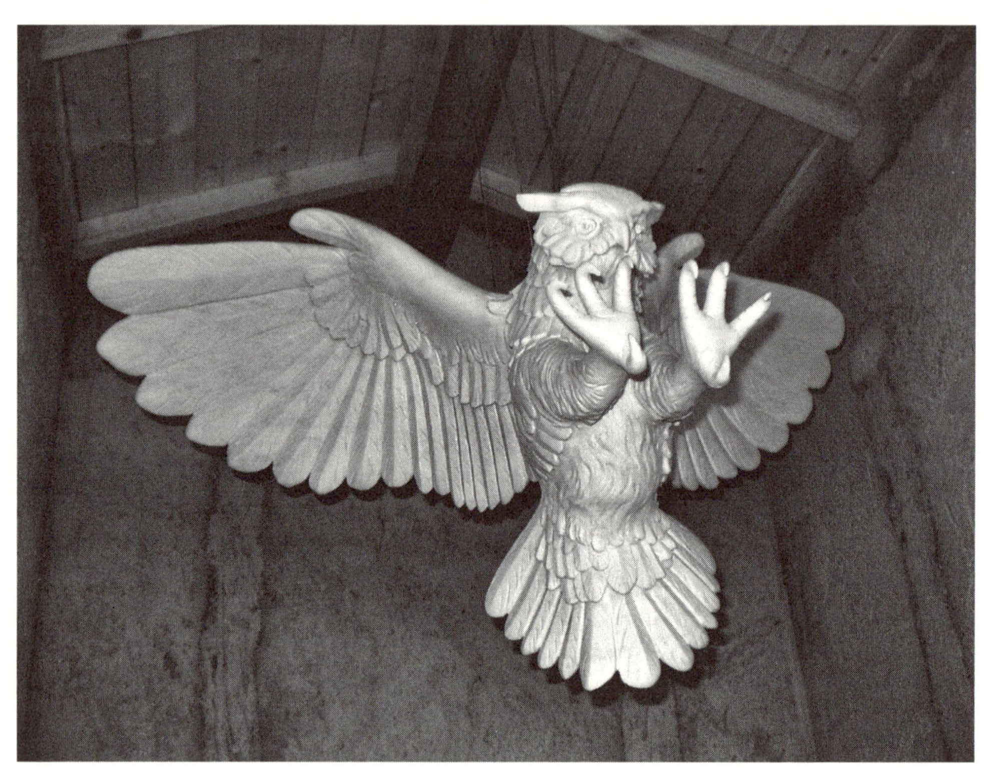

THOUGHTS ON *HEGEL'S OWL* | 2002

Why work outside? Isn't nature enough? How about the chaos of modern development? What does art add to either the fullness of the natural order or the spectacle of human disorder? George Mallory justified the climbing of Mount Everest "because it is there." Carl Andre once said he made art "because it is not there." But don't questions of value, both aesthetic and moral, hover at the edges of every impulse to put something where there was once not that thing? Traditionally these questions about permissibility are not asked. Art, being one of man's longest endeavors, just happens. Its appearance is justification enough. But we reach a new divide here on the cusp of the twenty-first century. A divide where more things are questioned. As Noam Chomsky put it, "It's part of moral progress to be able to face things that once looked as if they weren't problems." Is the luxury of art to be permitted when for the first time we seriously begin to ask ourselves whether the human may have been a fatal mutation. The earth itself seems on the verge of irreparable ruin. Or is it the case, *pace* Chomsky, that we in the West now see problems where before we only saw opportunities? Hasn't our idea of the "universal" been a hopelessly local Western outlook all along? The chilling thing is, we have no real answers to the problems we face or the questions we pose to ourselves. So much for the vestiges of a guiding Enlightenment rationality. But of course the argument is that art was never a rational endeavor and its goals were of another order. But it is just this other order—one in which the aesthetic makes no move toward the moral that looks ever more feeble and irrelevant.

Once upon a time in modernism (and not so long ago) the story was told that outside art, so-called public art, could, by virtue of its formal permutations, touch some "universal" aesthetic chord in the viewer. But such a story is but another of the fairy tales narrated by an optimistic modernism. It joins those of economic and psychic liberation told by Marx and Freud.

Hegel's Owl perhaps subsides into just another outside art amusement of which there seems to be no end in sight. Just more irrelevant aesthetic tonnage

---

97. *Hegel's Owl*, 2002. Detail (interior view). Photo courtesy of Bill Schillinger.

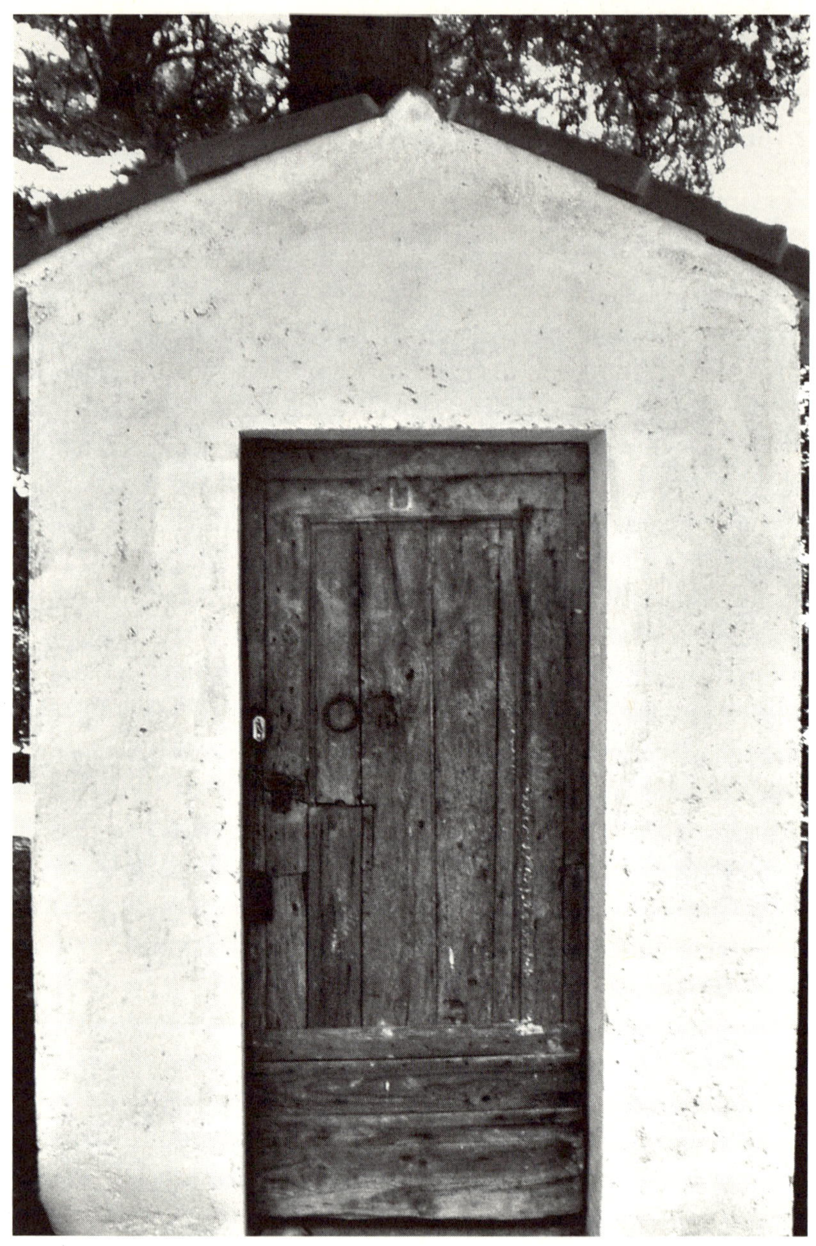

98. *Hegel's Owl*, 2002. Detail (exterior view). Photo courtesy of Bill Schillinger.

burdening the earth and providing a distracting moment to out-of-breath viewers who tramp the landscape looking for the aesthetic thrill. Still *Hegel's Owl* offers no monumental scale with which to awe. *Hegel's Owl* offers no special fit to a given, site-specific landscape. In fact its presence is characterized by no extroverted, confident assertion of "form" for its own sake. Rather it addresses the fading light of dusk when objects begin to lose their palpable physical presence and unambiguous identity. *Hegel's Owl* occupies that anxious hour "between the dog and the wolf." *Hegel's Owl* celebrates no physical monument but rather addresses itself to interior questions. To "see" *Hegel's Owl* is to stop looking at the monument in its landscape and peer into an interior gloom. It shuts out that physical world we never tire of trying to ruin in the name of progress. Squint your eyes, peer into the interior dimness. Does a question form itself? Does this question abrade and reverse the smooth flow of perception that was there an instant ago?

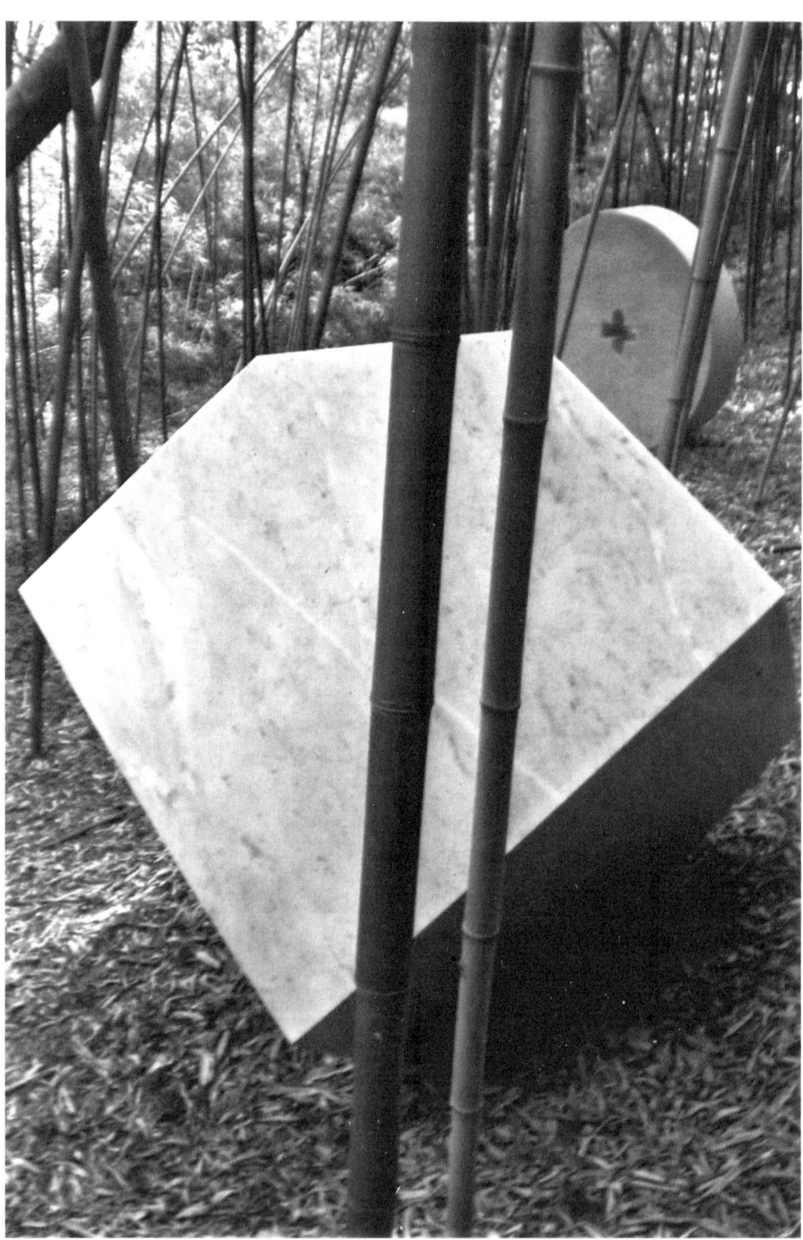

MAYBE THE ANGEL IN DÜRER | 2003

Maybe the angel in Dürer's print is blind. Maybe the angel could feel around the landscape for the polyhedron, the sphere, the mill wheel, the bell. But what would the angel learn? Vision is not the issue in this image, it seems to me. Anyway not literal seeing. The angel stares off into space. Unseeing or blind. Maybe the angel is thinking. But we would not know what such thoughts are about. We humans are, according to Chomsky, somewhere on a scale between rats and angels. A rat could not solve a maze requiring the application of prime numbers. So why should we have answers to questions about the self, the mind/body relation, consciousness, a priori knowledge, etc.? And would we really want to know what the angel knows about these things? We should be satisfied with our blindness about such questions. But of course we are not. Anymore than the angel is satisfied with not having answers to those unimaginable questions angels ask. The angel's is a superior brand of blindness. Melancholia is the condition of mourning for answers that don't arrive—on whatever level the questions might be asked. Let the relations between disc, polyhedron, and sphere stand as allegory for relations between sets of questions without answers—whatever level these might exist on. Off in the distance a bat holds the scrolled inscription "Melencolia"—thought flying blind, mocking the angel who sits immobile, the tools surrounding him/her (I don't think this angel has a sex, or is both) abandoned. We are witnessing a scene of great restraint: the angel sits passively and blind. Universes might collapse in fiery implosion should the angel lose its patience and actually act. Wouldn't we like to think. Wouldn't we like to think the massive physique beneath that robe was a metaphor for potentiality. But look again. Dürer went deeper. There is only mockery here. Mockery of the great Other. Or rather mockery of our impulse to extend authority to the Other. Mockery of our incorrigible compulsion to first dream up the Other and then endow him with power. Dürer mocks transcendence itself in the image of this hulking incompetent sitting passively, surrounded

---

99. *Melencolia II*, 2002. Detail. Permanent site-specific installation. Collaboration with Claudio Parmiggiani. Collection of Giuliano Gori, Fattoria di Celle, Santomato, Pistoia, Italy. Photo courtesy of Bill Schillinger.

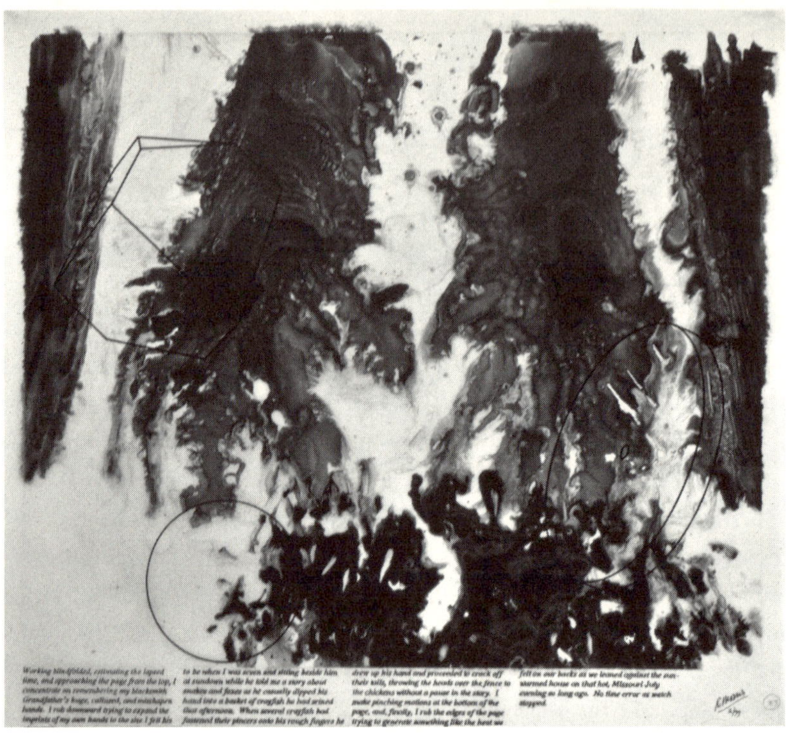
Working blindfolded, estimating the lapsed time, and approaching the page from the top, I concentrate on remembering my blacksmith Grandfather's huge, callused, and misshapen hands. I rub downward trying to expand the imprints of my own hands to the size I felt his to be when I was seven and sitting beside him at sundown while he told me a story about snakes and foxes as he casually dipped his hand into a basket of crayfish he had seined that afternoon. When several crayfish had fastened their pincers onto his rough fingers he drew up his hand and proceeded to crack off their tails, throwing the heads over the fence to the chickens without a pause in the story. I make pinching motions at the bottom of the page, and, finally, I rub the edges of the page trying to generate something like the heat we felt on our backs as we leaned against the sun-warmed house on that hot, Missouri July evening so long ago. No time error as watch stopped.

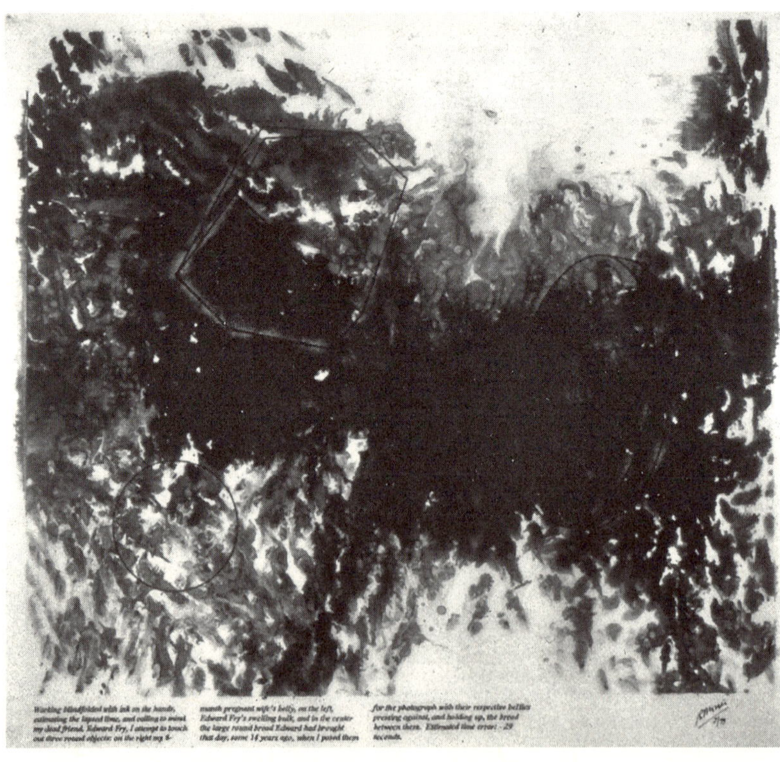
Working blindfolded with ink on the hands, estimating the lapsed time, and calling to mind my dead friend, Edward Fry, I attempt to touch out three round objects: on the right my 8-month pregnant wife's belly, on the left, Edward Fry's swelling bulk, and in the center the large round bread Edward had brought that day, some 14 years ago, when I posed them for the photograph with their respective bellies pressing against, and holding up, the bread between them. Estimated time error: -29 seconds.

by scattered tools he doesn't know how to use, staring blindly into space. This strapping angel can make sense of nothing, make use of nothing, get off his butt and do anything. The dividers, the balance, the hourglass, the carpentry tools, the ladder, the nails—these will wait for all eternity for this brainless ox of an angel to act. The image is subversive in the extreme. Melancholia is the condition of never learning, of being taken in by our own inflated hopes. Melancholia is the condition of expectation. Melancholia is the bet placed on the long shot. Of course the most melancholy condition imaginable would be no more horse races, no more making fun of angels.

On the drawings I always started with the sphere, the polyhedron, and the disc. I traveled from one to the other in my blindness, learning nothing. I am always reduced in the *Blind Time* drawings to my lowest levels. Groping and pathetic, absent the illusions of sight. Fragmented and spastic, absent the illusions of wholeness. Subhuman, beneath the angel's suffocating skirt. And freed into a chthonic realm where it is easy to hold my breath. Freed to act outside of expectations set for the enterprise by others. Freed to feel for my darker lump of being.

White marble and bamboo and the steep ravine. A dim but visible scene. The bell is reassuring, and it makes a bell-like sound. The anxiety between the five objects is mild. And the available names reassure. Maybe a certain smug nominalism prevails, but there are no dark lumps lying around. I can still hear the echo of the conversation with Parmiggiani. The suffocation of blindness does not threaten. No bat flits through the bamboo with inaudible screams of warning. It is of course possible that Kesselring walked the ravine sixty years ago with dried blood on his boots. We know he was in the area and we know what he did. But *Melencolia II* commemorates no past atrocity. Nor does it mark any site of angelic blindness. The angel has long ago taken leave of the site with a smirk. And that's a relief. There is air here and a certain filtered light and the earth is soft underfoot. It is quiet and contemplative. There are no inhuman demands placed upon us here. That sudden drop of soft, heavy blindness, that suffocating weight of the angel's skirt falling over our breathing does not threaten here. Neither threat nor mockery presides at this site because we have banished that overbearing lout of an angel.

---

100. *Blind Time V: Melancholia*, 1999. Ink on paper, 29½ × 27 inches (74.93 × 68.58 cm). Private collection, New York. Photo courtesy of Bill Schillinger.

101. *Blind Time V: Melancholia*, 1999. Ink on paper, 29 × 30 inches (74.30 × 76.20 cm). Collection of the artist. Photo courtesy of Bill Schillinger.

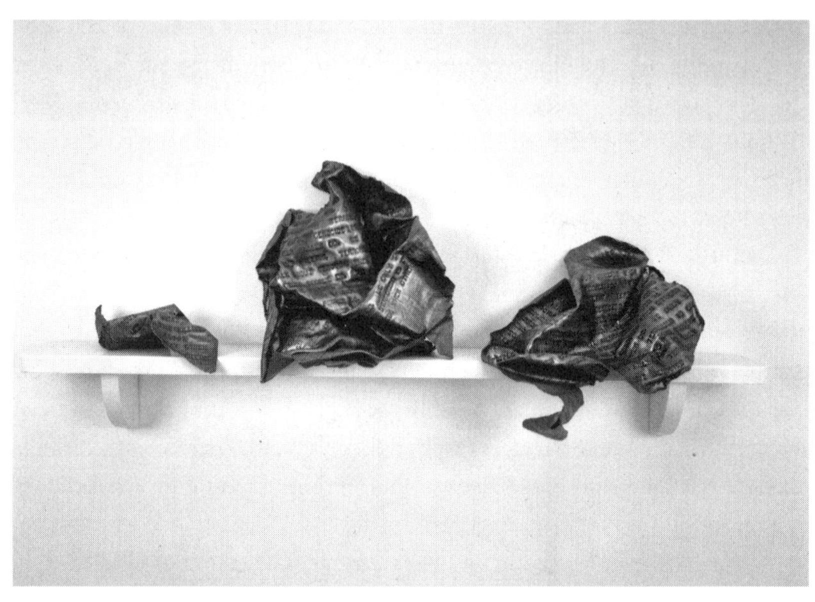

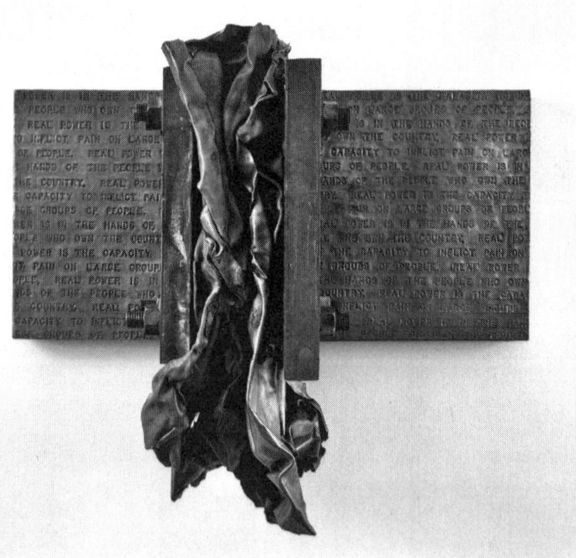
REAL POWER IS THE
OF PEOPLE. REAL POWER
HANDS OF THE PEOPLE
THE COUNTRY. REAL POWER
CAPACITY TO INFLICT PAI
GROUPS OF PEOPLE.
IS IN THE HANDS OF
WHO OWN THE COUNT
POWER IS THE CAPACITY
PAIN ON LARGE GROUP
REAL POWER IS IN
OF THE PEOPLE WHO
COUNTRY. REAL
CAPACITY TO INFLICT
CAPACITY TO INFLICT PAIN ON LARGE
THE CAPACITY TO INFLICT PAIN ON
GROUPS OF PEOPLE.

FROM A CHOMSKIAN COUCH: THE IMPERIALISTIC UNCONSCIOUS | 2003

Dr. Chomsky sits impassively behind the black leather couch. I lie down. Minutes pass in silence. I look up at the sign on the wall that reads It's part of moral progress to be able to face things that once looked as if they weren't problems.[1] *I imagine a faint smile crossing the lips of the doctor. He uncrosses his legs and recrosses them. And to help me along, says . . .*

Dr. C: There need be no objects in the world that correspond to what we talk about, even in the simplest cases, nor does anyone believe there are.[2] A lexical term provides us with a certain range of perspectives for viewing what we take to be things in the world, or what we conceive in other ways. . . . The terms themselves do not refer . . .[3]

Me: Okay, Doc, I'll just say what comes into my mind as I recline here on your couch. What could the perspectives be to the phrase *A century of unimaginable violence?* Or should the question be, What are yours? since mine might very well be different. Century? Unimaginable violence? The terms are too diffuse, general, multiple, and complex for any expectation of a common reference. Reference is not needed for language to work. And meaning may not be produced by truth, or even use. Meaning may be innate, presupposed by the concatenation of the sentence. And isn't the ethical connected to this thought? Aren't we anxious to be right about things? And does the aesthetic underlie this? Or is the aesthetic supervenient on the ethical? Or are the ethical and the aesthetic inseparably entangled, as well as basic? Have we reached bedrock yet?

Silence again. Then Dr. C reminds me of some words of Charles Sanders Peirce

---

102. *Noamian Fragments*, 2002. Lead, 16 ½ × 47 ½ × 11 inches (41.91 × 120.65 × 27.94 cm) overall. Collection of Leo Castelli Gallery, New York. Photo courtesy of Robert Morris.

103. *Squeeze*, 2002. Lead, 20 × 24 × 12 inches (50.80 × 60.96 × 30.48 cm). Collection of Leo Castelli Gallery, New York. Photo courtesy of Robert Morris.

who he notes in passing was crazier and smarter than either of us could ever hope to be. He quotes at me from memory:

Dr. C: Aesthetics is the science of ideals, or of that which is objectively admirable without any ulterior reason. . . . Ethics, or the science of right and wrong, must appeal to aesthetics for aid in determining the *summum bonum*.[4]

Me: In the dream there was Duchamp's *Given: 1. The Waterfall, 2. The Illuminating Gas* . . . But the liquid fall was of blood and the illumination that of a metal behaving like a gas and moving faster than anything in the universe. By mid-twentieth century both holocaust and nuclear detonation had shaded the usual perspectives. And in retrospect, what perspective is to be taken on the American work of art in the first years of the twenty-first century? And what aesthetic does the ethical now appeal to here on the edge of the millennium?

Dr. C: It may be expected that conscious beliefs will form a scattered and probably uninteresting subpart of the full cognitive structure.[5]

Me: From Charles Wilson Peal's *Exhuming of the Mastodon* to the Twin Towers: the evolution of the **Mega Image** (MEGIG), the sublime that begins in the "natural world" of a vast new continent. Allegories of a certain **American Phenomenological Awe** (AMPHENA) repeated endlessly. Tall tales, railroads, vast western spaces, gold rushes, gunfighters, all to be balanced by an aesthetic prescription for gigantism in art. From Gutzon Borglum to Robert Smithson, Frederic Church to Michael Heizer, John Ford to Bruce Nauman. If Mount Palomar chagrins James Turrell, what do the Twin Towers tell us of Mark di Suvero? We approach cautiously here beneath the shadow of an urge. Dangerous territory. Artists in berets equipped for secret ops. Standing at attention, ready for aesthetic assaults. No, it's a dream, another bad Schwarzenegger movie on too large a screen. One of those exploding patriotic docudramas. Good art wouldn't be so . . . unconscious. Artists wouldn't *enlist*, would they? Artists don't *serve*. Artists aren't dragged down by the past. Anyway America doesn't have a past, only a future. And AMPHENA? Well, you've got to make yourself heard in a culture of spectacle. Can't blame anybody for that. Then that 9/11 spectacle. Big art event, so Karlheinz Stockhausen claimed. Well, a German said it, not one of us. Super spectacle. No getting around that. When the dust settled, as it is still doing, American art somehow looked different.

Dr. C: Now you're cranking.

Me: Everybody knows what Dr. Johnson said so long ago—patriotism is the last refuge of the scoundrel. But haven't we all been patriots in this vast land? No, that's not the right way to put it. Things are more elusive, more . . . unconscious. Something vast stands behind us. We are obliged to stand tall. It looms behind us and we hear it on rare occasions like the roll of summer thunder. It is something large and we sense it is there even though we never see it directly. We hear only the rumble of blurred words. But America presents only . . . its great variety. So great a variety it can be said to own no reference. Anything so vast, so greatly varied, eludes reference. To begin a sentence, *America is* . . . is to feel oneself step off into empty space. And when the bunting is taken down and the band has gone home power vanishes behind the marble facade. Or around a corner like Mack the Knife. But art was listening while the band was playing, tapping its foot . . . unconsciously.

Dr. C: Let me deal with the unconscious. Just talk.

Me: The ideology of the monumental. From Frederic Church to Richard Serra. The numbing sublime. From nature to abstract art. The Wagner effect.[6] Overwhelming the human scale. Self-importance and grandiloquence. In classical times monumental art was in the service of military victories. Now the U.S. is the dominant world power, the planetary imperial force. A nation where bigger was always better. And today the monuments are to what? Today, at the beginning of the twenty-first century, the idea of justifying the monumental in purely formal terms reeks of that blind ideology of art as autonomous, uninfected by the culture that produces it. Large abstract art is of course the most deluded example of such modernist denials. Spectacle is dedicated to avoiding consciousness and is always transporting in delivering the phenomenological ride. AMPHENA is always dedicated to forgetting. And there is always that spot of residue in large contemporary works of art. It feels like a bit of grit in the eye of memory.

Dr. C: Is this criticism or confession?

Me: Is there a difference?

Dr. C: You may be beyond help.

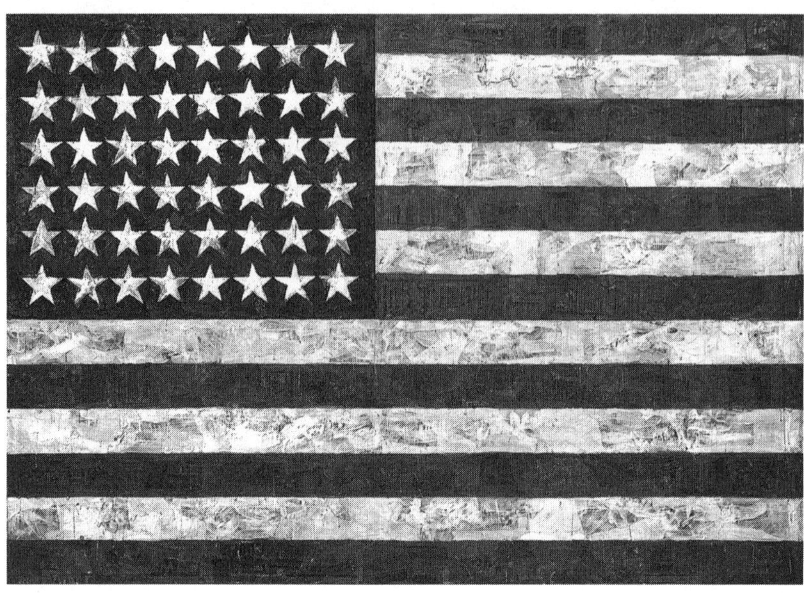

104. Jasper Johns, *Flag*, 1954–55. Encaustic on fabric mounted on plywood, 42¼ × 60⅝ inches (107.3 × 154 cm). The Museum of Modern Art, New York: Gift of Philip Johnson in honor of Alfred H. Barr, Jr. Copyright © Jasper Johns/Licensed by VAGA, New York.

Me: The challenge of ambitious American art since the mid-twentieth century was to be up to the task of producing cultural icons befitting a world empire. What makes Jackson Pollock's canvases function as banners for an empire? First, their implicit defeat of European painting; second, their focus on energy to sustain the agonistic triumph; and, third, their pragmatism in harnessing process. Besides the large-scale requirement, these characteristics—the agonistic, the energetic and the pragmatic—have remained requirements of ambitious American art regardless of genre affiliations. A pessimistic attitude, always judged anti-American, has generally disqualified, but if writ large, even a Claes Oldenburg could be run up the flagpole.

The exception in the last half of the twentieth century to official American icons of the big, the loud and/or energetic was the work of Jasper Johns, who almost never worked on a monumental scale. But then there were the iconic American flags and maps. His work, always filled to the seams with ambivalence, was never pessimistic. More significantly, he was the most historically pregnant American artist of the last century. Johns rewrote Pollock's pragmatism of material process into one of logical structure. Beginning with his influence on Frank Stella, Johns's lessons in the pragmatism of the structural device that unfolded to complete the work also made minimal art possible. Johns, the cold-eyed strategist, was nothing if not agonistic toward European art—but with such European elegance. It was as if General Erwin Rommel had switched sides to give demonstrations on how to achieve victory by eschewing material and energy for strategic logic. As much code breaker as strategist, Johns the cryptologist general stood as the paradigmatic American aesthetic cold warrior of the 1950s and early '60s. No other American artist of the last century emblematizes the aggressivity of the unconscious imperialistic impulse more than Johns. Miniaturizing while the others bloated up scale, he demonstrated that with the right signs you could have the right stuff and finesse scale. The national flag General Johns marched under was large in every way but size. If Johns was the ultimate aesthetic cold warrior he was hardly responsible for the burgeoning manifestations of imperial-sublime art. Abstract expressionism of the '50s proclaimed a near religious faith in both abstraction and large scale. Johns denied both tenets of the doxology. Looking back at abstract expressionism today a kind of self-hypnosis is required. Without being possessed by a quasi-religious stupor those stained and painted acreages of Clyfford Still, Barnett Newman, Jackson Pollock, Franz Kline, and Robert Motherwell appear vapid and inane. Only Ad Reinhardt, the most politically aware and active of all of them (signing every petition, appearing in every civil rights and anti-Vietnam march), had the consciousness to resist the rhetorical, all-American, self-congratulatory monumental scale which continues down to today, that American art of the imperialistic unconscious (IMPUNC).

Dr. C: There you go again with that word . . . but there were precedents to numbing scale.

Me: Well, there was Albert Speer.

Dr. C: And his proposed *Hall of the Volk* for the Third Reich . . .

Me: Sixteen times the size of St. Peter's in Rome. But let's get back to some really big American art. In the '60s earth art recapitulated the conquest of the West as an aesthetic allegory. Expansion into space is the growth of empire. Space is never free but acquired by aggressive occupation. Space is one of the commodities the planet is running out of. To have it locked up in large-scale art speaks of luxury and excess. The art of grand spaces from Rome to the Third Reich to Bilbao all speaks of empire. Michael Heizer's grandiose *City* in the desert may be the most demented and blatant metaphor yet for the IMPUNC gesture.

Dr. C: The Grand Inquisitor is articulating the view that freedom is dangerous and people need, and indeed at some level even want, subordination, mystery, authority, and so on.[7]

Me: Aggressively large-scale, grand spatial occupation, the buzz of spectacle. A long list could be drawn up. From Pollock and Newman on down to Stella, di Suvero, Heizer, Turrell, Kelly, Serra. From Andy Warhol's yard goods of camouflage to Jeff Koons's flowering puppies. From Chuck Close to Jeff Wall, plus all that screaming big screen video from Bruce Nauman to Bill Viola . . . the list goes on . . .

Dr. C: Hmmm, all males so far . . .

Me: . . . and, just wait, includes virtually all ambitious American art regardless of genre. By this point the aesthetic strategies that can be combed out of this work yield little more than art lint. But a meaning leaks from the MEGIG at the unconscious level of desire—a desire to limn a metaphorical sign for American power. As Edmund Burke noted long ago, allegories of the sublime are always ultimately political. Our version of the sublime valorizes neither nature nor revolution but rather that peculiarly American status quo of domination and blindness. A refusal of memory and the other is to be expected from such an unconscious enterprise that asserts the present as the only temporal dimension: a depthless phenomenological now where awe and entertainment encircle one another.

Dr. C: And those few examples of miniaturization that run counter to your thesis—those forays into a bioart of invisible microbes and viruses?

Me: I'm not saying that the MEGIG is completely unopposed. But in the last few years we have seen a surfeit of large, multimedia installations (Ann Hamilton, Matthew Barney, and others) and multiscreen video installations (Nauman, Viola, Douglas Aitken, and others). In these genres the MEGIG has expanded to a kind of multisensory spectacle in which viewers are engulfed. Here they are no longer independent observers so much as passive particles floating within the sublime surround. Installation art of the spectacle has moved far beyond those forms of theatricality that used to keep Michael Fried up at night.[8]

If conceptual art wanted to give up the object in favor of the word, **multi-screen video installations** (MUSCRVIT) and multimedia **installation art of the spectacle** (INARSE) gives it up in favor of an expanded, multisensory theatrical space. A different perceptual space actually. The object, or even the single screen of projected imagery, delivers a single perceptual focus. MUSCRVIT and INARSE deliver a more peripheral, pulsating multifocus—a space of de-differentiation. Here our attempt at focusing must give way to the vacant, all-embracing stare.[9] Of course this perceptual space is not without precedent. Giambattista Tiepolo's vast painted ceilings, impossible to take in from a single point of view, touch on the dedifferentiated space. But we must look to cubism's shattered surfaces to find the first modernist attempt to systematically disrupt representation from being encompassed by either proximate or distal vision. MUSCRVIT literalizes this by temporal and spatial expansions. And by foregrounding this fracture of focus MUSCRVIT attempts to solve that problematic of what to do with time. The hiccup in time of the looped repetition, or the heavy-footed recording of "real time," the two strategies pioneered by single screen video, were failures. What was so massively boring on the single screen (which, in fact, still occupies the perceptual space of painting)—lives far better in a space of dedifferentiated focus provided by MUSCRVIT.

Dr. C: So MUSCRVIT gets to it better than INARSE?

Me: Sometimes you get INARSE with MUSCRVIT in the same place.

Dr. C: Sounds like the old neuritis and neuralgia. But what about the IMPUNC?

Me: We're talking large-scale here. That plus the passivity required of the viewer of INARSE and MUSCRVIT make them divine vehicles for the IMPUNC. You could say that INARSE is the very emblem of the IMPUNC. Rome had the Colosseum and we have the Dia.

Dr. C: You mentioned conceptual art. Wasn't it an exception to the case you are making?

Me: In the beginning when it said no to modernism, but by now conceptual art has seeped into everything. Now there is a version of it you might call *Conceptual Folk Art*, a rubric that covers bread bakers, tattooers, back rubbers, body huggers, quilters, feet washers, masochists of self-inflicted suffering . . .

Dr. C: That sounds like body art . . .

Me: *Body Art!* The first bad body art was the Crucifixion, Smithson used to say.

Dr. C: But the artist as gift giver and sufferer might be a form of penance for all those past MEGIGS of the IMPUNC. Maybe we are seeing a form of resistance and implicit critique here.

Me: Well, Doc, I think your hopes are illusory. Nobody is apologizing.

Dr. C: The idea that we might apologize for having left maybe half a million dead or hideously deformed fetuses lined up in Saigon hospitals, that we might apologize for it, or even help the victims, that idea doesn't arise. [*P*, 56]

Me: The one time the phenomenological sublime attempted to turn itself toward memory was with the Vietnam Veterans Memorial in Washington, D.C. These minimalistic walls for staging nativistic grief are also effective screens against consciousness (perhaps one wall obliterates the memory of the North Vietnamese dead while the other suppresses the criminality of the war). There is nothing like the monumental minimal for suppressing the gruesome aspect of the political behind impregnable martial forms—whether this takes the form of those long steps at Nuremberg or the sinking black walls of the VVM. Names of the American dead carved on the VVM's polished minimal flanks reflect back the images of the mourners whose glances will never penetrate the granite to see causes and responsibility, level accusations, or exact justice. Nothing works like the minimal sublime for performing this *Aufhebung* of canceling consciousness by raising up formal, phenomenological awe. The VVM is the most prominent national monument of/to our unconscious imperialistic sublime. That it was designed by an Asian American female also indicates that the IMPUNC is not an exclusively gendered or racial category.

Dr. C: You are feeling lightheaded?

Me: We feel there is something buoying us up. There is a momentum, and it is always forward and never looks back. A force from somewhere. Unseen, we feel it has always been there, urging pride on us. Oh, but when those towers fell, something went out of the force. In those dreadful moments of collapse a different reference became attached. Or uncovered. Could those two monstrous towers have been masking out something other than the sun?

Dr. C: These are things people need to know if they want to understand anything about themselves. They are known by the victims, of course, but the perpetrators prefer to look elsewhere.[10]

Me: It was nothing we *consciously* signed up for. It was just a tradition, this scouting of the MEGIG. It was expected. Not exactly a rule. But everyone was moving toward it, buoyed up by that unseen force. We never had a name for it. Now I'm trying to find one. But if I found it could I say it? Would it be part of a private language that everybody from Wittgenstein on said couldn't exist? Maybe I could whisper that name to Mary or to Peter . . .

Dr. C: Successful communication between Peter and Mary does not entail the existence of shared meanings or shared pronunciations in a public language (or a common treasure of thoughts or articulations of them), any more than physical resemblance between Peter and Mary entails the existence of a public form that they share.[11]

Me: But we wanted to be public. We believed in it. Something open to all. Nothing hidden, private. Everything above board and transparent. Then it could be really grand for those grand, public spaces. No narcissistic belly button stuff. And go easy on the shaggy expressionism. And nothing political either—unless of course those knee-jerk, liberal, overdetermined gestures toward race and gender. I mean shouldn't we remember modernism for having done *something?* Well today of course we can laugh at the idea of an old-fashioned autonomy. It seems like a faded photograph from another time. So what if today our grand public space throbs with entertainment? Isn't it better lit for all that? And who says we shouldn't entertain? Who says we shouldn't mesmerize with size? Who says MUSCRVIT and INARSE should not overwhelm? Who says the MEGIG is hiding anything? Who says AMPHENA is not still the way to go?

Dr. C: The intellectual class is supposed to be so well trained and so well indoctrinated that they don't need a whip. They just react spontaneously in the ways that will serve external power interests, without awareness, thinking they're doing honest, dedicated work. [*P*, 80]

Me: *Serve?* Us? What? How? Who's got the time? We're holding up the MEGIG and it's a hell of a lot of work. We're doing our job, which is to furnish that grand space with something for people to come and see and marvel at.

Dr. C: In a democracy you have to control people's minds. You can't control them by force. There's a limited capacity to control them by force, and since they have to be controlled and marginalized, be "spectators of action," not "participants." [*P*, 152]

Me: You are pulling us toward what is irrelevant to our concerns. All we started out to do was to compare our MEGIGS to those vanished Twin Towers, just for the sake of a little perspective. And now the tone of accusation. What we really resent here are insinuations of a lack of innocence on our part. We work in intuitive ways, ways that have to be more or less . . . unconscious. We may be serving forces we don't want to look at, filling up spaces provided by the ruling class, taking their vows of amnesia and no questions asked. But we're American artists and our power depends on that saturated and resplendent now.

Dr. C: [uncrosses and recrosses legs]

Me: But did it what? Allegorize some distribution of power? The only kind of power we ever had in mind was the power of the MEGIG—big, bold, clean, sweeping you off your feet. That's what you came for, wasn't it? And you want to suggest there is some readable iconography behind all that formal variety? All that grand space of INARSE and the practice of AMPHENA might . . . what? Be screening something off? Well, it wasn't all just big, galumphing formalism. There was lots of ironic stuff in there about the empty, tinny aspects of America. And we can't be accused of ever being a violent group.[12]

Dr. C: Part of the reason why the U.S. is trying to look as violent and vindictive and out of control as possible is to frighten off Europe and others, to say, We know we can't convince you, but get out of our way, because we're violent and dangerous. [*P*, 51]

Me: That's going too far. Those things are for the others. We remain innocent and sort of . . . unconscious. With certain exceptions, doubt, resistance, memory, and the contemplative mark the European aesthetic. American art, with certain exceptions, is distanced and distinguished from this by an aesthetic of immediacy and the aggressively invasive and occupying impulse. These are not merely formal categories.

A common language and dominant religious outlook are said to characterize a national culture. But Peirce's insight suggests we look to culturally specific aesthetic tendencies for a deeper assessment. It is not a question of stereotypes here but of tendencies, predilections, assumptions, tropes and desires that move in ways that are less than . . . conscious.

Dr. C [quoting Carl Schmitt, jurist of the Third Reich]: "Tell me who your enemy is and I'll tell you who you are."

Me: Space may or may not be God as the great American Puritan, Jonathan Edwards, once said,[13] but it is surely a source of anxiety, maybe even a form of anxiety. What we do with space tells us who we are. The kinds of spaces we make, what we put in them, and how we put ourselves into them come to define us. Different cultures have different personal and public spaces. The spaces of Red Square or Tiananmen Square are not those of Pennsylvania Avenue. Foucault has spoken about such overdetermined, politicized spaces as prisons and schools. But there are also those more diffuse cultural spaces. Spaces that one goes up to. "Meaning something," Wittgenstein said, "is like going up to someone."[14] But there are also those spaces that come up to oneself. Perhaps there is no mind/body problem, only a mind/space problem.

Dr. C: [rolls eyes upward, looks at watch]

Me: Every cultural space has a certain semantic/pneumatic aspect. Meanings are read within a certain pressure and density of affect. There are spaces that invite and those that command. Cultural spaces do both. Once these commands were given a little more sotto voce. And what commands are heard today in those spaces of the new museums sprouting up everywhere? In the 1920s and '30s there were the movie palaces—the Fox of Atlanta, Grauman's Egyptian and Chinese theaters of Hollywood.[15] Today Frank Gehry, Santiago Calatrava, and others fashion new fantasy palaces of entertainment in the shape of the art museum where the spaces of spectacle once again benumb, lull, and command.

Spaces of AMPHENA, spaces framing the MEGIG. Within these quintessential American spaces one hears a slight buzzing sound. Perhaps that low, vibrating rumble is the echo of Pennsylvania Avenue. Listen too closely and it fades. Maybe it is just a ringing in the ears due to the vast amount of enclosed cubic feet of space. But inside or outside a certain commanding rhythm animates things. One can almost hear the sound of martial music. John Philip Sousa echoes across the tumbling volumes. A stirring, imperial strut animates those soaring arches. Here in the spectacle of the new museum/pleasure palace we hear the hymn to the IMPUNC.

Dr. C: Then you should ask whether policies and the shaping of information reflect the distribution of power. That's what any rational person would expect. [*P*, 27]

Me: It is not a big step from the large, aloof, chromed, corporate spaces of the Chelsea galleries to the pleasure-palace art museum. But it is a different step. You must go up to the former; the latter rushes up to you. The former might deign to part with a fetish, for a price, in private; the latter gives you a feel in public. Both spaces exude overconfidence and condescension. Both flaunt the force. Both have folded within themselves the electric tingle of Pennsylvania Avenue. The MEGIG slides from the former to the latter on greased rails. The MEGIG services these two imperial spaces that were made for one another.

Dr. C: And these sublime spaces and things are saying to the world . . .

Me: America is saying to the world, Get out of the way.

Dr. C: You're quoting me.

Me: A Freudian slip.

Dr. C: And the American culture of AMPHENA, MEGIG, INARSE, MUSCRVIT, and IMPUNC?

Me: "Hit me again, Li'l Dahlink," as Krazy Kat said to the brick-throwing mouse, Ignatz. "And may his eelbow neva wicken."

Dr. C: Settle down.

Me: Besides the building of museums as pleasure palaces, which are springing up like mushrooms across the country, there will no doubt soon be a more sober American public monument on the site of the former World Trade Center. A temporary monument in the form of a "theater of lights" marked the site of the two most monstrous and egregious pieces of architecture to have ever burdened the island of Manhattan. The temporary memorial also marks a kind of amnesia about another large, flat space: the Nuremberg Parade Ground of the Third Reich where some seventy years ago Albert Speer installed his memorable searchlights. But the IMPUNC has always been dedicated to the self-righteous suppression of history and to the forgetting of the other. The values, norms, and aspirations of every past civilization have been read through its art. Ours is going to be interpreted in the same way.

Dr. C: But you are not waiting for the ruins to arrive to prowl through the fragments.

Me: The ruins are already here.

Dr. C: If we want to consider this question seriously, we should recognize that in much of the world the U.S. is regarded as a leading terrorist state, and with good reason.[16]

Me: There has been no program guiding the extensive catalogue of American IMPUNC monumental art that reaches back almost two centuries and shows no signs of abating. Self-congratulatory grand scale, the entertainment spectacle of awe and buzz, the obliviousness to the past, the optimism of domination—such attitudes are packed into the IMPUNC impulse. But since 9/11 the breeze of an overt nationalism has arisen. Has it blown the camouflage cover off? Can the beliefs in American pragmatism, liberalism, and corporate capitalism as non-ideological guides of purity (a purity so lofty as to have, in Francis Fukuyama's words, "evaded history") any longer be credible? Or will art come to the rescue to head off consciousness of our national belligerent, predatory, power-driven presuppositions? It did it before by folding into the work a phenomenology of dominating affect that submerged and screened from consciousness the implications of the values it promoted. Will it do it again? I think we can count on it making the effort.

Dr. C: I see our time is up.

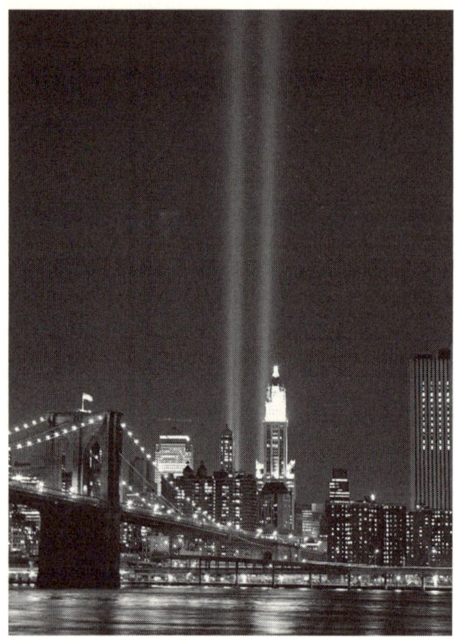

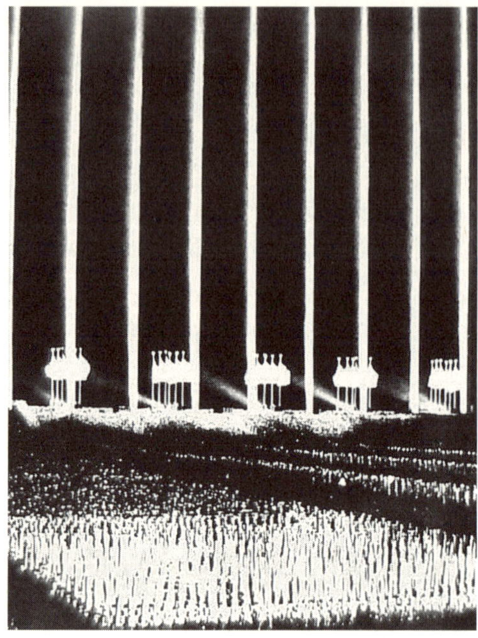

105. *Towers of Light*, 2003, New York. © Brigitte Stelzer, New York.

106. The Nuremberg Parade, 1936.

NOTES

1. Chomsky, *Understanding Power: The Indispensable Chomsky*, ed. Peter R. Mitchell and John Schoeffel (New York: New Press, 2002), 356.
2. Chomsky, *Language and Thought* (Wakefield, R.I.: Moyer Bell, 1993), 22.
3. Chomsky, *New Horizons in the Study of Language and Mind* (Cambridge: Cambridge University Press, 2000), 36.
4. Peirce, "Philosophy and the Sciences: A Classification," *Philosophical Writings of Peirce*, ed. Justus Buchler (New York: Dover, 1955), 62.
5. Chomsky, *Reflections on Language* (New York: Pantheon, 1975), 163.
6. For a discussion of Wagner-effect art, see Robert Morris, "Size Matters."
7. David Barsamian and Chomsky, *Propaganda and the Public Mind: Conversations with Noam Chomsky* (Cambridge: South End Press, 2001), 80; hereafter abbreviated *P*.
8. See Michael Fried's early prescient essay, "Art and Objecthood," *Art and Objecthood: Essays and Reviews* (Chicago: University of Chicago Press, 1998), 148–72.
9. See Anton Ehrensweig, *The Hidden Order of Art: A Study in the Psychology of the Artistic Imagination* (Berkeley: University of California Press, 1967), 74.
10. Chomsky, *9-11* (New York: Seven Stories Press, 2001), 57.
11. Chomsky, *New Horizons in the Study of Language and Mind*, 30.

12. Unlike some groups. From World War II to 2001 America engaged in military adventurism in China (1945–46, 1950–53), Korea (1950–53), Guatemala (1954, 1957–69), Indonesia (1958), Cuba (1959–60), the Belgian Congo (1964), Peru (1965), Laos (1964–73), Vietnam (1961–73), Cambodia (1969–70), Grenada (1983), Libya (1986), El Salvador (1980s), Nicaragua (1980s), Panama (1989), Iraq (1991–2001), Bosnia (1995), and Yugoslavia (1999). List compiled by Arundhati Roy, *Power Politics* (Cambridge, Mass.: South End Press, 2001), 128.
13. "But I had as good speak plain: I have already said as much as that space is God" (Jonathan Edwards, "Of Being," *A Jonathan Edwards Reader*, ed. John Edwin Smith, Harry S. Stout, and Kenneth P. Minkema [New Haven: Yale University Press, 1995], 10).
14. Wittgenstein, *Philosophical Investigations*, trans. G. E. M. Anscombe (New York: Macmillan, 1953), § 457, 133.
15. Stanford White's assassin, Harry K. Thaw, traveled to Hollywood after his release from prison. Seeing Grauman's million-dollar Egyptian Theater he was reported to have exclaimed, "My God, I shot the wrong architect." Of course today most urban architecture has been reduced to a low, grubby form of white-collar crime.
16. Chomsky, *9-11*, 23.

TOWARD AN OPHTHALMOLOGY OF THE AESTHETIC AND AN ORTHOPEDICS OF SEEING | 2004

Speculating beyond the little that is known, we might take the mind/brain to be a complex system with a highly differentiated structure, with separate "faculties," such as the language faculty, those involved in moral and aesthetic judgment . . .

—NOAM CHOMSKY, *LANGUAGE AND THOUGHT*

Aesthetic and moral faculties—two or one? Chomsky says "those," so maybe he means two. Does it make a difference? One or two, we have here innate capacities to respond to the environment in ways not concerned with truth predications. Charles Sanders Peirce's holism would have cemented the two together at the external level, as well as given the aesthetic more weight to bear, when he said

> aesthetics is the science of ideals, or of that which is objectively admirable without any ulterior reason. . . . Ethics, or the science of right and wrong, must appeal to aesthetics for aid in determining the *summum bonum*. It is the theory of self-controlled, or deliberate, conduct. Logic is the theory of self-controlled, or deliberate, thought; and as such must appeal to ethics for its principles.[1]

Bertrand Russell, while not linking the aesthetic to the moral, might have been more sympathetic to Chomsky's innate notions when he said that "*a priori* knowledge is knowledge as to ethical value."[2]

Kant tied the aesthetics of the sublime to the moral when he said that "in the case of the sublime the link to morality is not, as it is in the case of the beautiful, merely explanatory or interpretive. Here this link justifies the claim of judgments about the sublime to universal validity, on the (legitimate) presupposition that man does in fact have moral feeling."[3] He links the faculty for such a response not to the culture that shapes and conditions it but to the innate when he notes that the response is not "initially produced by the culture and then introduced to society by way of (say) mere convention. Rather, it has its foundation in human nature."[4] The feeling for the sublime in nature is tied to "a mental attunement similar to that for moral feeling."[5]

The early Wittgenstein said that "ethics and aesthetics are one and the same."[6]

Do we have a reference yet for the aesthetic? Beyond pointing to its innate nature, do we need anything more precise? Donald Davidson's holism would dispense with reference.[7] Chomsky echoes Davidson when he says that words are used to refer to things and to talk about them, but "it is quite a leap to conclude that the *words* refer to these things."[8] Certainly complex terms such as "aesthetic" need no precision. Rather they provide "a complex perspective from which to think about, talk about, and refer to things, or what we take to be things."[9]

The Aesthetic: an innate faculty, a capacity concerned with affective responses. Leave it at that. What has been endowed in us by what Hume called "the hand of nature" may be beyond introspection and conscious human knowledge. Kant cautioned that the "schematism of our understanding, in its application to appearances and their mere form, is an art concealed in the depths of the human soul, whose modes of activity nature is hardly likely ever to allow us to discover, and have open to our gaze."[10] So far art has not come through the door. But it hovers in the hall and I can hear its heavy breathing.

Gottlob Frege ushered in the "linguistic turn" coincident with the turn of the twentieth century by asserting that only in the context of a sentence does a word have meaning. Analytic philosophy is born out of the conviction that only the sentence delivers truth. Frege's analysis of how the *sense* of a sentence is prior to delivering a posterior *reference*, which locates its truth value, was problematic but influential. The early Wittgenstein was influenced by Frege, and in the *Tractatus*[11] he tried to establish the priority of sense over reference. In any case meaning and truth are bound together in the Fregean analysis. As Michael Dummett has noted, "Almost anything could be taken as rendering some sentence true: it depends on what the sentence *means*."[12] The history of analytic philosophy could be written in terms of attempts to define truth and meaning. By assigning meaning to use the later Wittgenstein displaces the concept of truth as central to meaning.[13]

In 1927 Frank Ramsey put forth his "redundancy theory," which argues that assertions of "is true" add nothing to assertions of fact and, pending some difficulties that Ramsey thought could be overcome, could be eliminated from statements. The redundancy theory is the simplest of a class of theories termed "deflationary." In general deflationists see truth as a property of sentences rather than of propositions. Truth is regarded as a not metaphysically deep term. Donald Davidson is perhaps the most well known recent thinker associated with the deflationary. He regarded truth as a primitive concept, left it undefined, but considered it central to his theory of meaning. Since the mission of philosophy, as generations and generations have seen it, has been to deliver truth, the radicalness of the deflationary stance is striking.

The question is, can the deflationary be generalized as a strategy that is operative outside the confines of analytic philosophy? Could the deflationary name a strategy that certain earlier philosophers shared? Could it be broadened to other areas of the culture? Is the deflationary as a strategy summed up in Kenneth Surin's remark that it is "the desire to deflate or make transparent our recourses to principles that confer on our thinking this or that manifestation of invariance and stability"?[14] Or is the deflationary much more negative and aggressive than a mere desire for transparency? Could the desire in question be one of Nietzschean negation? Davidson's desire to squeeze truth down to a kind of primitive squeak that carries meaning on its back would seem to go beyond a concern for transparency. And Davidson's infamous remark "there is no such thing as a language, not if language is anything like what many philosophers and linguists have supposed,"[15] sounds Nietzschean to me. I think the notion of the deflationary has to be broadened and refocused to include an underlying negativity. Philosophizing with an attitude, a combative, take-down attitude. It could be argued that Socrates' program was mainly negative. If so, he started it all. But deflation is much more than aggressive negation. It involves the dismantling of those boundary presuppositions of implicit limits that are assumed to be necessary for activity in a given field. Paradoxically, the negations of the deflationary have the function of the *Aufhebung* and subsequently open up the field for new production. This binding of "removal" and "renewal" suggests the neologism *remowal* as a term for this contradictory phenomenon.

There is a commotion in the room next door making it difficult for me to concentrate here. I hear loud arguing, banging on the wall, and sounds of pushing and shoving. It seems that Ace wants to get into the room and take the chair beside Art. Big D, the deflationary, is blocking the door and yelling at the Aesthetic, whom they call Ace. "Get out, bitch!" Big D yells. Art is shoving Big D away from the door. "She just wants to sit down and visit," Art says. "Yeah, yeah, sit in your lap, you mean," Big D says. "I can't stand the two of you making eyes at each other." But Ace has slipped inside and is running around knocking over chairs. Big D's mascot, Little T, is yapping and whimpering at the commotion and pulling at its leash. Real pandemonium next door.

Analytic cubism of 1909–11 would be the first twentieth-century deflationary manifestation in the arts. And, characteristic of the deflationary, it manifests the dualism of *removal.* Cubism opens toward a new production while the consequences of its negativity take some time to surface. In cubism the world of light, that world of previous painters, is converted into mud, into black and white and brown. Painting involuntarily impoverishes itself in order to become combative, to go against the world in a way representation never had before. There is great pathos in this assertion by negation. T. J. Clark sees this attitude as one in which the work was done "under the sign of failure."[16] That is, the failure to remake representation. In cubism the image of the body is flattened into a kind of map comprising unresolvable convex/concave planes that hinge together and multiply across the surface. A shallow spatiality flickers here that speaks of confinement and flatness more than space. The rejection of salience, or the figure/ground distinction, was a paradigmatic assumption of all previous representation. Cubism's dismissal of this assumption constitutes its deep deflationary thrust. Space is negated, or rather what little is allowed suggests its imminent absence. A profound skepticism legislates the airless compression that flickers between figure and ground in these half-burials of the figure beneath shallow planes scattered across the surface like dead leaves.

Analytic cubism is a denial of modernism's transcendent and utopian spirit. Of course a profound sense of anxious doubt is already there in those last works of Cézanne, which so inspired Braque and Picasso. Analytic cubism lasted only a few years. Synthetic cubism set aside the pessimism that saturated the analytic period, and the *removal* cycle was set in motion.

. . . . .

The anthropologist Colin M. Turnbull studied and lived with the Pygmies of central Africa in the 1950s. The "Molimo" was an object spoken of with both awe and amusement. It was brought out in times of crisis, and could be seen only by the men; women would be struck blind, so they said, if they laid eyes on this object of great reverence. Turnbull assumed it was the one great Pygmy art masterpiece. "I had expected an object elaborately carved, decorated with patterns full of ritual significance and symbolism, something sacred, to be revered, the very sight or touch of which might be thought of as dangerous. I felt that I had a right, in the heart of the tropical rain forest, to expect something wonderful and exotic. But now I saw that the instrument . . . was not made of bamboo or wood, and it certainly was not carved or decorated in any way. It was a length of metal drainpipe."[17]

It must have been in 1964 that I went to a panel at the Museum of Modern Art that consisted of Marcel Duchamp, William Rubin, and Alfred Barr. Rubin questioned Duchamp in a scholarly, if overly loud way, while Barr nearly whispered in his misty-eyed reverence. The discussion turned to the readymades. Duchamp claimed that he never really understood them, only that he was inherently lazy but felt that from time to time he should nevertheless make some art. He once referred to himself as a defrocked artist. So he, Duchamp, made appointments with himself: on such and such a day, he would just have to make art. When the day arrived, he would choose something just to get it over with, and that would be that. A readymade: not an object he had labored over or crafted, but a mass-produced artifact available to anyone. "But how did you go about this?" queried Rubin. "Well, I would usually find myself in a hardware store on these days. I would look around and choose something. That would be the readymade," Duchamp replied. Ever the academic, Rubin persisted, "But what criteria were employed in the selection of the object?" "Well, I tried to predict which object there I might always remain indifferent toward, and that would be the one I would select," Duchamp said. At this point, Alfred Barr piped up and said, "But, oh, Marcel, why do they look so beautiful today?" Duchamp turned toward him and said, "Nobody's perfect."

Thierry de Duve has pointed out that the readymades of Duchamp nominalized the term "art," demoting it from a concept to a name.[18] Big-time deflation here. The readymade delivered a blow from which art never really recovered, not to mention the license it extended for the production of mountains of the most egregious art. But the *removal* cycle makes way for renewed production, which is almost invariably oblivious to the negative insights of the deflationary act. Of course the possibility exists that Duchamp may not have been telling the truth about his indifference. The bottle rack, the snow shovel, the urinal, the bicycle wheel . . . Was Alfred Barr right, aren't they all "beautiful"? (And weren't they beautiful from the beginning?) Could the Aesthetic have been holding Marcel's hand there in the hardware store? After all, Marcel did not object that Barr was wrong. Rather he seemed to be saying that he, Duchamp, had failed. Our perception, being functionally selective, does not allow the experience of chaos. And our choices? We know what we like (a privilege we share with all the lower animals, as Oscar Wilde remarked), and we know what repels us. Our affective responses have an immense range and the aesthetic response can and has also been elicited by destruction and violence.[19] But doesn't the notion of choice based on non-affective indifference suggest the oxymoronic? Do we just want to think that the aesthetic can be liposuctioned out of art? If so, don't we have here a misplaced philosophical longing for a testosterone-drenched strategy that could banish the aesthetic? Don't we genderize a masculine philosophy and a feminine art by making such an opposition? If so, how bizarre, given Rrose Sélavy and all those Ready-Maids.

Take a few ordinary kitchen matches, dip them in paint, and by means of a toy cannon, shoot the matches at a large sheet of glass. Then drill holes in the glass where the paint marks show up. Photograph three squares of gauze ruffled by air currents and use these as patterns. Well, more or less "presto," Duchamp introduced a note of chance into art making in the *Large Glass*. Better, drop three one-meter-long threads from the height of one meter, use these to make templates . . . But do threads really fall into such lovely parabolic curves as displayed in Duchamp's *3 Stoppages Étalon*, 1913–14? No matter how gravity behaves, or was assisted here, it is what is *said* about the intention that raises a large sign that reads CHANCE.

The party in the next room is getting loud and there is more banging on the wall. I can hear Big D yelling at Ace, whom he insists on calling "Ms. Ace," in his loud, gravelly voice. The note of contempt is obvious. Ace has grabbed the mascot's leash and is running around the room trying to get Little T to jump over chairs. Art is on a fourth vodka in the corner and looking really out of it.

Given: an aesthetic waterfall and illuminating gas lighting up the readymades. This only lends them the aura Barr saw, an aura they deserve. Barr's judgment was only exercising an innate faculty. True, the dampness and gaseous haze of the aesthetic shrinks their tough, deflationary dimension somewhat. Still, the subtraction of labor and the reduction of artmaking to mere choice (whatever the criterion) is deflationary enough. And the accusation that Donatello cast the legs of the Holofernes figure from life instead of modeling them? And the photograph? Such prior examples do not dilute the status of the readymade, but stand as precedents for it.

David Hume was, hands down, the greatest deflationary thinker. And Kant, awakening from his "dogmatic slumbers" to plow his vast fields of the systematic, testifies to the inevitability of the cycle of *removal*. Hume's skepticism about any substantive basis for belief, as well as his deconstruction of induction, probably did keep Kant up nights. But didn't Descartes found the "Club Déflationnaire"? The membership was quite small then, consisting of Descartes alone, sitting before his fire and perusing his doubt all the way down.

John Cage looked for imperfections in a sheet of paper over which he dropped musical staff lines drawn on acetate. The imperfections became musical notes. Later, following the readymade, Cage admitted all sounds, except those of pain, into the house of music, thereby nominalizing the term "music" as henceforth the calling of any sound into the pantheon. Even so-called silence, like the

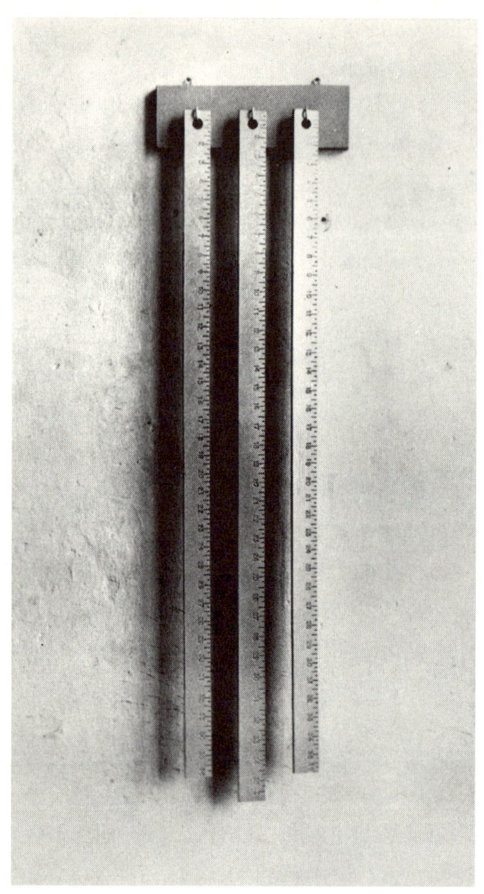

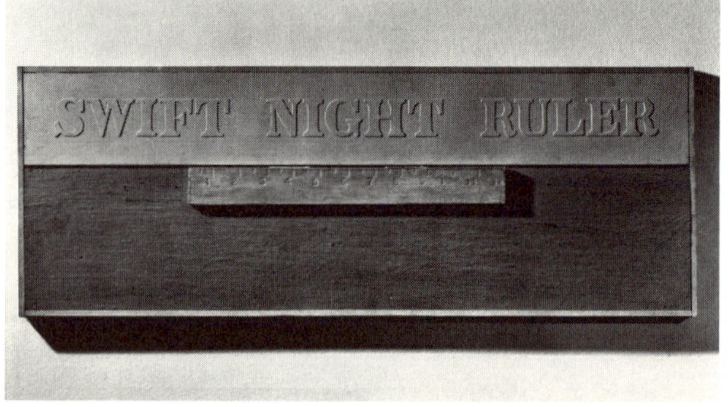

107. *Three Rulers*, 1963. Painted wood and metal hooks, 42 × 11 inches (106.7 × 27.9 cm). Estate of Harry N. Abrams. Photo courtesy of Robert Morris.

108. *Untitled (Swift Night Ruler)*, 1963. Sliding ruler and wood, painted, 10 × 28½ × 1 inches (25.4 × 72.4 × 2.5 cm). Collection of Mr. and Mrs. Leo Castelli, New York. Photo courtesy of Robert Morris.

proverbial quantum vacuum, pulses with something. Cage said in effect, "Listen to what is going on because I'm calling it music." Did Cage like the noises he heard sitting motionless at the piano in a tuxedo for four minutes and 33 seconds—all that coughing and mumbling and grumbling in the audience? He said he never heard a sound he didn't like (excepting the sound of pain). Get as deflationary as you like, and Cage liked the deflationary, and you just get much more grist for the aesthetic faculty to mill. The aesthetic is not shut out by the deflationary, only extended into new realms. Cage, who admitted to having a "sunny personality," did not need Duchamp's indifference when he had Zen's equivalencies. The aesthetic is set free with the readymade and chance.

Jasper Johns, the third member of the twentieth-century Art Club Déflationnaire, squeezed the last breath out of painting at mid-century by flattening it beneath the readymade in his *Flags*, *Targets*, *Numbers*, and *Alphabets*. But he did far more. "Johns rewrote Pollock's pragmatism of material process into one of logical structure. Beginning with his influence on Frank Stella, John's lessons in the paradigm of a structural device that unfolded to complete the work also made minimal art possible."[20] And minimal art demonstrates once again, in its excessive and repetitious productions, the inevitability of the *removal* cycle.

Someone said that the most dangerous class of people in the world is "young unmarried men between the ages of eighteen and thirty five."[21] Duchamp, Cage, and Johns were young, unmarried men when they assaulted art and left their deflationary cultural scars. But the twentieth-century Club Déflationnaire had a fourth member and she was female. In the early '60s Simone Forti introduced her "rule games" and the manipulation of objects (including other performers' bodies) into dance. The following of rules, which often required concentration on and responses to clues coded in other performers' actions, or by manipulating or traversing objects small and large, generated movement—movement that was often effortful and workmanlike, unselfconscious and clearly devoid of any vestiges of ballet-inspired gesture. Like the other members of the Club, Forti's work admitted the "ordinary" to the arena of art. Her work dealt a heavy blow to the elitist culture of ballet-dependent choreography. And, characteristic of the *removal* cycle, her work opened the flood gates to new activity in dance. How much the spirit of the late Wittgenstein hovered over the Club Déflationnaire is an open question. The readymades came too early. But by the early '50s, ideas of the "ordinary" had risen from the *Investigations*[22] and were in the air.

The deflationary is not initially focused on either the aesthetic or negation as such. It is first of all an inspired adventure of thinking the possible. There is something detached and—the term is not too strong—psychopathic about

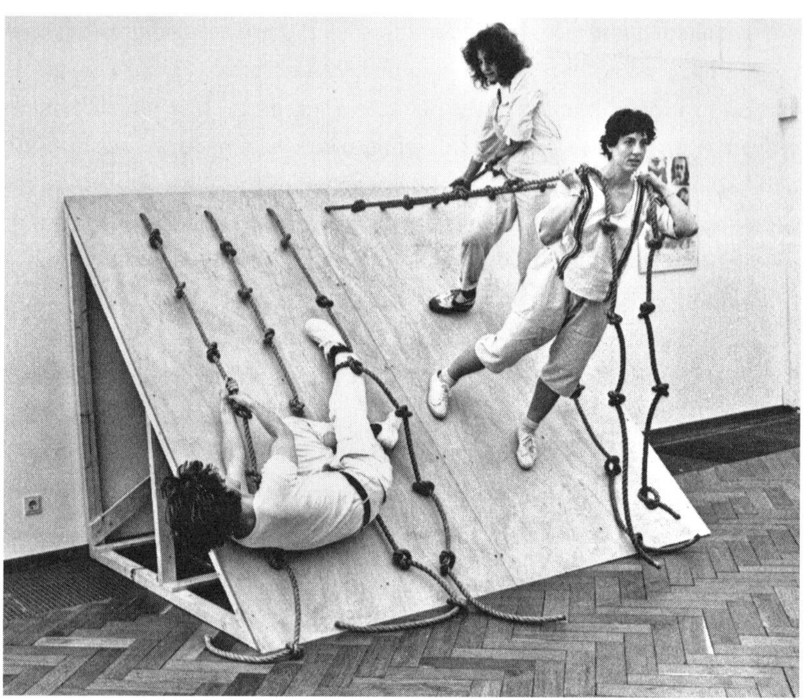

109. Simone Forti, *Slant Board*, 1961. Prop by Robert Morris. Restaged at the Stedelijk Museum Amsterdam in 1981. Photo courtesy of Robert Morris.

the space of the deflationary. A Nietzschean imbrication of the creative and destructive has to be posited, as well as left unexplained. The deflationary act taps a surge of insight seldom repeated in the individual's career. Nobody shouts "Eureka!" more than once. But the question can be asked, didn't the avant-gardes of modernism follow a deflationary program? There was to be sure a certain regression into the rules of the game in Modernism's moves. But such a strategy stopped short of the demolition of premises.

Awfully quiet in the next room. Let's look in. Art is sprawled on the floor passed out. Big D is looking fatigued and slouched in a chair. Little T is licking Big D's hand trying to cheer him up. Big D keeps mumbling to himself . . . "a cross-dresser all along, hmm . . . Ms. Ace was always also Mr. Ace. Hmm . . . Mr. and Ms. He/she . . . her/him . . . Now Ace is gone." Ace has slammed the door on both of them. "Give me some air," Ace says. "I'm out of here and I'm sick of those two creeps. It's the big world for me." Looks like the party is over.

The always feeble theoretical ideology of Modernist abstract art was by the mid-twentieth century dead on its feet. But the larger question is why did visual art production cease bearing cultural weight after the '70s? The short answer is because of the massive increase in the flood of imagery across a vast array of visual reproduction modalities that had been building in the culture for some time. Besides the expansions of television and advertising imagery, one could point to the "computer-aided design, synthetic holography, flight simulators, computer animation, robotic image recognition, ray tracing, texture mapping, motion control, virtual-environment helmets, magnetic resonance imaging, and multi-spectral sensors," noted by Jonathan Crary.[23] These modes constitute but a part of the rubric of a "visual culture" so multiple and profuse that it has been called a "pictorial turn" by W. J. T. Mitchell.[24] The engine of such visual multiplicity was of course commodity capitalism, which powered the new visual democracy and destroyed art's elitist aura of the unique and special image. Eric Hobsbawm has noted that shortly after the mid-twentieth century, classical high culture was undermined by the "universal triumph of the society of mass consumption. From the 1960s on the images that accompanied human beings in the Western world—and increasingly in the urbanized Third world—from birth to death were those advertising or embodying consumption or dedicated to commercial mass entertainment."[25] Language, no less than the visual, was demoted from the high holy books of elitist culture and even came to rest on such places as T-shirts, where, "like magical charms," they lent the wearer "the spiritual merit of the (generally youthful) life-style which those names symbolized and promised."[26] The mass market had replaced modernist dreams of utopia. High Art had fled but the aesthetic had not. As Hobsbawm has noted, "Technology had drenched everyday life in private as well as in public with art. Never had it been harder to avoid aesthetic experience. The 'work of art' was lost in the flow of words, of sounds, of images, in the universal environment of what would once have been called art."[27] The culture had become saturated with visual imagery as well as awash in information. Of course this may be too mundane an explanation for the death of High Art. Some have proposed a more mythical explanation in which Art knelt down to Hegel, heaved a terminal sigh of totalizing, suicidal self-knowledge, and then expired.[28] But naturally art proliferated and expanded in the wake (both senses) of High Art's demise. A kind of democratic conceptual folk art rose to take its place toward the end of the '70s. Anyone could do it. Only the smallest idea was required. And the video camera was cheap. Turn it on and let it run and be kind to your aesthetic faculty.

We have to assume that the aesthetic faculty, always shaped by the existing culture, has been refashioned, remolded, perhaps skewed and broadened by the cultural changes wrought by late-capitalist consumer society with its constant blitz of imagery. Such changes can be highlighted by considering the implosion and irrelevance of Nelson Goodman's differences in sign-types articulated in his *Languages of Art*. Here Goodman notes that nonlinguistic signs differ from linguistic systems by virtue of what he calls "density." Echoing Jakobson and Saussure, Goodman emphasizes the gaps and discontinuities in the linguistic system, which at the simplest level allows for a "p" to be distinguished from a "t" (phonetic differentiation). On the other hand, an image presents no distinctive breaks but is rather a continuous field. It is dense and continuous as compared to the discontinuities of the linguistic. Goodman compares the two systems of signs to the "analog" and the "digital." But he is careful to note that it is history, not an inherent metaphysical character, that determines whether something is read as digital or analog.[29] It is a sign of the changed times that Goodman's distinction between an analog system in which "every difference would make a difference,"[30] and the digital system read through discontinuities, no longer guides our visual processing in an environment flooded with a constant blitz of imagery. It is no accident that the demise of Modernism coincides with the ascendancy of a digital system of "reading" images, which has surely also reordered aesthetic responses. Today everything is scanned or "read."[31] There is no time for the contemplation of the continuous, which is associated with previous aesthetic attention to the densities of an image.[32] A post–High Art culture is a visual culture in which perception is compressed into the digital mode as a necessary response to the continuous assault of images. The innate aesthetic faculty can only be expected to have shifted with the "pictorial turn." I stop short here of theorizing a new observer, one who is born with a visual attention deficit, but could a post–"baby boomer" stand today in hushed contemplation before, say, Velàzquez's *Las Meninas*, noting how every small difference makes a difference in the continuous flow of the image?[33]

Are we freer now that our aesthetic faculty is exercised on the discontinuities of the post–High Art general spectacle? Hasn't a democratized visual culture, which returns the possibility of aesthetic reading to everything in sight, fulfilled John Dewey's demand for the merging of art and life?[34] Or has the aesthetic faculty been further dulled by the constant ratcheting up of scale and spectacle, encountered at an ever accelerating pace in the old sites of the museum space as well as outside it? Has the fractious terrain of the perpetual media blitz also honed our aesthetic faculty to triage the incoming barrage and made us quicker on our feet—or with our eyes, as the case may be? As the ophthalmologist asks, replacing one lens with another, "Better or worse?"

I hear a persistent tapping on the wall and feel I should investigate what is going on in the other room, since the party noise has died down . . . Well, I see Ace has gone, Art is still out cold, Big D is slumped in his chair dozing. Only Little T sits staring at me, motionless, except for a hesitant wag of the tail.

Me: "You're the only one left, Little T?"

T: "I'm always around. And you can drop the diminutive," the mascot replies. I have to admit I'm startled at speech from such a small being.

Me: "Well, I heard the tapping and I thought I should . . ."

T: "I was doing the tapping and I think it is about time you remembered your Edmund Burke."

Me: "But it is the deflationary and the aesthetic I've been worrying about."

T: "You are falling into Burke's trap of subliming things."

Me: "Me?"

T: "Yes, you and your Club Déflationnaire to begin with. Add to that the murky and mysterious innate aesthetic faculty as that which is forever out of sight. You end up with a few big guys and how they changed history, and all of it shrouded by the murky penumbra of the elusive aesthetic. It's all dark and sublime and Burkean, and . . ."

Me: "And one gal, don't forget. And I've tried to show how it was the celebration of the ordinary that set the members of the Club Déflationnaire apart. Implicit in this is a rejection of the sublime as an always reactionary strategy."[35]

T: "There is ordinary and there is ordinary. I hung around Davidson long enough to know about the hard ordinary, as opposed to the romantic ordinary."

Me: "What about the Wittgensteinian ordinary? He got pretty iconophobic in the *Investigations*. And you can't have Davidson without the late Wittgenstein."

T: "I don't like to keep defending Davidson—after all, look what he did to me. But he wasn't one of the iconophobic *philosophes*. And his sense of the ordinary was pretty well developed."

Me: "You mean his Principle of Charity, that notion that what most people believe is true, that we all seem to believe in things such as it is either raining or it isn't, or that none of us has been far from the surface of the earth, or that . . ."

T: "Without our agreement in belief about the mundane ordinary, there could be no meaningful disagreement about the more complex issues. Davidson's ordinary does some heavy lifting."

Me: "Well, T, we seem to have lost sight of the metastasized image and all our wayward ways of looking at things, not to mention those unpredictable effects of the aesthetic shade that is always drawn over our seeing. And now that Ace has fled the party for the big world, shouldn't we say a word to remember her by?"

T: "Well, we could remind ourselves of Stanley Cavell's remark that 'epistemology is obliged to keep aesthetics under control, as if to guard against the thought that there is something more [and better] seeing can be, or provide, than evidence for claims to know.'"[36]

Me: "Perish the thought that there might be pleasure in looking, huh? But I guess that Leonardo's *Paragone*[37] doesn't go away. Obviously the image is still a threat to some. But you are not so iconophobic, T? Not so Puritanical? Wouldn't Jonathan Edwards have cut us more slack than Cavell?"

T: "We all peer out into the same bleakness that has descended. Maybe Cavell is right, we can't afford not to know what we are seeing. And what we can least afford not to see through are the sublimities of imperialistic war."

Me: "So we should constrain our vision, and keep Ace at arm's length?"

T: "We know Kant was wrong about a lot of things, one of which was his idea of where the sublime led. As for Ace, she can take care of herself, and she will always be around."

Me: "But could we practice a way of seeing that allows us to look out onto the ordinary world, somehow seeing through the bleakness, to secure appreciation as well as criticality? Isn't there some therapy for vision?"

T: "We never seem to be able to say what we see, or see what we've said. And there is always too much to see that can never be said."

Me: "Don't talk in conundrums."

T: "Ace promised to take me for a walk, and I think I hear her calling. Enough of this blather. Here, take my leash, and let's go outside and see what she is pointing at."

NOTES

1. Peirce, *Philosophical Writings of Peirce*, ed. Justus Buchler (New York: Dover, 1955), 62.
2. Russell, *The Problems of Philosophy* (New York: Oxford University Press, 1959), 76.
3. Kant, *Critique of Judgment* (Oxford: Clarendon Press, 1952), lxxi.
4. Ibid., 125.
5. Ibid., 128.
6. Wittgenstein, *Tractatus Logico-Philosophicus*, trans. D. F. Pears and B. F. McGuinness (London: Routledge and Kegan Paul, 1961), 147.
7. See Donald Davidson's essay "Reality without Reference," in his *Inquiries into Truth and Interpretation* (Oxford: Clarendon Press, 1984), 215–24.
8. Chomsky, *Language and Thought* (Wakefield, R.I.: Moyer Bell, 1993), 22.
9. Ibid., 23.
10. Kant, *A Critique of Pure Reason*, 110–11.
11. Wittgenstein, *Tractatus Logico-Philosophicus*.
12. Michael Dummett, *Origins of Analytical Philosophy* (Cambridge, Mass.: Harvard University Press, 1994), 15.
13. Wittgenstein, *Philosophical Investigations*, trans. G. E. M. Anscombe (New York: Macmillan, 1953).
14. Surin, "Getting the Picture: Donald Davidson on Robert Morris's *Blind Time Drawings IV (Drawing with Davidson)*," *South Atlantic Quarterly* 101, no. 1 (Winter 2002): 164.
15. Davidson, "A Nice Derangement of Epitaphs," *Truth and Interpretation: Perspec-*

tives on the Philosophy of Donald Davidson, ed. Ernest LePore (Oxford: Blackwell, 1986), 433–36.

16. See T. J. Clark's brilliant remarks on cubism in his *Farewell to an Idea* (New Haven, Conn.: Yale University Press, 1999), 187, and throughout chapter 4.
17. Colin M. Turnbull, *The Forest People* (New York: Simon and Schuster, 1961), 75.
18. Thierry de Duve, *Kant after Duchamp* (Cambridge, Mass.: MIT Press, 1998).
19. One only need recall Marinetti's and Fascism's glorification of war, which, as Walter Benjamin has reminded us, "can experience its own destruction as an aesthetic pleasure of the first order." See Benjamin's essay "The Work of Art in the Age of Mechanical Reproduction," in *Illuminations* (New York: Schocken, 1969), 242.
20. Morris, "From a Chomskian Couch: The Imperialistic Unconscious."
21. I had thought Eric Hobsbawm had made this remark, but my search through his work did not turn up the quote. It is possible that I've imagined he said it.
22. Wittgenstein, *Investigations*.
23. Jonathan Crary, *Techniques of the Observer: On Vision and Modernity in the Nineteenth Century* (Cambridge, Mass.: MIT Press, 1990).
24. See Mitchell's essay "The Pictorial Turn" in *Picture Theory* (Chicago: University of Chicago Press, 1994), 11–34.
25. Eric Hobsbawm, *The Age of Extremes* (New York: Random House, 1996), 513.
26. Ibid., 513.
27. Ibid., 520.
28. See Arthur Danto's "The End of Art," *The Philosophical Disenfranchisement of Art* (New York: Eastern European Monographs, 1986), 81–115. Hegel's philosophy of history did of course greatly influence political theory. But most of Hegel's doctrines are patently false. See Bertrand Russell's satirical remarks on Hegel's notions of the "whole" in *A History of Western Philosophy* (New York: Simon and Schuster, 1945), 732–33.
29. See Nelson Goodman's *Languages of Art* (Indianapolis: Hackett, 1976), and W. J. T. Mitchell's incisive analysis of Goodman's thought in *Iconology* (Chicago: University of Chicago Press, 1986), 63–74. I stray from Mitchell's critique of Goodman's formalism in my remarks here.
30. Mitchell, *Iconology*, 69.
31. Recent cognitive science pictures a modular brain in which visual perception is broken down into a number of separate tasks such as recognition of shape, movement, edges, constancy of form through rotation, etc. Language is a different system, and the study of its innate features will, as Chomsky has noted, "neither provide a useful model for other parts of the study of mind, nor draw from them significantly" (*Language and Thought*, 34). According to Goodman, when one of the two codes (that of density or discontinuities) becomes operative, it is not a function of physiology but history. That history now favors the discontinuous code does not indicate that the brain could suppress or has suppressed visual perception. What may never be made clear by cognitive science is how the interface between the visual and verbal operates, not only in terms of the seamless connection that facilitates the interchange between what is seen and said, but the complex and endless conflict between the one and the other. "Reading" is of course the wrong

word for this processing of the visual. The fact that it is in play indicates a lag in theorizing the complexities of what Mitchell has called the "pictorial turn."

32. This shifting of perception did not happen only yesterday. Richard Wollin in his *Labyrinths* (Amherst: University of Massachusetts Press, 1995), 68, notes how Walter Benjamin, writing "On Some Motifs in Baudelaire" in the late 1930s, "laments the fact that in the modern world the powers of consciousness must be enhanced as a defense against the shocks of everyday life (a problem that is especially acute in the modern metropolis, the locus classicus of shock experience). As a result of this need for constantly vigilant consciousness, our natural and spontaneous capacities for experience are necessarily diminished."
33. Michel Foucault's remarks on *Las Meninas*, which open his book *The Order of Things* (New York: Pantheon, 1973), 3–6, unpack the Velàzquez work by subjecting its surface to an inch by inch analysis. There could be no more relentless pursuit of differences across an image. That its most every difference is a difference in relation to a standard, "classical" space which stands outside the work's representations speaks not only to Velàzquez's historical moment before representation had swallowed the world but to that of Foucault's, when the perception of such densities was still available.
34. See John Dewey's *Art as Experience* (New York: Minton, Balch and Company, 1934).
35. See Morris, "From a Chomskian Couch," for a development of this argument.
36. Stanley Cavell, *In Quest of the Ordinary* (Chicago: University of Chicago Press, 1998), 84.
37. Here Leonardo takes the other side, valorizing the visual over the verbal when he says, "If you, poet, describe the figure of some deities, the writing will not be held in the same veneration as the painted deity, because bows and various prayers will continually be made to the painting. To it will throng many generations from many provinces and from over the eastern seas, and they will demand help from the painting and not from what is written." *Treatise on Painting*, ed. A. Philip McMahon (Princeton, N.J.: Princeton University Press, 1956), 22.

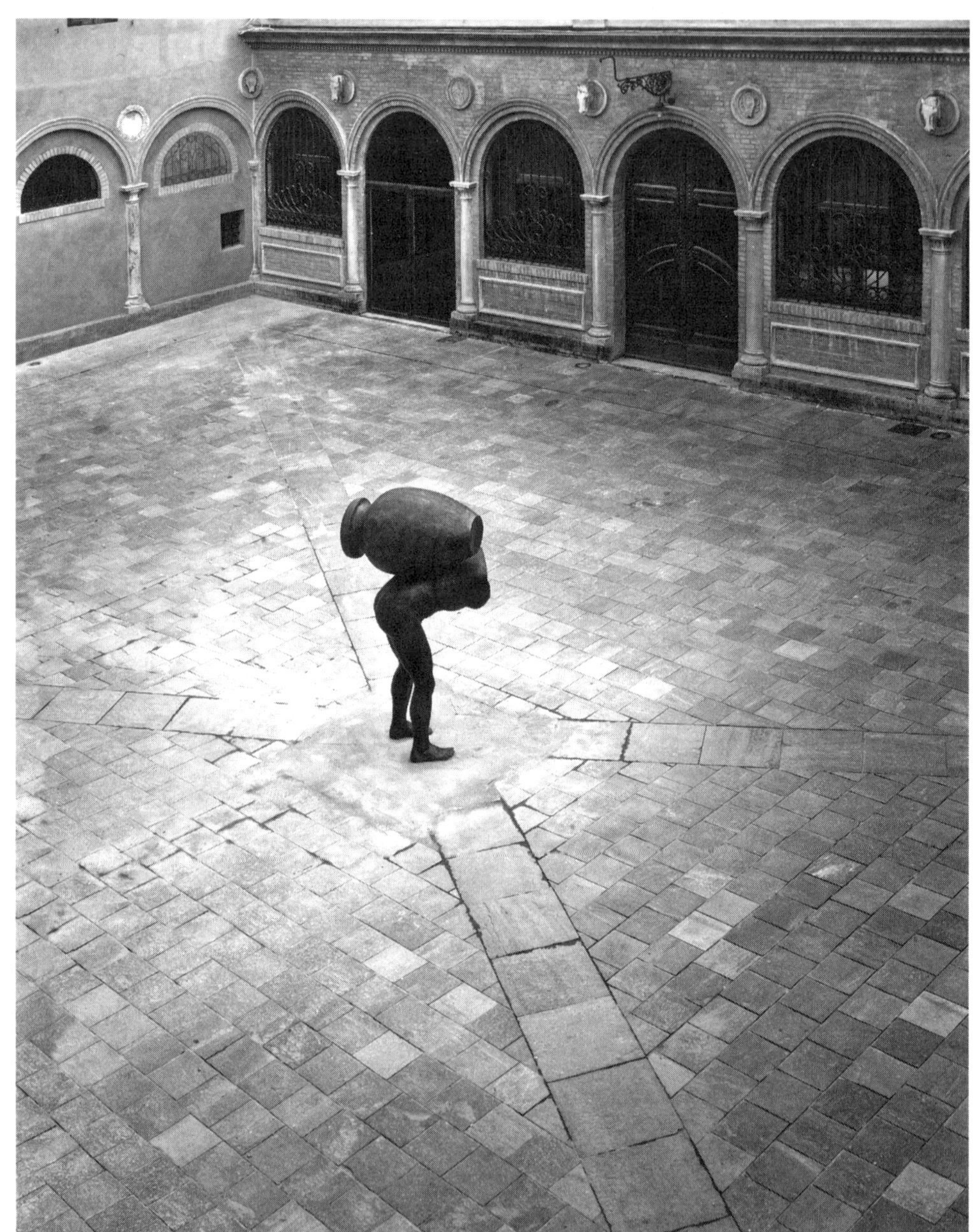

Marcel Duchamp spoke of the artist as half the equation. The artist makes the work and the public tells him (or her) what it is. The artist's intentions count for nothing. Like everyone, the artist always says more and less than he intends. There is no final publicly shared meaning for art or language. Communication is not the mission of either. Both allow us to express ourselves.

Our historical moment is one in which we are assaulted by an ever-increasing barrage of information and images, most of which is forgettable. Modernism's always feeble utopian ideology has been dead for half a century. Its formalism proved incapable of either mounting resistance to or offering compensation for the excesses and assaults of a virulent and metastasizing visual culture. As the edge of the descending bleakness what can art now offer?

When the stopper was removed from Pandora's jar, so the Greek myth goes, all the evils of the world flew out, leaving Hope inside at the bottom. Aquinain and Irenean theologies were two Christian attempts to explain evil. But since we exist on a scale somewhere between rats and angels, as Noam Chomsky has reminded us, why should we assume ourselves capable of answering such questions as the nature of consciousness, have the capacity to solve the mind/body problem, or unlock the problem of evil? Perhaps evil is abyssal and beyond discourse, approachable only on an allegorical level. (Of the artists, only Goya looked it in the face.)

In our time we have witnessed art assuming a variety of stances and identities. We have seen it strike the mystical and metaphysical pose. We have seen it ally itself with kitsch entertainment. We have seen it become a tool of identity politics. We have seen it try to persevere with a dead formalism. We have seen it retreat into an airless, elite aestheticism. We have seen it pump itself up with spectacle and overwhelming scale. We have seen it shrink its ambitions to pure

110. *Less than*, 2005. Bronze, 86.6 × 49.2 × 29.5 inches (220 × 125 × 75 cm); audio: approximately six minutes, light sensor–activated, begins at dusk softly, builds in volume and then fades, recorded on four separate tracks quadriphonia, four amps, four speakers. Chiostro piccolo, Chiostri di San Domenico, Reggio Emilia. Musei Civici Collection, Reggio Emilia. Photo by Miro Zagnoli, courtesy of Comune di Reggio Emilia.

decoration. We have seen it try to exploit every new technological medium. We have seen its ambition reduced to a kind of conceptual folk art. But nowhere does it now bear any significant cultural weight. And none of these stances has allayed its diminution toward irrelevance in the face of the descending, high-decibel bleakness.

Of course art has always been allied with the myth of Hope that remains stuck at the bottom of Pandora's jar. That art is also tied to an innate aesthetic faculty is no guarantee that art will have a significant place in the culture. And the aesthetic has in the past found outlets in violence and destruction. That art should lose its significance does not mean art will fade from memory. Myth, even at its most threadbare, is always necessary. Or, as Nietzsche put it, "We have art lest we perish of the truth."

THE BIRTHDAY BOY | 2004

Stage directions: a middle-aged male art historian actor stands at lectern. A glass of red wine (grape juice) sits on a table beside lectern. Actor drinks throughout lecture. Hand and arm (body off camera) with bottle refills glass when empty—either by pouring into glass on table or holding bottle in frame so that actor notices and holds out glass for refill.

Camera: still shot throughout. Framing: just above actor's head to just below waist.

Male Voice:
Let me raise a glass, a toast to the five-hundredth birthday of Michelangelo's *David*. It is an honor to be asked to say a few words celebrating this event.—*drinks, sets glass back on table*—Let me begin by trying to give a little context to the masterpiece that stands before us. And for this we must go back to the Quattrocento and look briefly at the works of Donatello. Specifically, to his marble *David* of 1408 [*slide 1 of marble David*], created almost exactly a hundred years before Michelangelo's work. And we should also look as well at Donatello's bronze *David* (c. 1440) [*slide 1 of bronze David*].—*pause, turns, looks at screen*—Both works are, of course, precedents to the Michelangelo work. In contrast to the *David* of Michelangelo, the earlier Donatello marble [*slide 2 of marble David*] seems modest, restrained, and is of course not naked but carefully garbed. It can also be described as projecting an air of non-heroic, inner contemplation. But a certain ambiguity hovers over the expression of body and visage [*slide 3 of marble David*]. Do we witness a kind of serenity or is this just blankness; a relaxation after the event of killing Goliath, or a kind of indifference?—*pauses, drinks, looks at glass*—

Donatello's later bronze *David* [*slide 2 of bronze David*]—*turns, points at screen, pauses, turns back to text*—well, this is from another world. Here is a *David* in prepubescent nakedness. It is dark, sleek, polished, life-size, inviting, glorious, somewhat elaborate. This first freestanding bronze figure since classical antiquity seems to announce that a certain "gayness" can now be celebrated in the Renaissance worship of the body. Neither of Donatello's *David*s can be described as heroic, but the later one is typical of his mature work in its pen-

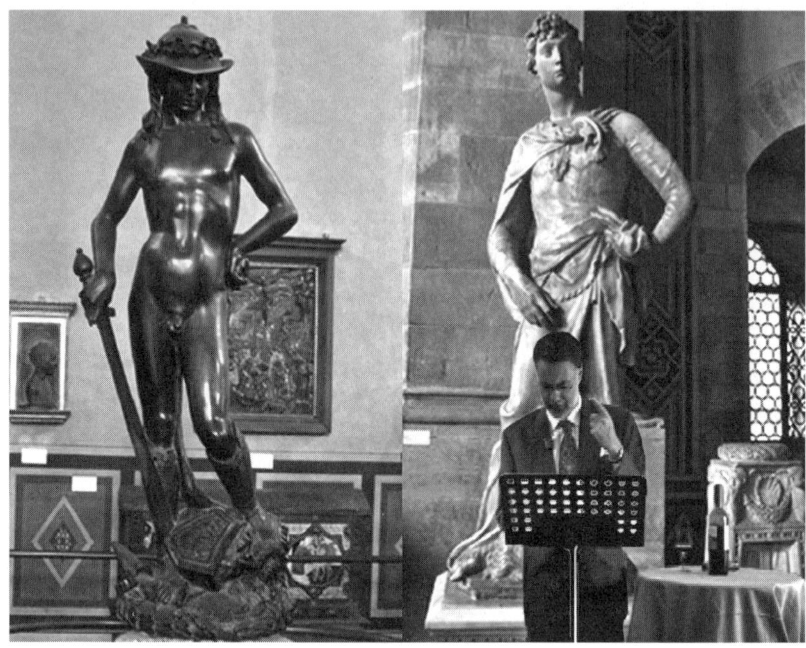

III. *The Birthday Boy*, 2004. Two-screen video with sound installation at the Galleria dell'Accademia, Florence. Photo courtesy of Vincenzo Capalbo.

chant for the shocking. His constantly innovative oeuvre resisted the repetitive, signature style. Look closely at this bronze *David*. The elaborate hat [*slide 3 of bronze David*] and boots [*slide 4 of bronze David*], which seem to make the sensuous surface of nakedness all the more startling. The tumbling locks [*slide 5 of bronze David*], the soft, protruding belly, the arms akimbo, and the head almost bowed beneath the wide brim of the hat shading the face—all of these features seem to frame the focus on the pudenda [*slide 6 of bronze David*].—*pauses, turns, looks at screen, drinks, turns back to text*—Then there is the pun implied by the bird's wing from Goliath's helmet, which slides so sensuously up the inside of *David*'s thigh—the word "uccello" being slang for the phallus [*slide 7 of bronze David*]. Part of the tension that hovers over this work has to do with its mocking irony. A child warrior stands dreamily contemplating the huge giant's head, which he has just severed with his massive sword, a weapon his delicate arms could never have brandished. By exaggerating the contrast between the hoary, yet oddly handsome severed head of the adult giant, and the dreamy pubescent boy who teases Goliath's mustache with his toe [*slide 8 of bronze David*], Donatello puts an uneasy twist on the narrative that informs the work. The artist had no trouble giving a cast of madness to children. Look at his marble *Cantoria* (1433–39) [*slide of marble Cantoria*] where the dancing angels are more like miniature monsters. But in his bronze *David* [*slide 9 of bronze David*] an aura of eroticism bordering on child pornography suffuses the work, flooding every polished, undulating surface. Is there something inherently pornographic about the encounter of giant and child? Did Goliath "fall" for the child? There is in any case a very different kind of homoeroticism in this work than in Michelangelo's later monumental *David* [*slide 9 of bronze David off*]. *—pours glass of wine, drinks, fidgets at lectern, looks out at audience—*

Well, it's the Renaissance here. The big awakening from the Middle Ages. Rebirth of classical themes. Although, of course, God still runs things from afar. But man is the big ticket. Humanism and all that in the sixteenth century. But what almost nobody says is that thought in the Middle Ages was far more original than anything those guys in colored tights were doing strolling around outside the Palazzo Vecchio. I mean who's the equal of old Abelard and Ockham in the sixteenth century? The big problem of universals came up in the Middle Ages, not the Renaissance. Likewise the argument between the realists and the nominalists was a medieval debate. Bear with me for a moment while we think about dogs instead of this great block of white marble. Take universal doghood. Does it exist in each individual dog [*slide of dog*] ? Well, of course, if it is universal. But then how can it be in two animals at once [*slide of two dogs*]? Doesn't that divide doghood in two? And then we have half the universal doghood in each dog. Doesn't compute. A realist could not explain how it could be in both. Well, I stray from art into ideas, always the rotten plank in any art platform [*slide of two dogs off*]. *—takes sip of wine, unbuttons jacket—*

The old argument runs this way: Donatello and the fifteenth century is about dramatic intensity and tension. Michelangelo and the sixteenth is about grandeur. Yeah, let's concede the point. Dramatic intensity can swallow all the perversity you want to throw at it, all those puns, and double entendres. It is comfortable with ambiguity. Narrative infects the visual and the very notion of purity in art is irrelevant. Skepticism and irony are always tucked up its sleeve, ready to be played as trump cards. Grandeur on the other hand allows for no jokes. I would not go so far as to say that the goose step is at home here [*slide of World War II German soldiers marching*], but heroic self-importance is essential. The ironic is never welcome and doubt can only take the form of a tortured mannerism. Massive, intimidating scale is de rigueur. Everybody must look up and hum Wagner [*slide of Wagner opera*] in this temple of art. So how to explain this shift in mind set from the fifteenth to the sixteenth centuries, from Donatello's quirky range of styles to Michelangelo's thundering themes? Theories abound. But theories as Saul Kripke has reminded us, are always wrong [*slide of Wagner opera off*]. —*drinks, rearranges papers, takes handkerchief from pocket, wipes face, looks out at audience—*

In the Michelangelo work all iconographic traces of the giant are absent. The effect is to truncate and nearly cancel any narrative. Here the scale of the absent giant has been morphed into the child who has ballooned into a huge young manhood. The narrative of event, of just terminated combat, so important to the Donatello, is absent from the aura of self-conscious stasis that seems to rise upward around the towering white marble by Michelangelo. Here stands a robust and muscular young man, an athletic specimen that might have just stepped out of the gym. The self-involved, self-satisfied and autonomous seems to emanate from the huge white figure. No severed giant's head lies at this *David*'s feet to divert one's purely visual contemplation of the resplendent male narcissism. Does *David*'s perturbed frown imply he is staring down Goliath? It could just as well be read to indicate he is in the process of forgetting, or trying to recall the event that required the use of his sling. Iconographic narrative is elided and replaced by a static sign. We are intended to read this sign first as that of universal heroic maleness (white, of course), and secondly, as metaphor for confident, latent power. Of this sign writ large, we are to stand in awe. It is the formula for the sublime. Some 253 years after the birth of the *David*, Edmund Burke would articulate the sublime as an image that elicits awe by means of a large, threatening presence, always identified with the masculine. —*drinks, polishes glasses, shifts body position—*

The *David* presages much in the centuries that follow this large art sign of the sublime unveiled in Florence five hundred years ago. Under the sign of the *David* we can collect that mass of Western art sold as the uplifting, the positive, the confidently optimistic, and the sublime. Such a cultural production has the hubris to appeal, as does the *David*, to a universalism which would stand outside its past.

The *David* stands as a sign for an entire culture of art devolving from Renaissance humanism. One of the main assumptions underlying both the ideology of humanism and the art it gave rise to is the belief in a confident autonomy. The aesthetic allegory of autonomy, let us argue, is visual immediacy. Visual immediacy is best achieved by submerging narrative. Iconographic signs and the verbal meanings they elicit can of course never be completely eliminated. Everything is first of all a sign. But the history of Western art is also a long story of trying to rid the visual of stories. Renaissance art purged the text that had been literally inscribed on medieval paintings, displacing the story into images that could be ready iconographically. By the twentieth century we arrive at Modernist abstract art. Here the signs of art seek pure, non-narrative self-referentiality. Here the logophobic strategy has displaced text into the separate activity of critical exegesis [*slide 1 of Krazy Kat*]. This drive for visual purity illuminates our inherent fear of images. Hence the iconophobic disciplining of images by critical interpretation. But does the purging of text from images also shed light on our discomfort with the linguistic [*slide 2 of Krazy Kat*]? Images and words: forever at war, their signifiers forever unstable [*slide 3 of Krazy Kat*].—*drinks, turns to look at screen, spills drink*—Sorry, folks. I don't know how these slides got in here.

Memory is built of stories. The other side of the purging of inconography and narrative from the image is a form of forgetting. How can we name this desire for a forgetful, dominating image that has informed the production of Western art for five hundred years since the *David* showed how to do it? More than aesthetic production is at stake here. Veneration for the immediate and the impact of a visual splash unburdened by the past and a desire for the spectacle of size and power—these would seem to be the quintessential features of the current American cultural psyche. And here we must pause to ponder the ease with which this great white icon, Michelangelo's *David*, has been converted into kitsch. In the tourists stalls of Florence one can buy a miniature *David* in a variety of sizes [*slide of little Davids in tourist stall*]. What is the pop appeal? *David* as pin-up boy? *David* as rock musician without a guitar? *David* as a nude dude with attitude? *David* as a sign of the Renaissance with sex? *David* as Barbie Doll with balls?—*lifts glass to drink but drops glass, shrugs. Off screen hand proffers another glass of wine, which he takes, nodding thanks*—[*slide off*]

We have tried to trace various threads of cultural desire back to this gigantic white marble figure. Michelangelo's *David* broke with Donatello's complex, ironic, narrative-dependent art in favor of the sublime, the static, and the autonomous. Beneath the kitsch image the *David* embodies there lies at a deeper level an aesthetic allegory of Western power driven by whiteness, maleness, and militaristic predilection. Did Mussolini take a good long look at this towering figure? The recent meticulous and laborious cleaning of this icon of Western power perhaps stands itself as a further kind of allegory. This careful caressing with Q-tips mirrors a kind of writing, or re-writing. One that mirrors the writing of five hundred years of European history, a text written by white victors who would carefully document the advances of Western civilization, highlighting its military glories. The victims of course never write history. I wonder how

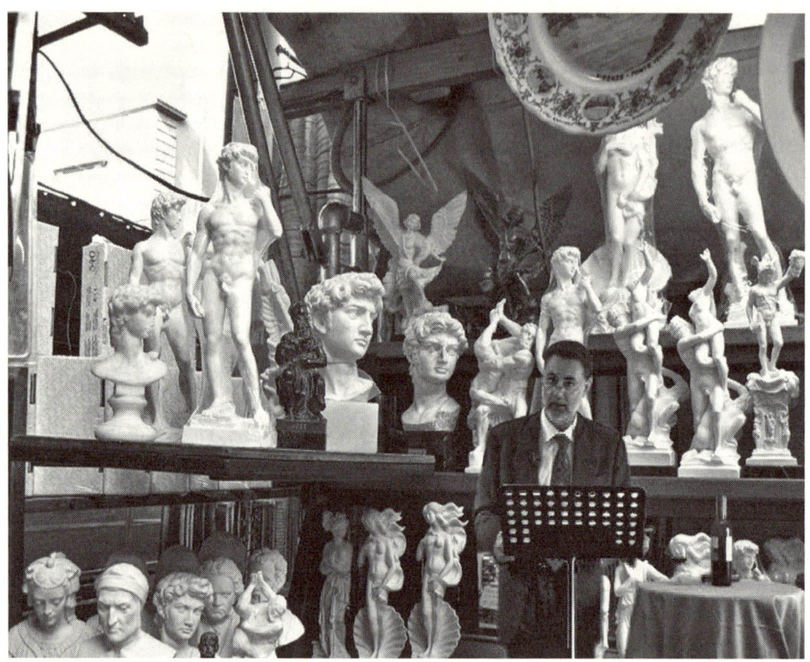

112. *The Birthday Boy*, 2004. Two-screen video with sound installation at the Galleria dell'Accademia, Florence. Photo courtesy of Vincenzo Capalbo.

repositioning the *David*—say removing this oversize, erect work from its pedestal and laying it horizontally on the floor [*slide of David horizontal without pedestal*]—*bends from waist to examine image*—would affect the great Western narrative of art and culture. Hmmm . . .—*straightens up, staggers slightly, grips lectern, drinks*—[*slide off*]

David stands for more than half of art. Maybe three-quarters. Art of the uptick. Jesus has morphed into *David* in this icon of Renaissance humanism. Renaissance humanism is still soaked in, and guaranteed by, Christian belief. Christianity is a time religion that promises the millennium and undoes the pagan view, which is cyclic and static and non-triumphal. Christianity is triumphal with dogmatic hope. Hope, the future, and change: this is Christianity's subtext trinity that *David* also embodies. The promise of youth triumphant and bursting with potentiality. Greek rationalism, which Christianity replaces with faith, is pessimistic by comparison. True, Christ gets nailed to the cross [*slide of Donatello's Crucifixion*]. But before that he kicks the moneychangers out of the temple and promises a Second Coming [*slide off*]. *David* wouldn't have much trouble as a temple bouncer. He looks as tough as they come. Bring on the bad

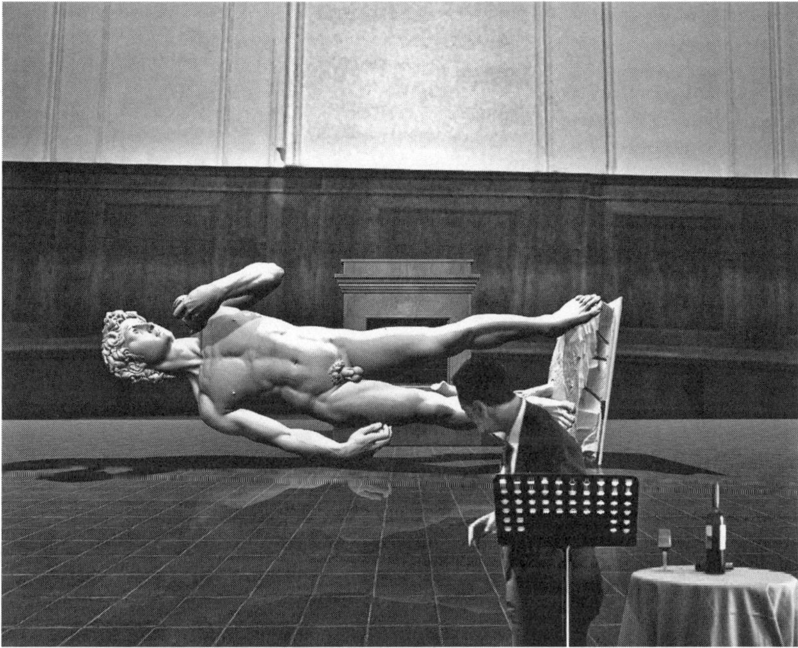

113. *The Birthday Boy*, 2004. Two-screen video with sound installation at the Galleria dell'Accademia, Florence. Photo courtesy of Vincenzo Capalbo.

old giants. *David* will lay these devils low. Cast them out, cut off their ugly heads. *David*'s got the balls and fights for the light and the right. Give *David* a few clothes and helmet and he's an onward-marching Christian Soldier. He's so tough, though, he can do it naked with just a rock and a sling. We identify with his forwardness, his confidence edging up to arrogance, and oh, those swelling muscles. Here is more than Boy Scout preparedness. Here is optimism and reassurance. What three-quarters of art has always been selling: positive energy and the thrust of the uplifting. Thank God, Goya worked small and we can close the book of etchings quickly. We want heroes and thunder. Fast-forward a bit. All of modernist abstract art seeks the transcendent surprise. Faith and youth. Hope and form. The new must point up not down. Belief, so American pragmatism asserts, is what we are prepared to act upon. Belief and action. Modern secular marching orders with the Christian cross slightly displaced. But glance down one of those dark alleys the parade went by without noticing, and recall Noam Chomsky's remark that "it is a sign of moral progress to be able to face things we once thought weren't problems." It is definitely time to change *David*'s position. Remove the pedestal [*slide of David horizontal without pedestal*]. Lay him out flat on the ground so we can get a good, close-up look at him.—*drinks, turns, cocks head to the side, examines horizontal image, turns back to face audience*—[*slide off*]

What else besides that kind of confidence that shades off into arrogance? Wanting to be the center of the universe? As if one were immune. Well, of course, this is the desire to be forever. Immortal. Always in the memory of others. But this requires a great achievement. Causing the deaths of thousands works very well. Napoleon's losses in the Russian winter still sends shudders. Stalin did better. Who can forget his remark that "the death of one man is a tragedy, the deaths of a million is a statistic"? Only the big numbers count.—*makes large gesture and spills wine, staggers slightly, recovers, grips lectern with one hand*—After genocide comes the image. Of course there can be no genocide without images. Words alone were never enough. And ideas? Weren't they always first? Socrates, Kant, Marx. But isn't that over with now that we have information? Now that we have the massive now of ever-new information. Memory is buried. Forgetting is the flush of new information washing away, eroding the old. All the better for youth. That ever-present newness. But wait. Something's got to last. Can an image last? But our images constantly accelerate. They are built for speed, it would seem. Yet some icons hang around. The Beatles didn't die. Il Duce's chin [*slide of Mussolini posturing*] doesn't get erased any more than FDR's cigarette holder [*slide of FDR*]. Well, maybe these last two are now forgotten. Did World War II really happen? Sixty million dead in the forties? Forget it. [*slide off*]—*pauses, polishes glasses, drinks*—

All we need to remember about the last century is that it was, as Elizabeth Bishop reminded us, "the worst so far." But the millennium has turned. Let's think about the new, let's think about youth instead. Brash, loud, confident, adventurous, optimistic, narcissistic, wrinkle-free, gobbling up every new electronic twitch. The future in capitals, say the marketeers. March them this way into the market's yawning maw. Tattooed and pierced with an attitude. Fierce fashion their only law. Well, you say, they have their anxieties. They think about things you never noticed. The oceans turning murky. The butchery and eating of animals. Green architecture. Gender liberation. And don't they all hate war? They claim they are prisoners of spectacle, yet addicted to it. Marx thought capitalism brought both the best and the worst. They say so without having read him. They're too wise for idealism, for utopia, for movements, for the old stories. The rock musician becomes their supreme icon. The lyrics short, repetitive, loud, puerile and pertinent, callow and caustic. Stand up there, *David*, put on some pants and play the air guitar. They don't want to look at your dick, they want to see that big time scowl. They want to hear a deafening wail about how you plonked Goliath. They want to hear you rap about your sling, Dude. And how you did the man with an eighty-eight-millimeter rock. Oh yeah. Rock about that rock. Rap on that rumble. And then stand there with that "Don't fuck with me, Dude" mean old look. Cause it says it all. That's what it's all about. Taking the Man down. The bigger they come, the harder they fall. The eternal war is not, after all, between the short and the tall, but between the young and the old. Goliath must have been ancient, over thirty when David whacked him. Something's not right here. David, that Jew boy slinging rocks? Wasn't that Goliath a Palestinian? Something's wrong with the story.—*throws a few pages of text over shoulder, drinks, looks around at screen, shakes head*—

Five hundred years of whiteness. White boys calling the tune. Five hundred years of the northern hemispheres stomping the southern hemispheres. What counted was what was above the equator. Five hundred years of a capitalist market economy. Winning out in the end, at the end of history. Five hundred years of no planning, since all the plans were utopian and didn't take into account human nature [*slide of Boccioni work*]. What about Futurism [*slide of the dictator*] and Il Duce. More white boys strutting their stuff. Stomp a few Ethiopians, glorify war. Adolescent white boys aestheticizing the political [*slide of Mussolini off*]. Socrates and Wittgenstein: two white boys who went to war. But only to endure it. One stood barefoot in the snow, the other whistled Beethoven in a prisoner of war camp. The most dangerous class on earth: young, unmarried males sixteen to thirty-five. Give them a rock and a sling, a bow and arrow, a sword, a rifle, and watch the world burn. We are strong white boys and we will rule the world by force, so George W. Bush tells us. But we need enemies, preferably dark, hairy little bastards. But big ones will do just as well. Ajax wasn't all that light-skinned under his armor. Dark, stumbling giants we will lay low.—*large gesture with arms flung up, sloshing wine from glass*—Well, we tell the story about those big bastards we took down, urging each other on. Maybe they weren't all that large, but they were dark and they looked like they had weapons. And the winners tell the tale. The dead victims don't write history. And the women can stand around clapping when we march by.

—*turns, looks at screen, lifts glass, looks at glass, back at screen (David now fully morphed into nude young black woman), sets glass down carefully, turns to audience*—I don't know what's happened to our great white hope. *David*, where did you go? Sorry, folks. I can't explain this. I wonder if this is a dream. A nightmare maybe. Did I say the wrong thing? Talking about victims and all that. Well, we do see art differently as the ages pass. Our changing vision

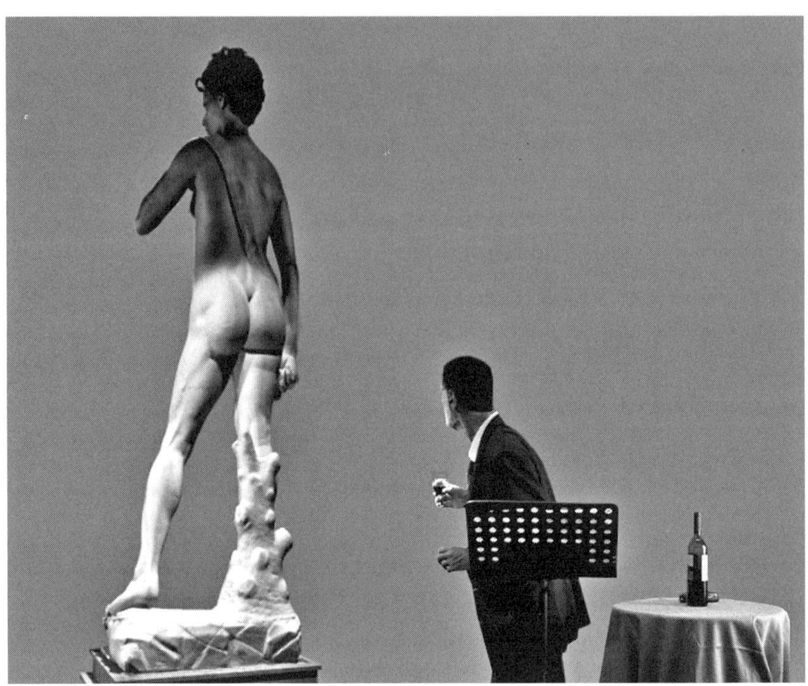

114. *The Birthday Boy*, 2004. Two-screen video with sound installation at the Galleria dell'Accademia, Florence. Photo courtesy of Vincenzo Capalbo.

changes the art. No doubt about that. We see other things than what was seen in its day of creation. As Leonardo said, "With time everything changes." But this is going too far. Yes, too far. *David*, where are you? What has happened to you?—*throws arms out in questioning gesture*—Have you slipped beneath the waves of history? This is not the *David* I once knew. I'm sorry, folks [*slide of exploding* Hindenburg air ship]. I'm beginning to feel like that man who announced the *Hindenburg* disaster in New Jersey . . . "Oh, the humanity . . ." Well, things are changing so fast these days [*slide off*]. Maybe some new force has risen up. Some force of change moving too rapidly for us to stop it and it infects everything. Some kind of art virus, which has penetrated even our most venerated art objects. And even as we speak perhaps the world's masterpieces in all the museums are morphing according to this virus of revenge.

Stage Directions: middle-aged female art historian actor stands at lectern. Glass of red wine (grape juice) sits on table beside lectern. Actor drinks throughout lecture. Hand and arm (body off stage) refills glass from time to time—either by pouring into glass on table or presenting bottle so that actor notices and holds glass out for refill.

Camera: still shot throughout. Framing: from just above actor's head to waist level.

Female Voice:
It is an honor to be asked to say a few words about this great masterpiece before us. Indeed, I raise a toast to the five-hundredth birthday of our beloved *David.—turns, raises glass, drinks, turns back to audience, sets down glass*—Let me begin with a little archaeological background. For the great white block of marble from which the *David* emerged has itself a history. In the 1460s a program was started to furnish giant statues of the Prophets for the Cathedral. Donatello may have been behind the commissioning of the sculptor Agostino di Duccio to carve a giant or Hercules, read in Christian iconography as symbol of fortitude and courage. Duccio was set to make a second statue when Donatello died in 1466, and Duccio's second commission was quietly dropped. The sixteen-foot-tall block, acquired in 1464, was intended for this second Duccio work. One Antonio Rossellino took over the job in 1474 and started carving the block. But he abandoned the task very quickly and with apparently almost no result. The great block lay in the Cathedral workshop yard for twenty-seven years until Michelangelo took on the commission for the gigantic *David* in 1501.—*drinks*—We do not know what state the stone was in at the time, or just how much Rossellino had done. The work is referred to at the time as "a certain figure of marble called *David* badly blocked out and supine. . . ." What did Michelangelo really have in mind for this work? Nobody knows. A Michelangelo sketch exists of a *David* figure [*slide of drawing*], which resembles the earlier Donatello bronze. On this page a muscular arm not unlike the right arm of the finished *David* is rendered. And written beside it are a few words from a Petrarch sonnet: "Rocte lalta cholonna el ver [de lauro . . .] (Broken the high column and the green laurel felled . . .)" Fortitude was symbolized by a broken column in the Quattrocento and the biblical hero David was seen as a personification of courage. Somehow in Michelangelo's mind—here I take the liberty of imagining the goings-on of his genius mind—this gigantic marble rendering of a Hellenistic athlete must have incorporated these virtues.—*drinks, adjusts glasses, glances at screen*—

In 1504 the finished work was set outside the Palazzo Vecchio in the Piazza della Signoria. Was the work seen as a republican, anti-Medici sign? Was the

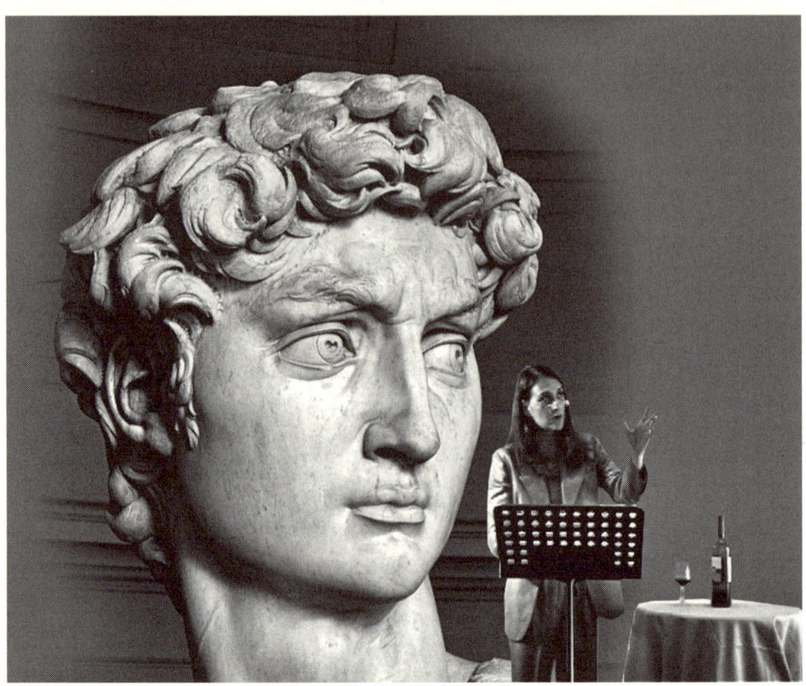

115. *The Birthday Boy*, 2004. Two-screen video with sound installation at the Galleria dell'Accademia, Florence. Photo courtesy of Vincenzo Capalbo.

left-turned head of the *David* read as facing south, staring down the Florentine enemy Rome? Why did some hostile citizens pelt the statue with stones on that night of May 14, 1504, when it was moved into the piazza? And how should the iconography of the figure be unpacked? Does the *David* look toward Goliath, Rome, or the Medicis—anticipating conflicts with all of them? How much Christianity adheres to the shocking nudity of the figure? Or is it just an emblem of fifteenth-century humanism?—*takes off glasses, polishes glasses, drinks, puts glasses back on*—

Well, it's the Renaissance here. The big awakening from the Middle Ages. Rebirth of classical themes. Although of course God still runs things from afar. But man is the big ticket. Humanism and all that in the sixteenth century. But what almost nobody says is that thought in the Middle Ages was far more original than anything those guys in colored tights were doing strolling around the Piazza della Signoria. I mean who's the equal of old Abelard and Ockham in the sixteenth century? The big problem of universals came up in the Middle Ages, not the Renaissance. Likewise the argument between the realists and the nominalists was a medieval debate. Bear with me for a minute while we think about cats instead of this great block of white marble art [*slide of cat*]. Take universal cathood. Does it exist in each individual cat? Well, of course, if it is universal. But then how can it be in two animals at once? Doesn't that divide cathood in two [*slide of two cats*]*?* And then we have half the universal cathood in each cat. Doesn't compute. A realist could not explain how it could be in both. Well, I stray from art into ideas, always the rotten plank in any art platform [*slide off*].

The old argument runs this way: Donatello and the fifteenth century was about dramatic intensity and tension. Michelangelo and the sixteenth century is about grandeur. Yes, let's concede the point. Dramatic intensity can swallow all the perversity you want to shovel at it, all those puns and double entendres. It is comfortable with ambiguity. Narrative infects the visual and the very notion of purity in art is irrelevant. Skepticism and irony are always tucked up its sleeve, ready to be played as trump cards. Grandeur, on the other hand, allows for no jokes. And when doubt about it creeps in there is no distancing irony, only mannerist exaggeration. I wouldn't go so far as to say that the goose step [*slide of German soldiers marching*] is at home here, but heroic self-importance is essential. Doubt and the ironic are never welcome. Massive, intimidating scale is de rigueur [*slide of Wagner opera*]. Everybody must look up and hum Wagner in this temple of art. So how to explain this shift in mind set from the fifteenth to the sixteenth century, from Donatello to Michelangelo? We could theorize endlessly about the reasons. But as the philosopher Saul Kripke has reminded us, theories are always wrong [*slide off*].*—shuffles papers, drinks—*

And what about the iconography of the youthfulness of our *David* figure? Male of course. No doubt about gender here. And white of course. But we must remember this is the beginning of the sixteenth century in Italy. Macho is the way it is. The representation of women tends toward either the Madonna or the whore. The High Renaissance was just as misogynist as those classical themes it sought to imitate. Men had all the power, so the image of a giant, young male athlete was going to go down well in 1504—among the cognoscenti anyway. Some thought the total nudity went too far. The homoerotic was all right, just not so blatantly hanging out in public. The bestiality of *Leda and the Swan* was permitted [*slide of painting*], but Leda getting it on with, say, Gloria? Well, you can imagine what would have happened to the artist who dared to make such an image. And I don't need to remind you that women artists were few and far between in those days. In fact they were virtually nonexistent in the High Renaissance.*—turns to look at screen, elbows on hips, shrugs, slide off, turns back to lectern, drinks—*

The *David* initiates a five-hundred-year effort to deface narrative and precipitate it out of visual production. But immediacy of the image unburdened by an involved iconographic narrative is a necessary but not sufficient requirement for maximum visual impact. Grand scale and some sense of hovering threat, however nuanced this shading of the sublime, must also be present. For the first time in Western art the *David* organizes all these necessary and sufficient features and therefore stands as a model for five centuries of what counts as high art in the West.

Does the homoerotic aura that emanates from the *David* account for its elevation to a universal, transcultural status? That and the fact of its size? Youthful male grandeur in a militaristic mode. Here we have it all: youth, maleness, whiteness, grandeur, hero, killer. A formula that is as rampant today as five hundred years ago. The main difference is that today it is framed by movies and not by gigantic sculpture. One other significant difference about the image of the testosterone-charged young male hero of today is skin color. White is no longer exclusive. Steroid-drenched body builders and Kung Fu artists of all colors—black, yellow, brown, whatever—have stepped into the film role today in our culture of spectacle and celebrities. Today *David* would be competing with hordes of young muscled males trying to escape the ghetto by getting into professional athletics or acting in films. Today *David* might get his start in a Calvin Klein underwear ad [*slide of David in costume*]. Or with the addition of a modest pair of camouflage shorts and a cartridge belt he might land the lead in a TV commercial made for the military recruiting office. But he would not be up there strutting his stuff without competition—of course I speak about what might go on in America where the military is as big as God.—*turns toward slide, makes gesture, drinks*—[*slide off*]—*turns back to lectern*—

If *David* was the Arnold Schwarzenegger of his day, he turned out to be just as good a politician. Although so far as we know Arnold didn't have to kill any giants to get the job, although he seems to have manhandled a number of women on his way to the top. I am straying, I know. I'll get back to the art. But the images of art are not innocent. We can't have wars without images. Words alone won't do it. The great and the heroic, the promise of adventure and risk, the moralism of shining causes, and above all the nasty otherness of an enemy—all these things need images in order to be sold to the young, the gullible, the uncritical. All those who take their slings, or M-16s, or Kalashnikovs out into the dusty fields to do the dying need the image of some kind of sexy glory to get them going. No, images are not innocent. Death must be masked and aestheticized. And art, or something like it, has always been will-

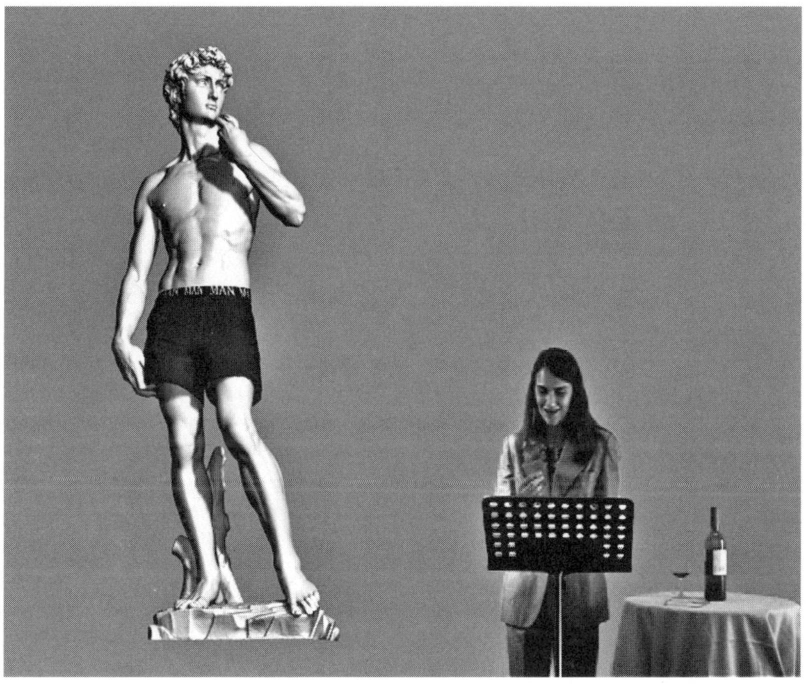

116. *The Birthday Boy*, 2004. Two-screen video with sound installation at the Galleria dell'Accademia, Florence. Photo courtesy of Vincenzo Capalbo.

ing to serve power. Art can always be hired to emblazon a gigantic and heroic image over the nothingness of death. Art can always be hired to show you the glory before the battle, before the dying, before the stench of rotting bodies and maimed flesh. The heroic young soldier stands stalwart and courageous, looking to his left at the coming enemy and not flinching. Standing tall, weapon in his hand. What an image. Truly inspiring. Of course it takes a Goya to show what happens after the battle.—*drinks, fidgets, looks around*—

When Goya was shown the image of the *David* he laughed and laughed and laughed. He laughed all day long. Then he did a series of black-and-white ink and crayon drawings based on the great white figure. To one he gave the head of an ass, another he wrapped in an enormous white sheet blowing in a high wind [*Goya slide*]. Yet another showed the figure as a French soldier raping a Spanish nun. One had the figure of *David* squatting over a ditch defecating while strange bird-like creatures flew over his head. Still another showed the proud figure standing on a dunghill with his own head under his arm. Goya devoted an entire album of drawings to the *David*. I'm sorry I have but one

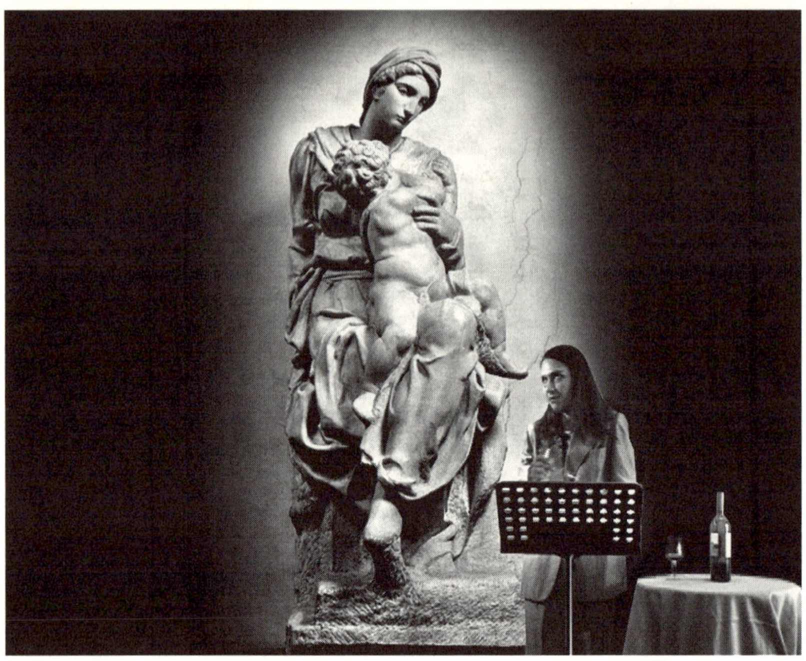

117. *The Birthday Boy*, 2004. Two-screen video with sound installation at the Galleria dell'Accademia, Florence. Photo courtesy of Vincenzo Capalbo.

image to show you here. Unfortunately this small bound volume of drawings has been lost. I only know them from some rather bad reproductions of copies made by an obscure Spanish artist who owned the volume briefly.—*turns, looks at screen, drinks, shrugs, turns back to lectern, pushes hair up from face, etc . . . signs of inebriation showing now in her gestures*—[*slide off*]

Humanism, as we know, put man at the center. Man, not woman. Woman was left out. Michelangelo left them out. Look at the Medici Tombs [*slide of Night*]. Neither *Night* nor *Dawn* [*slide of Dawn*] are convincing, let alone sympathetic, representations of women. Rather what we have here are two male athletes with breasts stuck onto their chests. The Madonnas he carved, for example the *Medici Madonna*, begun in 1521 [*slide of Madonna*], are voluminously draped, disguising their gender more than asserting their femininity. The misogynous representations of Michelangelo are too well known to dwell on here and I only note them in passing to underline the machismo at the heart of humanism.—*raises glass, spills some wine*—[*slide off*]

Man's addiction to killing has not lessened since the sixteenth century. Sixty million died in World War II. Technology, ramping up from the rock and sling to nuclear weapons, just makes the killing easier. Although recent studies have shown that in some so-called primitive societies more men die in fighting in proportion to the population than what went on in the industrialized nations of the twentieth century—hardly cause for celebrating an advance in the pacific tendencies of the male.

Only white boys put up the monuments—to themselves, to their victories, their heroes, their dead, their glory, their certainty, their maleness, their conquests, their sublimity. So we let *Victory* be a woman with wings [*slide of Victory*]. Well, we couldn't very well heap up thousands of enemy corpses and stick a victory sign on them. And we only list the names of our fallen heroes [*slide of Vietnam Veterans Monument*]. Showing them legless and blind is out. And always make it larger than life. The sublime can't be small [*slide off*]. But then again we don't want to make it too frightening. How about showing, say, a young man before he suffers any wounds. Go through the ranks and find someone fit. So what if he is a thug with hands like sledgehammers. Give him the line about glory, the barbarians, and humanism. Pump him up with the old stories and pose him looking serious and confident and like he owns the place. Better have him buck-naked. And give him some kind of primitive weapon. Just a rock in his hand will do the trick. Now turn his head slightly, have him look out and frown. Perfect. Freeze frame. What? He's big enough but not white enough? Well, he's been standing there for five hundred years with pigeons shitting on him. Clean him up, give him a bath so he will again blaze out his whiteness and glory, his oversized manhood.—*knocks over wine glass, staggers, arm comes in from off-stage and replaces full glass on table*—

Oh, we all get old. We always have. Only now we are taking the earth itself into our declining old age. Melt the ice caps, poke a hole in the ozone clouds, piss in the ocean, shit in the streams, vomit in the lakes. The market goes on valorizing youth, but everybody over thirty knows how much we resent age. Otherwise why would we be dragging down the planet into ecological senility? The old adage, "After me the deluge," doesn't apply here. No, we resent aging so much that we have decided to watch the earth die of old age. Arthritic mountains and sludged-up arterial rivers. Why should art be immune to the aging process? If the earth is to perish of old age why should the art hang around pretending to offer some kind of illusory renewal? Why did they bring the *David* inside? He should have remained where they put him on that night in May 1504. Let the acid rain wash away his youth, erode his muscles, darken his

Caucasoid skin, slump his militaristic strut. Let him get old with the earth we are forcing into senility.—*takes off jacket and throws over her shoulder at screen, drinks, grabs lectern for support*—

It is not hard to see from our perspective how Renaissance humanism, in its self-centered confidence, implied racism, colonialism, corruption, militarism, and misogyny. Just take a look at Machiavelli. The question then arises, why should we go on venerating and conserving the art humanism generated? It surely isn't to remind ourselves about what should be avoided. Is Michelangelo's pompous, portentous, and overstuffed sculpture a norm to be emulated? Or can we somehow ignore its baroque self-involvement and mannerist doubt, which are so heavy-handed and glaringly transparent? It is possible. But we need a certain kind of faith. Then we can see that there is something in the work to be isolated, extracted, and preserved. Some kind of Neo-Platonic essence. This is its "form." Oh, you can find it if you just go into that aesthetic trance that purges the historical and the political from the object, and numb yourself to the iconographic levels. As Renaissance humanism wrapped itself in Christianity, so too can we wrap its art in an equally transcendent substance—that immaterial essence called aesthetic form. This reductive ideology reaches its peak in the modernist formalism of the last century. Seeing things this way, where the so-called content collapses into the form, also offers the comfort of forgetting. A kind of forgetting about the culture that produced it. A forgetting of the powers it served, the contradictions it mediated, the unconscious needs that impelled it. All that drains away. Then form emerges as an apolitical, transcendent essence that wafts up from the material embodiment like a grand perfume of promise. This promise even fooled Immanuel Kant. But Kant was selling the aesthetic as a disinterested formal judgment of taste—subjective but nevertheless commanding universal consent—as another kind of Calvinist duty to be performed by the enlightened white European. Kant's claims to the universal were Eurocentric and had nothing to do with Asia or Africa, or any other place very far from Königsberg. And pleasure had little to do with it either in his system where the sublime was charged with leading one up to the moral. But when the Kantian God died, or was killed off, as Nietzsche would have it, the unbelievers were left to worship aesthetic form as a substitute spirituality. Humanism, Neo-Platonism, Kantianism, formalism. Junk. Trash. Waste. Cultural amnesia. Self-delusion. A gigantic heap of metaphysical junk with the miasma of the aesthetic condensing like a toxic waste over this great heap of dead European thought. Open the door and let in the dark. Paint it black. Don't breathe that yucky, pure white, quasi-spiritual aesthetic crap down my

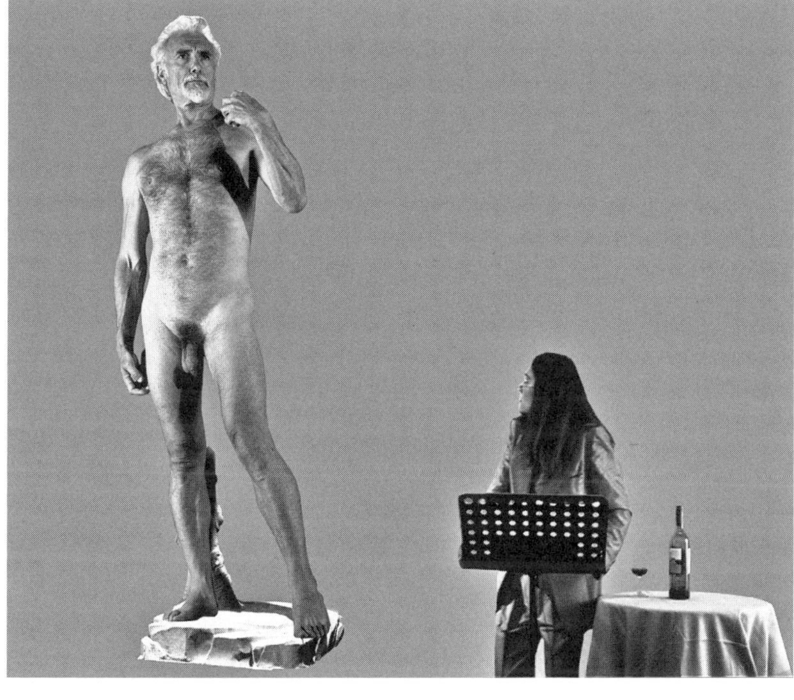

118. *The Birthday Boy*, 2004. Two-screen video with sound installation at the Galleria dell'Accademia, Florence. Photo courtesy of Vincenzo Capalbo.

neck.—*flings glass of wine at David image on wall behind her, staggers around behind lectern, lecture pages fall on floor*—

But wait, isn't the ambition for grandeur and wanting to know who one's enemies are truly universal? (Machiavelli again?) Isn't it, finally, just part of the male genetic makeup? Isn't it the same old record, the same old song, just with a different beat in different cultures? Isn't what really matters what is made out of these impulses, what they leave behind as works? Sure, Auschwitz or the killing fields of the Khmer Rouge are more likely than the Parthenon. So when a block of stone is turned into a *David*—instead of, say, five hundred cavalry turned into hamburger in the Charge of the Light Brigade—shouldn't we celebrate? But then again, isn't the Charge of the Light Brigade celebrated? And for some of the same reasons the *David* was celebrated. Heroes. Dead or alive. We need heroes. And the heroic. Grandeur demands the heroic. And, of course, we can't get by without our enemies because without enemies we could not invent heroes. So let's hear it for Michelangelo. He knew two things. One, that the young and sexy hero lasts the longest if he can be freeze-dried into art.

And two, only the awe and spectacle of the monumental will do the job. So let a million tongues of art lovers of form lick the *David* clean, back to its pristine whiteness. Back to its gigantic adolescent youthfulness. Lick. Lick. There, with tongue sliding over the cold whiteness, eyes focused in extreme close up, we enter the myopic, amnesiac trance where only form comes into focus. There we are suspended, buoyed up in that hazy space of grandeur where death is denied.—*shrugs shoulders, drinks, smirks at the David image now completely morphed into eighty-year old man, does a double take*—

But, oh, wait a minute. What's happened here to our youthful giant? Crumbling into old age? Unthinkable. The *David*, before he was anything else, he was a kind of guarantee of eternal youth. Ageless. It's a little frightening. Terrifying actually. A statue aging? Are my eyes deceiving me? Has the story of Dorian Gray taken over here, like some form of art virus? Yes, that must be it. And if it has got to our perfect *David*, even after being cleaned with a million Q-tips, where else might it have found a host? What is happening at the Louvre? Has the *Mona Lisa* grown a moustache [*slide of Duchamp's postcard*], has her face wrinkled, her smile become a sneer? And all the Botticelli ladies, have they become dreadful old crones [*slide off*]? Nietzsche promised that "we have art lest we perish of the truth." Looks like this art virus has been gnawing at that remark as well. Oh, it looks like it is over. Downhill from here. All the art getting old. Forget it. Turn on the TV.

JASPER JOHNS: THE FIRST DECADE | 2005

Half a century ago a recently discharged, young army veteran began his cultural assaults. In a decade-long campaign he raised the *Flag*, dared them to fire at his *Target, Numbered* the prisoners taken *0 through 9*, *Mapped* out a strategy, and *Dived* from a height heretofore not attempted.

Much has changed since Johns produced these works just after midcentury. America was then not only a guaranteed safe place with a middle class, but also lender to the world. Recently we have become unsafe, debt-ridden, and absent a middle class. Since 9/11 we have become an unapologetically imperialistic and militaristic nation squandering its treasure on war while waiting for the next disaster to be played and replayed as the spectacle of entertainment on TV. America is anxious, insecure, self-righteous, and dangerous, with an ever shorter fuse and attention span.

America's large museums have also changed by becoming virtually unrecognizable from the introverted, mostly empty, silent places they were at midcentury. Those somber spaces that sat halfway between church and bank have given way to new architectural pleasure palaces—recalling the movie palace extravaganzas of the 1920s—in which "gee whiz" art of the spectacle replaces sober masterpieces. But the museums only reflect the culture at large, which is a culture of spectacle. Fun is serious business, and no museum can ignore serving up the entertainment that will pull in a paying crowd.

We have always wanted art to intrigue us with its physical achievements and tell us about itself. We want to be seduced by its wiles and graces. But we also look to art to tell us about our culture and ourselves. The better art always tells us about those aspects that are not apparent or easy to accept. Lesser art speaks to what we already know.

Modernism, with its claims of autonomy, valorization of the heroic, and utopian sentiments, seemed to want to deny Elizabeth Bishop's remark that the twentieth century was "the worst century so far." Likewise, modernism wanted to prove wrong Max Weber's idea that modernity had disenchanted the world. By midcentury modernism was dead (largely euthanized by Johns in the plastic arts) and the disaster of the twentieth century could no longer be denied. But neither could it be easily accepted. That culture has turned toward the distractions of spectacle is proof enough of this denial. Anything not to face a failure so vast as to be unthinkable. Today demographic, political, economic, social, and ecological areas are out of control and there are no answers available to rescue the world for us. After the Cold War was won, the market and technology were deified by the West. It is now clear that these were false gods. The demand for the right to entertainment, perhaps the patron saint of this dual divinity, drives toward ever larger, more relentless, and ubiquitous staging of spectacles of distraction from the coming disasters. Large museum shows have for some time very often been in the service of the hysteria of the spectacular. What then can this exhibition of quiet, unspectacular paintings just this side of the grim deliver to museumgoers today?

I want to argue that some of these works from 1955 to 1959 held a proleptic edge, and today we can see in them a beacon from the horizon of the past. Perhaps these works were more profoundly pessimistic than they seemed at the time they appeared. Targets, numbers, flags, maps: icons always hoisted amid the clank and grind of gearing up for the enemy, anticipating the coming shock and awe. Whether red stars or crescents fly on the flags above their trenches, the targeting of the other was always a targeting of just numbers. Trying hopelessly and absurdly to make the edges of our homeland map safe in the face of the imagined threat—all this was better than facing what could not be solved. Johns' works of 1955 to 1961 stand as a painful reminder of what we have done and have not done in the half century that followed their creation. How better to be reminded of our collective failure than by such gracious signs? And if we can take this, then there is also—as might be expected from work that is also always something else—that breathtaking ride of complexity, intricate thought, and aesthetic glory that the works deliver.

. . . . .

An overarching allegory of art as of and from the body haunts all of the work, regardless of its formal or structural dispositions, or apparent subject matter. And the subtheme is, in my opinion, the self-confined body's endurance of oppression or suffering. The obliqueness of the handling of this reference gives the work the subtle sense of the tragic which rises from it. If there are many European affinities in the work it is in the nature of this "tragic" aura that the artist is revealed as quintessentially American. The suffering of which the art speaks arises from isolation and loneliness. Only a massive, hermitic solipsism of the defended, vulnerable self could generate the kind of flat, gorgeous, airless space, where, generally, only icons of the already represented are permitted entry. A voluntary inner exile has been the fate of many American poets and artists, driving a number to the depths of not only their art. Herman Melville, Edgar Allan Poe, Albert Ryder, Delmore Schwartz, and Hart Crane were but a few.

The world and its disturbing evils has for Johns always been *Out the Window*, and that window is never raised. If Johns sensed what was outside in his early exposure to the military, the window was closed tightly by the end of the 1950s, and the *Shade* lowered. Knowing even indirectly about the European slaughter is enough to make most want to draw the shade. And no artist has better illuminated the somber pleasures of our isolated confinement in our innermost rooms, where we wait with and on the body, where flesh numbers its losses, where skin wears its memories, and where every mark is a solemn, careful counting toward our mortality.

. . . . .

Tell me who your enemy is and I'll tell you who you are.

—CARL SCHMITT[1]

On May 25, 1951, Jasper Johns was drafted into the Army. He was stationed for a year and a half at Fort Jackson, South Carolina, where he developed an art exhibition program for the soldiers. From December 1952 until May 1953, Johns was sent to Sendai, Japan. The military environment is characterized by the impersonal, the anonymous, and the insistently repetitious. Targets, flags, numbers, and maps form a ubiquitous set of iconic signs within the closed military environment. These icons constitute the subjects of the paintings Johns made, beginning two years after his discharge from the Army in May 1953. I don't think it is too much of a stretch to regard these works as allegories of revenge. Military life is at best regimented, demeaning, repetitive, stupefying, and alienating. Outside the chaos of battle the military environment is characterized by the rigidly hierarchic and symmetrical. The U.S. flag is seldom out of sight. Every button on the soldier's uniform must be fastened to maintain bilateral symmetry. The soldier is first and last a number. And military life is completely regulated by numbers. On the rifle range the target is raised, the soldier fires, and his score is denoted by a number that is hoisted in the place of the target. The soldier marches within a squad of bodies dressed in identical uniforms and rigidly aligned. Life in the barracks is strictly supervised and disciplined. Personal freedom of choice does not exist. Standing at rigid attention in a symmetrical field of unmoving bodies, the soldier shouts the anonymous "Yo!" in response to the roll call of his name. Sometimes he is required to shout his enlistment number as well. Johns' particular experience in the Army—whether difficult or easy—is irrelevant. The culture of the military could not have been avoided. No, it is not too much of a stretch to see the depiction of the early *Targets, Flags, Maps*, and *Numbers* as allegories of revenge and, perhaps, redemption. It is doubtful that these works sprang from a conscious intention. But the intention of the artist is irrelevant. Art of any weight and significance rises from unconscious compulsions.

ZERO THROUGH TEN

A single death is a tragedy; a million deaths is a statistic.

—JOSEPH STALIN[2]

Under organized power. Subject to tremendous controls. In a condition caused by mechanization. . . . In a society that was no community and devalued the person. Owing to the multiplied power of numbers which made the self negligible.

—SAUL BELLOW, *HERZOG*[3]

I. *Figures*, 1955

In 1955 Johns painted some *Figures*. Each canvas limned a number from zero to nine. Each is roughly 17 by 14 inches. Each depicted figure is more or less the same size, fills most of the rectangle, and is of the same, standard serif typeface. A thin black outline distinguishes each number, or figure, from its field or ground. Collaged newspaper is visible beneath the brushy encaustic white paint. The entire surface from edge to edge, as well as running beneath the outlined figure, is rendered in collage and white wax. Let us read this family of signs—these standardized and anonymous icons of quantity, these crisp yet somehow shabby figures, each so lovingly rendered in a wistful haze of unreadable, mute text and sensuous, translucent white wax—as punning metaphors for the human figure. Figures as figure. Each so alike, yet different. Allegorical portraits of the anonymous dogface soldier. Maybe. But the "messy" beauty of the brushwork and diaphanous collage of surface does more than undermine the spit and polish of the compulsive, oppressive, minimal military aesthetic.

Nothing is ever simple, immediate, singular, straightforward, innocent, undisguised, or undisplaced in Johns' early work. Logic is always burdened with contradiction, language and image remain adversarial, puns abound, origins are hidden, ambivalence reigns, and the allegorical is seldom out of sight. Simplicity of image never equates with simplicity of experience. Revenge lies locked in an embrace with redemption. If one were to search for a law governing these early works it might be this: "Everything is really something else."[4] The art in the *Figures* displaces the image from its origin in revenge. Redemption of the bloodless, singular "figure" is achieved by the *Aufhebung* of converting revenge into pathos. The thick, waxy, clotted, translucent white paint running down the surface of these works is of course encaustic. But what are we to make of the resemblance here to semen running down a newspaper? The aestheticized surface functions as a decoy, a disguising delay that ever so slowly refocuses itself as an act of witnessing on the part of the artist. Eventually it dawns on us that the artist has seen for us, felt for us, redeemed for us, the dehumanizing of human numbering. But the cost of the original dehumanizing is never forgotten in the work of Johns—where, if there is pathos, there is never sympathy—and it haunts all the early works based on the diagrammatic icons of flag, target, number, and map.

Existence is terrifying.

—PAUL CÉZANNE[5]

2. *Target with Plaster Casts*, 1955

To reiterate the place that the early works of Johns hold in that narrative of the collapse of modernism is to trivialize and officialize them, allowing their contradictions, complexities, and origins to slip away. The more familiar the works are allowed to become, the less we need to face the morality that underlies them. If the dehumanized saturates the military emblems of the flag and target, the diagrammaticism of the numbers and the maps extends further Johns' investigation into the field of alienated signs, which forms the dehumanizing language of the military.

Heraclitus was right, war is the father of everything. All I know I learned in the army.

—JOSEPH BEUYS[6]

Shoot the foot, the face, the breast, the ear, the genitals, the heel, or the bull's eye: the large *Target* of 1955 offered a choice (even the bull himself was offered metonymically via a beef bone in the last box on the right). Looking is conflated with a .30-caliber weapon. Military life flattens and confines the body, controls it and puts the body in boxes. Desire is objectified, regimented, fragmented,

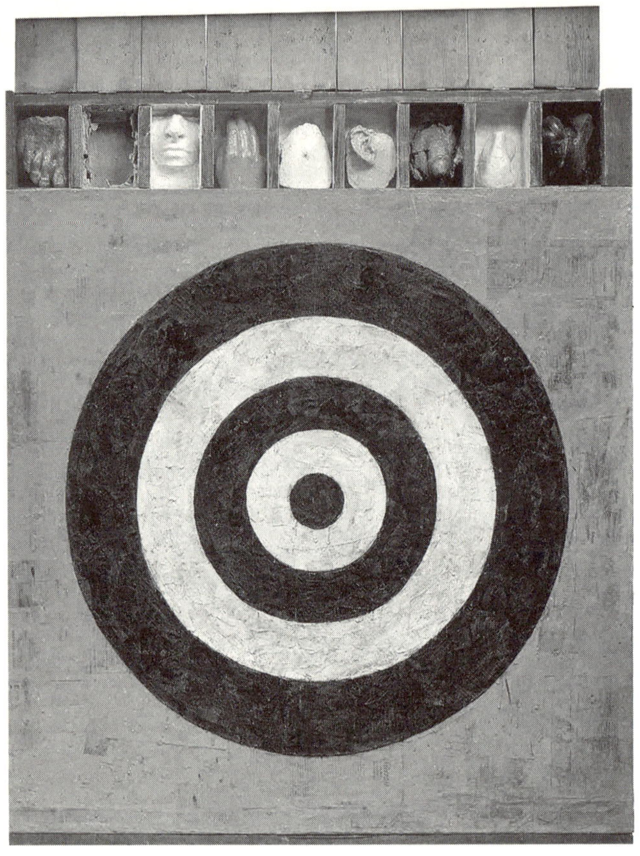

119. Jasper Johns, *Target with Plaster Casts*, 1955. Encaustic and collage on canvas with objects, 51 × 44 × 3½ inches (129.5 × 111.8 × 8.8 cm). Collection of David Geffen, Los Angeles. Copyright © Jasper Johns/Licensed by VAGA, New York.

compartmentalized. Get drunk on payday, fuck on Saturday, shoot a Gook on Monday. Everything in its box. And if you failed inspection on Tuesday, you got to sleep with your M-1 rifle for the rest of the week.

But out there in civilian life the Abstract Expressionists were dripping paint, throwing paint, screaming paint, and Clem Greenberg was telling them they were macho geniuses. Out there in civilian life subjectivities were untucked and it was hard to tell who had the biggest one. A kind of American adolescent male athleticism was in place, and only the really big sweat-soaked canvas counted. Of all the twentieth-century American artists, Johns has been the least American (the flag notwithstanding). Here was an aesthetic subversive who would temper his innate suspicious mistrust and a grim, arrogant, detached derisiveness with redemptive loving care. Here was a skeptic who took back any large gesture and covered it with an embroidery of doubt. Here was a sensibility with an itch for mockery that would not be denied. Here was the predatory, remorseless aesthetic of a compassionless, dead-eyed art sniper who "targeted" the cant in big-time American art. But a deeper, more subtle revenge is delivered by the target paintings. They stand as a mockery of the notion of focus itself. The kind of vision the target invites, focused and conscious, will always deliver the fragmented, the partial thing in its box. The targets impugn conscious thought itself insofar as the "targeted," what one consciously focuses on, is a kind of tunnel vision condemned to miss the whole.

The *Targets* speak to a deep given in the culture—that sacred tenet of capitalism—competition. Winning, the best score, hitting the bull's eye, getting the prize, defeating the other, being the best, etc., etc. And for the consequences of this first rule of American freedom, open the boxes above the target.

3. *White Flag*, 1955

Why so large? Almost 7 by 10 feet. The size of the Old Glories I remember tacked up in the mess halls. A ballsy, intimidating military size and "bigger than you, soldier." It was up there watching you and demanded a salute. But cut one in two places and let the blood colors of red and blue drain out. Make it a big cut. Not exactly that "Y" cut of the autopsy. Not exactly. Dead flag. Cut and drained and stuck back together with the scar showing. A big, anemic, dead sign. A bloodless sign. Yet a sign resurrected as flesh. Dead flesh perhaps. An embalmed flesh of the sign. A white, waxy necrophilia for the autopsied remains. A murderous aesthetic act and a caressing mummification of the corpse wrapped in white, waxed strips, or stripes. Revenge taken. Resurrection delivered. The redeemed corpse as a trinity of dissected and reassembled parts. Transfiguration of the oppressive, dominating sign by transgressive encaustic bleaching. Encaustic, the medium of second-century tomb décor. Nothing but the finest funerary accouterments for that patriotic shroud which has wrapped so many public scoundrels. The large *White Flag*, ghost banner of countless, officially sanctioned criminal acts. But flattened, bled white by Johns, and filed away as flat forensic evidence. No wonder Johns kept this work so long for himself.

4. *0 through 9*, 1960

The outline of one number on top of the next, superimposed (confined?) in a space 29 by 23 inches. Drawn in charcoal on white paper. A few smudges, but on the whole fairly neatly executed. Each number skillfully drawn free-

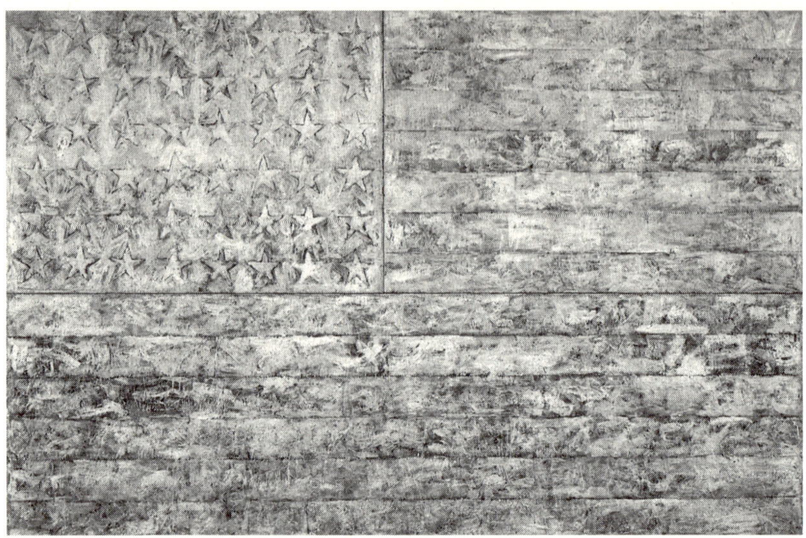

120. Jasper Johns, *White Flag*, 1955. Encaustic and collage on canvas, three panels, 78 5/16 × 120 3/4 inches (198.9 × 306.7 cm) overall. The Metropolitan Museum of Art, New York. Copyright © Jasper Johns/ Licensed by VAGA, New York.

hand. At first glance the "3" snaps into focus, then the "4." The rest take longer to extract. A collapsing of quantitative signs, an implosion of the numerical, counting compressed to a single point in time and space. An endless, repetitive rush of the act of dividing done at warp speed. Zeno's paradox. In some ways this can be seen as a pendant to Marcel Duchamp's *Three Stoppages-Étalon* of 1913–1914. Duchamp's use of chance to point up the absurdity of standards of measurement is echoed by Johns (whose early works are almost all "assisted readymades") in *0 through 9*, when he applies a vacuum to suck out the space that is assumed to be needed to enumerate anything. But the pessimism that lies below *0 through 9* goes much deeper. The suggestion that numbers imply an infinite sublime is inverted and cancelled in this work. The very process of enumerating the series shuts down the action. At a deeper level *0 through 9* is an allegory of foreclosure, stasis, ending—a counting toward death.

> But how can a rule show me what I have to do at *this* point? Whatever I do is, on some interpretation, in accord with the rule. . . . Is what I call "obeying a rule" something that would be possible for only *one* man to do, and only *once* in his life?
>
> —LUDWIG WITTGENSTEIN[7]

After some thought he [Albert Speer] hit on the idea of covering the distance from Berlin to Heidelberg by walking around the garden—four hundred miles as he calculated. As he had no tape-measure, he marked out the path by shoe-lengths. It came to 870 units, which he multiplied by the twelve inches of a shoe, concluding that one circuit would equal roughly 295 yards. Then he fixed an approximate daily route, and after four weeks recorded that he had covered 149 miles.

—JOACHIM FEST[8]

5. *Gray Alphabets*, 1956
6. *White Numbers*, 1958

These paintings allow for a lateral, two-dimensional space that is denied in the later *0 through 9*. Once the units—whether running across a two-dimensional space (*Gray Alphabets, White Numbers*) or collapsed into a temporal superimposition (*0 through 9*)—are run through, the work finishes itself by exhausting the sequence. What the three works share is a logical structural device, which might be described one way as an entropic rule for exhaustion. Another way to describe it is as a self-enclosed and self-completing mechanism, or as an a priori, spring-loaded algorithm or rule for sequences, which nullifies the freedom for certain aesthetic decisions. Part of the pathos of these works issues from that march of patient, encaustic marks across and within the imprisonment of the device.[9] Johns' focus on the ordinary iconic signs of numbers, flags, targets, and maps as subjects for art carries more than aesthetic significance. A morality of resistance is implied in taking on these signs, which, if so apparently ordinary, are also freighted with connotations of domination. For in mass society numbers are not innocent. Neither is the nationalism implicitly signified by flag and map. And targets are of course in the service of weaponry. The defamiliarization of these signs through the frame of art can be read as an oblique rhetoric of resistance which is also a form of redemption.

7. *Map*, 1961 (With a note on *Device Circle*, 1959)

The gestalt singularity of flags, targets, and numbers is missing in the map imagery. Space in the sense of an implied figure/ground opposition, and the arbitrary designations of state boundaries in the U.S. map don't hold the image. There seems to be a special anxiety evident in the somewhat hysterical brushwork that delineates and obliterates the boundaries in these works.

Johns' work is especially powerful when he employs the mnemonic, public, gestalt image that he can then haunt with a brushwork that never violates the

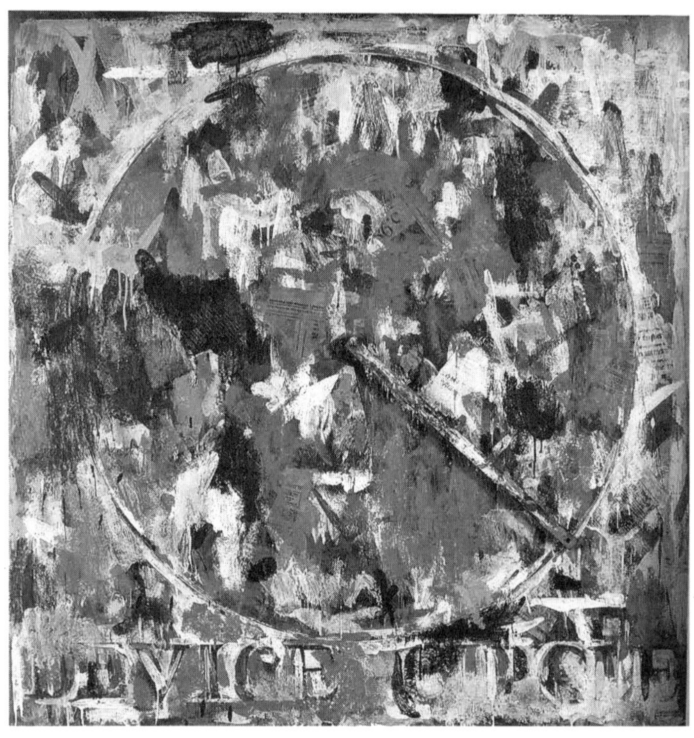

121. Jasper Johns, *Device Circle*, 1959. Encaustic and collage on canvas with wood, 40 × 40 inches (101.6 × 101.6 cm). Collection of Denise and Andrew Saul. Copyright © Jasper Johns/Licensed by VAGA, New York.

inner divisions. The earlier *Device Circle*, 1959, which literalizes the inscribing compass and hints at the coming of indexical signs, is attacked with a riot of paint, the excesses of which never endanger the loss of the gestalt. Perhaps because of this security, as well as the lack of a "public" tension-making sign to work against, *Device Circle* seems too self-consciously devicelike and finally too didactic. The *Flag*, *Numbers*, and *Target* works are powerfully mnemonic signs against which the pathos of the art can press.

There is something of the folk-art sampler in those works in which the image coincides with the physical limit of the painted object. Patchwork quilts that respect the interior divisions of stripes and bands, stars and numbers, are distant relatives of that family of a priori images that Johns embroidered with the wistful delicacy of newspaper and collage. That and the use of the mechanical instruments of ruler, compass, and stencil, which eschew the "creative" mark and lend a further pathos to this family of early works in which the artist abdicates the skill of drawing to merely "copy" given public signs. And this cool, insouciant reticence is of course the strategic Trojan Horse with which Johns invades and decimates the fervid existential pretentiousness of originality in American art in the 1950s.

8. *Tennyson*, 1958

Be near me when my faith is dry,
And men the flies of latter spring,
That lay their eggs, and sting and sing
And weave their pretty cells and die.

—ALFRED LORD TENNYSON, "IN MEMORIAM"[10]

Monochrome gray, about 6 by 4 feet. Two vertical panels covered with an unstretched piece of canvas starting about one fifth of the way down and ending before the bottom edge, where it terminates just above the name TENNYSON. This large, loosely attached patch of canvas does not quite reach the edges. It is like a cover, or a shade drawn (the use of an actual window shade would appear a year later). This seems to be an early instance of a word interrupting the image of a painting in Johns' work. *Diver* comes five years later, citing the second poet, Hart Crane, in dedication rather than the label, which names the act rather than the man. A faint vertical line appears on the left side of this "shade" in *Tennyson* and runs across the bottom edge. Part of a canvas ripped from its stretcher bars? Second thoughts about what is under this shade? This seems to be one of the first works Johns made that abandoned the a priori given of both internal divisions and external limits. It is not a work that copies a given scheme as do the maps, flags, targets, and numbers. Yet *Tennyson* maintains a strict bilateral symmetry. The expected newspaper collage beneath the wax is abandoned and the embroidery of gray encaustic is laid on in a subdued, almost mechanical way. We could be looking at a badly painted wall, except for clues that emerge from the bottom edge where a few inches of nearly bare canvas show spatters of color, which lend credibility to the speculation that the large shade covers and suppresses a previous, more colorful effort. We seem to be looking not so much at a salvaged mistake as at a subdued and suppressed first impulse. Tennyson always said too much in too heated and lyrical a way. But those overheated, romantic scenes of Camelot, where the Lady of Shalott is confined and condemned to see the world through a mirror on pain of death, must be set aside for now, covered over. Her corpse and mirror will not be forgotten. Johns will revisit them a couple of decades later. But here, in this work, naming for the first time not only asserts itself as invasive equivalent of the image, but becomes

122. Jasper Johns, *Tennyson*, 1958. Encaustic and collage on canvas, 73½ × 48¼ inches (186.7 × 122.6 cm). Purchased with funds from the Coffin Fine Arts Trust, Nathan Emory Coffin Collection of the Des Moines Art Center, 1971. Copyright © Jasper Johns/Licensed by VAGA, New York.

image itself. The slightly earlier *Tango* of 1955 does of course place the name clearly in the upper left corner of this monochrome blue picture, which also contains a music box hidden behind the canvas and a key located near the lower right side to do the winding. Duchamp's object entitled *With a Hidden Noise* is the obvious reference. But neither word nor implied sound seem to come together here to rescue this work from a rather inert monochrome image. (The convention of looking at paintings rather than touching them would seem to override Johns' stated intention which went something like this: the invitation to turn the key protruding from the surface would induce a kind of close-up looking into the surface or field of the work and then the limiting edges of the picture would disappear).[11] In *Tennyson* the linguistic sign supports the entire weight of a visual mass above it. The large letters can put an edge on a painted space, as well as lend tension to the word itself, which it otherwise would not possess as modest script.[12] But what does "Tennyson" name in this work? The poet? the poetry? or both? If we follow the American philosopher Saul Kripke's argument that, contrary to Bertrand Russell's claim, proper names are not descriptions but "rigid designators" that hold true in "all possible worlds," and trace back through time to their original referent, then perhaps Tennyson sleeps somewhere beneath the shroud of gray shade in this work. We might theorize this, but bearing in mind again Kripke when he said he had no theories, because if he did they would be like all theories, wrong.[13]

9. *Voice*, 1966–67

This is one of the most mysterious and un-device-like of all of Johns' early works. Actually it slips just beyond the wire of the first decade, which runs from 1955 to 1965. I refer not to the painting of 1964–67 but to the 48 ¼ by 31 ¼ inches black-and-white lithograph of 1966–67. As in the earlier *Tennyson* the word of the title runs prominently across the bottom of the image. The surface seems smudged or scraped with the swath of a lighter form cascading down and across the darker areas. But the entire surface is mottled and there are no distinct linear divisions in the work, except for the letters of the word "voice" at the bottom edge. No representation of an image seems to emerge from what appears to be an abstract design in black and white—until one stares for a while at the work. Then I begin to see an endless assembling, dissolving, and re-assembling of monstrous faces, not unlike what emerges from staring at the surfaces of Goya's *Black Paintings*. I would not argue that this imagery was intentional, any more than I would argue that the swath of a lighter form was a kind of synesthetic visual equivalent of the interior of the throat, but it feels like a throat/voice. It is not a representation but a kind of subjective mapping of the body's interior, as if the imagery of the *Skin* works, in which the body, pressing and distorting against the surface of the page as though it were a sheet of glass, has given way and we now have access to what is within the epidermis of the body, and have passed into the interior passages of the vocal chamber itself where we find ourselves within the very stream and origin of the linguistic. Although it may not be language we feel rushing around us, for we may be within the voicing of the artist himself, hearing what we have always heard from him—a quiet melancholy humming. *Voice* does and does not sing

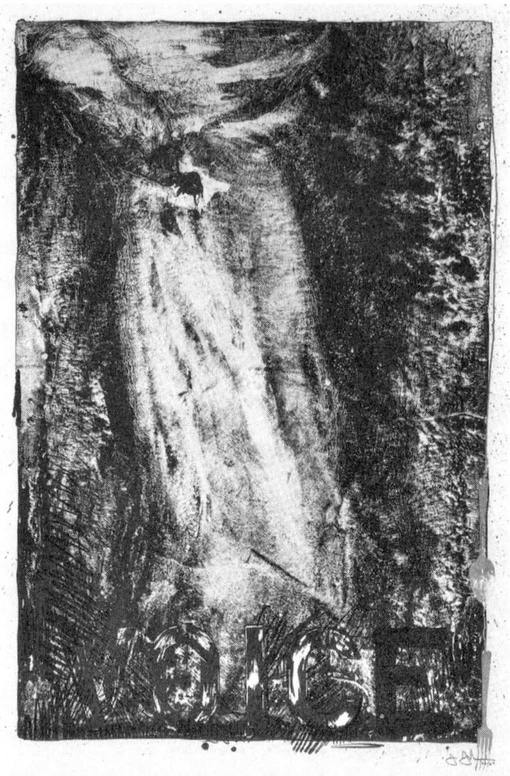

123. Jasper Johns, *Voice*, 1967. Lithograph, 48⅜ × 31¹¹⁄₁₆ inches (122.9 × 80.5 cm). Published by Universal Limited Art Editions. Copyright © Jasper Johns/Licensed by VAGA, New York.

the song the abandoned child sings to keep up his courage in the face of the monstrous that hovers nearby. Along with *Diver* and *Tennyson*, the work looks inward and to the past, turning its back on the exterior, public themes of flags, maps, targets, and numbers.

10. *Diver*, 1962–63

> An object that tells of the loss, destruction, disappearance of objects. Does it speak of itself. Tells of others. Will it include them?
>
> —JASPER JOHNS[14]

This work has its roots in the earlier *0 through 9*, 1960. These roots are not imagistic but temporal. Roots in time that have collapsed, in the dense moment when an action is run through in a flash of time, leaving an indexical sign of

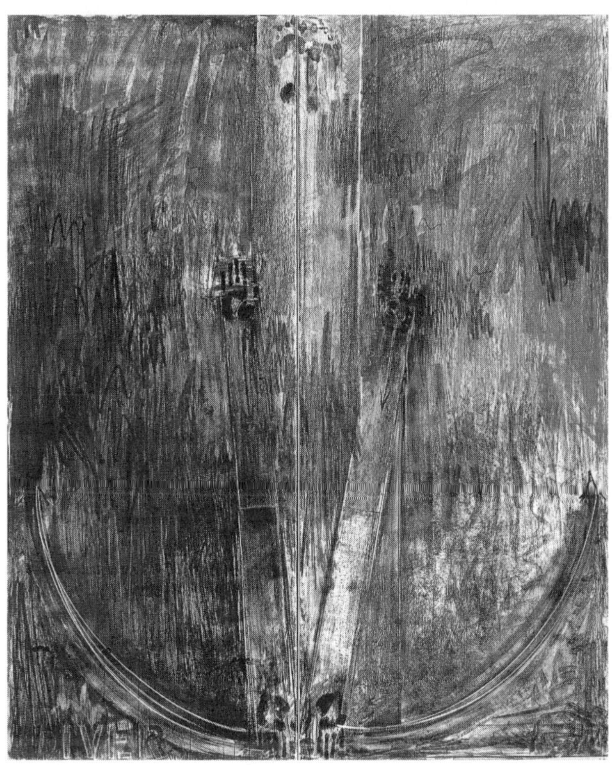

124. Jasper Johns, *Diver*, 1962–63. Charcoal, pastel, and watercolor on paper mounted on canvas, two panels, 86½ × 71¾ inches (219.7 × 182.2 cm) overall. The Museum of Modern Art, New York. Copyright © Jasper Johns/Licensed by VAGA, New York.

good-bye. The "figures/figure" of *0 through 9* has transited to an elsewhere in *Diver*. But that quintet composed of *Target, Flag, Numbers, 0 through 9, Diver*, forms a family of related signs. Of the five, *Target* vibrates with a threatening imminence awaiting the violence of an impending impact. But *Diver* exists in the space of the immediately past instant, after an irreversible action has left its indexical trace. Nevertheless this family of signs, related at some deep, irrepressible genetic level by the innate trait of revenge—which can be admitted into the light only with the promise of redemption—bears the family resemblance of the disenfranchised and the alienated, surrounded by a hovering absence of either before or after.

Diver is the only work in which Johns maps the extension of the fully unfurled body. Johns is himself a large man, and the reach and movement indicated by the indexical signs of hands and feet seem to loom enormous here.

The traces of a body just unfurled are all the more emphasized by the board-like tracks and radial marks of feet and hands, which are laid out in bilateral symmetry and seem to indicate the terminations of the extended body. Yet in spite of the sense of a body having just previously occupied the space—where it paused to address the void and make a sweeping gesture before disappearing into oblivion—we cannot resolve these indexical tracks into any prior logical bodily coherence. Some extended set of symmetrical bodily motions does seem to have just occurred and the indications of limits made by the radial swing of arms and hands resonate with Leonardo's *Vitruvian Man*.

Diver—the one time the artist permits the full gesture of the expanded body suggesting wholeness—is dedicated to the suicide of Hart Crane. Pessimism and the self-punitive will cancel any moment of bodily joy, and the artist will never again allow the implication of a full bodily presence through an indexical sign.[15]

In other works of 1963, an arm and hand swing through an arc in imitation of the mechanical *Device Circle*,[16] and in still other works we can look through the invisible glass into the face and hands as in the *Skin* works of 1962,[17] but the whole body perishes in the dive with Hart Crane.

A diver stands poised between earth and water. If Johns appeared to be standing on the firm ground of hard public signs in the first years of his production, his skepticism and mockery of this public space was apparent from the beginning. And as early as 1955 the liquid blue depths of *Tango* announces the nearness of the shoreline of the subjective. *Diver*, 1962–63, limns the pivot from the former to the latter as an allegory of farewell to the public, external world. The drawing generates a wake formed by the plunge into the terrors of the self. If the world is as hard as targets, flags, numbers, and maps picture it, the risk of a downward voyage into a shaded interior is the other perilous option. Up above, the public space is a vicious, implacable, unforgiving, intolerant, self-righteous, hypocritical, fickle space, lit by a shadowless, accusatory glare. Take the plunge downward out of the light. Take the risk, death wish and all.

Or was this work based on military calisthenics, say the "side straddle hop," and just later given the sexy dedication linking it to the poet? It would not be too much of a stretch to posit both, given the artist's perverse and hidden humor. There are many decoys in Johns' work set up to shunt us away from his profound vulnerability, which will reveal itself only at the last minute, by which time he has fled. For *Diver* also says, "You are too late. I have gone before you had the chance to fail me."

Seven of the works examined in some detail here are informed by and preoccupied with the structuring "device." Such devices as the public signs of flag, target, and map constrain the image and deliver a limit as whole images more or less coincident with the limit of the painting.[18] The repetitive use of the numbers one to nine, as well as the alphabet paintings, forecloses the works in slightly different ways. *Diver, Tennyson*, and *Voice*, while unconstrained by the limiting device, nevertheless seem to be even more deeply introverted works of melancholy and mourning. Never was a body of work further from modernist utopian impulses to "re-enchant the world." What redemption this art achieves is wrenched from its losses, losses made bearable in the ten works we have lingered over here by a mourning that forgets and forgives nothing.

Seven of the works discussed above remain today as the proleptic and admonitory conundrums they were half a century ago. They alluded then, among many other things, to a chilling spiritual, moral, and political bleakness hovering on the horizon. Standing as we do now in the midst of such an achieved bleakness, do we see these works differently? Certainly we read these early works from a much darker place, and we should be aware of how our present condition shades our outlook.

COUNTING MARKS

The early Johns is to marking as Descartes was to thinking. Descartes' doubt brought him to the undeniable idea of himself thinking and therefore existing. Johns' skepticism brings him to confront the repetitive stroke of marking as the digitalized body. Ten fingers connect us to the world. The numbers 0 through 9 are not only metaphors for the "figure." They are in the hands of Johns the recursive affirmation of hands counting and being in the world, but at the same time they are displaced from the anthropomorphic image. Later, in 1963, Johns makes a lithograph of his two hands in which all ten fingers are clearly readable. Perhaps he does this to mark the ground with a clue? I count therefore I am. We are digitalized beings incapable of not dividing the world with our fingers. Johns' reduction of the body moving as a digital marker delivers simultaneously the pathos and accusation of how we inescapably divide and reduce the world by counting it. But as Johns knew, numbers count. And in his hands, hands count with a vengeance. That the first few, special *Figures* of 1955, which resisted serial completion, become the *Numbers* of the serial sequences beginning two years later is already a narrative of pathos.

Johns' early meditation on *Figures* and then *Numbers* recalls us to Edmund Husserl's early phenomenological thought in which "the concept of plurality, for example, was explained in terms of our mental act of combining different contents of consciousness into one representation, of, for example, seeing distinct people as a single group."[19] Johns inverts and deconstructs this plurality in the *Figures*, reinvesting the plural name of the counted (a "3," "5," "7," etc.) as metaphor for a single "figure" which, in all of its physical particularity, still remains anonymous.

In the early *Figure* works Johns' skepticism finally delivers that ecstatic leap from doubt to the "Eureka!" of insight, undeniable newness, and a fresh beginning. His rejection of what counted in the past as art demanded a radical deflationary stripping and discarding of certain premises deemed necessary for art to occur at all. Johns delivers the *coup de grace* to the already tottering dragon of modernism and its fire-breathing, transcendent attempts at enchantment. On this lumpy, still febrile corpse, Johns raises his flat *Flag* and begins *Numbering* the dragon's last breaths. When the smoke starts to clear one looks down to see the world of the ordinary, so sinister and so intimate, looking back from his art.

Johns' phenomenological meditation bridges thought and the body. The *Figures* show a necessary connection between the body and thought, anchoring thought to the counting body. And here it is the body that counts in both senses. This digital, Cartesian meditation is first embodied in the sensuous metaphor of figure as figural "4" or "7" or "5," etc., but not in sequence or completed as a 0 through 9 series. There is something of the vulnerability of lament or mourning, as well as defiance, in preserving the intense particularity of only a few *Figures* in the face of that generality personified by the mathematical infinity of numbers. But it is characteristic of Johns' sensibility that he will not allow this element of pathos without soon mocking it by letting the series go, submerging the *Figures* of 1955 into the march of sequential, anonymous *Numbers*, which begin in 1957. "Count off!" shouts the drill sergeant and the ranked soldiers yell out their numbers in sequence (excepting zero).

Thought is not colored. Color adds nothing to thought. Thought is black, white, and gray. Infinity may be gray. Why add color to numbers? Color in Johns, one might think, is not so much a weakness as an irrelevance. Then why is it there? It is not immediately apparent. Perhaps it is an additional form of enumeration. Red, yellow, blue are often named in the early works, such as *False Start*, 1959, as well as applied to the surface. But as someone remarked about the movies, the old black and whites are more powerful and even more realistic than the later Technicolor. The white encaustic *Figures* and *Flag* have, like every instance of white, all the colors already. In his early works, Johns is essentially a graphic artist of thought. (Color in the first *Targets* and *Flags* is simply a given that arrives with the image.) And throughout his long, subsequent meditation on figures and numbers, the black-and-white work remains the more arresting. And this is partly because light, as well as dark, opens to the world of thought by allegorical implication—the penumbra of black and gray opening to the white light of illumination. Color is given to the lower world as compensation for the absence of the light of illumination.

The large black-and-white drawing *0 through 9* of 1961 conveys a pathos through its majestic modulation of dark and light, line and shadow, rubbed and incised surfaces, multiple and contrapuntal edges that move from crisp to soft to the glint of the erased white line. All this stands mocked in the heavy-handed, clotted, colored *Figures* of 1959. But this illustrates the second rule in Johns' work: for every instance of the exquisite flight of the aesthetic, there is an equal and opposite instance of the mocking and self-consciously crude. The corollary is to let color do the grunt work of self-mockery. *Figure 0*, 1959, is a perfect example of the way color, and its heavy-handed application, is a hostile pendant to the graphic instances of the same subjects. Although in this particular case, *Figure 0*, 1959, predates the large graphic *0 through 9* of 1961. Here the dynamic of exquisite/crude runs the other way, in which case we could invoke the notion of the redemptive. Here strategic color in a "loaded" brush is used to "execute" these *Figures*. It is a weapon, as well as a shield, against the vulnerability of the intimate, exquisite, undefended, black-and-white thought-mark. Or maybe John Locke was right after all: color is only a secondary quality. It is not until gray is called in to subdue color in a work like *By the Sea, 1961*, that color is allowed to speak with any sensibility in the work. In works he completed in his first phase Johns often sets color loose like a pit bull to maul his ideas, which like Minerva's Owl—to mix the metaphors and invoke Hegel's mascot of philosophical thought—takes flight only in the grayed, colorless dusk of black, white, and especially gray, after the colorful tumult of the day has died down. This brings us to the third Johnsian law, and to its corollary: everything springs from the penumbra of the hidden, and all tracks and origins will be covered—almost.

SIGNS AND ICONS

The American philosopher Charles Sanders Peirce believed that nothing escapes its destiny of appearing as a sign. Every percept is destined to precipitate into a propositional sign. Underlying his famous semiotic classification of types of signs as index, icon, and symbol, was a tripart system of categories derived from the logic of relations. The predicate "This painting is red" is a one-place predicate. "No red painting respects the law" is dyadic, or two-place. And "The policeman gives the law to the red painting" is a three-place relation. Underlying this was a corresponding triadic phenomenological metaphysics of oneness or firstness as mere presence; secondness as brute actuality; and thirdness as a mediation and intelligibility to which Peirce assigned chance, law, and habit taking.[20] Signs themselves are inescapably interactive. As Peirce put it:

> The whole purpose of a sign is that it should be interpreted in another sign and its whole purpose lies in the special character which it imparts to its interpretant. When a sign determines an interpretant of itself in another sign, it produces an effect external to itself.[21]

What was essentially new in Johns' early works in which the readymade signs of flags, targets, and numbers functioned as subjects for the art was the compression into triadic relations of "apparent" one-place predicates. "That is a flag" is a one-place predicate which is destabilized beneath the dyadic "is/is not a flag, but is also a painting," which is compressed into the triadic "This flag, which is/is not a flag, is also a painting and this changes art expectations"—not to mention the multiple references these predications bring in their wake. The precedent here is Duchamp's readymades which deflate art by means of utilitarian, apparently one-place predicate signs (snow shovels, urinal, bottle racks, etc.) forced into three-part predication of "is manufactured object/is also art/changes art." There may be more signs of this type that could have been adapted to painting than those "flat" ones of flags, numbers, and targets (the defect of the maps is that this sign was already inherently dyadic before its designation as art), but Johns found no others and was *forced* (I think the term is not too strong) rather quickly into beginning with the tertiary predication of "is a painting/is art/does not change art," which is already occurring in such works as *Jubilee* and *Out the Window*, both of 1960. The bilateral symmetry of the early works (which closely follow the one-place signage of flags, targets, and figures) was probably an unconscious attempt to hold on to this compressive tension (here I refer to such works as *Tennyson, Shade, Thermometer, Painting with Two Balls*, and a number of others which conform to symmetrical layouts). Is there a diminution in those nonsymmetrical works which begin with the triadic predication of "this object/ is (clearly) a painting/is like many others"? I think the answer is yes. It was as if some powerful muse (half Cartesian skeptic and half relentless, Hannibalesque warrior general) disciplined and sustained the earliest work—work that issued out of doubt and was transmuted into the impersonal attack mode of revenge for about five years during which the compressive density of the work was at an almost unsustainable level.

. . . . .

The iconic sign is said to represent its object by resemblance or similarity. The definition is problematic. Some similarity can always be found between any two objects. On the other hand one identical twin does not represent the other.[22] Flags, targets, and maps fall under the problematic heading of iconic signs. Are such signs looked at but not really seen, perceived but not experienced? Johns forces his iconic signs to become flesh. Such embodied icons are eroded of their iconic status in Johns' oeuvre where seeing is always both reading and experiencing, and sometimes even identified with eating.

But what do we mean by the term "experience," and what do we mean by the term "perception"? And are some percepts experienced and others "read"? Does every act of perception imply a propositional attitude? Are signs read and not experienced? Or should all awareness fall under the term experience? The answers to these questions will vary depending on whether an empiricist or a rationalist is being asked. Pragmatist empiricism has long been identified with an American outlook. Postmodernism, first theorized in France, was dedicated to textualizing experience by a reduction to "reading." Experience then becomes an empty signifier, a mere effect of language and power. But on the other side, from the empiricism of Locke and Hume down to American Pragmatism, experience is claimed to be all there is.[23]

Four plaster casts of faces cut just below the eyes are placed side by side and above the painted surface in *Target with Four Faces*. Here blindness is presented as both sign and metaphor of non-experience—vision denied and experience foreclosed. The iconic target below the faces is subdued and slowed, wrested from its transparency as unseen sign and made flesh by the sensuously painted surface on the one hand, and by the nominalism of calling a target art on the other. This art-icon-non-icon reverberates against the dead, sightless faces above. The work is suspended between the sign made flesh and the representation of a blindness incapable of experiencing the flesh of sight. Johns does not unify our experience but mocks it, stretches it between two irreconcilable polarities, metaphorizing and displacing the iconic sign as sensuous flesh while desiccating the body as a wounded sign. The simple gestalt imagery resolves nothing. In the Johnsian world flesh (experience) is always tortured by the connotations of the sign—via manipulations of blindness, the oppressions of patriotism, the numbing of repetitive counting, and in myriad other ways. No other artist of the twentieth century delivered so much pain and pleasure in such simple packages. But the density of the irony informing this work deflates any foothold for the sublime. The aesthetic gorgeousness of these early works would caress our bodies only for an opening through which the mind could be seared. Redemption and torture were never cinched more closely together.

THE INWARD TURN

No artist of the last half of the twentieth century carried more weight than Johns. No other possessed the necessary cruelty, resentment, arrogance, and thirst for revenge, which would enable him to drive himself so far into dismantling the presuppositions of existing art while at the same time redeeming the ground he had laid waste. No other changed the course of art as much as he. No other could wield an arsenal of grim, ordinary object-signs with such fearlessness, yet without ever losing his self-possession, restraint, and reticence. And no other possessed so many mirrors with which to reflect back and forth across his oeuvre his aggression and his vulnerability, his complexity and simplicity. Finally, no other moved so relentlessly toward hermetic self-sufficiency, which, as the years passed, turned from an increasingly grim external world toward an increasingly melancholy inner one.

Never before had the command for flatness in painting been so enforced and obeyed, while being presented with such sly mockery. But there is a flickering between mockery and pathos here. From the very beginning Johns presents his flags, targets, numbers, and maps with a pathos that redeems their tawdry, alienated status. And yet, these ordinary public signs are freighted with accusation and boil up with aesthetic *pharmakon*. Holding in balance his ambivalent feelings, he transmutes the aesthetic into the critical and the moral. But when Johns leaves the public, militaristic arena of flags, maps, targets, and numbers, for the darker inner worlds of *Diver, Tennyson*, and *Voice*, the work turns melancholy. After *Land's End*, his more conventionally "composed" pictures (*In Memory of My Feelings—Frank O'Hara*, 1961, *Fool's House*, 1962, and others) are somber inner meditations.

Johns was not a cold-blooded, impersonal, cynical, and depressive personality, as was Duchamp, who sustained the aggressive tension of compressed predicate signs for much of his career. His strategy of the readymade involved overloading the one-place sign (for example, "is urinal") into the triadic predication: "is manufactured object (urinal) / is art / changes art." But such expansion does not obliterate from the obstinate, existential, one-place predicate "is urinal," its hardness as a non-art thing. This hard, cold-bloodlessness of the readymade was not softened by any added aesthetic touch. As we have argued, Johns sought redemption through his art and it follows that he would turn toward (inward?) iconologies of *need* rather than Duchampian ones of *desire*. Duchamp would never have conflated seeing with eating as Johns does in the iconography of tableware found in so many works. There is at times a coyness, a beseeching of the "hidden" that pervades Johns' work—especially after the early symmetrical phase that suggests a profound insecurity (a vulnerability?) and the need to be "found out" (understood, loved?). Johns quickly turned from works that struck out at the world through public signs to those of the inward gesture that might save his own *Skin*.

On one level the works of the first decade can be described as moving from resentment to mourning. Johns' military experience may have been no more than a catalyst precipitating the first works—the military environment of repression, regimentation, and conformity stirring earlier, more deeply seated resentments. The aesthetic realizations of *Flags, Targets*, and *Numbers* then gave way to an unlocking of, and permission for, a confrontation with feelings rising from the deepest sense of personal loss and suffering. And this second space, opening after 1960, is illuminated by a pathos of mourning that increasingly suffuses all the work.

But how different it is, after 1960, to try to find Johns than to be confronted with his accusatory signs of the first five years. Both *False Start* and *Jubilee*, both from 1959, say what we see before we see it. And on first acquaintance, they seem to be two of the worst paintings Johns ever produced. Red, yellow, and blue are splashed over the surface in crude, mocking imitation of abstract expressionist brushwork. The words "red," "yellow," and "blue" are stenciled over the surface in colors that correspond neither to the colors of the named word nor to the splotches of color on which they appear. The irony here seems tedious. Although the treatment of the surfaces resembles that of *Shade* of the same year, both *False Start* and *Jubilee* are absent any attached object or a priori, readymade image, multiple panels, or division of the canvas surface that are found earlier (see *Canvas*, 1956, *Gray Rectangles, Drawer*, and *Newspaper*, all of 1957). One of the connotations of the word "jubilee" is emancipation. And perhaps the artist felt certain jubilation in being rid of these things. But the uniform density of an allover surface uninflected by physical division or attached objects was a "false start" in that these previous aids would quickly reappear to structure his pictures. But the title *False Start* is also ironic and mocking in view of the fact that the play of the linguistic red, yellow, and blue across the surfaces of both works announces a theme that would be relentlessly repeated. The linguistic nominalism also announces Johns' confrontation with color, which must have held much trepidation for an artist who showed no facility for it. The irony of the nominalistic would have been a way to ease into this new world of color. The play of word against thing, name against color, is explored in a number of canvases divided horizontally into three and four panels—a format that runs from *Out the Window* of 1959 to *Land's End*, 1963, and beyond.

The 1955 work of the early *Figures*, *Targets*, and *Flags* may be as close as Johns ever comes to looking directly at the world. By allegorizing counting and the quantitative as our pathetic and manipulative grip on the world, we could read the earliest Johns as a kind of proto-Goyaesque artist pointing out our tendencies toward the pathetic and the monstrous. But for whatever reasons, by 1959 his work had turned inward. If *Tennyson* announces this, *Device Circle, Jubilee, False Start* were by 1959 all following a change of course. In this sense one of the other ironies of *False Start* is that it was one of the earliest works to hint at the coming inward turn.

What accounts for the work having turned so resolutely inward at such an early stage? Had that dragon of modernism bitten Johns as he stood atop its dying body? Did recognition come too early, fast and furious? How much guilt does revenge bring with it? And after success can it be sustained as a motive force? Does redemption feel hollow in the face of success? Did a point come around 1961, when he knew and felt these things—and expressed them in the bleak and knowing *No?* Had these burdens pushed him to an edge, to an unstable *Land's End* by 1963? I think it took ten years for the artist to recover his balance, density of structure, exuberance of high mental concentration and purpose, when in the early 1970s he again caught the *Scent* (1973–74) of his muse.

The cry a peacock makes in the early morning after it has had its first drink of water at some forest pool: a raucous, tearing cry that should have spoken of a world refreshed and re-made but seemed after the long bad night to speak only of everything lost, man, bird, forest, world . . . later it was possible to work out the stages by which he had moved from what he would have considered the real world to all the subsequent areas of unreality: moving as it were from one sealed chamber of the spirit to another.

—V. S. NAIPAUL[24]

Johns' work has been seen largely in the context of what it did to art: what it closed off and what it opened up. That and its aesthetic gorgeousness seem to have preoccupied past commentaries, and much of this one. But as art recedes into the past, even this aesthetically complex work, the question begins to be asked: what does it tell us about ourselves and the world? I started by asking about affect in the work. But how in the end can the overarching question about the epistemic be avoided? The question always arises at the end, when we try to sort out our feelings. Just as there is no ontology without epistemology, there are no aesthetic judgments without assumptions of the epistemic. Affects arise from effects. Art exists in a world that impinges on us. Art is part of a world that presses against us. And we respond by asking what is the nature of this weight we feel against us. The epistemic reverberations from both Kant and Hegel have still not faded completely. Heroic notions about art, how it mediates even a little freedom in the causal, downward crush that surrounds, can still be heard. Not to mention that narrative of how history proceeds and increases the consciousness of art, both ours and its. Today wisps of this epistemic fog bank still rise from much so-called critical writing. But in clearer, bleaker air questions of minuscule increments of liberation, asked within the gritty walls of the market (questions still smelling of K & H & Co.), are the wrong questions.

And that bleakness I spoke of seems at this point to be less and less ascribable to a set of totalized effects of the world. Or to say it differently, what we know of the world through art is always mirrored by a glass smudged by our desires. Subjectivity, which already threatened Descartes, will always be part of the equation. And its consequences are never innocent. That affect which focuses our vision does not just passively receive the world; it changes it. The twentieth century was a lesson in how our defective vision lost our world. Johns' first five years of work started to speak of how certain failures of feeling account for the grimness accompanying the loss of our world. His first five years of production arose from epistemic meditations that allegorically targeted, numbered, flagged, and mapped the affects of a ruthless vision (or a vision of ruthless affects). He kept a precarious balance on this exposed and threatening site by beating time with aesthetic flourishes, but after half a decade he turned inward toward a more personal melancholia.

REASONS

There is far more in the works of Jasper Johns than reason can enumerate. And we have no doubt that Johns, always so full of apparent reasons, has operated on that other side of those reasons and according to mysterious impulses we will never fully grasp or name. We are prompted to recall here Wittgenstein's question, '"Have I reasons?' the answer is: my reasons will soon give out. And then I shall act, without reasons."[25] Nothing is more important than acting without reasons in art, unless it is acting with so many that they never quite come to rest. And here we arrive at a cultural turning point over "reasons" in art in the mid-1960s.

> Recent cognitive science pictures a modular brain in which visual perception is broken down into a number of separate tasks such as recognition of shape, movement, edges, constancy of form through rotation, etc. Language is a different system, and the study of its innate features will, as Chomsky has noted, "neither provide a useful model for other parts of the study of mind, nor draw from them significantly" (*Language and Thought* 34). . . . What may never be made clear by cognitive science is how the interface between the visual and verbal operates, in terms not only of the seamless connection that facilitates the interchange between what is seen and said, but the complex and endless conflict between the one and the other.[26]

Not being a rational enterprise, the kinds of meanings, or problems, expected of art are not those expected of linguistic discourse. At least this was the case up until the 1960s when a new rationalization of art was set in motion. First came minimalism, followed by conceptualism, then the rise of the photograph as an art object, and finally, now, the democratization of art as spectacle. We look back at forty years of a progressive simplification, a reduction of ambiguity of meaning, and a thinning of art as cultural engagement.

If Johns initiated this with his rationalizing methodology of the a priori device—that final, fatal arrow in the Saint Sebastian of modernism—the rising market's demand for nominally simple and distinct commodities completed the emptying out of art. (Johns himself moved toward mannerism after the 1970s and mocked the rational/a priori aspects of his art in the self-parody of self-quotation.) The "plurality" that was said to characterize the art market of the 1980s and 1990s nominalized art by demanding style-star recognition to negotiate the exponential increase in gallery activity. The expanding market demanded ever more artists to supply it with that contradictory demand for commodities both new and name-recognizable. Thus art progressed, over the last four decades, toward a kind of stupefying of expectation that had more to do with labels and commodity identification and ever less with the experience of ambiguous, shifting, multiple, and relative meanings. Nominalization in itself does not militate against rich experience. Johns' use of his readymade icons of target, flag, numbers, and maps demonstrated that. But the very success of this combination of simple images, which belied their potency for experience in the form of a kind of delayed detonation, did not travel. Nothing demonstrated this more clearly than minimalism's supreme easiness. Anybody could get it, because there was very little to get. As Stella remarked, "What you see is what you see." Of course nothing was more American than that kind of flat-footed empiricism. And minimalism was nothing if not an all-American, anti-European art practice—the term "practice" slipping so easily into the jargon of the day. Minimalism was that performative art unwaveringly stamped out from a few blunt premises. There was not much to experience or to "get" here, but you knew what it was from a mile away. And of course what little there was to get beyond the inherent, simple decorativeness were the *reasons* for minimal art, its dogma of justifications. It was minimalism (though coming out of Johns) that so resoundingly set art on that course of dumbing down that permeates all "art practices" today. Practices justified by reasons (euphemized as "ideas" in conceptual art) that guide us through the extensive bleakness that now surrounds us.

THE LIVERIED LIFE

Artists are the elite of the servant class.

—JASPER JOHNS[27]

Art has always been dependent upon and served one set of forces or another with little regard for the morality of those people or forces it served (pharaoh, pope, nobilities, capitalism).

—ROBERT MORRIS[28]

In the Museum of Modern Art a woman said to him, "Jasper, you must be from the Southern Aristocracy."

He said, "No, Jean. I'm just trash."

—MAX KOZLOFF[29]

The people who own the country ought to govern it.

—JOHN JAY, FIRST CHIEF JUSTICE OF THE UNITED STATES[30]

For one artist to think about another is to think about other "possible worlds." Could Kripke aid me here? Or are those other "possible" worlds Kripke imagined as bleak as ours? Could there be another possible world similar to ours, but more advanced in its historical cycle? What might we see in such a world that had come to the end of its history? Perhaps it would be this: The two last men fighting to the death. Inevitably one would gain the advantage in the struggle. As the vanquished felt the blade against his throat, he would plead, "Spare me and I will be your slave." The victor, curious as to whether being a master would give him more satisfaction than the murder he loved, relented. Thus began a relation between the two in which the master lived in idle luxury while the slave worked (in the beginning out of fear of death) to provide the master with food and shelter. One day the master called his slave and said, "This is not enough, I want more than necessities." The slave returned to his labors and invented art and brought it to his master. "Ah," said the master, "this is what I have always wanted. It is magnificent. And although I get no prestige from recognizing you, slave, who I regard as trash, perhaps owning this art will bring me prestige." The slave smiled a hidden smile and thought to himself, "Through my work I have found my freedom, and though I am still a slave I have achieved my prestige through the recognition of my master—not to mention a kind of quiet revenge, allegorical though it may be."[31] Of course such a story (a nightmare, actually) could only be about another world. Here in our world we already have art. Part of this art is the magnificent works Jasper Johns made between 1955 and 1965.

. . . . .

After speculating on the sources of the works, and after tracing the arc of their development, enumerating the motifs, innovations, devices, ironies, and contradictions—after all of the explanations—much of the work, like all great art, remains elusive, unexhausted by analysis. In the end we stand before these icons, which have become part of the memory images of our time, and listen to their silences. On the other side of all the complexities a kind of majestic grief rises from such works as *Target with Four Faces*, 1955, *Tennyson*, 1958, *0 through 9*, 1961, *Diver*, 1962–63. Whatever else these works may be about, they loom as monuments of melancholy and mourning. Their dark origins in Johns' personal suffering become irrelevant when we realize that these works seem to resonate to an indelible darkness at the bottom of our own being. We are held, stilled by these icons of loss and perseverance, these images so saturated with pathos, yet so understated by having been handmade from that grit and grain of the ordinary, which forms the very texture of our lives.

The underlying tragic edge of much of Johns' work may be alien to the irrepressible optimism of the American pragmatist outlook. Johns' work speaks of exhaustion and paralysis, the termination of options, and often displays a blatant mockery of action. The work is founded on an implicit pessimism and critique of enthusiasm, immediacy of experience, and the assumption of the transparency of signs. Its doubt approaches Humean dimensions. The skeptical thought at the bottom of the work, beneath its aesthetic splendors, has in the past perhaps been misidentified as mere Johnsian irony. The depth of negativity in the work should be acknowledged. That this is disguised by the exquisite aesthetic touch of the artist as he skates over the surface of the abyss—with one innovation after the other appearing in the first decade of production—can lead us astray. The strategy of an exquisite formal presence sliding over and shading the abyssal has been practiced by few. Goya and Edward Hopper come to mind.

Perhaps the redemptive capacity of these early works, these icons of melancholy which now feel somehow ancient, lies in how they confront us and open us to accept the darker shadows within ourselves, and to meditate on that fallen world into which we have been cast.

NOTES

1. Carl Schmitt, *Glossarium: Aufzeichnungen der Jahre 1947–1951*, ed. Eberhard Freiherr von Medem (Berlin: Dunker and Humblot, 1991), 243.
2. This maxim is widely attributed to Stalin (though not by Stalin scholars), and has also been attributed to Lenin and Hitler; see Ralph Keyes, *The Quote Verifier: Who Said What, Where, and When* (New York: St. Martin's, 2006), 41–42.
3. Saul Bellow, *Herzog*, introduction by Philip Roth (New York: Penguin, 2003), 219.
4. Palle Yourgrau, *A World without Time* (New York: Basic Books, 2005), 146.
5. "C'est effrayant, la vie!" Joachim Gasquet, *Cézanne*, 2nd. ed (Paris: Editions Bernheim-jeune, 1926), 208.
6. Joseph Beuys, private conversation with the author, Düsseldorf, 1964.
7. Wittgenstein, *Philosophical Investigations*, trans. G. E. M. Anscombe (New York: Macmillan, 1953), §198, 80e.
8. Joachim Fest describing one of the strategies Albert Speer employed to deal with

his long confinement in Spandau Prison. See Fest's *Speer: The Final Verdict*, trans. Ewald Osers and Alexandra Dring (New York: Harcourt, 1999), 316.

9. I use the term "device" to refer to three aspects of the works: (1) the indexical mark made by stretcher bar, ruler or hand rotated through 180 degrees and appearing to leave a screeded track of wet paint, (2) the readymade image that is more or less coincident with the edges of the canvas, and (3) a sequential rule which when followed completes the work. If titles are any indication, Johns himself uses the term only in the first sense, i.e., in reference to works generating circular or semicircular marks. See not only *Device Circle, 1959*, but the paintings and lithographs from 1961–62 entitled *Device.*
10. Alfred Lord Tennyson, "In Memoriam," in *A Choice of Tennyson's Verse* (London: Faber and Faber, 1971), 16.
11. "I wanted to suggest a physical relationship to the pictures that was active. In the targets one could step back or one might go up very close and lift the lids and shut them. In TANGO, to wind the key and hear the sound, you had to stand relatively close to the painting, too close to see the outside shape of the picture." Quoted by Michael Crichton, *Jasper Johns*, exhibition catalogue (New York: Harry N. Abrams and Whitney Museum of American Art, 1977), 30.
12. A lesson not lost on Ed Ruscha. Although I do not think we can hold Johns responsible for what now amounts to a kind of conceptual folk art: that tedious practice of writing large on walls.
13. See Kripke's *Naming and Necessity* (Cambridge, Mass.: Harvard University Press, 1972).
14. Quoted by John Cage in "Jasper Johns: Stories and Ideas," in Alan Solomon, *Jasper Johns*, exhibition catalogue (New York: Jewish Museum, 1964), 22.
15. Of course in the later 1987 paintings, *The Seasons*, the silhouette of a nearly complete bodily shadow appears. Presumably this is that of the artist and as such a kind of indexical sign. But rather than implying the recent presence of an active body springing to its death, which in *Diver* is associated with Hart Crane, the shadow in *The Seasons* pictures seems to refer to the future absence of the artist and a death arrived at by a process of decay.
16. The half circle described by a pinioned ruler appears as early as 1961 in *Good Time Charlie*, and is doubled in *Device*, 1961–62, where two stretcher bars appear to screed paint beneath double arcs—a thematic repeated in the lithographs of 1962. Again the ruler performs this motion in *Passage* and *Out the Window Number 2*, both of 1962, the same year that a broom in *Fool's House* does double duty as a swinging paintbrush. The following year a hand and forearm, apparently pinioned at the elbow, indicate the indexical, windshield-wiper-like mark of swiped half circle. If this anthropomorphic version of the image, so obsessively repeated in works of the early 1960s, conveys a note of temporal motion through the indexical sign, the waving gesture also seems to convey a signal for help—or perhaps futility, or worse, since it is anatomically impossible for the forearm to rotate a full 180 degrees palm down while pinioned at the elbow.
17. The 1960 *Anthropometries* of Yves Klein, while precedents for using the surface of the rotating body to generate indexical marks, are decorative and detached, not to

mention absurdly sexist in their use of the female body as paintbrush. Johns' use of the device seems to reek of airless confinement and compression of the body in two dimensions.

18. Of course the margins between the outer ring of the target and the four edges of the painting in the *Target* works vary from one *Target* painting to another; as early as 1955 a flag floats above a lower field of arbitrary dimension; in 1957 a flag is painted floating in an orange field; in 1958 three flags of diminishing sizes are stacked one on the other. Clearly the found image did not obviate every compositional decision Johns made in the "device" works. The sizes of the *Numbers* and *Alphabet* works are in no way given by the series run-out of 0–9 or A–Z. And colors are not suggested by any prior logical decisions. But this caveat does not weaken the general argument about the importance of the device or found object in Johns, or for those who came after him.
19. *The Oxford Companion to Philosophy*, ed. Ted Honderich (New York: Oxford University Press, 1995), 382.
20. See Joseph Brent, *Charles Sanders Peirce, A Life* (Bloomington: Indiana University Press, 1998), for Peirce's notions about perception and logic, as well as the triadic nature of his systems.
21. *The Collected Papers of Charles Sanders Peirce*, ed. Arthur Burks (Cambridge, Mass.: Harvard University Press, 1958), vol. 8, 191. On the other hand, Wittgenstein thought that the practice of interpreting every sign—those for rules, for example—could only lead to skepticism. For whatever one might do would be, "on some interpretation, in accord with the rule" (*Investigations* §198, 80e). Not interpreting rules saves us from skepticism. Or, as Wittgenstein put it, "When I obey a rule, I do not choose. I obey a rule *blindly*" (§219, 85e). But such salvation from skepticism only delivers us to ethical questions.
22. See Nelson Goodman's *Languages of Art* (Indianapolis: Hackett, 1976) for a discussion of the difficulty encountered by semiotics in attempting to define the icon, and how resemblance is neither a necessary nor sufficient condition for representation.
23. Abstract art of the 1960s and beyond, especially minimal sculpture, was American modernism's last gasping attempt to protect an aestheticized zone of phenomenological "experience." Increasing scale was the main tactic utilized in this conservative operation. Gigantic objects impinging on the body in environmental spaces sought to restrict art to pure perception. Johns belonged to neither the abstract camp of empiricist-modernist "experience," nor to the rationalist, deflationary signage camp of postmodern conceptual art. Yet he heavily influenced both.
24. From the prologue of *Magic Seeds* (London: Knopf, 2004).
25. Wittgenstein, *Philosophical Investigations*, §212, 84e.
26. Morris, "Toward an Ophthalmology of the Aesthetic and an Orthopedics of Seeing."
27. Crichton, *Jasper Johns*, 17.
28. Morris, "Notes on Art as/and Land Reclamation." *October* 12 (Spring 1980): 102.
29. Max Kozloff, *Jasper Johns* (New York: Harry N. Abrams, 1969), 15.

30. This maxim is attributed to John Jay by Frank Monaghan, *John Jay, Defender of Liberty against Kings and Peoples* (Indianapolis: Bobbs-Merrill, 1935), 323.
31. Hegel tells the story slightly differently, leaving out the art. See G. W. F. Hegel, *Phenomenology of Spirit*, trans. A. V. Miller (Oxford: Clarendon Press, 1977), and especially Alexander Kojève, *Introduction to the Reading of Hegel*, ed. Allan Bloom, trans. James H. Nichols Jr. (Ithaca, N.Y.: Cornell University Press, 1980), 48–49.

CHRONOLOGY

A selected chronology of events, solo exhibitions, and works

1931

February 9: Robert Morris is born in Kansas City, Missouri.

1948–50

Studies at the Kansas City Art Institute and the University of Kansas City.

1950–51

Studies at the California School of Fine Arts in San Francisco.

1951–52

Serves in the Army Corps Engineers; posted to Korea, Japan, Hong Kong, Formosa (Taiwan).

1953–55

Studies philosophy and psychology at Reed College in Portland, marries the dancer and choreographer Simone Forti.

1955–59

San Francisco, starts theater workshop with Simone Forti.

1957

August 31–October 1, first one-man exhibition, Dilexi Gallery, San Francisco.

1961

Moves to New York; meets Marcel Duchamp.

Creates *Box with the Sound of its Own Making*; *Box for Standing; Portal; Column.*

June: Creates *Passageway.*

1962

Graduate studies in art history at Hunter College; studies with Ad Reinhardt.

Creates *Slab; Cloud*; *14 Minutes.*

1963

Choreographs first dance performances.

June: Performs *Arizona* and *War* at Judson Memorial Church, New York.

October 15–November 5, one-man exhibition, Green Gallery, New York.

Creates *Card File; Electroencephalogram; Brains; Wheels; Metered Bulb; Litanies*; *Document (Statement of Esthetic Withdrawal); Memory Drawings.*

1964

February: Performs *21.3* at Surplus Dance Theater, New York.

March: Performs *Site* with Carolee Schneemann at Surplus Dance Theater, New York.

October 26–November 21, one-man exhibition, *Robert Morris*, Galerie Alfred Schmela, Düsseldorf, Germany.

Begins teaching art history at Hunter College.

Creates *Corner piece; Stairs; Footprints and Rulers.*

1964–65

December 16–January 9, one-man exhibition of seven plywood pieces, Green Gallery, New York.

1965

March 10–April 3, one-man exhibition, *Robert Morris*, Green Gallery, New York.

March: Performs *Waterman Switch* with Yvonne Rainer and Lucinda Childs at the Festival of the Arts Today in Buffalo; and later that month at the Judson Memorial Church, New York.

Creates *L-Beams; Battered Cubes; Mirrored Cubes.*

1966

March 15–April 1, one-man exhibition, *Robert Morris*, Dwan Gallery, Los Angeles.

Master's thesis at Hunter College: "Form-Classes in the Work of Constantin Brancusi" with William Rubin.

1967

Joins Leo Castelli Gallery.

March 4–28, one-man exhibition, *Robert Morris*, Leo Castelli Gallery, New York.

Creates *Stadium; Stacked and Folded; Nine Fiberglass Sleeves.*

Creates first *Felts* in Aspen, Colorado.

1968

February 16–March 31, one-man exhibition, *Robert Morris*, Stedelijk van Abbemuseum, Eindhoven, the Netherlands.

February 20–March 16, one-man exhibition, *Robert Morris*, Galerie Ileana Sonnabend, Paris.

Creates *Threadwaste* and *Dirt.*

1969

March 1–22, one-man exhibition, *A Continuous Project Altered Daily*, Leo Castelli Warehouse, New York.

November 24–December 28, one-man exhibition, *Robert Morris*, Corcoran Gallery of Art, Washington, D.C.

Creates *Mirror* (16 mm black-and-white film).

1970

January 8–February 8, one-man exhibition, *Robert Morris*, Detroit Institute of Arts, Detroit.

April 9–May 31, one-man exhibition, *Robert Morris*, Whitney Museum of American Art, New York.

1971

April 28–June 6, one-man exhibition, *Robert Morris*, Tate Gallery, London, England.

June 10–July, one-man exhibition, *Robert Morris*, Galerie Ileana Sonnabend, Paris.

1971–77

Creates *Observatory*, a permanent site-specific installation, Oostelijk, Flevoland, the Netherlands.

1972

April 18–May 6, one-man exhibition, *Robert Morris: Hearing*, Leo Castelli Gallery, New York.

October 24–November 16, one-man exhibition, *Robert Morris: Projects on Paper*, Western Gallery, Western Washington State University, Bellingham, Washington.

1973

January 23–March, one-man exhibition, *Robert Morris: Felt Pieces*, Galerie Ileana Sonnabend, Paris

February 17–March 16, one-man exhibition, *Robert Morris*, Galerie Konrad Fischer, Düsseldorf, Germany.

Creates first *Blind Time Drawings*.

1974

March: Creates *Philadelphia Labyrinth*.

April 6–27, one-man exhibition, *Labyrinths—Voice—Blind Time*, Leo Castelli Gallery and Ileana Sonnabend Gallery, New York.

Creates *Steam*, a permanent site-specific installation at Western Washington University, Bellingham, Washington.

October: Creates *Grand Rapids Project*, a permanent site-specific earthwork at Belknap Park in Grand Rapids, Michigan.

1975

November: One-man exhibition, *Robert Morris*, Galleria D'Alessandro Ferranti, Rome, Italy.

1976

October 9–30, one-man exhibition, *Robert Morris: Black and White Felts*, Leo Castelli Galley, New York.

1977

March 11–April 19, one-man exhibition, *Portland Mirrors*, Portland Center for the Visual Arts, Portland, Oregon.

April 22–June 2, one-man exhibition, *Robert Morris: Blind Time II*, Galerie Art in Progress, Düsseldorf, Germany.

April 23–May 30, one-man exhibition, *Het Observatorium van Robert Morris in Oostelijk Flevoland*, Stedelijk Museum, Amsterdam.

1978

Creates *Bent Mirror* works.

1979

Creates *Reclamation Project* (Johnson Pit no. 30), a permanent site-specific earthwork in King County, City of Kent, Seattle, Washington.

March 3–24, one-man exhibition, *In the Realm of the Carceral*, Ileana Sonnabend Gallery, New York.

March 3–24, one-man exhibition, *Six Mirror Works*, Leo Castelli Gallery, New York.

Creates *Preludes (For A. B.)*.

1980

October 25–November 15, one-man exhibition, *Robert Morris: First Study for a View from a Corner of Orion (Night)* and *Second Study for a View from a Corner of Orion (Day)*, Leo Castelli Gallery, New York.

1981–82

December 12–February 14, one-man exhibition, *Robert Morris: Selected Works, 1970–1980*, Contemporary Arts Museum, Houston, Texas.

Creates *Labyrinth*, a permanent site-specific installation in marble, Collection of Giuliano Gori, Fattoria di Celle, Santomato, Pistoia, Italy.

1982

Creates first Hydrocal works; *Psychomachia* series; *Firestorm* series.

1982–83

May 1–June 27, one-man exhibition, *The Drawings of Robert Morris*, Williams College Museum of Art; July 6–August 29, Institute of Contemporary Art, Boston; November 27–January 15, Seattle Art Museum, Seattle, Washington.

1982

January 8–29, one-man exhibition, *Psychomachia: Drawings*, Leo Castelli Gallery, New York.

January 8–29, one-man exhibition, *Hypnerotomachia: Reliefs and Firestorms: Drawings*, Ileana Sonnabend Gallery, New York.

May 4–June 2, *Robert Morris: Oeuvres récentes*, Galerie Daniel Templon, Paris.

Creates *On the Death of my Father* and *House of the Vetti*.

1984

January 28–April 3, one-man exhibition, *Robert Morris: Drawings*, Malmö Konsthall, Malmö, Sweden.

July–August, one-man exhibition, *Robert Morris: Genom tiderna med honom/Genom tiderna utan henne; Through the Times with Him/Through the Times without Her*, Malmö Konsthall, Malmö, Sweden.

August: Marries Lucy Michels.

1984–85

December 14–January 20, one-man exhibition, *Robert Morris: Drawings, Firestorm and Psychomachia*, Portland Center for the Visual Arts, Portland, Oregon.

December 12–February 14, one-man exhibition, *Robert Morris: Selected Works, 1970–1980*, Contemporary Art Museum, Houston, Texas.

1985

January 5–26, one-man exhibition, *Robert Morris: Works from 1967–1984*, Ileana Sonnabend Gallery, New York.

January 12–February 9, one-man exhibition, *Robert Morris: Works from 1967–1984*, Leo Castelli Gallery, New York.

October: Daughter Laura is born.

Creates *Blind Time III* series

1986

January 4–February 5, one-man exhibition, *Felts: 1973–1976*, Galerie Daniel Templon, Paris.

February 14–April 13, one-man exhibition, *Robert Morris: Works of the Eighties*, Museum of Contemporary Art, Chicago.

1987

Creates *Memoria (For Alan Buchsbaum)* and *Holocaust.*

1988

January 7–February 11, one-man exhibition, *Robert Morris: Selected Work, 1961–1988*, Margo Leavin Gallery, Los Angeles.

January 9–31, one-man exhibition, *Robert Morris*, Leo Castelli Gallery, New York.

January 9–31, one-man exhibition, *Robert Morris*, Ileana Sonnabend Gallery, New York.

1989

January 7–February 11, one-man exhibition, *Robert Morris: Selected Works, 1961–1988*, Margo Leavin Gallery, Los Angeles.

May 23–July 14, one-man exhibition, *Robert Morris: The Felt Works*, Grey Art Gallery and Study Center, New York University, New York.

1990

April 7–28, one-man exhibition, *Robert Morris*, Leo Castelli Gallery, New York.

October 11–November 3, one-man exhibition, *Robert Morris: Feutres et dessins, 1964–1984*. JGM Galerie, Paris.

Creates *Investigations* series.

1990–91

December 8–February 17, one-man exhibition, *Inability to Endure or Deny the World: Representation and Text in the Work of Robert Morris*, Corcoran Gallery of Art, Washington, D.C.

1991

Creates *Blind Time IV (Drawing with Davidson)* series.

1992

Creates *Bull Wall, American Royale*, AIA commission, a permanent site-specific work in steel, Kansas City, Missouri.

1993

August 7–October 30, one-man exhibition, *Robert Morris*, Akira Ikeda Gallery, Taura, Japan.

September 25–October 23, one-man exhibition, *Blind Time IV (Drawing with Davidson)*, Leo Castelli Gallery, New York.

Creates *La Stanza*, a permanent site-specific installation, Collection of Giuliano Gori, Fattoria di Celle, Santomato, Pistoia, Italy.

1994

January 16–April 4, *Robert Morris: The Mind/Body Problem*, retrospective exhibition, Solomon R. Guggenheim Museum, New York.

June 12–August 2, one-man exhibition/installation, *Terra Moto: The Fallen and The Saved*, Alyce de Roulet Williamson Gallery, Art Center College of Design, Pasadena, California.

1995

January 28–April 30, one-man exhibition/installation, *Mirrors*, Williams College Museum of Art, Williamstown, Mass. Work in the collection of Williams College Museum of Art.

March 9–May 7, *Robert Morris: The Mind/Body Problem*, retrospective exhibition, the Deichtorhallen Museum, Hamburg, Germany.

March 17–September 2, one-man exhibition/installation, *Steam*, site-specific work filling the interior courtyard of the Musée d'art contemporain, Bordeaux, France.

June 10–September 20, one-man exhibition, *Tempora Caeca*, installation of wall drawings and *Blind Time IV: Drawing with Davidson*, 1991, Fattoria di Celle, Santomato, Pistoia, Italy.

July 5–October 23, *Robert Morris: The Mind/Body Problem*, retrospective exhibition, Musée national d'art moderne, Centre Georges Pompidou, Paris.

1996

June 29–September 29, one-man exhibition, *Robert Morris: Felt Works*, Lieu d'art contemporain, Sigean, France.

Fall: One-man exhibition, *Robert Morris: Felt Works*, Galerie Philomene Magers, Cologne, Germany.

1997

Creates *Based on a Section from Mont Saint-Victoire Seen from Les Lauves 1904–1906, Cézanne.*

January 11–February 8, one-man exhibition, *Horizons Cut: Between Clio and Mnemosyne*, Leo Castelli Gallery, New York.

June–September, one-man exhibition/installation, *Tar Babies of the New World Order*, Nuova Icona, Venice, Italy.

1997–98

September 27–March 20, one-man exhibition of steel sculptures, Pietro Sparta Gallery, Chagny, France.

1998

Appointed Distinguished Professor of Art, Hunter College, New York.

April 23–June 7, *Robert Morris: Retrospective of Prints and Multiples 1952–1998*, Cabinet des estampes du Musée d'art et d'histoire, Geneva, Switzerland.

June 4–September 5, first of three installations filling one floor of the museum and involving *Mirror Works* and the film *Mirror*, 1969, Le Musée d'art contemporain, Lyon, France.

September 26–November 30, one-man exhibition/installation, *Robert Morris: The Rationed Years and Other New Work*, Leo Castelli Gallery, New York.

1999

Creates *Blind Time V: Melancholia* series.

April 17–June 20, *Robert Morris: Retrospective of Prints and Multiples 1952–1998*, Maison Levanneur, Centre national de l'estampe et de l'art imprimé, Chatou, France.

June 4–September 5, second of three installations filling one floor of the museum, titled *Labyrinth*, Le Musée d'art contemporain, Lyon, France.

1999–2000

Completion of commission for a permanent installation of a granite labyrinth for the Isla de Escultuas, a sculpture park in Pontevedra, Spain.

2000

Completion of commission by the French Ministry of Culture for seventeen stained-glass windows installed in the Maguelone Cathedral, an eleventh-century Romanesque church designated a French national historical monument. Site: near Montpellier, France.

February 15–March 31, one-man exhibition, *Robert Morris: Early Felts*, Leo Castelli Gallery, New York.

June 9–September 17, third installation, titled *White Nights*, a work involving projected images, sound mirrors, film, and scrim labyrinth occupying the third floor of Le Musée d'art contemporain, Lyon, France.

October: Installation of two labyrinths in *Changing Perceptions: The Panza Collection at the Guggenheim*, Solomon R. Guggenheim Museum, Bilbao, Spain.

2001

January: One-man exhibition, *Fiberglass, Lead, Felt, 1963–1966*, Ileana Sonnabend Gallery, New York.

March 20–August 31, *Finch College Project, 1969*, a film installation, recreated for the Whitney Museum of American Art and mounted in the exhibition *Into the Light: The Projected Image in American Art, 1964–1977*.

May 9–June 16, one-man exhibition, *Blind Time Drawings*, Lance Fung Gallery, New York.

Creates *Blind Time VI* series.

Creates encaustic paintings.

October 6–November 18, one-man exhibition, *Robert Morris: Drawings and Performances on Video*, Samuel Dorskey Museum of Art, New Paltz, New York.

2002

February 22–April 4, one-man exhibition, *Drawings*, Leo Castelli Gallery, New York.

October 30–December 15, one-man exhibition/installation, *American Beauties; Noam's Vertigo*, Joseloff Gallery, University of Hartford, Connecticut.

Completion of commission for illuminated marble altar, bronze ambon, bronze and marble candelabrum for the Cathedral of Prato, Prato, Italy.

Creates *Melencolia II*, a permanent site-specific installation in marble. Collaboration with Claudio Parmiggiani. Collection of Giuliano Gori, Fattoria di Celle, Santomato, Pistoia, Italy.

Creates *Hegel's Owl*, a permanent site-specific installation in Parco della Padula in Carrara, Italy. Work commissioned by Pina and Giuliano Gori.

2003

February 18–March 29, one-man exhibition, *The Lemma Leads*, Leo Castelli Gallery, New York.

September 12–November 1, one-man exhibition, *Blind Time Drawings*, Haim Chanin Fine Arts, New York.

2004

Completion of commission by Fondazione della Cassa di Risparmio di Pistoia e Pescia for a fabricated steel entry gate for the Ospedale del Ceppo, il nuovo padiglione per l'emodialisi, Pistoia, Italy.

2004–05

November 29–September 4, "*The Birthday Boy*," a two-screen video with sound installation, created in commemoration of the restoration and five-hundredth anniversary of Michelangelo's *David*, in Galleria dell'Accademia, Florence, Italy, for the exhibition *Forme per il David*.

2005

January 28–February 28, one-man exhibition, *Small Fires and Mnemonic Nights*, Leo Castelli Gallery, New York.

Completion of *Less than*, a permanent site-specific bronze sculpture with sound installation for the Cultural Center of Reggio Emilia, Italy.

February 25–May 29, *Robert Morris: Blind Time Drawings, 1973-2000*, retrospective exhibition, Centro per l'arte contemporanea Luigi Pecci, Prato, Italy.

June 22–July 30, one-man exhibition, *Early Sculpture*, Sprüth Magers Lee Gallery, London.

July 2–31, one-man exhibition, *Robert Morris: Sculptures and Drawings*, Abbaye Saint-Jean d'Orbestier, Château d'Olonne, France.

2006

June 25–September 25, one-man exhibition, *Blind Time VII: After Goya*, Lieu d'art contemporain, Sigean, France.

2008

September: One-man exhibition, *Less than*, Hunter College/Times Square Gallery, New York.

BIBLIOGRAPHY

BOOKS BY THE ARTIST

Continuous Project Altered Daily: The Writings of Robert Morris. Cambridge, Mass.: MIT Press, 1993.

TELEGRAM / THE RATIONED YEARS. Geneva, Switzerland: JRP Editions, 1998.

Hurting Horses. Brussels, Belgium: MFC-M. Didier, 2005.

ESSAYS BY THE ARTIST (IN CHRONOLOGICAL ORDER)

"Notes on Dance." *Tulane Drama Review* 10, no. 2 (Winter 1965): 179–86.

"Notes on Sculpture." *Artforum* 4, no. 6 (February 1966): 42–44.

"Notes on Sculpture, Part 2." *Artforum* 5, no. 2 (October 1966): 20–23.

"Form-Classes in the Work of Constantin Brancusi." Unpublished master's thesis, Hunter College, New York, 1966.

"A Method for Sorting Cows." *Art and Literature* (Lausanne) 2 (Winter 1967): 180–81.

"Notes on Sculpture, Part 3." *Artforum* 5, no. 10 (June 1967): 24–29.

"Anti Form." *Artforum* 6, no. 8 (April 1968): 33–35.

"Notes on Sculpture, Part 4: Beyond Objects." *Artforum* 7, no. 8 (April 1969): 50–54.

"Some Notes on the Phenomenology of Making: The Search for the Motivated." *Artforum* 8, no. 8 (April 1970): 62–66.

"Observations on the Observatory." In *Sonsbeck* 71, vol. 2. Edited by Geert van Berjeren and Coosje Kapteyn. Arnhem, The Netherlands: Sonsbeek Foundation, 1971, 57–59.

"Aligned with Nazca." *Artforum* 14, no. 2 (October 1975): 26–39.

"The Present Tense of Space." *Art in America* 66, no. 1 (January–February 1978): 70–81.

"Mirror Works." In *Robert Morris: Mirror Works, 1961–78*. Exhibition catalogue. New York: Leo Castelli Gallery, 1979.

"Notes on Art as/and Land Reclamation." *October* 12 (Spring 1980): 87–102.

"American Quartet." *Art in America* 69, no. 10 (December 1981): 92–105.

"Three Folds in the Fabric and Four Autobiographical Asides as Allegories (or Interruptions)." *Art in America* 9 (November 1989): 142–51.

"Words and Images in Modernism and Postmodernism." *Critical Inquiry* 15 (Winter 1989): 337–47.

"Writing with Davidson: Some Afterthoughts after Doing *Blind Time IV: Drawing with Davidson*." *Critical Inquiry* 19 (Summer 1993): 617–27.

"The Beaded Knot." In Barbara Rose, *Memory in Search of Truth: Robert Morris Works at Villa Celle*. Pistoia, Italy: Fattoria di Celle, 1994.

"Five Labyrinths." In Bruno Corà, *Robert Morris: A Path Towards the Center of the Knot*. Pistoia, Italy: Fattoria di Celle, 1995.

"The Room." In Bruno Corà, *Robert Moris: A Path Towards the Center of the Knot*. Pistoia, Italy: Fattoria di Celle, 1995.

"Tar Babies of the New World Order." In *Robert Morris: Tar Babies of the New World Order*. Exhibition catalogue. Milan, Italy: Edizioni Charta and Nuova Icona, 1997.

"Professional Rules." *Critical Inquiry* 23 (Winter 1997): 298–322.

"Cézanne's Mountains." *Critical Inquiry* 24 (Spring 1998): 814–29.

"The Art of Donald Davidson." In *The Philosophy of Donald Davidson*, edited by Lewis Edwin Hahn. The Library of Living Philosophers, vol. 27. Chicago: Open Court Press, 1999.

"Size Matters." *Critical Inquiry* 26 (Spring 2000): 474–87.

"Threading the Labyrinth." *October* 96 (Spring 2001): 61–70.

"From a Chomskian Couch: The Imperialistic Unconscious." *Critical Inquiry* 29 (Summer 2003): 678–93.

"Solecisms of Sight: Specular Speculations." *October* 103 (Winter 2003): 31–49.

"Notes on *Less than*." In *Robert Morris: Less than*. Exhibition catalogue. Prato, Italy: Gli Ori, Prato Comune di Reggio Emilia, 2005.

MONOGRAPHS

Berger, Maurice. *Labyrinths: Robert Morris, Minimalism, and the 1960s*. New York: Harper and Row, 1989.

Tsouti-Schillinger, Nena. *Robert Morris and Angst*. New York: George Braziller, 2001.

SOLO EXHIBITION CATALOGUES

Beeren, Wim, Irene Veenstra, et al. *Robert Morris: Recent Felt Pieces and Drawings*. Exhibition catalogue. Hannover: Association L.A.C. Lieu d'art contemporain Sigean, 1996–97.

Bertrand, Anne. *From Mnemosyne to Clio: The Mirror to the Labyrinth (1998–1999–2000)*. Exhibition catalogue. Lyon: Musée d'art contemporain, 2000.

Cherix, Christophe. *Notes on Print: With and After Robert Morris.* Geneva: Cabinet des estampes du Musée d'art et d'histoire, 1995.

———. *Robert Morris: Estampes et Multiples 1952–1998.* Catalogue raisonné. Genève: Cabinet des estampes du Musée d'art et d'histoire and Chatou: Centre National de l'estampe et de l'art imprimé, 1999.

Cherix, Christophe, Nadine Wasserman. *Robert Morris: Drawings.* Exhibition catalogue. New Paltz: Samuel Dorsky Museum of Art, SUNY, 2001.

Compton, Michael, and David Sylvester. *Robert Morris.* Exhibition catalogue. London: Tate Gallery, 1971.

Corà, Bruno. *Robert Morris: A Path Towards the Center of the Knot.* Pistoia: Fattoria di Celle, 1995.

Criqui, Jean-Pierre et al. *Robert Morris Blind Time Drawings, 1973–2000.* Exhibition catalogue. Prato: Centro per l'arte contemporanea Luigi Pecci, 2005.

Davidson, Donald, *Robert Morris and Donald Davidson.* Exhibition catalogue. Allentown, Pa.: Frank Martin Gallery, Muhlenberg College, 1992.

Fry, Edward, Paul Schimmel, et al. *Robert Morris: Works of the Eighties.* Exhibition catalogue. Newport Beach, Calif.: Newport Harbor Art Museum, 1986.

Grenier, Catherine, et al. *Robert Morris: Contemporains Monographies.* Paris: Editions du Centre Pompidou, 1995.

———. *Robert Morris à Saint-Pierre de Maguelone.* Paris: Editions Ereme, 2003.

———. *Robert Morris: Less than.* Exhibition catalogue. Prato: Gli Ori, Comune di Reggio Emilia, 2005.

Karmel, Pepe, and Maurice Berger. *Robert Morris: The Felt Works.* Exhibition catalogue. New York: Grey Art Gallery and Study Center, 1989.

Krauss, Rosalind, Maurice Berger, et al. *Robert Morris: The Mind/Body Problem.* New York: Solomon Guggenheim Foundation, 1994.

Krens, Thomas. *The Drawings of Robert Morris.* Exhibition catalogue. Williamstown, Mass.: Williams College Museum of Art, 1982.

Mayo, Marti. *Robert Morris: Selected Works 1970–1980.* Exhibition catalogue. Houston: Contemporary Arts Museum, 1981.

Michelson, Annette. *Robert Morris.* Exhibition catalogue. Washington, D.C.: Corcoran Gallery of Art, 1969.

Sultan, Terrie, and Barbara Rose. *Robert Morris: Inability to Endure or Deny the World.* Exhibition catalogue. Washington, D.C.: Corcoran Gallery of Art, 1990.

Tsouti-Schillinger, Nena, and Kenneth Surin, *Robert Morris: Blind Time Drawings.* Exhibition catalogue. New York: Haim Chanin Fine Arts, 2003.

Tucker, Marcia. *Robert Morris.* Exhibition catalogue. New York: Whitney Museum of American Art, 1970.

INDEX

abstract art, 122–27, 143, 173
Abstract Expressionism, 122–23, 175
Aitken, Douglas, 176
Akhmatova, Anna, 119
Allen, Fred, 73
Analytic Cubism, 188–89
analytic philosophy, 187
Andre, Carl, 125–26, 163
Aristotle, 52

Babbage, Charles, 61
Bal, Mieke, 146
Barney, Matthew, 176
Barr, Alfred, 122, 189–91
Barthes, Roland, 54
Bellamy, Dick, 1, 101
Benjamin, Walter, 200 n. 19, 201 n. 32
Beuys, Joseph, 40, 129–30
Bishop, Elizabeth, 57, 212, 225
Borch-Jacobsen, Mikkel, 48 n. 8
Borglum, Gutzon, 172
Bourdieu, Pierre, 121
Brancusi, Constantin, 9, 62
Braque, Georges, 189
Brodsky, Joseph, 82, 119
Bryson, Norman, 146
Burke, Edmund, 123, 176, 197, 208
Bush, George W., 213

Cage, John, 77, 191–93
Calatrava, Santiago, 181
Callas, Nico, 139
capitalism, 31, 66, 130, 135, 195
Castelli, Leo, 82
Cavell, Marcia, 53, 58–59
Cavell, Stanley, 114–15, 198
Cézanne, Paul, 22, 103–19, 189
chance, 191, 233
Chomsky, Noam, 13, 139, 142, 146, 163, 167, 186–87, 200 n. 32, 203, 211, 251
Christianity, 210
Church, Frederic, 127, 172–73
Clark, T. J., 189
Close, Chuck, 123, 176
Cole, Thomas, 127
conceptual art, 124, 177–75, 252
Courbet, Gustave, 48 n. 6, 153–66
Crane, Hart, 236, 240
Crown Center complex, 31

da Vinci, Leonardo, 60, 198, 214, 240
Dante Alighieri, 61
Danto, Arthur, 139
Davidson, Donald, 13–14, 41–43, 45–47, 51–59, 115–16, 187–88, 197–98
de Duve, Thierry, 139, 190
deflation, 187–94, 197, 243
Descartes, René, 144, 191, 242, 250
Dewey, John, 123, 126, 196
di Duccio, Agostino, 215
di Suvero, Mark, 172, 176
Donatello, 93, 191, 205–9, 215, 217
Duchamp, Marcel, 3, 43–44, 48–49 n. 8, 71, 123, 139, 150, 156, 172, 189–91, 193, 203, 233, 237, 245, 248
Dummett, Michael, 187
Dürer, Albrecht, 167–69

earth art, 127, 129, 175–76
Edwards, Jonathan, 123, 125–26, 128–29, 181
Egyptian art, 34
Emerson, Ralph Waldo, 123
empiricism, 43, 122–23, 125–27, 151, 246

experience, 46, 123, 125, 201 n. 32, 246–47

Fermi, Enrico, 139
Flavin, Dan, 125–26
Ford, John, 172
formalism, 122, 126–27
Forti, Simone, 1, 151–53, 193
Foucault, Michel, 181, 201 n. 33
Frege, Gottlob, 187
Freud, Sigmund, 44, 53, 58–59 n. 11, 163
Fried, Michael, 135 n. 8, 151, 177
Fukuyama, Francis, 144, 183

Gates, Bill, 66, 118
Gehry, Frank, 133–34, 181
gestalt, 125, 127–28, 131, 234–35, 247
Goodman, Nelson, 67, 103, 123, 196, 200 n. 32
Goya, Francisco, 130, 203, 211, 219, 238, 253
Greek rationalism, 210
Greenberg, Clement, 122–23, 144, 231

Hamilton, Ann, 176
Hegel, Georg Wilhelm Friedrich, 195, 244, 250
Heidegger, Martin, 33, 44
Heizer, Michael, 129, 139, 172, 176
Heraclitus, 57, 61
Hitchcock, Alfred, 150
Hobbes, Thomas, 57
Hobsbawm, Eric, 95, 195
Holbein, Hans, 48 n. 8
Hopper, Edward, 253
horizontality, 97, 99
humanism, 207–8, 216, 218, 220, 222
Hume, David, 67–68, 187, 191
Husserl, Edmund, 243

iconography, 126

James, William, 127
Jameson, Fredric, 69, 134
Johns, Jasper, 174–75, 193, 225–57
Johnson, Phillip, 101
Joyce, James, 55, 58
Judd, Donald, 125–26

Kandinsky, Wassily, 122
Kant, Immanuel, 142, 186, 191, 198, 212, 222, 250
Kelly, Ellsworth, 129, 176
Kesselring, Albert, 169
Kiefer, Anselm, 129
Klein, Yves, 129–30, 256 n. 17
Kline, Franz, 175
Koons, Jeff, 176
Kripke, Saul, 67, 115, 208, 217, 237, 253

Lacan, Jacques, 44, 48 n. 8, 108, 156
Léger, Fernand, 156
Lessing, Gotthold Ephraim, 189
LeWitt, Sol, 135–26
Liberty Memorial Museum, 30–31
Lichtenstein, Roy, 129
Lin, Maya, 129–30
Livestock Exchange building, 36

Mallory, George, 163
Marx, Groucho, 44–45
Marx, Karl, 59, 163, 212
Masson, André, 156
Medici Tombs, 220
Merleau-Ponty, Maurice, 125
Michelangelo Buonarroti, 9, 205–9, 215, 217–18, 220, 222–23
Middle Ages, 207, 216
Mies van der Rohe, Ludwig, 126
minimal art, 122–28, 134, 175, 193, 252
Mitchell, W. J. T., 13, 66, 132, 195, 200 n. 32
modernism, 49 n. 11, 144, 163, 177, 225
Motherwell, Robert, 175
Mussolini, Benito, 209

Nagel, Thomas, 115
Nauman, Bruce, 172, 176

Nelson, William Rockhill, 34
Nelson-Atkins Gallery, 34
Newman, Barnett, 122–23, 175–76
Nietzsche, Friedrich, 135 n. 9, 139, 145, 204, 222, 224

Oedipus, 43–44
Oldenburg, Claes, 130, 174
Olmstead, Frederick Law, 127

Panofsky, Erwin, 15 n. 7
Parmenides, 57, 61
Parmiggiani, Claudio, 9, 169
Peale, Charles Wilson, 132–33
Peirce, Charles Sanders, 137, 142, 171–72, 181, 186, 245
perception, 44, 125, 143, 165, 200 nn. 32–34, 246
Petrarch, 215
phenomenology, 125
Picasso, Pablo, 44, 118, 189
Pollock, Jackson, 123, 125, 128, 130, 174–76, 193
Poons, Larry, 101
pop art, 123, 127, 130
postmodernism, 246
pragmatism, 123, 128, 175, 246
presence, 126, 254–55

Quine, Willard van Orman, 43, 51, 115–16

Ramsey, Frank, 187
readymade, 190–91
Reinhardt, Ad, 123, 175
Renaissance, 205, 207, 216
Richter, Gerhard, 129
Rodin, Auguste, 193
Rommel, Erwin, 175
Roosevelt, Franklin Delano, 212
Rorty, Richard, 44, 46–47
Rossellino, Antonio, 215
Rothko, Mark, 122–23
Rubin, William, 189–90
Russell, Bertrand, 114, 137, 142, 186, 237

Sartre, Jean-Paul, 34
Schwartz, Delmore, 58
Scully, Thomas, 133
Serra, Richard, 125–27, 129, 173, 176
Smithson, Robert, 172, 178
Socrates, 52, 188, 212–13
Sonnabend, Illeana, 157
Sousa, John Philip, 182
Speer, Albert, 132, 139, 175, 183, 234
Stalin, Joseph, 212
Stella, Frank, 127, 174–76, 193, 252
Still, Clyfford, 123, 175
Stockhausen, Karlheinz, 172
stockyards, 35–37
Stuart, Gilbert, 134
Surin, Kenneth, 188

Tarski, Alfred, 52
Tennyson, Alfred, Lord, 236–37
Tiepolo, Giambattista, 177
Turnbull, Colin M., 189
Turrell, James, 129, 172, 176

van Rijn, Rembrandt, 66
Vietnam Veterans Memorial, 131, 178
Viola, Bill, 129, 176
von Neumann, John, 61

Wagner effect, 128–35, 173
Wall, Jeff, 176
Warhol, Andy, 66, 176
Watt, James, 61–62
Welles, Orson, 58
Wilde, Oscar, 190
Wilson, Robert, 129, 139
Wittgenstein, Ludwig, 13, 51, 56, 63, 65–67, 69, 79, 85, 93, 97–98, 104–6, 114–15, 181, 187, 193, 197–98, 213, 251, 256 n. 21
World Trade Center, 183

Zeki, Semir, 143–44
Zeno, 61, 234
Zoser, King, 34

ROBERT MORRIS is an artist and writer.

NENA TSOUTI-SCHILLINGER is an independent art historian. She is the author of *Robert Morris and Angst* (2001).

Library of Congress Cataloging-in-Publication Data
Morris, Robert, 1931–
Have I reasons : work and writings, 1993–2007 / Robert Morris ; edited and with an introduction by Nena Tsouti-Schillinger.
p. cm.
Includes bibliographical references and index.
ISBN 978-0-8223-4138-3 (cloth : alk. paper)
ISBN 978-0-8223-4292-2 (pbk. : alk. paper)
1. Morris, Robert, 1931– I. Tsouti-Schillinger, Nena. II. Title.
N6537.M654A35 2008
709.2—dc22 2007033640